Springer Proceedings in Business and Economics

More information about this series at http://www.springer.com/series/11960

B.S. Sahay • Sumeet Gupta
Vinod Chandra Menon
Editors

Managing Humanitarian Logistics

 Springer

Editors
B.S. Sahay
Department of Operations and Systems
Indian Institute of Management Raipur
Raipur, Chhattisgarh, India

Sumeet Gupta
Department of Operations and Systems
Indian Institute of Management Raipur
Raipur, Chhattisgarh, India

Vinod Chandra Menon
Former Member, National Disaster
   Management Authority
New Delhi, India

ISSN 2198-7246   ISSN 2198-7254   (electronic)
Springer Proceedings in Business and Economics
ISBN 978-81-322-2415-0   ISBN 978-81-322-2416-7   (eBook)
DOI 10.1007/978-81-322-2416-7

Library of Congress Control Number: 2015949924

Springer New Delhi Heidelberg New York Dordrecht London

Printed on acid-free paper

Springer (India) Pvt. Ltd. is part of Springer Science+Business Media (www.springer.com)

To
Our Parents

Preface

The worldwide rise in natural and man-made disasters in the last two decades has questioned the very preparedness to cope with them. Although less frequent, such disasters occur with high impact and completely disrupt the daily lives of people resulting in huge loss of lives and capitals to the extent of wiping out the entire city. Countries the world over have been developing mechanisms to deal with such disasters, but recent disasters reveal that the existing preparedness is still far below normal. Particularly, in emerging economics like India, such preparedness is hardly given any preference. The key to cope up with such disasters is logistics, termed as Humanitarian Logistics, organized to make life-saving drugs, food products, and other necessary amenities available to the affected people.

This book is a compendium of selected best papers presented at ICHL 2013 (International Conference on Humanitarian Logistics), organized by IIM Raipur on the 2nd and 3rd of December 2013. ICHL 2013 is the first conference organized in India to address the key issue of Humanitarian Logistics. This book addresses global call for effective Humanitarian Logistics.

The holistic approach to the management of Humanitarian Logistics requires addressing four key areas, namely, designing and planning humanitarian response strategies, developing strategies for efficient Humanitarian Logistics, modeling Humanitarian Logistics, and preparedness for emergency humanitarian response. This book addresses these key areas for Humanitarian Logistics.

Part I discusses about the importance of design and planning in a disaster situation. With the ever-growing natural and man-made disasters reaching epic proportion, the need for nodal agencies with appropriately trained manpower, know-how, and machinery to reduce, avoid, and hedge the uncertainty is paramount. Thus, design and planning are the primary aspects of Humanitarian Logistics that deal with preparedness for emergency well in advance with various logistics designs and planning strategies. Sahay et al. (2014) discuss the inherent issues in managing Humanitarian Logistics from the perspective of design and implementation. Papers presented in this section also discuss about the barriers and critical success factors of an efficient humanitarian supply chain. The section presents the importance of logistics in designing a humanitarian supply chain. If the logistics is poor, then all the three stages of dealing with a disaster, namely, preparedness, response, and recovery, will suffer. The planning aspects of logistics during natural disasters are covered in this section. Improving logistics response times is essential for improving response to a disaster situation, and this section discusses how logistics response capacity can be improved by combining it with the local commercial mobility through a truck sharing solution.

Part II discusses about developing strategies for improving humanitarian response. Research and preparedness for humanitarian response is not sufficient, unless backed up with proper humanitarian response strategies. A poorly designed humanitarian response will not work well even if all the other necessary ingredients of humanitarian response are in place. Formulation of strategies during the preparedness stage is therefore essential for effective and efficient response and recovery from a disaster. A number of papers presented in this section emphasize the use of technology for disaster response. Particularly the use of ICT and RFID has been presented in this section for developing effective humanitarian response strategies. Several strategies have been presented in this section and include the IT-based network relief model; supply chain configurations for identifying the best configuration and developing collective capacity as a strategy for improving disaster response and recovery are the major frameworks presented in this section.

Part III discusses about modeling of Humanitarian Logistics from various perspectives. Humanitarian Logistics modeling includes integrative, analytical, conceptual, inter- or multidisciplinary approaches and methods of dealing with the logistics, transport and supply chain management and emergency, crisis and disaster preparedness, and response and management. The models and approaches form the backbone for the decision support systems in logistics operations. These various perspectives presented include a comprehensive model for finding the optimal location of suppliers for designing humanitarian efforts that mitigates and reduces the risk of a disruption in the humanitarian aid; modeling of human elements, namely, donors and frontline staff, involved in delivering humanitarian aid for efficient relief operations; modeling of supplies for effective humanitarian response using p-median approach; modeling for multi-period demand allocation of relief items in a humanitarian supply chains; modeling of reverse supply chains for improved cost benefits, reclaiming value of used products and profits in secondary markets and indirect benefits such as gaining customer confidence and enhancing the green image of the organization, compliance of regulations, etc., that can be appropriated; and modeling of post-disaster Humanitarian Logistics structure. The section also presents a case study of an existing rural healthcare system deployed in a slum community in India for modeling of a sustainable and successful humanitarian effort.

Part IV of this book discusses about the relief supply chains required for disaster management from various perspectives. A relief supply chain requires trained manpower, understanding of peculiarities of disasters in difficult terrain, logistics for relief operations, and reverse logistics of disposing human remains in a disaster. The studies presented in this section discuss about challenges in management of human resources in a disaster, strategies for developing trained manpower, and simplistic methods of logistics for effective and efficient disaster response, dealing with disaster situations in a high altitude area and also dealing with the human bodies/remains after the disaster.

The collective discussions help understand managing Humanitarian Logistics from design, preparedness, response, and recovery perspective apart from usage of technology for managing the logistics involved. We hope that this book will help academicians and researchers in defining their research and practice, respectively, towards improvement of Humanitarian Logistics towards both natural and man-made disasters.

Raipur, India	B.S. Sahay
Raipur, India	Sumeet Gupta
New Delhi, India	N. Vinod Chandra Menon

Acknowledgments

First of all, we express our sincere thanks to the Honorable Governor of Chhattisgarh, Shri Shekhar Dutt, who spent valuable time with us in designing the theme and coverage of the ICHL 2013 and helping us connect with eminent personalities and stakeholders in the field of Humanitarian Logistics. We are thankful to him for identifying and connecting us with the key speakers from Atomic Energy, Indian Army, Air Force, and Naval and Coast Guard. Meeting with him gave us enthusiasm to pursue ICHL 2013 with full determination.

We express our sincere thanks to our Conference Cochair, Mr. N. M. Prusty, who helped us in connecting with key players in the field of Humanitarian Logistics, eminent personalities from National Disaster Management Authority (NDMA), New Delhi, and key NGOs and in helping us with sponsorships.

We express our sincere gratitude to the members of the Advisory Board who provided us with an international perspective to the conference. The members of the Advisory Board include Prof. Amrik Sohal, Monash University Australia; Prof. Anthony Roath, University of Bath, the UK; Prof. Aristides Matopoulos, Aston University, the UK; Prof. Ashish Chatterjee, Indian Institute of Management, Calcutta, India; Prof. Ben Wisner, University College London (the UK) and Oberlin College (USA) UK; Prof. Beverly A. Wagner, Strathclyde Business School, the UK; Prof. Christenson, David, National Advanced Fire & Resource Institute, the USA; Prof. David Moore, Cranfield University Defence Academy of the UK; Prof. Dong-Wook Song, Edinburgh Napier University, the UK; Prof. Ediz Ekinci, Embassy of the Republic of Turkey; Prof. Emmanuel M. Luna, the University of the Philippines; Prof. Felix T. S. Chan, Hong Kong Polytechnic University; Prof. Gyongyi Kovacs, Humanitarian Logistics and Supply Chain Research Institute, Finland; Prof. Ivan Russo, the University of Verona, Italy; Prof. Jaideep G. Motwani, Grand Valley State University, the USA; Prof. James R. Stock, the University of South Florida, USA; Prof. Janat Shah, Indian Institute of Management Udaipur, India; Prof. J.C. Gaillard, The University of Auckland, New Zealand; Prof. Jock Menzies, American Logistics Aid Network (ALAN), the USA; Prof. Juliana Hsuan, Copenhagen Business School, Denmark; Prof. K. N. Singh, Indian

Institute of Management Lucknow, India; Prof. M. J. Xavier, Indian Institute of Management Ranchi, India; Prof. Kevin Cullinane, Napier University, the UK; Prof. Linet Ozdamar, Yeditepe University, Turkey; Prof. Marina Dabic, the University of Zagreb, Croatia; Prof. Martha C. Cooper, Ohio State University, the USA; Prof. Paul D. Larson, the University of Manitoba, Canada; Prof. Paulo Goncalves, University of Lugano, Switzerland; Prof. Peter Schmitz, CSIR Built Environment South Africa; Prof. Peter Tatham, Griffith Business School, Australia; Prof. Peeyush Mehta, Indian Institute of Management Calcutta, India; Prof. R. Glenn Richey Jr., the University of Alabama, the USA; Prof. Ravishankar, Indian Institute of Technology Delhi, India; Prof. Robert De Souza, The Logistics Institute-Asia Pacific, Singapore; Prof. Richard Oloruntoba, the University of Newcastle, Australia; and Prof. Trond Hammervoll, Harstad University College, Norway.

We also express our sincere gratitude to our key speakers who spared their valuable time from their busy schedule to garner this conference and share their invaluable views in the conference. It is because of their presence that ICHL 2013 took altogether a different dimension. Prominent speakers include Shri Shekhar Dutt, Honorable Governor of Chhattisgarh; Shri J. K. Sinha, Honorable Member, NDMA; Dr. Anil Kakodkar, DAT Homi Bhabha Chair Professor and Former Chairman, Atomic Energy Commission, Government of India; Mr. B. Bhattacherjee, Member, NDMA; Shri Sudhir Vasudeva, Chairman, ONGC; Prog. Gyongyi Kovacs, Director, Humanitarian Logistics and Supply Chain Research Institute, Finland; Mr. N. M. Prusty, Founding Chairperson, Sphere India, and Conference Cochair; Prof. N. V. C. Menon, Former Member, NDMA, and Conference Cochair; Mr. Ali Illiassou, H.E. Ambassador, Embassy of Niger; Shri Anil Kumar Sinha, Vice Chairman, Bihar State Disaster Management Authority; Lt. General Anil Chait, CISC, Headquarters-IDS; Air Marshal Jasvinder Chauhan, AVSM, VSM, Central Air Command; Vice Admiral Anurag G. Thapliyal, Director General, Indian Coast Guard; Dr. P. K. Mishra, Director General, Gujarat Institute of Disaster Management; Mr. P. P. Shrivastav, Former Member, North East Council, Government of India; Mr. Pierangelo Gandini, In Charge, Consular Affairs, Embassy of Columbia; Mr. B. Bhattacherjee, Member, NDMA; Mr. Bhaskar Barua, Former Secretary, Ministry of Agriculture; Prof. Prem Vrat, Former Director, IIT Roorkee and VC, ITM University; Prof. Devanath Tirupati, Director In Charge, IIM Bangalore; Prof. G. Raghuram, IIM Ahmedabad; Prof. Gautam Sinha, Director, IIM Kashipur; Prof. Prafulla Agnihotri, Director, IIM Trichy; Prof. Ravi Shankar, IIT Delhi; Prof. Janki Andharia, TIIS Mumbai; Dr. Santosh Kumar, Director SAARC Disaster Management Center; Mr. Kuldip Nar, Managing Director, Aidmatrix; Prof. Bernhard Blessing, FH Vorarlberg, Austria; Mr. Ashutosh Bajpai, Director of India Operations, DHL Express; Mr. Aslam Perwaiz, Head, Disaster Risk Management Systems, Asian Disaster Preparedness Center, Bangkok; Mr. Derek Glass, Programme Director, ADRA; Dr. Ram Boojh, Programme Specialist, Natural Sciences, UNESCO; Dr. Richard Oloruntoba, the University of Newcastle, Australia; and Ms. Margarita Tileva, UNICEF.

We are thankful to our sponsors, Oil and Natural Gas Commission, National Disaster Management Authority, UNICEF, and Aidmatrix, for supporting the conference in different capacities. We are also thankful to the Directorate of Culture and Archeology, Government of Chhattisgarh, for sponsoring the cultural program during the eve of the conference. We are also thankful to our print media partner, Business Standard, for providing adequate coverage to our event.

We are thankful to the organizing committee including Group Captain Vivek Dubey, CAO IIM Raipur; Shri B.R. Khairnar, AFA, IIM Raipur; Dr. C. K. Swain, Librarian, IIM Raipur; and Mr. Hemant Debata, FA & CAO, IIM Raipur, for helping us with administrative efforts in organizing this conference. We are also thankful to Mr. Ghanshyam Sohoni, Mr. Pratik Bakshi, Mr. Shakib Ahmed, Ms. Sparsh Lunkad, and Mr. Tanmoy Kundu in helping us with organizing this conference. We are also thankful to Mr. Shubham Singh, Ms. Namrata Sharma, Ms. Thalla Monika, Mr. Sourav Mandal, and Ms. Vikita Pawar who helped us in designing and disseminating information about ICHL 2013.

We are thankful to the faculty colleagues, particularly Prof. Vinita Sahay and Prof. Sanjeev Prashar, for their whole-hearted cooperation and support for ICHL 2013. We are also thankful to the students of IIM Raipur for their support in anchoring and taking care of conduction of the conference. As we may miss out names of valuable partners in the conference, we thank one and all who supported in whatever form for ICHL 2013, the outcome of which is presented in the form of this edited book.

Contents

Contributors

Editors' Profiles

B.S. Sahay is the founder director, Indian Institute of Management (IIM), Raipur. Prior to joining IIM Raipur, he served as director of reputed Indian institutes such as Management Development Institute (MDI), Gurgaon, and Institute of Management Technology (IMT), Ghaziabad. Dr. Sahay has obtained his Ph.D. from Indian Institute of Technology, Delhi. He has been to Germany (1997) and Japan (1994) under fellowship programmes. His teaching, research and consulting interests include logistics and supply chain management, productivity management, business modelling, higher education and accreditation. Dr. Sahay serves on the Editorial Board of journals such as *International Journal of Logistics Management*, *Supply Chain Management: An International Journal*, and *Business Process Management Journal*, to name a few. He has authored six books and edited thirteen books in the area of supply chain management, world-class manufacturing, total quality management and productivity management. He is a recipient of the IIT Delhi Alumni Association Award and Distinguished Alumnus award.

Sumeet Gupta is currently affiliated with IIM Raipur as associate professor and chairman (research). He received his Ph.D. (information systems) as well as MBA from the National University of Singapore. He has worked as a research fellow with the Logistics Institute – Asia Pacific, Singapore. He has worked on several high-profile national and international consultancy assignments such as with SAP A.G., DFS Gallerias, ASEAN secretariat and EDB Singapore. He has published several papers in top-tier international journals (such as Journal of Management Information Systems, Decision Support Systems, *European Journal of Operations Research*, Omega) and conferences (such as ICIS, ECIS, POMS). He is also a reviewer of top-tier international journals in the field of information systems.

N. Vinod Chandra Menon is a former member of NDMA, GOI. He is an alumnus of Kerala University and Jawaharlal Nehru University, New Delhi. He joined the UNICEF India Country Office, New Delhi, in August 2002 in charge of Emergency Preparedness and Response till August 2005, when he was nominated by the Prime Minister of India as one of the founder members of the National Disaster Management Authority (NDMA), Government of India, with the status of a Union Minister of State in the Government of India. He worked as a member of NDMA till 27 September 2010. For his contributions in the field of disaster management in India, Prof. Menon was awarded the Skoch Challenger Award 2010 for Disaster Management. He has been a consultant to UNICEF, UNDP, World Bank and ADPC on various aspects of disaster management before joining the Government of India.

Authors' Profiles

A. Ramesh graduated in Production Engineering from Madras University and M. Tech in industrial engineering from NIT Trichy. He completed his doctoral research in the area of supply chain management from IIT Delhi in 2011. Currently he is working as assistant professor in the Department of Management Studies at IIT Roorkee. Prior to that he has worked in the Department of Mechanical Engineering at National Institute of Technology Calicut, Kerala, as assistant professor for 2 years. His research interests include Humanitarian Supply Chain Management, Sustainable Supply Chain Management, Six Sigma and Data Mining.

A.K. Vij is affiliated to ITM University, Gurgaon, India.

Ajay Bohtan has done his B.Tech and M.Tech in mechanical engineering with award of degrees from Jawaharlal Nehru University, New Delhi. He has a rich practical experience of functioning in high-altitude areas, managing disaster response policies and formulation of logistics and supply chain norms for heavy automotive equipment. At present he is working as a research fellow with the National Maritime Foundation, New Delhi, and is also enrolled at the ITM University, Gurgaon, to pursue Ph.D. in Supply Chain Management.

Ali M.S. Zalzala is associated with Institute of Management Technology, Dubai as Associate Professor.

Amol Singh is a faculty in the area of operations management at IIM Rohtak. He did his Ph.D. in Industrial Engineering from IIT Roorkee and M. E. in Production Engineering from Motilal Nehru National Institute of Technology, Allahabad. He has published several research papers in international journals and conferences. His research work appeared in international journals like *The International Journal of Advanced Manufacturing Technology* (Springer), *International Journal of Simulation Modelling* (European journal), *International Journal of Purchasing and Supply Management* (Elsevier), *International Journal of Modelling in Operations*

Management (Inderscience), *Journal of Modelling in Management* (Emerald), *Procedia Engineering* (Elsevier), etc., and in international conferences like MAT-ADOR, DAAAM, SIMTECH, etc. His research interests include operations management, project management and supply chain management.

Ashish Agarwal is affiliated to Indira Gandhi National Open University, New Delhi, India.

Ashwini Sharma is working as assistant professor in the Department of Mechanical and Automobile Engineering. He did his postgraduate diploma in steam engineering from Forbes Marshall Ltd., Pune, and M.Tech (production) from GNDEC, Ludhiana, and is pursuing his Ph.D. from NIT Kurukshetra. He has a total of more than 13 years of teaching experience. His area of specialization is supply chain management and industrial engineering. He is a faculty advisor of the Society of Automotive Engineers at ITM University and life member of ISTE and IIIE.

Darshan Suresh Rathi is affiliated to Institute of Management Technology, Ghaziabad, India.

Debashish Naik is a management consultant at Mevocon, Bangalore, India.

Devendra Kumar Dewangan is a Ph.D. research scholar of the Department of Management Studies at IIT Roorkee. He received his Master of Technology in Industrial Engineering and Management from IIT Kharagpur and Bachelor of Engineering in Mechanical Engineering from the Govt. Engineering College, Bilaspur (C.G.). He has more than 8 years of teaching experience and supervised more than 50 students in B.Tech and M.Tech. He has published more than 15 papers in journals and international and national conferences.

Divya Choudhary is affiliated to the Indian Institute of Technology, Delhi, India.

Dixit Garg is a professor in the Mechanical Engineering Department, National Institute of Technology Kurukshetra (Haryana). He has more than 28 years of teaching experience. He also acted as a project coordinator of two prestigious DST-TIFAC, Govt. of India Projects on Technology Gap Study of (i) Karnal Agriculture Implements Industry and (ii) Ambala Scientific Industry Clusters. He has also been awarded 'Eminent Engineering Personality Award' on the occasion of Engineer's Day. He has also been selected for 'Shiksha Rattan Puraskar' and 'Best Citizens of India award'. His area of interest includes operations and quality management, just-in-time (JIT), production planning and control, manufacturing processes, supply chain management, educational planning, industrial engineering, productivity, entrepreneurship, etc.

Gaurav Kabra is a research scholar in the Department of Management Studies in IIT Roorkee. He did his B.Tech information technology and MBA from ABV-Indian Institute of Information Technology and Management, Gwalior, and has published various research papers in journals of national and international repute. His areas of interest are supply chain management, humanitarian logistics and application of IT in business.

Jitendra Madaan is affiliated to the Indian Institute of Technology Delhi, India.

Joy Mukhopadhyay received his master's degree from IIT Kharagpur and Ph D. from the Indian Institute of Science, Bangalore. He has a total experience of 38 years in research, industry, consulting and academics and has authored more than 50 research papers. His corporate experience includes working for HUL, Asian Paints, Blue Star Ltd., Waters and Pharmacia Ltd. He travelled abroad to Japan, Malaysia, Singapore, Sweden and USA. At present he is an academic supervisor for Engineering Management Programme, University of Warwick, UK, a visiting professor in many business schools in India and technical and management consultant to many industries.

Kailash Gupta is the executive director of the Center for Development and Disaster Management Support Service, New Delhi, India.

Kuldeep Malik is affiliated to Jain University, Bangalore, India.

Laxhminarayan Das is currently working as a faculty member at Ravenshaw Business School, Ravenshaw University, Cuttack, in the area of marketing. He has around 13 years of post-educational and consulting experience. Besides core teaching and research, he is actively involved in few educational projects; a consultant for few management institutions and manpower consulting firms, working on a book in Green Marketing; a corporate trainer for few government brands of Odisha; and a freelancer to students' community as a career counsellor and placement activities.

Lijo John is currently pursuing his doctoral studies at the Indian Institute of Management Kozhikode. His research areas include humanitarian logistics, supply chain management and risk management. Prior to joining the Indian Institute of Management Kozhikode, he did his undergraduate studies in production engineering from the University of Kerala and graduate studies in industrial engineering and management from the National Institute of Technology Calicut. He has published papers in refereed international journals as well as in national and international conferences.

Micha Hirschinger is doctoral student at the Chair of Supply Chain Management at the Friedrich-Alexander-Universität Erlangen-Nürnberg. He has obtained Master of Science from Wirtsch.-Ing., Friedrich-Alexander-Universität Erlangen-Nürnberg). His research interests cover studies on purchasing performance, foresight in emerging markets and supply chain business model innovation.

Milind Kumar Sharma is affiliated to JNV University, Jodhpur, India

Parikshit Charan is assistant professor in operations management at IIM Raipur. He has obtained his Ph.D. from the Department of Management Studies, IIT Delhi, and master's from MNIT Jaipur. He has been associated with various other institutions like IIM Rohtak, JIIT Noida, AIM Jodhpur, etc. He has also been awarded 'Best Professor in Operations Management' at the 20th Dewang Mehta Business School Awards held at Mumbai. He has published various papers in national and international journals and conferences. His research areas include supply chain management, supply chain performance measurement system, productivity measurement and management and various others.

Prem Vrat is the vice chancellor and professor of eminence at ITM University, Gurgaon. He is a former professor of eminence, MDI Gurgaon, and also the former director, IIT Roorkee. He has had an outstanding academic record and is a product of IIT system throughout. He obtained B.Tech (Hons.) in mechanical engineering in 1966 from IIT Kharagpur and M.Tech (industrial engineering and operations research) from the same institute in 1968. He received his Ph.D. degree from IIT Delhi in 1974 in industrial engineering and operations research. During 1975–1976 he was honorary research fellow at the Department of Engineering Production, University of Birmingham (UK). He was professor and chairman of the Div. of Ind. Engg. and Management at Asian Institute of Technology in Bangkok during 1989–1991. He was an international visiting fellow at the University of Western Sydney, Australia, in June–July, 2003. He has visited 21 countries. He is also an honorary visiting professor at IIT Delhi. IIT Bombay has appointed him as distinguished guest professor.

Purvishkumar Patel is a graduate in computer science and engineering, pursuing postgraduation (M.Tech) in disaster mitigation and management at IIT Roorkee, with a research topic 'Humanitarian Logistics and Relief Supply Chain Management'. He is a founder of a firm which provides solutions for mainstream logistics, supply chain, transportation and tour and travel companies. His hobbies include travelling to different places and interacting with different people.

Rachita Gupta is affiliated to the Indian Institute of Technology Delhi, India.

B.R. Raghukumar is presently pursuing doctoral studies and is working for the Armed Forces and DRDO. He holds a degree in industrial and production engineering and has master's in aerospace engineering from IIT, Madras. He has a vast experience in the maintenance of armoured fighting vehicles and helicopter fleet. He has published papers in maintenance management-related areas such as zero breakdown maintenance, apart from collaborative networks, business process reengineering and lean management. His research interests are basically supply chain management and other logistic functional areas.

Rajat Agrawal is working as assistant professor at the Department of Management Studies, IIT Roorkee. He has more than 14 years of teaching experience besides 2 years of industry experience. Four students got their Ph.D. degree under his supervision, and eight students are currently working under his guidance. He has published more than five research papers in refereed journals and conference proceedings. His research interest is in supply chain management and manufacturing strategy on one end and spirituality at the bottom of the pyramid on the other.

Repaul Kanji is a computer science engineer at heart with the aim of finding scientific and logical solutions for disaster mitigation and management while pursuing postgraduation in the same field at IIT Roorkee. He is interested in diverse fields like algorithms and corporate social responsibility, the latter being the M. Tech research topic. Sports, music and travelling are the primary hobbies, and accolades in the first two encourage to keep on exploring more and more.

Roger Moser is assistant professor of International Management (Focus India) at the University of St. Gallen, Switzerland, and Visiting and Adjunct Faculty at IIM Bangalore and IIM Udaipur, India. Dr. Moser focuses in his research on access-based infrastructure solutions especially in rural India including healthcare, water and transportation. Among other awards, Dr. Moser received the CK Prahalad Excellent Contribution Award from the Strategic Management Society in 2011. Dr. Moser is also the director of the ASIA CONNECT Center-HSG at the University of St. Gallen supporting European and Asian companies during their internationalization processes.

S.K. Mukul Ali holds a B.Tech in computer science and engineering from West Bengal University of Technology and MBA in operations and finance from NITK Surathkal. Currently, he is working as a lecturer in Business Mgt Dept. in Rajiv Gandhi University of Knowledge Technologies, Basar Campus. He is also the director and founder of Alam Human Hair Pvt Ltd., an export-oriented company.

Sancharan Roy is affiliated to New Horizon College of Engineering, Bangalore, India.

Sheelan Misra is a professor of marketing; is an AIMA-accredited management teacher; has doctorate in marketing; is a postgraduate in international business (gold medalist); has a rich academic, research and industry experience of 12 years; is currently working with New Horizon College of Engineering, Bangalore, as a professor and head of Department of Management Studies; and is also heading the Center for Innovation and Entrepreneurship, New Horizon College of Engineering. She holds her doctorate degree from Jamia Millia Islamia, New Delhi, in the area of international marketing and MBA from Guru Jambheshwar University, Haryana, and BSc from the University of Delhi.

Sravani Bharandev is affiliated to Rajiv Gandhi University of Knowledge Technologies, Basar Campus, Basar, India.

Subhash Kumar is a PGP student at the Indian Institute of Management Raipur, Raipur, India.

Sumit Agarwal is a PGP student at the Indian Institute of Management Raipur, Raipur, India.

Vijayta Fulzele is affiliated to the Indian Institute of Technology, Delhi, India.

Vinay Sharma is affiliated to the Indian Institute of Technology, Roorkee, India.

Vivek Roy is a fellow student at the Indian Institute of Management Raipur, Raipur, India.

Part I
Humanitarian Logistics Design and Planning

With the ever-growing natural and manmade disasters reaching epic proportion, the need for nodal agencies with appropriately trained manpower, know-how and machinery to reduce, avoid and hedge the uncertainty is paramount. Knowing what to do before, during and after the disaster is an essential part of preparedness and disaster relief operations. During necessary chaos, when every second is crucial in saving life and material property, capacity building, although costly, is the only differentiating factor in ensuring the safety and security before, during and after the disaster. Furthermore, the role that the stakeholders play in improvising, learning, unlearning and relearning from the disaster experience would lead to a better response in the humanitarian circumstances. What needs to be explored is how the stakeholder's behaviour impacts the operational and executional capability? The first paper presents the theme of this section and discusses the design, development and implementation of humanitarian logistics. This section also covers a discussion on the identification of critical success factors in a humanitarian supply chain. The major issue whether in preparedness stage or while responding to a natural disaster lies with logistics. If the logistics is poor then all the three stages of dealing with a disaster, namely, preparedness, response and recovery, will suffer. The planning aspects of logistics during natural disasters are covered in this section. Improving logistics response times is essential for improving response to a disaster situation. One of the papers discusses how logistics response capacity can be improved by combining it with the local commercial mobility through a truck-sharing solution. A discussion on the barriers to humanitarian supply chains with a view to overcome them has also been presented in this section.

Chapter 1
Humanitarian Logistics and Disaster Management: The Role of Different Stakeholders

B.S. Sahay, N. Vinod Chandra Menon, and Sumeet Gupta

1.1 Introduction

The increasing frequency and devastating impact caused by natural and man-made disasters in the last two decades, as witnessed in the loss of lives, disruption of livelihoods, and damage and destruction of property, infrastructure, and assets, has exposed the multi-hazard preparedness and response capacity of governments, business sector enterprises, international humanitarian assistance agencies, civil society organizations, and local communities. The Orissa supercyclone in India in 1999, the Gujarat earthquake in India in 2001, the Bam earthquake in Iran in 2003, Hurricane Ivan in 2004, the Indian Ocean tsunami in 2004, Hurricane Katrina in 2005, the Muzaffarabad earthquake in Pakistan in 2005, Cyclone Sidr in Bangladesh in 2007, Cyclone Nargis in Myanmar in 2008, the Sichuan earthquake in China in 2008, the Haiti earthquake in 2010, the Pakistan floods in 2010, and the triple disaster triggered by the earthquake, followed by a tsunami and ultimately the Fukushima nuclear emergency in Japan in 2011, the Pakistan floods in 2011, the Uttarakhand floods in 2013, Cyclone Phailin in Odisha and Andhra Pradesh in India in 2013, and the Typhoon Haiyan in the Philippines in 2013 were a few of the most devastating disasters in the recent past.

This article is based on the background paper prepared for the International Conference on Humanitarian Logistics 2013, organized by IIM Raipur on 2–3 December 2013 at Raipur, India. A brief report was also published earlier in the Summary of Proceedings of ICHL2013, published by IIM Raipur.

B.S. Sahay (✉) • S. Gupta
Department of Operations and Systems, Indian Institute of Management Raipur, Raipur, Chhattisgarh, India
e-mail: bssahay@iimraipur.ac.in; sumeetgupta@iimraipur.ac.in

N.V.C. Menon
Former Member, National Disaster Management Authority, New Delhi, India
e-mail: nvcmenon@gmail.com

India itself faced the threat of three cyclones in the year 2013, namely, Phailin, Helen, and Lehar, which shows the unprecedented increase in the frequency of natural disasters. The devastation caused by the increasing number of disasters in India, like the Odisha supercyclone of 1999, the Bhuj earthquake of 2001, the Indian Ocean tsunami in 2004, the Kashmir earthquake in 2005, the Kosi floods in 2008, the floods in Andhra Pradesh and Karnataka in 2009, the Leh cloudburst in 2010, the Sikkim earthquake in 2011, the floods and landslides in Uttarakhand in 2013, Cyclone Phailin in Odisha and Andhra Pradesh in 2013, and the recent floods in Jammu and Kashmir, has repeatedly alerted us to the critical imperative for strengthening the humanitarian logistics and supply chain management of relief supplies in India.

According to UNISDR (2013), "between 2002 and 2011, there were 4,130 disasters recorded, resulting from natural hazards around the world where 1,117,527 people perished and a minimum of US$ 1,195 billion was recorded in losses. In the year 2011 alone, 302 disasters claimed 29,782 lives; affected 206 million people and inflicted damages worth a minimum of estimated US$ 366 billion." UNISDR (2013) further observed that the proportion of world population living in flood-prone river basins has increased by 114 %, while those living on cyclone-exposed coastlines have grown by 192 % over the past 30 years. Over half of the world's large cities, with populations ranging from 2 to 15 million, are currently located in areas highly vulnerable to seismic activity.

Rapid urbanization further increases exposure to disaster risk (UNISDR 2013). Shyam (2013) observed that "the losses from natural disasters to mankind are undoubtedly massive—on average, globally every year over 100,000 people were killed and some 246 million people affected by natural disasters during the period 2002–2011 and the estimated average economic loss was US$ 131 billion per year."

Apart from the loss of lives, livelihoods, and damage and destruction of property, infrastructure, and assets caused by the natural disasters, in the immediate post-disaster phase, the affected countries face the challenges posed by bottlenecks in humanitarian logistics: the identification of sources for the supply of relief materials; the choice of the optimal way in which these relief materials can reach the disaster-affected communities; the transportation, warehousing, and distribution of relief supplies to the disaster-affected households; etc.

In other words, logistics is a major challenge in dealing with disasters, and therefore, there is a need for a comprehensive management of humanitarian logistics in disasters. Several research studies (Nilsson et al. 2010; Granot 1999; Trim 2004; Akhtar et al. 2010) have advocated the need for a well-coordinated effort in dealing with disasters, and therefore, it is imperative that the roles of various stakeholders in a disaster are defined properly and their responsibilities chalked out in advance. This paper looks into the roles that various stakeholders can play in the effective management of a disaster and develops a humanitarian action matrix that summarizes the roles of various stakeholders in humanitarian logistics for improving the effectiveness of disaster management.

1.2 Disaster Statistics and Response Mechanisms

The world has been a witness to various types of disasters since time immemorial. Table 1.1 presents a list of major disasters all over the world. These are representative worst disasters and such disasters have been increasingly common during the recent years.

From the statistics, we can note a few interesting things. First, earthquakes and cyclones have caused severe damages. They arrive for a short period but bestow huge damage. Second, epidemic used to be the cause of major deaths during early years, but its toll on humanity has subsided in recent years. Epidemics used to reign for a long period and sometimes even hundreds of years. Third, hurricanes cause major disasters usually in North America, whereas earthquakes are more common in Asian countries. We can also note that epidemics are more common in European countries and famine/drought are more common in South Africa.

According to UNEP-SBCI (2007) in the reconstruction of damaged houses immediately after the Indian Ocean tsunami which devastated Banda Aceh in Indonesia, the masonry needs for the construction of 120,000 houses in Aceh province were projected to be more than 1 million tons of cement and 3.6 million cubic meters of sand, while the timber requirements for the housing construction were estimated to be between 300,000 and 400,000 m^3. The logistics of sourcing the sand, cement, and timber and getting them across to the house reconstruction sites in Banda Aceh posed very serious challenges, similar to those faced in moving building materials from the mainland to Andaman and Nicobar islands in India for the construction of intermediate shelters and permanent housing reconstruction after the Indian Ocean tsunami.

According to UNISDR (2013), direct disaster losses are at least 50 % higher than internationally reported figures: Total direct losses in 40 low- and middle-income countries amount to USD 305 billion over the last 30 years; of these, more than 30 % were not internationally reported. The Global Assessment Report 2013 observed that disasters directly affect business performance and undermine longer-term competitiveness and sustainability: When business leaves, it may never return. Prior to the 1995 Kobe earthquake in Japan, the port of Kobe was the world's sixth busiest port. Despite a massive investment in reconstruction and efforts to improve competitiveness, by 2010, it had fallen to the 47th place.

Following the 2011 earthquake and tsunami, automobile and electrical component production in Japan declined by 48 and 8 %, respectively. But automobile production also fell by 20 % in Thailand, 18 % in the Philippines, and 6 % in Indonesia. Electrical component production fell by 18 % in the Philippines and 8 % in Malaysia (Ye and Abe 2012).

The Renesas Electronics Corporation, the world's largest custom manufacturer of microchips for the automobile industry, and which serves Japanese automobile manufacturers, suffered estimated losses of USD 615 million. Toyota lost USD 1.2 billion in product revenue owing to parts shortages that caused 150,000 fewer Toyota automobiles to be manufactured in the United States, production stoppages

Table 1.1 Major disasters all over the world

Sl. no.	Year	Disaster	Type	Affect	App. aid[a]
1	Sep 3, 2014	India-Pakistan floods	Flood	557 deaths, 2,500 villages affected, and 80,000 homeless	USD 0.1 billion
2	14–17 Jun 2013	North India floods	Flood	5,748 deaths, 4,200 villages, 110,000 people evacuated	USD 0.17 billion
3	Jul 2011 to Aug 2012	East Africa drought	Drought	12.4 million in need of food, 9.5 million under threat of livelihood, 50,000–260,000 deaths	USD 1.3 billion
4	Jan 12, 2012	Haiti earthquake	Earthquake (7.0 on Richter scale)	0.2 million death, 2 million homeless, and 3 million in need of emergency aid	USD 0.315 billion
5	Mar 11, 2011	Tohoku, Japan, earthquake and tsunami	Earthquake (9.0 on Richter scale)	15 million dead or injured and 2,814 missing, 18 prefectures, and 250,000 buildings damaged/destroyed	USD 235 billion
6	Feb 22, 2011	Christchurch, New Zealand, earthquake	Earthquake (6.3 on Richter scale)	185 deaths, 238 missing, and 164 injured	USD 16 billion
7	Oct 8, 2005	Pakistan earthquake	Earthquake (7.6 on Richter scale)	75,000 death and 106,000 injured	USD 5.400 billion
8	Aug 23, 2005	US Hurricane Katrina	Hurricane (Cat 4)	1,833 killed	USD 108 billion
9	May 2, 2008	Myanmar Cyclone Nargis	Cyclone (Cat 4 on Saffir-Simpson scale)	84,500 people killed with 53,800 missing, devastated 37 townships	USD 10 billion
10	Feb 5, 2008	Afghanistan blizzard	Blizzard	926 deaths, 100,000 sheep and goats and 315,000 cattle dead	
11	Dec 26, 2004	Indian Ocean earthquake and tsunami	Earthquake (9.1–9.3 on Richter scale)	0.23–0.31 million	USD 14 billion

12	Jul–Aug 2003	European heat wave	Heat wave/drought	75 % of wheat crops lost, 70,000 deaths	NA
13	Jan 26, 2001	Gujarat earthquake	Earthquake (7.7 on Richter scale)	20,000 deaths, 167,000 injured, 400,000 homes destroyed, 600,000 homeless	NA
14	Feb–Mar 2000	Mozambique, South Africa, flood	Flood	800 deaths, 44,000 homeless, 1,400 sq. km arable land affected, 20,000 herds of cattle lost	USD 0.015 billion
15	1994–1998	North Korean famine	Famine	240,000–3,500,000 deaths	Aid for 4 years
16	Aug 14, 1992	Africa West Coast Hurricane Andrew	Hurricane (Cat 5)	65 deaths and 175,000 homeless	USD 26 billion
17	Nov 13, 1985	Nevado del Ruiz volcano	Volcano	25,000 deaths	USD 1 billion
18	Nov 12, 1970	Bhola, Bangladesh, cyclone	Cyclone (Cat 3)	500,000 deaths	USD 0.49 billion
19	Jul–Aug 1931	Yangtze River, China floods	Flood	3,700,000 deaths	NA
20	Dec 16, 1920	Haiyuan, China earthquake	Earthquake	240,000 deaths	NA
21	1918	Spanish influenza	Epidemic	40–100 million deaths	NA
22	July 28, 1876	China Tangshan earthquake	Earthquake (7.8 on Richter scale)	240,000 deaths and 164,000 injuries	NA
23	1775–1782	North American smallpox epidemic	Epidemic	11,000 deaths	NA
24	1600s	Europe, the Great White Plaque	Epidemic	Leading cost of death due to tuberculosis	NA

(continued)

Table 1.1 (continued)

Sl. no.	Year	Disaster	Type	Affect	App. aid[a]
25	1348–1351	The Black Death	Epidemic	Killed 25–60% of Europe's population (75–200 million)	NA
26	Oct 11, 1138	Aleppo, Syria earthquake	Earthquake	230,000 deaths	NA
27	526	Antioch, Syria earthquake	Earthquake	250,000–300,000 deaths	NA

[a]The amount in aid is based on the time of occurrence of disaster

at five plants in the United Kingdom, and reductions in production of 70 % in India and 50 % in China (Asano 2012).

The UNISDR's (2013) report also found that the globalized supply chains create new vulnerabilities: Toyota lost $1.2 billion in product revenue from the 2011 Japan earthquake and tsunami due to parts shortages that caused 150,000 fewer Toyota automobiles to be manufactured in the United States and reductions in production of 70 % in India and 50 % in China. The report concluded that disaster risk is a new multitrillion dollar asset class. Global capital flows have transformed the landscape of disaster risk, creating a new pile of toxic assets for businesses and governments that do not currently appear on balance sheets. Globally, USD 71 trillion of assets would be exposed to one-in-250-year earthquakes. In Honduras, already a one-in-33-year disaster would create a significant financing gap for the government with impacts on future GDP.

UNISDR's (2013) report also points out that most disasters that could occur haven't happened yet: Total expected annual global loss from earthquakes and cyclone wind damage alone now amounts to USD 180 billion per year. This figure does not include the significant cost of local disasters from floods, landslides, fires, and storms or the cost of business interruption. Agriculture is also at risk: In Mozambique, a one-in-10-year drought would lower maize yields by 6 % and GDP by 0.3 %.

The low penetration of insurance in disaster-prone areas is another critical issue. Insurance is critical to business resilience. Yet insurance pricing often does not reflect risk levels or provide an adequate incentive for risk-sensitive business investment, particularly in low- and middle-income countries with low penetration rates but rapidly growing markets (UNISDR 2013). In China, for example, only 3 % of properties are insured against earthquake and 5 % against typhoons and floods (McElroy 2013).

With the increasing frequencies of natural disasters, governments in various countries gathered themselves to develop disaster response mechanisms. In all such disasters, logistics play a major role in disaster aid administration. Christopher (1992) defines logistics as "the process of strategically managing the procurement, movement and storage of materials, parts and finished inventory and the related information flows through the organization and its marketing channels in such a way that the current and future profitability are maximized through the cost effective fulfillment of orders." When the same is applied to natural and man-made disasters, it is often referred to as humanitarian logistics.

Governments report significant progress in developing more effective disaster response and preparedness strategies and are investing to address these risks. Yet, the required shift to anticipate risks in public and private investment remains a challenge for most countries. The number of export-oriented special economic zones has expanded from 176 zones in 47 countries in 1986 to 3,500 zones in 130 countries in 2006. Many such zones are located in hazard-exposed areas increasing disaster risks.

A new wave of urbanization is happening in hazard-exposed countries, and with it, new opportunities for resilient investment are emerging. In India alone, the urban population is expected to grow from 379 million in 2010 to 606 million in 2030 and 875 million in 2050. Private construction company Mori Building has successfully invested in earthquake-resistant housing developments in Japan, where earthquake resistance is the most important criteria for choosing new offices for 92 % of businesses (UNISDR 2013).

Several best practices in humanitarian logistics and concerns like those mentioned above are required to be shared to make the lifesaving drugs, food products, shelter materials, and other necessary relief supplies available to the disaster-affected people. Humanitarian logistics demands a separate treatment in comparison to the commercial logistics operations undertaken by the corporate sector because of the sense of urgency, voluntary nature of the stakeholder groups, and the plethora of problems associated with the lack of effective coordination in the operations, especially in the immediate post-disaster context. The design, development, and implementation of appropriate mechanisms for humanitarian logistics are dictated by the need for understanding "the big picture" related to the complex task of matching demand and supply of post-disaster relief through a series of preparedness measures including pre-positioning of relief supplies in warehouses, identifying potential suppliers of relief materials, working out standardized specifications for relief supplies, entering into long-term agreements with manufacturers and authorized distributors for "just in time" dispatch of relief materials in the event of a sudden onset of disaster, undertaking training and capacity building of humanitarian staff to internalize best practices of humanitarian logistics, working out transportation logistics to collect relief materials from warehouses and reach them to the disaster-affected communities, identifying the most deserving sections of the disaster-affected communities for distribution of relief, etc.

The business case for stronger disaster risk management is threefold. It reduces uncertainty and strengthens confidence: Orion invested USD 6 million in seismic protection in New Zealand that saved the company USD 65 million. It opens the door to cost savings: Preventive investments by fishermen in Mexico saved each individual entrepreneur USD 35,000 during Hurricane Wilma in 2005. It also provides an avenue for value creation: An Economist Intelligence Unit survey records that 63 % of businesses see opportunities to generate value from disaster risk reduction. Businesses that have invested the most in risk management may financially outperform their peers[1].

The best practices in humanitarian logistics and supply chain management by developed countries and international humanitarian assistance agencies emphasize that humanitarian logistics plays a significant role in enhancing preparedness of communities and governments at the provincial and national levels to cope with the challenges posed by increasing frequency of natural and man-made disasters.

---

[1] http://www.globalnetwork-dr.org/gndr-blog.html

1.3 Coordination for Disaster Management in India

Although logistics mechanisms have been improved, it has been observed that the coordination has become the next big challenge. Disaster response mechanisms now call for effective coordination among various stakeholders. Coordination has been reported as one of the biggest challenges in humanitarian aid administration (Kovacs and Spens 2007).

The Indian Ocean tsunami of 26 December 2004 exposed the weaknesses in institutional mechanisms and techno-legal regimes in most of the tsunami-affected countries. The declaration of the Hyogo Framework of Action in 2005 by the United Nations and its endorsement during the World Conference on Disaster Reduction at Kobe, Japan, by 168 countries prompted many countries to introduce appropriate legislations to improve the disaster management architecture in these countries. A formal architecture of institutional mechanisms for disaster management was a long-articulated demand in India, as early as the deliberations of the high-powered committee established by the Ministry of Agriculture, Government of India in 1999. India finally enacted the Disaster Management Act in the year 2005[2] for the effective management of disasters in the country. A National Disaster Response Force (NDRF) was also established as a specialist first responder agency to respond effectively to disasters. Simultaneously, the National Disaster Management Authority (NDMA) as the apex agency at the central level and State Disaster Management Authorities at the individual state level and District Disaster Management Authorities at the respective district levels were formed to effectively manage disasters. A National Institute for Disaster Management was also established at the national level. The first visible impact of disaster management occurred in the year 2008 with the strategic evacuation of more than 1 lakh people during the Kosi floods in Bihar and later the evacuation of more than 1 million people during Cyclone Phailin in Odisha in 2013 within a very few days. However, post-disaster rehabilitation still continues to be difficult and challenging.

The NDMA envisions building a safer and disaster-resilient India by a holistic, proactive, technology-driven, and sustainable development strategy that involves all stakeholders and fosters a culture of prevention, preparedness, and mitigation[3]. NDMA, as the apex body for disaster management in India, lays down the policies, plans, and guidelines for disaster management to ensure timely and effective response to disasters[4]. One of its major responsibilities is to take measures for preventing the disaster, or the mitigation, or preparedness and capacity building for dealing with threatening disaster situations or disasters, as it may consider necessary.

The National Policy for Disaster Management states that NDMA's vision to build a safer and disaster-resilient India will be achieved through a culture of

---

[2] http://www.ndma.gov.in/en/disaster.html

[3] http://www.ndma.gov.in/en/about-ndma/vision.html

[4] http://www.ndma.gov.in/en/about-ndma/roles-responsibilities.html

prevention, mitigation, and preparedness to generate a prompt and efficient response during disasters. The entire process will center stage the community and will be provided momentum and sustenance through the collective efforts of all government agencies and nongovernmental organizations. In order to translate this vision into policy and plans, the NDMA has adopted a mission-mode approach involving a number of initiatives with the help of various institutions operating at the national, state, and local levels[5]. Central ministries, states, and other stakeholders have been involved in the participatory and consultative process of evolving policies and guidelines. This policy framework is also in conformity with the International Strategy for Disaster Reduction, the Rio Declaration, the Millennium Development Goals, and the Hyogo Framework 2005–2015. Some of the major themes that underpin the National Policy for Disaster Management are[6]:

- Community-based disaster management, including last mile integration of the policy, plans, and execution
- Capacity development in all related areas
- Consolidation of past initiatives and best practices
- Cooperation with agencies at the national, regional, and international levels
- Compliance and coordination to generate a multi-sectoral synergy

As envisaged in this policy, a well-coordinated effort among various stakeholders will improve disaster response strategies in the country. The most important function in managing disasters is the strengthening of multi-hazard preparedness which involves all stakeholders. The following section presents the essence of deliberations by various practitioners in humanitarian logistics and disaster management during ICHL2013.

1.4   The Role of Different Stakeholders in Disaster Management

Different stakeholders need to play different and specific roles in the management of a disaster. A humanitarian supply chain for both natural and man-made disasters consists of various stakeholders (Kovacs and Spens 2007), namely:

- The academic community
- The government bodies, private sector, and the disaster response organizations
- Other stakeholders (local community, disaster-affected communities and donors)

Technology plays an enabling role for strengthening humanitarian efforts in post-disaster situations.

---

[5] http://www.ndma.gov.in/en/policy.html

1.4.1 The Academic Community

The academic community plays an important role in teaching and researching on humanitarian logistics. The key roles of academic community are education, research, and developing a knowledge base for sharing of best practices.

1.4.1.1 Education in Humanitarian Logistics

Academia plays a key role in increasing awareness about dealing with disasters among all sections of the society. At the local community level, it is important for everyone to be proactive and understand his/her respective roles during various phases of the disaster management cycle. The academic community can conduct risk assessment and vulnerability analysis of specific disaster-prone areas and suggest appropriate strategies for dealing with the disasters that people of the local area are likely to face. Moreover, some kind of development programs should be carried on regarding natural disasters which may include raising the awareness levels about the disasters and the mechanisms to deal with them. This would include launching a short course or module which can be taught at undergraduate levels. With such modules, a few people could be trained at each district or block level who can work out disaster scenarios, map their vulnerability profiles, develop communication levels and systems, and prepare for the availability of response forces and assets. Then only we will be able to prepare ourselves starting from village panchayat to district, to state, and then to the national level.

Different bodies have undertaken the task for education in the field of humanitarian logistics. UNESCO, for example, has launched its own programs. Still there is a need for disseminating the scientific and technical knowledge in economy of local food systems, agriculture policies, management of supply chain, etc. This can be effectively done by local bodies only, and academic institutions can play a pivotal role in absorbing and disseminating such knowledge.

The death of school children due to fire in schools caused by the lack of trained teachers in handling midday meals raises the question of the need for awareness about dealing with such crisis situations. Disasters happen because the people who are handling the responsibility of midday meals, such as the teachers in local schools, are themselves not trained.

In summary, educational institutes can play an important role in disseminating knowledge of dealing with disasters. Different institutions may participate differently in such efforts. The institutions of national importance can launch advanced courses like "training the trainers" of other local institutions/schools through which such education can be disseminated to the masses.

1.4.1.2   Development and Sharing of Best Practices

A very important role of academic institution is in the development of knowledge base and sharing of best practices. In India, the government bodies such as National Disaster Response Force, Indian Defense Services, and National Disaster Management Authority play an important role in strengthening disaster preparedness, mitigation, disaster risk reduction, and emergency response. There is a serious need to develop and share a well-defined knowledge base of the experiences, strategies, and best practices of these agencies which are involved in humanitarian relief exercises. We need to learn the lessons of organizational management and standard operating procedures (SOPs) from the armed forces in dealing with such disasters. Academic institutions can play a strong role by disseminating education in management of disasters in conjunction with national bodies such as National Disaster Management Authority. Moreover, disaster management in India needs to be more professionalized by institutionalizing the lessons of preparedness, emergency response protocols, and simulation exercises from our armed forces and best practices from developed countries.

Institutions can also learn and develop knowledge base from the initiatives launched by other countries. For example, regarding food security, various governments have launched various initiatives to ensure food for all citizens of the country. The Government of India and state governments have launched different initiatives to strengthen food security to people below poverty line. The Government of Chhattisgarh has established CORE PDS for bringing transparency in the distribution of food. Such initiatives need to be assessed and documented and used as teaching and research materials for education in humanitarian logistics.

1.4.1.3   Research in Logistics Preparedness, Planning, and Optimization

The logistics efforts in humanitarian work absorb around 80 % of the total cost of humanitarian efforts, out of which major chunk of cost is absorbed in procurement. There is a need for serious research in this area for improving the effectiveness of humanitarian logistics in humanitarian efforts.

Humanitarian logistics is a peculiar area of supply chain where all normal parameters of a normal supply chain fail. In fact, disaster management situations can provide worst case scenarios in supply chain management. If somebody can successfully manage a disaster situation, he/she has proved his credentials to manage any other situation. Such situations require just-in-time response without knowledge of who, what, why of disasters. Therefore, different parameters need to be examined and set forth for measuring the effectiveness of humanitarian efforts. In India, none of the management institutions have taken disaster management as a research area. There are several studies whose results are not known to people.

We also need to study the capacity gap in preparedness and response to a disaster. Although we are prepared, but when it comes to response, we find so many hurdles as was demonstrated in the case of Uttarakhand flash flood due to sudden cloud burst caused by unprecedented rainfall.

Risk assessment is very important in managing disasters. Although we cannot stop natural and man-made disasters, still we can reduce the risk considerably by proper planning in advance. This requires substantial amount of research and research institutions to take up this task in the service of the society and the nation. We are also prone to several man-made disasters, such as that of failure of nuclear plant which may cause irreparable damages as in the case of recent tsunami in Japan, which led to failure of Fukushima nuclear plant. We need to examine the acceptable level of risk a technology may bring in so as to not lead to disastrous situations. The probability of occurrence of accidents must be minimized to zero. The ability to pick up precursors as early warning signals is very important at the time of disaster. Serious research can be conducted in this area.

There is also a need for research in the area of schemes such as midday meals. Several models, including both centralized and decentralized, have been developed for midday meal distribution in India, and these models need to be studied for their effectiveness at the grass roots level. There is also a need for research in rehabilitation. The people evacuated from a disaster area need to be rehabilitated. How to rehabilitate them is one of the areas which need to be examined in greater depth.

Another area that needs research is in developing an efficient network of supplies to the disaster-affected area. By establishing relationships with third party agencies which have long-term relationship with suppliers of drug and essentials and transporters, the disaster response could become more effective.

A different model needs to be evolved to strategically manage these networks, and management institutions can take up research projects in this area to identify best practices for management of disaster preparedness and response.

In other words, there is a strong need for research in the area of humanitarian logistics, and academic institutions should take the onus of conducting such research and disseminate its practices in the society. Such research should be need based and should be for the benefit of the entire society.

1.4.2 The Government Bodies and Disaster Response Organizations

Government bodies, such as Integrated Defense Services, INCOIS, NDMA, NDRF, and the national and the state governments, play a key role in the preparedness and response to disasters. They have been playing a key role during all the disasters experienced earlier.

1.4.2.1 Preparedness for Disasters

The need for logistics is different in different terrains, and therefore, proper preparedness will help in management of disasters. There is a need for conducting mock drills and the national and the state governments all have different responsibilities and their responsibilities have to be well coordinated, whereby participation is drawn from people and from the society so that everyone understands the need to be prepared.

Preparedness is also important for different supplies that need to be made available during disasters. Developing countries need to be ready for times when food won't be available to people, thus leading to starvation and which will have a long-term effect on the lives of the people. We also need to see that the middlemen are not taking the chunk of the cost in the food value chain, making it very expensive for the consumer. Government policies must ensure agility and transparency in the system.

Another aspect of preparedness is to train people in values of selflessness and helping each other during the disasters. Disasters bring people together. But if they are together before the disaster strikes, then they can render valuable help to each other.

People need to learn to cooperate with the disaster response organizations in their efforts to quickly evacuate and rehabilitate a disaster-affected area. In India, the Integrated Defense Services is one of the major contributors in disaster preparedness and humanitarian response efforts. The National Disaster Response Force is a dedicated first responder agency which has made significant contributions in responding effectively to several disasters in the past few years. The contributions such organizations make during disaster to save lives are commendable, and we must give them full support in their search and rescue and evacuation operations during disasters.

There is a need to establish formal agreements with the corporate sector entities who are suppliers of relief materials, transporters, or those who own warehouses. The corporate sector may also like to contribute to strengthening disaster risk reduction and disaster preparedness, apart from providing essential relief supplies after the onset of disasters to help the disaster-affected communities. Such partnerships with other stakeholder groups would assist the government in effectively dealing with disasters. NDMA has developed a Corporate Disaster Response Network in collaboration with AidMatrix, and this network helps in providing aid during disasters by leveraging its strong network of civil society partners and corporate donors across the country.

It is also the responsibility of the government to plan the urban critical infrastructure and amenities in such a manner that they do not cause any risk to human lives in case of a disaster. The procedure for quick evacuation must be clearly laid out, and the awareness of the same should be disseminated en masse so that people are always aware and prepared for the same.

1.4.2.2 Responding to Disasters

For an effective response to disasters, there is a need to move from benefit-cost models to the model of agility. In the case of disasters, cost-effective models have limited utility because the opportunity cost of late response is so high. The opportunity cost of quick response has to be seen holistically even if it appears to be expensive otherwise. In the present system, government agencies are ill-suited to respond to such disasters because they are always worried about Comptroller and Auditor General (CAG) and Central Vigilance Commission (CVC). Therefore, there is a need to devise an effective mechanism for disaster response, by considering the total cost of the system, which overcomes the hurdles of CAG and CVC, but still keeping the larger public interest as well as transparency and accountability in the system in the forefront.

The citizens also have a responsibility in responding to disasters, and they should not expect the emergency response to be the responsibility of government or first responder agencies alone. Although disaster preparedness and emergency response planning has been improved after NDMA inception, more effort is required to mobilize community participation in disaster preparedness and emergency response. Sometimes, communities find it difficult to extend their cooperation to armed forces or other first responder organizations when they are asked to evacuate their villages when early warning has been issued about possible threatening disasters. Ultimately, it is the responsibility of the community to assist the NDRF, armed forces, police, and paramilitary forces in their disaster management efforts.

The role of the state government and local administration is most crucial in strengthening disaster preparedness and in responding to disasters, and there are several weak areas that need to be addressed to improve the effectiveness of disaster management in the country.

1.4.3   Other Stakeholders (Disaster-Prone Communities and Donors)

The preparedness and management of disasters is not only the responsibility of the government but also of the local community, the disaster victims, and the donors. They need to cooperate in the efforts for improving the effectiveness of disaster management.

1.4.3.1 Cooperation in Disaster Management Efforts

The community that is affected by disasters also plays a key role in humanitarian efforts. The main principle is cooperation. They need to cooperate with the disasters management organizations. The local community best understands the local context. There is a need to develop local capacities to improve disaster preparedness and strengthen emergency response capacities at the local level.

The local communities have an equal responsibility for ensuring that the ecosystem does not become fragile due to human interference. The use of nonbiodegradable plastic bags can lead to a major disaster as was witnessed by the clogging of drains that led to the Mumbai floods in July 2005, when the unprecedented rainfall and the high tide choked the expressways and the roads. Therefore, a system for minimizing the damage to the ecosystem needs to be developed and put in place that will help in preventing such disasters. The fact that the frequency and intensity of disasters has been increasing in the recent past means that we are endangering our ecosystem due to our actions like deforestation, encroachment on floodplains and slopes, etc. The constant meddling with the ecosystem will lead to increase in disasters. Therefore, there is a need to study the traditional systems and coping capacities that were useful in dealing with disaster situations.

1.4.3.2   Developing Human Values

The importance of developing psychosocial support in dealing with disasters has to be acknowledged. Most of the people panic when they are suddenly faced by a disaster. There is a need to develop the capacity to stay calm and help others during such disaster situations. During most disasters, people tend to be selfish and therefore try to take advantage of the situation by claiming benefits meant for disaster victims. The value of selflessness needs to be built in our educational system for greater good of the society.

We must also develop a strong concern for our environment. The more we deplete forests and the more we become urban, the more we run the chances of accidents, fatalities, disasters, etc. India has been dealing with almost all varieties of natural and man-made disasters, and even in Chhattisgarh, the fatalities due to disaster in some form or the other are quite high. We must live a life of harmony with nature.

1.4.3.3   Donors Should Be Responsible Citizens

While there are donors who put their sincere efforts in helping to manage disasters, there are many who try to take advantage of disaster situations. They bring items, either advertently or inadvertently, that clog the supply chain as these items are useless for the affected people. Such clogging delays the supply of essential items as well as hamper disaster response efforts. While cash donations help the relief agencies to help disaster victims to purchase essential supplies which they desperately need to repair their house or to help them survive when their livelihoods have been adversely affected due to the disaster.

1.4.4 The Technology for Humanitarian Efforts

The role of technology in humanitarian efforts needs to be clearly understood and applied wherever necessary. The diffusion of technology is very poor in India, and therefore, it is important that such efforts are properly managed and appreciated. Technology can play a key role in strengthening disaster preparedness and in responding to the disaster. This has been demonstrated by the role played by information and communication technology applications in the Uttarakhand floods in 2013. The Google Crisis Mapper, Person Finder, and the use of Unmanned Aerial Vehicles (UAVs) by NDRF to locate marooned people in the remote areas where roads had been washed away due to the floods showed the positive ways by which ICT tools can be used to improve humanitarian response efforts in crisis situations.

1.4.4.1 Role of Technology During Preparedness

Government bodies, such as NDMA, have started using scientific tools such as Decision Support Systems, Geographical Information Systems, etc., for improving disaster preparedness and emergency response. It also uses digital elevation maps depending upon the type of disaster that may strike the local area. These must be in place as these may not be readily available on online sites of public domains. The preparedness for resources needs to be assessed again and again and preparedness to face worst case scenarios evaluated through mock drills so that we are prepared to face any kind of disaster.

1.4.4.2 Role of Technology During Emergency Response

Information and communication technologies (ICTs) and the Internet have been of great use in information management during disaster, and these technologies have come in handy in various disasters all over the world. India needs to leverage IT for effective use because we have a number of security issues as well. The democratization of ICT has empowered stakeholders to effectively use these applications in humanitarian response. The effectiveness of the application of these technologies depends specifically on the individuals and the leaders who participate in the use of that technology. In other words, although India has technology, it needs to be leveraged for improving the effectiveness of both preparedness and in emergency response to disasters.

Many humanitarian organizations have made several innovative efforts to make modular compact kits for disaster response. Examples include the development of collapsible water containers, emergency shelter, and Solar Chill refrigeration system. We can take advantage of such low-cost and appropriate technology for emergency response.

1.5 Conclusion

The action plan for different stakeholders is summarized in Table 1.2. Different stakeholders play different roles in managing a disaster right from the preparedness stage. These stakeholders must work in unison to ensure an effective response to disasters.

Table 1.2 Humanitarian action matrix

	Academia	Government bodies	Other stakeholders
Preparedness	Initiation of awareness and development programs, training programs at village, block, or district level; institute to take up advanced research courses	3 P's—planning, preparing, and practice; organizing mock drills; training to the people for inculcating the right value system	Communities to be made disaster resilient
Response	Collaboration of government/researchers/local ecosystem for better disaster response	Response effort to quickly evacuate and rehabilitate	Coordinate with govt. bodies for efficient logistics
Technology	Effectiveness of ICTs for coordination during disaster management and response. Examining the effectiveness of DSS and GIS in disaster preparedness and response	Agility and transparency in government policies and systems; efficient networks of supplies to disaster-affected areas; use of digital elevation maps/communication technologies/Internet	Build network of suppliers for emergency response and prepare long-term agreements
Coordination	Minimizing the damage to ecosystem; need to build the value of selflessness; development of a shared knowledge base	Participation from people and society; maintain relationship with third parties or the agencies involved; the request for resources to be properly routed and coordinated	Coordination between the demand from the disaster-affected community and matching supply by the donors
Procurement	Proactive, emergency, and accelerated procurement; effectiveness of procurement policies for disaster response; examination of agile vs benefit-cost-based models of disaster response	Disaster procurement rules are clear, but agencies are not always prepared, so there is need for an effective mechanism	

References

Akhtar P, Fischer C, Marr N (2010) Improving the effectiveness of food chain coordinators: a conceptual model. In: Paper presented at the third international symposium: improving the performance of supply chains in the transitional economies, Kuala Lumpur, 4–8 July

Asano K (2012) Rethinking a Business Continuity plan (BCP): what should companies learn from the Great East Japan Earthquake? Nomura Research Institute paper No. 173, May 1, 2012. Nomura Research Institute, Ltd., Japan

Christopher M (1992) Logistics and supply chain management: strategies for reducing costs and improving services. Pitman, London

Granot H (1999) Emergency inter-organizational relationships. Disaster Prev Manag 8(1):21–26

Kovacs G, Spens KM (2007) Humanitarian logistics in disaster relief operations. Int J Phys Distrib Logist Manag 37(2):99–114

McElroy (2013) Traditional approaches 'increasingly fail' insurance industry in time of climate change. Available at: http://www.unisdr.org/archive/33781. Accessed 10 Sep 2013

Nilsson S, Sjoberg M, Larsson G (2010) A civil contingencies agency management system for disaster aid: a theoretical model. Int J Organ Anal 18(4):412–429

Shyam KC (2013) Cost benefit studies on disaster risk reduction in developing countries. World Bank's Working paper. Available at: http://documents.worldbank.org/curated/en/2013/08/18136412/cost-benefit-studies-disaster-risk-reduction-developing-countries. Accessed 10 Sep 2013

Trim PRJ (2004) An integrative approach to disaster management and planning. Disaster Prev Manag 13(3):218–225

UNEP (2007) After the Tsunami: sustainable building guidelines for South-East Asia. UNEP SBCI (Sustainable Buildings and Construction Initiative). Published by Swiss Resource Centre for Consultancies for Development, Vadianstrasse

UNISDR (2013) Global assessment report on disaster risk reduction 2013. Published by The United Nations Office for Disaster Risk Reduction. Available online at: http://www.unisdr.org/we/inform/publications/33013. Accessed 10 Sep 2013

Ye L, Abe M (2012) The impacts of natural disasters on global supply chains. Asia-Pacific Research and Training Network on Trade. ARTNeT Working Paper Series N°. 115/June 2012. ESCAP, Bangkok

Chapter 2
Logistics Planning in Natural Disasters

Sravani Bharandev, S.K. Mukul Ali, and Sindhu

2.1 Introduction

Manmade or technological disasters can be avoided if all the people start working carefully without any negligence and their harmful intentions to kill the people change, but natural disasters arise because of nature and they cannot be avoided. So every country should plan properly when faced with disasters, for which a plan of how to manage a disaster is essential.

In general, disaster management is structured into four phases. The first phase is mitigation where the government of the country will focus on building safer communities. Mitigation activities are long run and policy integrated and helps in minimizing future threats posed by disasters. Preparedness is the second phase of disaster management in which the analysis of previous disasters is made and the strategies for the next period are formulated. If a country manages this phase of disaster management effectively, then the loss that a disaster can make to the country will be minimized. After the disaster took place, there is a need to serve the people who are affected because of it. This stage of disaster management is called the response phase. This phase concentrates on the immediate response to the needs of the affected people. Finally, if the disaster continues over a long period, all rehabilitation activities will take place; this phase is called reconstruction, and it is the final phase of disaster management.

S. Bharandev (✉)
Rajiv Gandhi University of Knowledge Technologies Basar, Basar, Telangana, India
e-mail: sravanibharandev@gmail.com

S.K. Mukul Ali • Sindhu
Business Management Department, Rajiv Gandhi University of Knowledge Technologies
Basar, Basar, Telangana, India

© Springer India 2016
B.S. Sahay et al. (eds.), *Managing Humanitarian Logistics*, Springer Proceedings
in Business and Economics, DOI 10.1007/978-81-322-2416-7_2

Every country should concentrate on its performance in each stage of disaster management in order to minimize all types of losses that a disaster causes. There will not be much impact on human life immediately if any activities of mitigation or preparedness got delayed, but in the phase of response people are affected by the disaster, so they need assistance immediately. Affected people may have the need for so many basic amenities like food, water, clothes, transportation, medicines, etc.; these needs can be met through proper logistics, for without which serving the people in these situations will be difficult. Seventy-percent of the total cost of managing the disaster is the cost of logistics. Because of these and the urgency in fulfilling the needs of the affected people, logistics planning in disaster management is very important.

2.2 Natural Disasters in India in the Last Decade

India is one of the disaster-prone countries in the world. It is vulnerable to natural disasters due to its geoclimatic conditions and various environmental factors. Urbanization, industrialization, population growth, inefficient technologies, and immoral intentions of the people made India a technological disaster-prone country also. In India, out of the 35 states and union territories, 27 are disaster prone: 58.6 % of the land is prone to earthquakes with a degree of moderate to high intensity, 12 % of land to floods and river erosion, 76.2 % of the coast line to cyclone, and 68 % of the agricultural field to drought; besides these, many disasters had not been counted because of improper communication and inefficient administration in remote areas. In the last decade India has experienced so many significant disasters, some of them created adverse affect on the lives and socioeconomic status of the country. The Bhuj earthquake occurred on 26 January 2001 with a magnitude of 7.7 and resulted in 13,805 deaths and damage of 1,205,198 houses. Indian Ocean Tsunami on 26 December 2004 affected 2.44 million people and 157,393 houses and caused 8,835 lives. In August 2006, the arrival of Barmer floods in Rajasthan affected 800,000 lives and damaged 300 million crops and 5,200 houses. It also resulted in the deaths of 103 people and 47,000 cattle. Kosi floods in Bihar on 18 August 2008 resulted in the deaths of 493 people and 3,500 people were missing. It also affected 3.3 million people, 608,000 acres of crops, 15,500 cattle and 236,632 houses. On 25 May 2009, Cyclone Aila in West Bengal caused the deaths of 175 people and affected the lives of 2.2 million people. It collapsed and damaged 61,000 and 132,000 houses respectively. It also damaged 236,609 ha of crops and 6,713 cattle and livestock. Because of the Cyclone Thane in Tamilnadu and Puducherry on 25 December 2011, 58 people died and 450,000 houses were damaged. It also affected 176,000 ha of crops. The recent Uttarakhand floods happened in June 2013 created a big loss in all aspects. Nearly 5,700 people were presumed to be dead and 4,200 villages were affected. Some of the parts of Uttar Pradesh, Delhi, Haryana, and Himachal Pradesh also got affected by these floods. Uttarakhand which is being a pilgrim spot due to Gangotri, Kedarnath, Badrinath, and Chardham made 70,000 and more people to be affected including the pilgrims and the local residents.

2.3   Disaster Management and Logistics Planning During Natural Disasters in India

National Disaster Management Authority (NDMA) headed by the prime minister of India plans all activities of disaster management in the country. It generates policies and communicates them to all states and is responsible for the allocation of funds for different phases of disaster management like mitigation and preparedness. State Disaster Management Authorities (SDMAs) headed by chief ministers of the states are responsible for their own state disaster management activities, but these SDMAs work under the guidelines of NDMA. SDMAs give instructions and distribute the policies or strategies, which are formulated by NDMAs to all the districts of its own state. In districts, District Disaster Management Authority (DDMA) headed by a district collector or district magistrate or deputy commissioner will look after all the activities of disaster management. Procurement of materials and provisions for rescue and relief operation in disaster situations will be planned and executed by NDMA. The National Institute of Disaster Management (NIDM) which works under the guidelines of NDMA is a research institute that studies previous disaster situations and forecasts upcoming disasters and also tries to find ways to avoid these disasters or to reduce their effects. The National Disaster Response Force (NDRF) is the trained army which has eight battalions of police force to take care of needs of the affected people in disasters; these battalions will be sent to the affected areas depending upon the need, the range of how much area got affected, and how severe is the impact of a disaster on the area. NDRF is bounded by the guidelines of the government of India and NDMA and is the main entity to serve the people in disaster situation, and the logistics and rescue operations will also depend on the strength of NDRF.

The National Crisis Management Committee (NCMC) is another special body of the central government of India which deals with some different cases of emergencies which require close involvement of security forces or intelligence agencies such as terrorism, law and order problems, serial bomb blasts, hijacking, air accidents, mine disasters, port harbor emergencies, forest fires, etc. Disaster management is multidisciplinary; if any action needs to take place, it has to be approved by so many different departments. The National Executive Committee (NEC), which has a union home secretary as its chairperson and has the secretaries from all other departments like agriculture, health, power, rural development, water resources, external affairs, mines, shipping, HRD, etc., develops the disaster management plan. Apart from these, there are some local authorities which participate in disaster management activities. They are Panchayati raj, municipalities, district and cantonment board, town planning authorities, etc. These local authorities mainly help in rehabilitation and reconstruction activities of disaster management.

NDMA, SDMAs, and DDMAs are responsible for disaster management in the country, states, and districts, respectively; these authorities along with some other local authorities plan logistic operations during disasters as well. These authorities concentrate on the procurement of required materials and acquiring of funds to procure the needed materials. The government will allot or sanction the funds for different activities as planned and suggested by these authorities. Once the procurement of required materials is done, the problem arises in transporting all these materials or goods and services to the affected area. Because during a disaster the infrastructure of the affected area will be damaged partially or completely sometimes, it is not easy to satisfy the needs of the affected people immediately. During disasters, the needs of the people affected are emergent; if response is delayed, a person may lose his/her life, so immediate response should be provided for which trained personnel is needed.

India has NDRF as its first and key responder in disaster situations because it is the only force in India which has personnel trained in logistics and rescue operations during disasters. For any disaster situation, if this force is not sufficient to take care of all the logistics operations, then the government may consult other departments for help. The departments which will take part in logistics operations if NDRF is not sufficient to handle are Indian Armed Forces, Central Paramilitary Forces (CPMF), State Police Forces and Fire Services, Civil Defense and Home Guards, State Disaster Response Force, National Cadet Corps (NCC), National Service Scheme (NSS), and Nehru Yuva Kendra Sangathan (NYKS).

The National Executive Committee (NEC) prepares the plan of how the logistics should take place during disaster by following the guidelines of the NDMA. The plan will be communicated and coordinated to all the above-mentioned authorities and different forces, which participate in the operations for better performance, which indeed minimizes the loss. In India, each department or ministry is concerned with disaster management with different standard operating procedures (SOPs) for different types of disasters. These SOPs are related to the rescue operations, medical assistance, restoration of essential services, and communication in disaster sites.

2.4   Analysis of Existing Situation and Improvements

Logistics deals with all operations that helps in transporting goods or services from the point of origin to the point of consumption. It involves procurement, transportation, and storage; distribution, planning, and preparation should also be done before procurement because needs assessment is crucial in case of humanitarian logistics—all the needs are very essential and emergent in nature. Currently in India the procurement during disaster situations is done by the government and some nongovernmental organizations (NGOs) along with some local authorities. The major part of procurement is done by the government and NGOs, but these two parties go for procuring in their own ways often from different markets which may lead to a difference in the prices of the required goods. Organizations may buy the goods from local markets. Because of the emergency, the inflation in those markets will increase due to the increase in demand and scarcity of the required goods. If all the entities want to take part in procuring the required materials to serve the affected people, an association and a committee should be appointed to organize all the activities of the association mainly regarding procurement. The committee should have members from all different organizations and should be headed by any person from the NGO; because if the NGOs want to do some favor for the affected people, mostly they don't let the credit to be taken by the government. The government should also compromise in giving the chairman position to a person from NGO because the ultimate purpose is to serve the people of disaster prone areas. Now bulk amount of goods can be ordered and purchased at one time, so the inflation in local markets can be controlled to some extent. The association will also enable distribution functions to be proper because the handling of goods and materials will be done by only one party. This also helps in avoiding sales in black markets, and currently, the government is following procedure of having labels affixed to the goods, which contain information that they are not for sale. In order to reduce the cost of procurement, the government can also take up another action, which does not exist currently. It should formulate a policy stating that all manufacturing firms should supply the products necessary during disaster situations at manufacturing cost without any profit as part of their corporate social responsibility (CSR) at the time of disasters.

To procure required goods or materials, funds are needed and they can be acquired either by government or through donations. Generally the funds allotted by the government are not sufficient to handle the situation, and the severity of disaster will also create a need for more funds. So there comes the importance of donations, and they can be made by individuals, organizations, nongovernmental organizations (NGOs), not-for-profit organizations, etc. The current mode of donating is through online banking or to go directly to any government body or NGO, which is collecting funds, and deposit the amount that they want to donate. If any person is interested in donating but does not have access to online banking and not able to contact any NGO or government body to donate the amount, then an opportunity to have some funds will be lost. So by creating a mode of donation through mobile phones will considerably increase the amount of funds because according to surveys in India 70.72 % of the total population are using mobile phones. For which to happen, the government has to create an agreement with all the network operators, and they should send messages which invite their customers to donate funds as soon as a disaster strikes. This can be a part of their CSR. A concept of issuing coupons can also be introduced as an option to raise funds. When customers go to government offices for payment of bills like electricity, telephone, etc., they will be issued these coupons instead of some small amount (i.e., less than Rs10) after payment is made. The total money collected from all the customers throughout the year will be transferred periodically to the government. Because the collection takes place every day irrespective of the occurrence of a disaster, good amount of money can be collected which may be helpful to serve the affected people once a disaster occurs.

If all manufacturing companies, network operators, or any other organizations will take these activities as part of their CSR, a good public image is created in the market with which customer satisfaction and loyalty can be achieved and the employees of those organizations will also feel motivated. A motivated employee can yield better results and by which the companies can also have increased profits.

After acquiring funds from all the parties, the procurement is made, after which transportation function takes place. Though there are trained personnel like NDRF and SDRF, etc., that can transport goods from one place to another with the worst conditions of infrastructure, the force will not be sufficient, and if the intensity of the disaster is becoming worse, it is further difficult to handle the situation. So the government should try to create some tie-ups with private business logistics companies like VRL, DTDC, DHL, Cargo, Blue dart, FedEx, TNT, etc. As these companies are experienced and well established in performing logistics operations. There is a certainty that in times of disasters the government will face problems of insufficient funds and there will be limited equipment which is needed in transportation of goods and in rescue operations. The government cannot invest in purchasing of equipment because they are highly expensive and will be used only during disaster situations. In such cases taking the help of private logistic companies will support the government in its operations to serve the people and save the people. They can easily provide assistance in technical aspects, trained staff and managers, facility for communication, fleet management, etc. A database should be created to store the information about all the manufacturing firms and logistics companies which gives a scope to add new companies to the database and to maintain good relationships with the existing companies which are already listed in the database. The creation of database will make the process of contacting the firms simple.

Once procurement is completed, the goods have to be stored at a place from where according to a plan they get distributed to the affected area. For this purpose, the government will need to look for regional or temporary warehouses because disasters will not affect the same area every time, so building permanent warehouses which involves high investment of funds is not a good option. In such cases, arrangement of temporary warehouses should be done; in some cases where there is a possibility that a disaster can affect the same area frequently, the government or the association should try to maintain good relationship with local authorities so that they can provide some buildings to store inventory on a temporary basis and when a disaster strikes in that region. Creating an association which tries to bring centralization possible in procurement activity will also help in the centralization of inventory and storage activities. Handling of goods by one person enables proper organizing of all the goods in performing functions such as analysis of existing inventory levels and replenishment.

Logistics is not completed without distribution function; once the goods are settled in their inventory, they need to be dispatched to the affected areas, which is quite difficult because of the damaged infrastructure in as a result of the disaster.

While distributing goods to the point of consumption, there may be a possibility that they can be robbed, so tracking and tracing of goods need to done to save them. Sometimes, if the affected area is very large, there is a possibility that the areas nearer to the warehouses can have more goods while the rest which are at considerably long distance from the warehouses will get less or none at all. To avoid such situations, tracking with the help of RFID (radiofrequency identification) can be implemented. At present barcodes are used to keep track of distribution activities, so adoption of RFID technology which is cost-effective can yield better results. RFID technology uses small tags which can be attached to goods, people, vehicles, etc., which works based on radio propagation.

2.5 Suggestions

Based on our study, we propose the following:

- Centralization in procurement and inventory management of required products for affected people by forming an association
- Creating a database about all the manufacturing firms and private business logistics companies
- Providing mobile donating facility to encourage people to donate more so as to increase the amount of funds
- Issuing coupons to raise funds all the time so as to maintain a considerable amount of funds to use in disaster situations
- Strengthening public-private partnership (PPP) for manufacturing firms to reduce procurement cost and for logistics companies to reduce transportation cost and for better logistics operations
- Implementation of RFID system in transportation and distribution of goods from warehouses to the affected areas

2.6 Conclusion

Logistics, though a very essential function in disaster management, often lacks recognition in India. Logistics planning was often started after a disaster strikes which will make it even more difficult, so a plan-do-check-act process should be followed to have better planning. Limited collaboration among all the parties involved in handling disaster situations results to the increase in the cost of logistics and ineffective and inefficient operations; to avoid these, it is suggested to form an association that will take care of all the activities of logistics. Lack of professional staff makes transportation and distribution activities of logistics complex, the collaboration or public-private partnership provides a facility to use the trained staff of business logistics companies in disaster situations. Inadequate use of technology increases the costs of operations and creates delay in responding; adopting technologies like RFID and using databases to be in contact with suppliers results to better tracing and tracking during distribution and immediate response to the needs of the people affected.

References

Argonne National Laboratory (2007) Emergency management logistics planning. From: http://www.dis.anl.gov/pubs/59061.pdf

Arun K et al (2012) Developing forecasting tool for humanitarian relief organizations in emergency logistics planning. World Academy of Science, Engineering and Technology 71 2012. From: http://www.waset.org/journals/waset/v71/v71-305.pdf

Business Civic Leadership Center US Chamber of Commerce, Washington (2012) The role of business in disaster response. Retrieved from: http://bclc.uschamber.com/sites/default/files/documents/files/Role%20of%20Business%20in%20Disaster%20Response.pdf

da Costaa SRA et al. (2012) Supply chains in humanitarian operations: cases and analysis. Retrieved from: http://www.lvmt.fr/ewgt2012/compendium_120.pdf

Federal Emergency Management Agency (2008) Washington. FEMA strategic plan fiscal years 2008–2013: Nation's Preeminent Emergency Management and Preparedness Agency. From: http://www.fema.gov/pdf/about/fy08_fema_sp_bookmarked.pdf

Government of India Ministry of Home Affairs (2009) National policy on disaster management. Approved by union cabinet on 22nd October 2009. Available from: http://nidm.gov.in/PDF/policies/ndm_policy2009.pdf

Government of India. Government of India situation report. New Delhi, Feb 2001

Howden M (2009) How humanitarian logistics information systems can improve humanitarian supply chains: a view from the field. In: Proceedings of the 6th international ISCRAM conference Gothenburg, Sweden, May 2009. Retrieved from: http://citeseerx.ist.psu.edu/viewdoc/download?doi=10.1.1.180.9783&rep=rep1&type=pdf

http://ndma.gov.in/ndma/cyclones.html

http://ndma.gov.in/ndma/dmdivision.html

http://ndma.gov.in/ndma/earthquake.html

http://ndma.gov.in/ndma/floods.html

http://ndrfandcd.gov.in/cms/Ndrf.aspx

http://top10companiesinindia.com/2013/07/05/logistics-companies-in-india

http://www.ndmindia.nic.in/management/ncmc.html

Kaul D, Ayaz MD, LohitKumar SN (2006). Department of Civil Engineering, IIT Kanpur, India. Disaster management in India. Retrieved from: http://unpan1.un.org/intradoc/groups/public/documents/apcity/unpan050292.pdf

Liu Ming, Zhao Lindu (2008) Institute of Systems Engineering, Southeast University, Nanjing, China. A collaboration model for multi level emergency rescue network. Published in POMS 19th annual conference La Jolla, California, USA, May 9–May 12 2008. Retrieved from: http://ebiz.uoregon.edu/poms2008/fullpapers/008-0033.pdf

National Disaster Management Authority (2010) The disaster management act, 2005. Government of India, New Delhi, p 1

Özdamar L et al (2004) Emergency planning in natural disasters. J Ann Oper Res 129(1–4): 217–245

Purohit J, Suthar CR, Department of Public Administration, M L S University, Udaipur, India (2012) Disaster statistics in Indian scenario in last two decades. Int J Sci Res Pub 2(5):1–5

Shivananda H, Gautam PK (2010) Reassessing India's disaster management preparedness and the role of the Indian armed forces. Available at: http://idsa.in/system/files/jds_6_1_Shivanandah.Gautam.pdf

Sinha A. Report on recovery and reconstruction following the Orissa Super Cyclone in October 1999. Asian Disaster Reduction Centre, p 1

Srinivasan K, Nagraj V (2006) The state and civil society in disaster response: post-tsunami experiences in Tamil Nadu. J Soc Work Disabil Rehabil 5(3/4):57–80

Van Wassenhove LN (2006) Blackett Memorial Lecture Humanitarian aid logistics: supply chain management in high gear. J Oper Res Soc 57:475–489. doi:10.1057/palgrave.jors.2602125

www.imd.gov.in

www.mha.nic.in

www.nidm.net

Chapter 3
Identification and Modelling of Critical Success Factors of a Humanitarian Supply Chain

Vijayta Fulzele, Rachita Gupta, and Ravi Shankar

3.1 Introduction

Nowadays, natural calamities are very frequent and it brings immense loss to lives and property. There is no specific pattern or pre-information for the occurrence of a disaster; it usually occurs all of a sudden and results in a lot of destruction. In more specific terms, disaster can be defined as disruption in the effective conduct of operations of an individual, system, organisation or nation. It may result into loss of infrastructure, resources and human lives. It is the disruption that physically affects a system as a whole and threatens its priorities and goals (Van 2006). The Federal Emergency Management Agency (FEMA) classifies disasters as natural (e.g., earthquakes, hurricanes, floods, wildlife fires, etc.) or technological (e.g., terrorism, nuclear power plant emergencies, hazardous materials, etc.). There are many other literatures in which authors have categorized the disaster based on its cause as 'natural' and 'man made' and also based on the speed of occurrence as 'sudden onset' and 'slow onset'. Hence, there can be four types of disaster: natural sudden onset, natural slow onset, man made sudden onset and man made slow onset. No matter what kind of disaster happens, its consequences are enormous, not only in short-term injuries and loss of lives but also in long-term changes in economic and social conditions.

Due to the increasing number of such destructive disasters, it is highly required to identify and implement some measures in order to reduce the occurrence or rather impact of disaster, as much as possible. Ergun et al. (2005) stated that the

V. Fulzele • R. Shankar
Department of Management Studies, Indian Institute of Technology, Delhi, India
e-mail: vijayta.fulzele22@gmail.com; ravi1@dms.iitd.ernet.in

R. Gupta (✉)
Bharti School of Telecommunication Technology and Management,
Indian Institute of Technology, Delhi, India
e-mail: rachitagupta1987@gmail.com

© Springer India 2016
B.S. Sahay et al. (eds.), *Managing Humanitarian Logistics*, Springer Proceedings
in Business and Economics, DOI 10.1007/978-81-322-2416-7_3

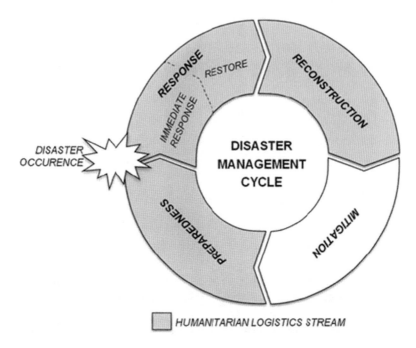

Fig. 3.1 The humanitarian logistics stream

occurrence of such events cannot be completely controlled, but its impact can be reduced to a certain level by using different means including disaster management. Whatever be the type of disaster, the management of these events typically follows four sequential stages: mitigation, preparedness, response and recovery (Ergun et al. 2005). These together constitute disaster management cycle (Cozzolino 2012; Van 2006). Van (2006) has depicted the four stages of disaster management, as in Fig. 3.1.

The description of each stage has also been defined by Van, as below:

Mitigation phase aims to retain the social and economic conditions and to reduce the destruction level by implementing various laws and mechanisms. In this phase, logisticians do not participate directly. These are issues that relate to the responsibilities of governments and do not involve the direct participation of logisticians.

Preparedness phase involves various operations that occur during the period before a disaster strikes. In this stage, strategies are adopted with the aim to avoid the gravest possible consequences of a disaster. To meet new challenges, various efforts are made on the basis of learning during disaster and based on the past experiences. This stage becomes more crucial and important as it involves development of physical network design, information and communication technology systems.

Response phase comes into picture after a disaster occurs. It is further subdivided into two sub-phases:

(a) Immediate-response sub-phase (involves activities/responses that are to be adopted immediately for providing relief to the affected ones via developing 'silent network' or 'temporary network')

(b) Restore sub-phase (involves restoration of basic services and delivery of commodities in the shortest possible time with the aim to serve as many affected as possible)

Recovery phase involves operations aftermath of a disaster. This phase involves various rehabilitation operations for a long-term perspective.

The success of all the four stages of disaster depends upon the proper functioning of involved supply chains. Supply chain plays an important role in disaster management. Gurnasekaran and Ngai (2004) defined supply chain as 'an integration of key business processes from end user through original suppliers that provides products, services, information and hence, add value for customers and other stakeholder'. To mitigate the effect of disaster and to reduce the number of loss of life, it is very important to have a proper understanding and implementation of the supply chain involved during disaster situation, i.e. effective implementation of the Humanitarian Supply Chain Management (HSCM). HSCM is concerned with the efficient flow management of aid materials, information and services to reduce the impact of disaster on human lives (Lijo and Ramesh 2012).

The humanitarian supply chain involves various operations for the provision of relief to the affected population and areas, such as rescue operation, medical aid, adequate food supply and distribution, transportation, provision of shelter, etc. (Munzberg et al. 2013). Implementation of this supply chains is not an easy task; there are so many factors affecting the supply chain and many barriers to the same. In the next sections, we will come to know what are those factors, what are its implications, and how does these factors affect the supply chain. In Sect. 3.2, we will be discussing literature review related to important factors affecting the HSCM. In Sect. 3.3, a hierarchy of factors has been created using ISM model on the basis of driving and dependence power.

3.2 Literature Review

Extensive research has already been done related to the Humanitarian Supply Chain Management (HSCM). For the timely relief operations, it is very important that the functioning of HSC is as effective as possible. But, as already been discussed in the previous section, this is not an easy task; there are many obstacles to it. Vorst and Beulens (2002) specified the issues as uncertainty and lack of data as to when a disaster will strike, number of people affected, what the available donations are, what the required infrastructure is, lack of adequate supplies, etc. Much research has also been done for the mitigation of various obstacles to HSCM. Still there is a research gap in terms of finding out the order of implementing various important factors that may result in successful HSCM. The ordering of these factors is performed using interpretive structural modelling (ISM), discussed in Sect. 3.3. All the identified factors lie in the category critical success factors (CSFs).

The concept of success factors was first developed by Daniel (1961). It was proposed that if certain factors critical to the success of that organisation are not achieved, the organisation will fail (Huotari and Wilson 2001). A number of definitions, for CSFs, have been given by many researchers. Hofer and Schendel (1978) state that CSFs are 'those variables which management can influence through its decisions' and which can affect a company's overall competitive position. A more specific definition was given by Korpela and Tuominen (1996); they stated that CSFs are 'the characteristics, conditions or variables that when properly sustained, maintained or managed can have a significant impact on the success of a company in a particular industry'.

In this study, various critical success factors have been identified. These factors are required to be considered and implemented in a way that these contribute to the overall success of the involved supply chains within a relief operation, during disaster situation. There can be a number of CSFs, out of which 11 most important factors are considered in this study. These factors are information management and technology utilisation, continuous improvement, effective utilisation of resources, strategic planning, distribution strategy, material movement, disaster assessment or prewarning system, risk mitigation, prompt response, rebuilding and minimisation of loss of human lives. Description of all these factors is given below.

3.2.1 Information Management and Technology Utilisation

During relief operation, communication and proper information management is one of the most important aspects, and the utilisation of existing telecommunications infrastructure is as important as other telecommunication methods (Gooley 1999). Real-time communications are 'the most important method of reacting quickly for affective coordination' (Long 1997).

Effective usage of communication technology is also crucial as it directly impacts the speed of the response at the time of relief operations and enables better coordination between the actors within the supply chain (Long and Wood 1995).

3.2.2 Continuous Improvement

It is recognised that commercial supply chain can meet the need of the market by focusing on the continuous improvement approach. The main requirement is over the capabilities of humanitarian supply chains and the measurement of their effectiveness. Few researches have already been conducted on the same (Davidson 2006; Beamon 2004; Van 2006). The improvements can be either radical or incremental. In case of radical, improvements are done at once, while in case of incremental, improvements are done over time. Continuous improvements can be done using the process of benchmarking in which processes and performances of relief operations for future disaster is evaluated and implemented by comparing it with the best practices from the previous relief operations.

3.2.3 Effective Utilisation of Resources

At the time of disaster, resources such as funds, donations, skilled human resources, aid supplies and other assets are very crucial, and these are required to be managed in an effective and optimised way.

The system to deliver humanitarian relief comprises of mosaic of actors that contract together in various ways, and the way in which they contract with each other affects the risks that can occur within the whole operation. This mosaic of actors is made up of donor organisations, bilateral and multilateral agencies, NGOs, Red Cross movement agencies, private contractors and military forces operating according to various norms and guidelines, but with significant diversity of approach (Ewins et al. 2006). As there are many actors involved within the humanitarian supply chain, there is a requirement to make proper planning and to implement same in a way that there is smooth functioning of relief operations with optimisation of resource usage. It has been a well-said and proven statement that effectiveness of any process depends upon the collaborative working of disparate teams with a common goal and the same applies to HSCM as well (Power et al. 2001).

3.2.4 Strategic Planning

This factor falls under the stage of preparedness, as this factor deals with making various plans and strategies before a disaster hits. A long-term approach is adopted which allows an organisation to be prepared for what must be done when an emergency occurs (Long 1997). Here, long-term decisions are made to identify the strengths and weaknesses of the involved activities within a relief operation, based on past experiences and learning, so that the conditions remain under control and the ultimate task of saving human lives can be achieved during disaster situation and post-disaster situation. As a preparedness measure, three types of planning are to be done: (i) pre-disaster planning, (ii) post-disaster planning and (iii) restoration planning (Pettit and Beresford 2009).

3.2.5 Distribution Strategy

Time and cost are major constraints in emergency relief operations. For the same, it is quite important to adopt some of the standard distribution strategies, such as direct shipping, cross-docking and centralized warehouse. In case of direct shipping, the supplies are transferred directly from source to destination. In cross-docking, supplies are not directly transferred from source to destination, rather there is a temporary storage unit in between, where the supplies are unloaded, sorted, loaded again and then shipped to the destinations. In case of centralised warehousing, supplies are collected from various locations to a central point, and then from there, the supplies are distributed to the destinations. An individual or a combination of these strategies can be adopted during HSCM. Whatever be the strategy, the supplies flowing through the relief chain primarily consist of pre-positioned stocks in warehouses, supplies procured from the suppliers and in-kind donations (De la Torre et al. 2011). Usually, supplies are shipped from various worldwide locations to a primary warehouse, which is usually located near a sea- or airport. Next, supplies are shipped to a secondary hub (a large, permanent warehouse typically located in a larger city). At this secondary hub, supplies are stored, sorted and transferred to tertiary hubs (local distribution centers). Finally, local distribution centers deliver relief supplies to beneficiaries. Supplies acquired from local sources may also be stored at secondary and tertiary warehouses or directly distributed to the beneficiaries (Beamon and Balcik 2008).

3.2.6 Transport and Capacity Planning

Material movement without proper planning of transportation is not even thinkable and implementable. Transportation of materials during disaster situation is completely different as compared to the usual condition faced by commercial organisation. While the latter have privately owned mode of transportation as well as stable infrastructure, in disaster situation, modes of transportation are unorganised and there is unavailability of infrastructure. Transportation is not just about transferring material; it also involves other aspects such as selecting transport mode, capacity, scheduling, maintenance and intermodality (Pettit and Beresford 2009).

During disaster situation, assessment of demand becomes unpredictable in terms of timings, location and scale and will be affected by a range of factors (Kovacs and Spens 2007; Barbarosa and Arda 2004). Capacity planning affects the decisions on the numbers of warehouses and distribution centers and their capacity, vehicles and other equipment and numbers of employees. Four key areas affecting capacity are warehousing, transport, material handling devices and human resources, and maximisation of use of capacity is key (Gunasekaran and Ngai 2003).

3.2.7 Disaster Assessment

This factor lies in the category of preparedness. Prewarning system helps in providing the information regarding volume and intensity of disaster that could affect the human lives and infrastructure as well. Daily communication with several meteorological stations keeps the organisation up to date with the local weather forecast and especially with the disaster threat in the region. Early warning system can make whole HSCM under control (Heeringen 2010).

3.2.8 Risk Mitigation

Risks are involved at every stage within a humanitarian supply chain. If no plans or strategies are adopted to remove or at least reduce the involved risks, then the whole relief operation during disaster situation might go in vain. The risk management process comprises of three elements: architecture, strategy and protocols, where risk management specifies the roles, responsibilities, communication and risk reporting structure; risk strategy involves various decisions to manage risks in an effective manner; risk protocols are the guidelines for the organization that include rules, procedures, tools and techniques that specifies risk management methodologies. Every organization should adopt various approaches towards risk mitigation in a formal way.

3.2.9 Prompt Response

Speed is a central value for emergency logistics stakeholders. Rapid response is the most important aspect during disaster situation. Speed of aid to disaster victims is often vital to their survival. There are many challenges that restrict the players within humanitarian logistics to respond quickly. These challenges include physical destruction, which limits logistical pathways (Kovacs and Spens 2007; Samii 2010), and constrained resources, which limit funding during the disaster (Long and Wood 1995; Oloruntoba and Gray 2006; Whiting and Ayala-Ostrom 2009; Benini et al. 2009).

3.2.10 Restoration

This factor lies in the category of recovery post disaster. Post disaster, there are many adverse affects such as socio-economic disparities, livelihoods, disruption of communities, environmental impacts, etc. (Ingram et al. 2006). Here comes the role of recovery phase for rebuilding everything and to bring life back to normal. Post-disaster recovery planning can be thought of as providing a blueprint for the restoration of a community after a disaster occurs. This can be done through long- and short-term strategies. Specific strategies might include planning, policy changes, programs, projects and other activities such as business continuity planning. Post-disaster recovery planning is a shared responsibility between individuals, private businesses and industries, state and local governments and the federal government (CSC 2012). Though this step is to be taken after a disaster happens, still pre-planning of such procedure can make things easier and reduce risks as well.

3.2.11 Minimisation of Loss of Human Lives

The overarching aim of humanitarian sectors is to save lives and provide the basic needs to the affected people. The objective of the disaster relief operation is always linked to how quickly and conveniently the resources reach the affected people (Roy et al. 2012). The relief distribution is the ultimate connector of the humanitarian sector with the beneficiaries. This is the ultimate stage of humanitarian supply chain. This involves the supply of relief items from local distribution centers to the disaster-affected area (Balcik et al. 2008). The necessity before, during and after disaster is to secure and move material efficiently.

3.3 Methodology

Interpretive Structural Modelling (ISM) depicts hierarchical relationships between various variables identified and produces structural models from poorly articulated mental models so as to make it more visible and well defined. ISMs are used in multiples of applications such as decision support system, waste management, vendor selection, product design, supply chain management, decision-making, value chain management, world-class manufacturing and so on (Sushil 2012).

3.3.1 Step by Step Procedure (Adopted from Sushil 2012; Mandal and Deshmukh 1993)

(i) Factors or attributes are identified, which are relevant to the issue.
(ii) Contextual relationship between various identified factors is established. This is done by pairwise comparison of each factor with other factors.

(iii) A structural self-interaction matrix (SSIM) is developed based on pairwise comparison of each factor, which analyses the contextual relationship of 'leads to'.

(iv) Reachability matrix is developed by converting SSIM matrix into binary matrix and the final matrix in check for any transitivity. Transitivity works on basic assumption; i.e. if factor A leads to B and factor B leads to C, then factor A necessarily leads to C and the modified reachability matrix is obtained.

(v) From the modified reachability matrix, reachability set and antecedent set for each factor are found. Then the intersection of these sets for all factors is derived and the reachability matrix is partitioned into different levels.

(vi) Based on levels obtained in step 5, a digraph is constructed after removing transitivity obtained in step 4 from the reachability matrix.

(vii) The resultant digraph obtained in step 6 is converted into ISM by replacing factor nodes into statements.

(viii) The ISM model developed is finally reviewed for any conceptual inconsistencies, and modifications are made accordingly.

On the basis of the above steps, ISM is applied on critical success factors in HSCM (discussed in Sect. 3.2).

3.3.2 Development of Structural Self-Interaction Matrix (SSIM)

Using available secondary data and opinions of expert, contextual relationships between identified critical success factors, say i and j, are established. Four symbols are used to describe the type of relationship that exists between two factors under considerations. The symbols are described below:

(i) V for the relation from factor i to factor j and not in both directions

(ii) A for the relation from factor j to factor i and not in both directions

(iii) X for both the direction relations from factor i to factor j and from factor j to factor i

(iv) 0 (zero), if the relation between the two factor i and j does not exist

The SSIM constructed is shown in Table 3.1.

3.3.3 Constructing Initial Reachability Matrix

The SSIM is converted into a binary matrix, called initial reachability matrix. The rules of substitution from the four symbols of SSIM discussed above to 1s and 0s in the reachability matrix are as follows:

Table 3.1 Structural self-interaction matrix

No.	Enablers	11	10	9	8	7	6	5	4	3	2
1	Strategic planning	V	V	V	V	V	V	V	V	V	V
2	Disaster assessment	A	O	V	V	V	V	V	V	X	
3	Information management and technology utilisation	V	V	V	V	V	V	V	V		
4	Effective utilisation of resources	V	V	V	V	V	X	A			
5	Distribution strategy	A	O	V	O	V	A				
6	Transportation and capacity planning	A	V	V	V	V					
7	Prompt response (C7)	A	V	V	V						
8	Risk mitigation	A	V	V							
9	Minimisation of loss of human lives	A	O								
10	Restoration/rebuilding	A									
11	Continuous improvement										

(i) If the (i,j) entry in SSIM is V, then the (i,j) entry in the reachability matrix becomes 1 and the (j,i) entry becomes 0.

(ii) If the (i,j) entry in SSIM is A, then the (i,j) entry in the reachability matrix becomes 0 and the (j,i) entry becomes 1.

(iii) If the (i,j) entry in SSIM is X, then the (i,j) entry in the reachability matrix becomes 1 and the (j,i) entry becomes 1.

(iv) If the (i,j) entry in SSIM is 0, then the (i,j) entry in the reachability matrix becomes 0 and the (j,i) entry becomes 0.

The initial reachability matrix derived from SSIM is shown in Table 3.2.

3.3.4 Constructing Final Reachability Matrix

The final reachability matrix is constructed from initial reachability matrix by adding transitivity rule; i.e. if A leads to B and B leads to C, then A must lead to C. This matrix also includes the driving power and dependence power of each of the involved critical success factors. The final reachability matrix is shown in Table 3.3.

3.3.5 Level Partitions

From the final reachability matrix, reachability set and antecedent set are derived for each factor. Intersection set is determined for each factor by identifying the intersection of corresponding reachability and antecedent set. If both reachability and antecedent sets are the same, then the corresponding factor is considered to be

Table 3.2 Initial reachability matrix

No.	Enablers	1	2	3	4	5	6	7	8	9	10
1	Strategic planning	1	1	1	1	1	1	1	1	1	1
2	Disaster assessment	0	1	1	1	1	1	1	1	1	0
3	Information management and technology utilisation	0	1	1	1	1	1	1	1	1	1
4	Effective utilisation of resources	0	0	0	1	0	1	1	1	1	1
5	Distribution strategy	0	0	0	1	1	0	1	0	1	0
6	Transportation and capacity planning	0	0	0	1	1	1	1	1	1	1
7	Prompt response (C7)	0	0	0	0	0	0	1	1	1	1
8	Risk mitigation	0	0	0	0	0	0	0	1	1	1
9	Minimisation of loss of human lives	0	0	0	0	0	0	0	0	1	0
10	Restoration/rebuilding	0	0	0	0	0	0	0	0	0	1
11	Continuous improvement	0	1	0	0	1	1	1	1	1	1

Table 3.3 Final reachability matrix

No.	Enablers	1	2	3	4	5	6	7	8	9	10	11	Driving power
1	Strategic planning	1	1	1	1	1	1	1	1	1	1	1	11
2	Disaster assessment	0	1	1	1	1	1	1	1	1	1^a	1^a	10
3	Information management and technology utilisation	0	1	1	1	1	1	1	1	1	1	1	10
4	Effective utilisation of resources	0	1^a	0	1	1^a	1	1	1	1	1	1	9
5	Distribution strategy	0	0	0	1	1	1^a	1	1^a	1	1^a	1^a	8
6	Transportation and capacity planning	0	0	0	1	1	1	1	1	1	1	1^a	8
7	Prompt response (C7)	0	0	0	0	0	0	1	1	1	1	0	4
8	Risk mitigation	0	0	0	0	0	0	0	1	1	1	0	3
9	Minimisation of loss of human lives	0	0	0	0	0	0	0	0	1	0	0	1
10	Restoration/rebuilding	0	0	0	0	0	0	0	0	0	1	0	1
11	Continuous improvement	0	1	1^a	1^a	1	1	1	1	1	1	1	10
	Dependence power	1	5	4	7	7	7	8	9	10	10	7	

[a] Addition of transitivity within initial reachability matrix

in Level I and is shown at the top in the ISM hierarchy. This procedure is repeated for every factor, in the form of iterations to determine the level of each attribute.

Partitioning of reachability matrix into different levels using various iterations.

Iteration 1

Variables	Reachability set	Antecedent set	Intersection set	Level
1	1,2,3,4,5,6,7,8,9,10,11	1	1	
2	2,3,4,5,6,7,8,9,10,11	1,2,3,4,11	2,3,4,11	
3	2,3,4,5,6,7,8,9,10,11	1,2,3,11	2,3,11	
4	2,4,5,6,7,8,9,10,11	1,2,3,4,5,6,11	2,4,5,6,11	
5	4,5,6,7,8,9,10,11	1,2,3,4,5,6,11	4,5,6,11	
6	4,5,6,7,8,9,10,11	1,2,3,4,5,6,11	4,5,6,11	
7	7,8,9,10	1,2,3,4,5,6,7,11	7	
8	8,9,10	1,2,3,4,5,6,7,8,11	8	
9	9	1,2,3,4,5,6,7,8,9,11	9	I
10	10	1,2,3,4,5,6,7,8,10,11	10	I
11	2,3,4,5,6,7,8,9,10,11	1,2,3,4,5,6,11	2,3,4,5,6,11	

Iteration 2

Variables	Reachability set	Antecedent set	Intersection set	Level
1	1,2,3,4,5,6,7,8,11	1	1	
2	2,3,4,5,6,7,8,11	1,2,3,4,11	2,3,4,11	
3	2,3,4,5,6,7,8,11	1,2,3,11	2,3,11	
4	2,4,5,6,7,8,11	1,2,3,4,5,6,11	2,4,5,6,11	
5	4,5,6,7,8,11	1,2,3,4,5,6,11	4,5,6,11	
6	4,5,6,7,8,11	1,2,3,4,5,6,11	4,5,6,11	
7	7,8	1,2,3,4,5,6,7,11	7	
8	8	1,2,3,4,5,6,7,8,11	8	II
11	2,3,4,5,6,7,8,11	1,2,3,4,5,6,11	2,3,4,5,6,11	

Iteration 3

Variables	Reachability set	Antecedent set	Intersection set	Level
1	1,2,3,4,5,6,7,11	1	1	
2	2,3,4,5,6,7,11	1,2,3,4,11	2,3,4,11	
3	2,3,4,5,6,7,11	1,2,3,11	2,3,11	
4	2,4,5,6,7,11	1,2,3,4,5,6,11	2,4,5,6,11	
5	4,5,6,7,11	1,2,3,4,5,6,11	4,5,6,11	
6	4,5,6,7,11	1,2,3,4,5,6,11	4,5,6,11	
7	7	1,2,3,4,5,6,7,11	7	III
11	2,3,4,5,6,7,11	1,2,3,4,5,6,11	2,3,4,5,6,11	

Iteration 4

Variables	Reachability set	Antecedent set	Intersection set	Level
1	1,2,3,4,5,6,11	1	1	

(continued)

Variables	Reachability set	Antecedent set	Intersection set	Level
2	2,3,4,5,6,11	1,2,3,4,11	2,3,4,11	
3	2,3,4,5,6,11	1,2,3,11	2,3,11	
4	2,4,5,6,11	1,2,3,4,5,6,11	2,4,5,6,11	IV
5	4,5,6,11	1,2,3,4,5,6,11	4,5,6,11	IV
6	4,5,6,11	1,2,3,4,5,6,11	4,5,6,11	IV
11	2,3,4,5,6,11	1,2,3,4,5,6,11	2,3,4,5,6,11	IV

Iteration 5

Variables	Reachability set	Antecedent set	Intersection set	Level
1	1,2,3	1	1	
2	2,3	1,2,3	2,3	V
3	2,3	1,2,3	2,3	V

Iteration 6

Variables	Reachability set	Antecedent set	Intersection set	Level
C1	1	1	1	VI

3.3.6 ISM Methodology and Model Development

Interpretive Structural Modelling (ISM) develops a hierarchy that depicts interrelationship between various factors. These factors are labelled and classified on the basis of their driving and dependence power. From all the critical success factors identified in this paper, the ISM model depicts that in order to minimise the loss of human lives, it is imperative to perform strategic planning (1) ahead of time, so as to prepare all stakeholders involved in HSCM to respond quickly to the disaster. Once the long-term decision-making process involved in the planning gets complete, the system continuously monitors the pre-warning system provided by meteorological department and assesses any occurrence of disaster in advance. Disaster assessment (2) would identify the intensity of disaster in terms of number of lives and infrastructure that might get affected due to disaster. Early assessment of disaster would facilitate authorities to make decisions related to distribution strategy (5) to be implemented, effective allocation and disbursement of resources (4) and transportation and capacity planning (6). From the ISM model, it is also clear that a good distribution strategy and accurate decisions related to transportation and capacity planning would help in optimising the utility of resources. Disaster assessment, distribution strategy, effective utilisation of resources, transportation and capacity planning should be well aligned with information management and technology utilisation (3), as the latter assists in real-time communication and coordination among various actors. The above said factors must be continuously improved

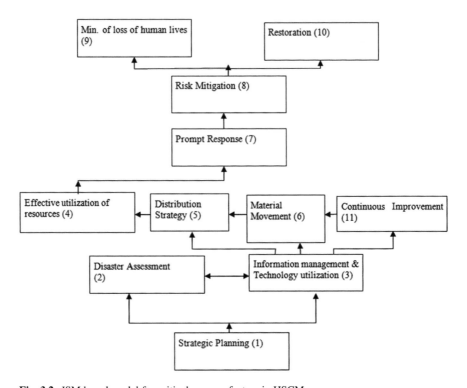

Fig. 3.2 ISM based model for critical success factors in HSCM

(11) using metrics and tools and benchmarking activities performed under each factor, against key performance indicators. In this way each link in the supply chain would learn and improve from this approach. IT performance measurement systems, which measure overall effectiveness of the supply chain, must be adopted for continuous improvement of activities involved in HSCM. This holistic approach will ultimately impact the response time (7) of providing relief operation to the affected population during disaster. Prompt response would mitigate the social as well as economic risks (8) that emerge at the time of disaster. Finally, risk mitigation further leads to minimisation of loss of lives (9) and assist in restoration (10) post disaster.

3.4 MICMAC Analysis

The intent of the MICMAC analysis is to classify and analyse the identified critical success factors on the basis of their driving power and dependence power. The first cluster consists of the 'autonomous CSFs' which have weak dependence as well as driving power. These factors are generally disconnected from the system. Second cluster consists of factors which have strong dependence power and weak driving power. Third cluster consists of factors which have both strong dependence and driving power. Such factors have effect on other factors and also take feedback on

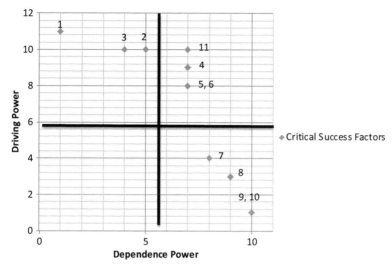

Fig. 3.3 Driving power and dependence power diagram

themselves. Fourth cluster includes factors which have strong driving power and weak dependence power. These factors are known as key factors as any adjustment or modification in this factor will automatically modify the subsequent factors.

The driving power and the dependence power of critical success factors identified in this paper are shown in the Table 3.3. Subsequently, the driver and dependence power diagram is shown in Fig. 3.3. For critical success factor 3, driving power is 10 and dependence power is 4. Therefore, in this figure, it is positioned at a place corresponding to a driver power of 10 and dependence power of 4. Also, in this figure strategic planning lies in cluster 4, which has strong driving power and weak dependence power. On the other hand, minimisation of loss of human lives and restoration or rebuilding have strong dependence power and weak driving power.

3.5 Results and Discussions

The outcome of ISM model for considered critical success factors within a humanitarian supply chain clearly indicates that the most critical factor among all is 'strategic planning' in terms of its ability to drive other factors for achieving the ultimate goal. This factor forms the lowest level in ISM model, whereas the target factor lies at the top level. In this study, the target factors are 'minimizing the loss of human lives' and 'restoration'. Since these are the top-level factors, their dependence power is maximum while driving power is least; i.e. these are the factors that are supposed to be achieved in the whole process of supply chain. Implementing the rest of the factors efficiently favours the situation to reach the goal. There should be no or less scope of error in implementing the rest of the factors, as this may adversely affect the whole humanitarian supply chain and ultimately people will have to pay for this loss, by compromising their own lives or rather their loved ones.

3.6   Conclusion and Future Scope

The objective of the ISM model in this research paper is to develop a hierarchy of CSFs in the humanitarian supply chain that would help in minimising the loss of human lives and in the quick restoration of infrastructure post disaster. These factors are considered to be critical because in the whole process of relief operation, it is not the individual organisation or actor that can make relief operation successful; rather it is the effective functioning of each link in the supply chain and coordination among them. Relief operation can be provided quickly to the affected population when all the partners in the supply chain prepare and implement strategic planning, so as to get well prepared before disaster hits the area. The driver dependence diagram helps to classify various critical success factors lying in a particular cluster. As there are no factors in the autonomous cluster, this means that there is not a single factor which is disconnected from the entire system; i.e. all the factors are strongly connected with the whole system of HSCM. In the next cluster, factors such as strategic planning, information management and technology utilisation and disaster assessment are having high driving power and modest dependence power. These factors play a key role in minimising the loss of lives and restoring the infrastructure hastily. The factors included in the next cluster are distribution strategy, effective utilisation of resources and transportation and capacity planning. These are influenced by the factors which are more critical compared to them, and in turn, they also impact other factors as well. The last cluster consists of factors such as minimisation of loss of human lives, restoration or rebuilding, risk mitigation and prompt response. In this, the factors at the topmost level (factor 9 and 10) are having the least driving power and highest dependence power. The rest of the factors together lead to the top-level factors.

The major contribution of this research paper lies in providing direction to the decision-maker to provide relief operation to the affected population as quickly as possible for the sake of human lives. Lastly, we examined the scope of further research. This research paper has considered only limited number of critical success factors. In real situation, there can be few other critical success factors that may impact the HSCM. Also, the ISM model developed can be statistically validated using structural equation modelling (SEM), which has a capability to test the already developed hypothetical model. Thus, this approach can be taken into consideration for future research.

References

Balcik B, Beamon BM (2008) Performance measurement in humanitarian relief chains. Int J Public Sector Manag 21(1):4–25

Barbarosa G, Arda Y (2004) A two-stage stochastic programming framework for transportation planning in disaster response. J Oper Res Soc 55:43

Beamon BM (2004) Humanitarian relief chains: issues and challenges. In: Paper presented at the 34th international conference on computers & industrial engineering, San Francisco, 14–16 Nov

Beamon BM, Balcik B (2008) Performance measurement in humanitarian relief chains. Int J Public Sector Manag 21:4–25

Cozzolino A (2012) Humanitarian logistics – cross-sector cooperation in disaster relief management, SpringerBriefs in business. Springer, Berlin/Heidelberg, ISBN: 978-3-642-30185-8, doi: 10.1007/978-3-642-30186-5_1

Daniel DR (1961) Management information crisis. Harv Bus Rev 39(5):111–116

Davidson AL (2006) Key performance indicators in humanitarian logistics. Massachusetts Institute of Technology, Massachusetts. Available at: http://dspace.mit.edu/bitstream/handle/1721.1/35540/72823316-MIT.pdf?sequence=2

De la Torre LE, Dolinskaya IS, Smilowitz KR (2011) Disaster relief routing: integrating research and practice. Socio-Econ Plann Sci 46(1):1–10

Ergun O, Karakus G, Keskinocak P, Swann J, Villarreal M (2005) Operations research to improve disasater supply chain management. Wiley. Available at: http://as.wiley.com/WileyCDA/Section/id-397133.html. Accessed Sept 2013

Ewins P, Harvey P, Savage K, Jacobs A (2006) Mapping the risks of corruption in humanitarian action. Overseas Development Institute and Management Accounting for NGOs (MANGO). A Report for Transparency International and the U4 Anti-Corruption Resource Center. Available at: http://www.transparency.org/content/download/8400/53941/file/ODI_corruption_risk_map.pdf

Gooley TB (1999) In times of crisis, logistics is the job. Logist Manag Distrib Rep 38(9):82

Gunasekaran A, Ngai EWT (2003) The successful management of a small logistics company. Int J Phys Distrib Logist Manag 33(9):25–842

Gurnasekaran A, Ngai EWT (2004) Information system in supply chain integration and management. Eur J Oper Res 159:269–295

Heeringen BB (2010) Risk management in regional humanitarian relief operations. Available at: http://dspace.ou.nl/bitstream/1820/3032/1/MWBBvHeeringenjan10.pdf. Accessed Oct 2013

Huotari M-L, Wilson TD (2001) Determining organisational information needs: the critical success factors approach. Inf Res 6(3):1–21

Ingram JC, Franco G, Rumbaitis-del Rio C, Khazai B (2006) Post-disaster recovery dilemmas: challenges in balancing short-term and long-term needs for vulnerability reduction. Environ Sci Policy 9:607–613

Korpela J, Tuominen M (1996) Benchmarking logistics performance with an application of the analytic hierarchy process. IEEE Trans Eng Manag 43(3):323–333

Kovacs G, Spens KM (2007) Humanitarian logistics in disaster relief operations. Int J Phys Distrib Logist Manag 37(2):99–114

Lijo J, Ramesh A (2012) Humanitarian supply chain management in India: a SAP-LAP framework. J Adv Manag Res 9(2):217–235

Long DC (1997) Logistics for disaster relief: engineering on the run. IIE Solut 29(6):26–29

Long DC, Wood DF (1995) The logistics of famine relief. J Bus Logist 16(1):213–239

Mandal A, Deshmukh SG (1993) Vendor selection using interpretive structural modelling (ISM). Int J Oper Prod Manag 14(6):52–59

Munzberg T et al (2013) Decision support for critical infrastructure disruptions: an integrated approach to secure food supply. 10th international ISCRAM conference – Baden-Baden, May 2013

Oloruntoba R, Gray R (2006) Humanitarian aid: an agile supply chain? J Supply Chain Manag 11(2):115–120

Pettit S, Beresford A (2009) Critical success factors in the context of humanitarian aid supply chains. Int J Phys Distrib Logist Manag 39(6):450–468

Power DJ, Sohal AS, Rahman SU (2001) Critical success factors in agile supply chain management. Int J Phys Distrib Logist Manag 31(4):247–265

Roy P, Albores P, Brewster C (2012) Logistical framework for last mile relief distribution in humanitarian supply chains: consideration from the Field. Aston University. Available at: http://windermere.aston.ac.uk/~kiffer/papers/Roy_ICMR12.pdf

Samii R (2010) The unique challenges of Haiti's emergency logistics. Available at: http://rsamii.blogspot.com/2010/01/unique-challenges-of-haitis-emergency.html

Sushil (2012) Interpreting the interpretive structural model. Glob J Flex Syst Manag 13(2):87–106

Van LN (2006) Blackett memorial lecture. Humanitarian aid logistics: supply chain management in high gear". J Oper Res Soc 57(5):475–489

Van der Vorst JGAJ, Beulens AJM (Spring 2002) Identifying sources of uncertainty to generate supply chain redesign strategies. Int J Phys Distrib Logist Manag 32(6):409–430

Whiting M, Ayala-Ostrom B (2009) Advocacy to promote logistics in humanitarian aid. Manag Res News 31(11):1081–1089

Suggested Reading

Chopra S, Meindl P (2004) Supply chain management, strategy, planning, and operations, 2nd edn. Pearson Education International, New Jersey. Retrieved from: http://www.kvimis.co.in/sites/default/files/ebook_attachments/Sunil%20Chopra,Supply%20Chain%20Management.pdf

Crainic TG, Laporte G (1997) Planning models for freight transportation. Eur J Oper Res 97:409–438

Davies P (2005) Mainstreaming security management. Secur Q Rev 1 (Spring):7–8. Available at: www.redr.org.uk/objects_store/SQR%20Issue%201.pdf. Accessed Oct 2013

Hoekstra S, Romme J (1992) Integral logistic structures – developing customer-oriented goods flow. McGraw Hill, London

Melo MT, Nickel S, Saldanha-da-Gama F (2008) Facility location and supply chain management-a review. Eur J Oper Res 2:401–412

Thomas A, Kopczak L (2005) From logistics to supply chain management: the path forward in the humanitarian sector. Fritz Institute, San Francisco, pp 1–15. Available at: www.fritzinstitute.org/PDFs/WhitePaper/FromLogisticsto.pdf. Accessed Sept 2013.

Chapter 4
Non-Ownership Commercial Mobility and Humanitarian Logistics: New Perspectives to Improve Response Times and Long-Term Impact

Micha Hirschinger and Roger Moser

4.1 No Vehicles Mean No Aid

The Centre for Research on the Epidemiology of Disasters (CRED) recorded in the year 2011 alone 332 natural disasters. Within these more than 30,770 people lost their lives, and about 244 million victims were affected. The total economic damage due to natural disasters amounted to an estimated USD 366.1 billion (Guha-Sapir et al. 2012). Unfortunately, the number of such serious natural and man-made disasters will rise up to an expected fivefold increase over the next 50 years (Thomas and Kopczak 2005).

Throwbacks around the Asian tsunamis in 2004 revealed that last-mile distribution is one of the key success factors for humanitarian aid. Since then, both researchers and practitioners have shown increasing interests in the emerging field of humanitarian logistics (HL) mainly focusing on immediate disaster relief. Van Wassenhove and Pedraza Martinez describe especially the role of transportation in last-mile distribution more drastically: "no vehicles means no aid" (Van Wassenhove and Pedraza Martinez 2012, p. 314). However, emphasis should also be paid on the long-lasting economic development of the affected regions. For example, the long-term support of community-based businesses to provide sustainable aid for impacted regions and exit strategies for NGOs is still a key challenge of economic development initiatives (Kovács and Spens 2011).

We apply a service-dominant logic perspective and suggest a business model based on value co-creation. We present a truck-sharing concept in rural India as an

M. Hirschinger (✉)
Department of Industrial Engineering, Friedrich-Alexander-University Erlangen-Nuremberg, Erlangen, Germany
e-mail: micha.hirschinger@wiso.uni-erlangen.de

R. Moser
Research Institute for International Management, University of St. Gallen, St. Gallen, Switzerland

© Springer India 2016
B.S. Sahay et al. (eds.), *Managing Humanitarian Logistics*, Springer Proceedings in Business and Economics, DOI 10.1007/978-81-322-2416-7_4

adaptation of successful car-sharing models in developed countries and combine it with the requirements of advanced humanitarian logistics concepts. We finally evaluate the applicability of such a truck-sharing concept in India using empirical data.

4.2 Efficacy of Humanitarian Logistics

Logistics in humanitarian aid are recognized as important to the success of disaster relief operations. Its efficacy can be understood as short-term disaster relief and long-term local development impact.

Humanitarian logistics (HL) is characterized by specific aspects that differentiate it from regular business logistics. First, the supply network of HL frequently consists of changing actors during the relief phases, including donors, military, governments, aid agencies, NGOs, logistics service providers, and volunteers, without clear relationships to each other (Balcik et al. 2010; Kovács and Spens 2007). Second, the uncertainty about when, where, what, and to which extent a disaster strikes combined with a typical shortage of resources and damaged infrastructure impedes the work of humanitarian logisticians and the setup of efficient supply chains above all in the aftermath of an unexpected event (Van Wassenhove 2006). Third, humanitarian operations suffer from a lack of experienced logisticians. Technical knowledge and logistics skills are scarce in many aid agencies preventing an efficient implementation of adequate supply chain solutions (Pettit and Beresford 2009).

As disasters are subject to lifecycles, the umbrella term humanitarian logistics generally covers two main streams, whereby varying factors and circumstances at different times necessitate diverse HL activities. On the one hand, disaster relief immediately responses to sudden-onset disasters like earthquakes and is set up to transport first aid to disaster regions very quickly. Thus, most of the emphasis is paid to quick response times minimizing human suffering at almost any monetary cost (Van Wassenhove 2006). On the other hand, the level of urgency in continuous aid work such as in the case of famines is much lower and also includes the development of the affected regions in the long term. In such a context, HL conditions are also challenging but more stable in both demand and supply (Barbarosoğlu et al. 2002; Holguín-Veras et al. 2012; Kovács and Spens 2007; Kunz and Reiner 2012). Always considering the overall humanitarian goal, the focus of this HL stream is consequently more on operational efficiency similar to commercial supply chains (Holguín-Veras et al. 2012; Oloruntoba and Gray 2006). Although the latter stream experiences a less urgent need to help, logistics and transportation are most critical for the success and effectiveness of the whole humanitarian aid program in terms of *order fulfillment* in the last mile (Balcik et al. 2008; Besiou et al. 2011; Kovács and Spens 2011; Kunz and Reiner 2012; Pettit and Beresford 2009). Therefore, the ideal case of HL in disaster management would be that vehicles are available every time and everywhere to maximize the aid for beneficiaries. However, resource restrictions (logistics is the second-largest overhead cost for NGOs after personnel) and technical challenges do not allow for an ideal solution so far (Pedraza Martinez and Van Wassenhove 2013).

4.2.1 Status Quo in Humanitarian Logistics

The international fleet size of humanitarian organizations amounts up to 80,000 units with costs above $1 billion per year and an estimated tripling of vehicles till 2050 (Pedraza Martinez et al. 2011). The fact that NGOs do not usually have own fleets locally in the affected regions (Balcik et al. 2010) necessitates them to import vehicles first before they can operate at large scale. The stages before and after arriving on site distinguish fleet management practices in HL from regular logistics operations. For instance, the International Committee of the Red Cross/Red Crescent (ICRC) operates three warehouses globally for the temporary storage of HL vehicles. From there it takes 4 weeks for arrival at national offices based on regular requests and 2 weeks in case of urgent requests due to disaster strikes. The arrival of the vehicles at national offices basically ends the influence of NGO headquarters such as ICRC in Geneva and with that the best opportunity for an efficient management of the fleet (Pedraza Martinez et al. 2011; Pedraza Martinez and Van Wassenhove 2013).

National offices assemble the demand of vehicles from their local aid programs and request it from headquarters mostly without standardized procedures or policies. The different objectives of headquarters and in-country programs lead to a misalignment of incentives. Headquarters are about to provide cost-efficient vehicles to national offices quickly, considering that bigger fleets will increase costs in total. As transportation capacity most significantly restricts last-mile distribution (Balcik et al. 2008, 2010), on-site vehicle allocation is limited to available resources (Kovács and Spens 2007; Pettit and Beresford 2009). As a consequence, national offices and their programs try to maximize the availability of vehicles in order to deliver items and staff immediately to aid recipients. Thus, they have an incentive to state higher demands for transportation than actually needed (Pedraza Martinez et al. 2011). In sum, the focus of each national office on its own operations and the fact that there is a fight for the limited vehicle resources on a global scale lead to low utilization rates of vehicles on average on a national level and a suboptimal operational efficiency of the total fleet (Pedraza Martinez et al. 2011; Pedraza Martinez and Van Wassenhove 2013).

Moreover, the misalignment of incentives may also result in further challenges. First, it leads to a lack of fleet visibility in terms of uncertainty on vehicle availability and global fleet sizes as well as oversized and aged fleets. Due to the difficult conditions in the countries of operations, fleet management further has to cope with rising fuel consumption, high operating cost of the vehicles (maintenances, insurances, etc.), and nonstandardized fleets (Besiou et al. 2011; Van Wassenhove and Pedraza Martinez 2012). Consequently, large parts of the total fleet costs are not optimized and provide opportunities for improvement in both capital and operating costs (Balcik et al. 2008; Pedraza Martinez et al. 2011). In short, in order to overcome the different trade-offs between vehicle availability to optimize response times and improved capacity utilization of the fleet, we might need to consider other HL approaches.

4.2.2 Quick Response and Long-Term Development to Improve Sustainable Livelihoods

Sudden disaster strikes require immediate worldwide responses. Reducing response time to a minimum is in line with the main objective of HL to ease human suffering at first. In this context, the availability of transportations means and short vehicle delivery lead times are crucial to enable an immediate response. Most research in HL focuses on this particular phase of disaster relief, while only a few papers cover continuous aid or long-term development from a HL perspective (Kunz and Reiner 2012). However, many humanitarian aid programs operate in countries parallel to long-term economic development activities and supply widely scattered beneficiaries with relief items and support the overall development of affected regions (Holguín-Veras et al. 2012; Kovács and Spens 2007; Kunz and Reiner 2012). Thus, HL needs to be embedded in economic development programs to ensure a long-term impact of humanitarian aid (Kovács and Spens 2011), enabling the sustainable development of affected regions.

In general, transportation networks to reach rural regions cover mid- to long-range travel distances (Holguín-Veras et al. 2012). Therefore, it faces mobility challenges due to mainly inadequate traffic infrastructure and increasing transportation demand (Kar and Datta 2009; TERI 2008). According to the sustainable livelihood approach, the improvement of the living conditions of low-income groups requires intact infrastructure such as access to healthcare, education, and logistics solutions among others (Carney 2002). Such infrastructure solutions are evaluated regarding their ability to improve natural, social, human, financial, or physical assets of rural communities (Scoones 1998). In this paper, we focus on physical assets since large parts of rural India suffer especially from a lack of mobility and transportation in particular (Gupta 2008; Schaefers and Moser 2011). The current access to diverse kinds of two- or three wheelers and public transportation systems can satisfy personal and low-weight transportation needs. However, small-scale producers in rural India are facing difficulties in getting access to light and especially heavy commercial transportation vehicles to satisfy their logistics requirements. Such vehicles are necessary for rural small-scale producers to overcome the mid- to large-range distances to additional consumer markets besides the local neighborhood (Gupta 2008; Ramachandran et al. 2012). As a consequence, goods produced by the rural, mostly low-income population hardly reach the next major city (Gupta 2008) impeding business opportunities and with that economic growth in rural areas (Schaefers and Moser 2011). In a nutshell, the importance of last-mile distribution in delivery processes (Esper et al. 2003) and the lack of transportation solutions in more remote and less developed areas highlight the importance of logistics connectivity as a key requirement for a sustainable economic and social development of rural livelihoods.

As international NGOs operate huge fleets, they might be able to improve logistics connectivity in rural areas by making their vehicles available to small-scale producers.

4.3 Service-Dominant Logic

Over the last decade, product-centered business models have shifted toward service-centered concepts offering access rather than ownership. This shift is described by Vargo and Lusch's (2004) concept of a service-dominant logic (SDL). They propose that goods are only a part of services instead of separating them in services and goods (Vargo and Lusch 2008b). The SDL focuses on services as central element of economic exchange since customers are always service consumers (Grönroos 1979; Vargo and Lusch 2004, 2008b). Services are understood as "the application of specialized competences" (Vargo and Lusch 2004, p. 2). The SDL serves as basis for non-ownership services, involving at least one user and the owner. Ownership focuses on the permanent access to a single object, satisfying the demand of one individual or of the owner. Non-ownership, however, tries to offer multiple individuals or users temporary access to an equally desired, single object which can be achieved through sharing (Lovelock and Gummesson 2004; Moeller and Wittkowski 2010). According to the SDL, specific services or products do not contain value per se, but the unique value is created by the actors during usage in a certain context. These actors are no longer regarded as functioning separately, but rather collaboratively co-create value (e.g., Grönroos and Ravald 2011; Vargo and Lusch 2008a, b; Vargo and Lusch 2004). Firms can thus only offer potential value (Ballantyne and Varey 2006) until the customers actively co-create individual value by using, applying, and adapting the provided appliances (Smith et al. 2011). In supporting customers' value creation, the process of interaction offers the opportunity for firms to co-create value (Grönroos and Ravald 2011).

Theories about social systems and social structures (e.g., Berger and Luckmann 1967; Giddens 1984) further emphasize the requirement to see customers within their social context or communities. These social construction theories can explain that different social contexts might cause different perceptions of the same service by the same customer. The concept of individual values has to be extended by the social context toward value in context (Edvardsson et al. 2011). Therefore, a community of different people with mutual objectives can jointly generate value in granting access for different people to a single object at different times. For instance, in the context of the classic car-sharing concept, ownership responsibilities remain with the offering company, while the user individually co-creates value in getting from A to B with the company's car. As a result, the customers focus on the function of the product, namely, transportation, rather than on ownership itself (Lovelock and Gummesson 2004; Moeller and Wittkowski 2010). However, a certain degree of capacity utilization is required to cover the high-fixed costs of vehicle ownership (Kilimann 2011). The larger the demand for such mobility solutions, the more services can be offered in terms of fleet size, availability, and vehicle types.

4.4 Service-Dominant Logic in Humanitarian Logistics

We propose an alternative humanitarian logistics model based on service-dominant logic and value co-creation in a social context. The model aims at both improving the response time and availability during a disaster and improving the long-term logistics connectivity of an affected region. The model is inspired by the well-functioning car-sharing concepts in cities in developed countries. For instance, Zipcar offers customers the access to cars at particular times and releases them from car-ownership costs and responsibilities (Lovelock and Gummesson 2004; Moeller and Wittkowski 2010), nevertheless satisfying the mobility needs of their customers. These car-sharing concepts are characterized by high utilization rates and car users free of vehicle ownership.

This model is now further developed for the perspective of NGOs, currently operating with their own vehicles outside of the centers of developing countries such as rural India. It evaluates how a truck-sharing concept (non-ownership commercial mobility) could contribute to faster response times as well as increased efficiency (high assets utilization) of the fleet by shifting fleet characteristics from the top left corner (ownership and low utilization) to the bottom right corner (non-ownership and high utilization) similar to car-sharing business model.

The first quadrant (I) of Fig. 4.1 indicates the basic situation of most of the NGO fleets and is characterized by vehicle ownership responsibilities, including cost of capital, insurances, maintenance, and repairs as well as low utilization rates (Pedraza Martinez and Van Wassenhove 2013). However, ownership is economically meaningful in case of high utilization rates (i.e., mileage) or low capital costs. The substantial international fleet owned by NGOs is used as buffer against stochastic uncertainty of aid. Its capacity should facilitate immediate responses but also represents massive costs of capital exceeding $1.6 billion (Pedraza Martinez and Van Wassenhove 2013).

In general, humanitarian fleets are characterized by low utilization rates which are further distorted by the use of vehicles for private needs and long distances for maintenance only. For instance, field data within the ICRC shows that annual mileage amounts to only 13,000 km on average (Pedraza Martinez and Van Wassenhove 2013). Before reaching operational stage, each vehicle further necessitates national registration. Registration is often delayed by governmental procedures and border clearance for at least 3 month and thus impedes the speed of vehicle delivery for in-country programs (Pedraza Martinez et al. 2011; Pedraza

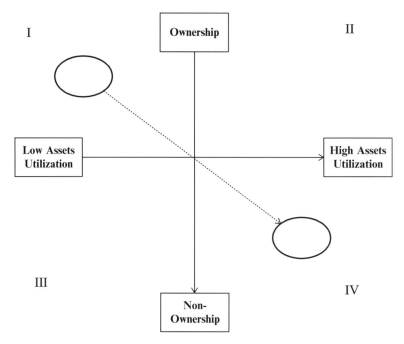

Fig. 4.1 Non-ownership model/utilization matrix

Martinez and Van Wassenhove 2013). Unforeseen breakdowns, political or administrative delays, and difficult condition on site further impede high utilization rates of vehicles in addition to the burdens of ownership.

The second quadrant (II) describes NGOs as truck-sharing service providers themselves to improve utilization rates of their vehicles. The lack of central planning and transportation coordination and the management of vehicles in silos by in-country programs, however, complicate the mutual share of vehicles between programs (Pedraza Martinez et al. 2011) or even small-scale producers located in the NGO's areas of operations.

The third quadrant (III) describes the option to assign third-party logistics providers (3PL) to fulfill last-mile distribution. This approach can release NGOs from their vehicle ownership responsibilities but does not solve the per se low utilization problem. Furthermore, the assignment of 3PL is expensive for NGOs as single user and limited to exceptions. Both quadrants (II) and (IV) describe only interim solutions and thus are beyond the scope of this paper.

In the fourth quadrant (IV), we have developed a truck-sharing concept in the case of rural India to overcome the outlined problems. In this model, both NGOs and small-scale producers have access to trucks offered by a service provider (owner) on site. In this concept, NGOs act as one user among other users. Together with a number of small-scale producers, a much higher level of utilization can be reached which is necessary for the service provider to perform economically. At the same time, response times can be dramatically improved as local disasters are handled like unexpected seasonal hikes "importing" vehicles from the overall truck-sharing system into a single region. A choice-based conjoint study with 300 small-scale producers in rural India confirms the willingness of small-scale producers to participate in such a truck-sharing concept.

All stakeholders could take advantages of a truck-sharing concept in rural India in collaboration with an NGO. Besides the economic potential for a service provider, NGOs and the local economy can benefit from such an approach. The high demand of NGOs and local small-scale producers for transportation means ensures a long-term high utilization rate of the offered fleet. In addition, local truck sharing can release NGOs from ownership responsibilities (i.e., insurance, maintenance) leading to cost reductions in both overhead and operational costs. As fleets would be locally operated by service provider, in-country transports of vehicles will be much less required. This does not only reduce the high emergency delivery costs for trucks (Pedraza Martinez et al. 2011) but also shorten vehicle delivery lead time and thus facilitate quick responses. The small-scale producers in rural India do not have to make high initial investments into transportation possibilities. Thereby they can reach more easily and flexibly the next factor markets creating new business opportunities for them.

4.5   Contributions

With this work we try to extend the academic thinking about fleet management in humanitarian operations. We propose such a truck-sharing model based on value co-creation to improve logistics connectivity in rural areas and with that economic and social growth as well as response time.

References

Balcik B, Beamon BM, Smilowitz K (2008) Last mile distribution in humanitarian relief. J Intell Transp Syst 12(2):51–63

Balcik B, Beamon BM, Krejci CC, Muramatsu KM, Ramirez M (2010) Coordination in humanitarian relief chains: practices, challenges and opportunities. Int J Prod Econ 126(1):22–34

Ballantyne D, Varey RJ (2006) Creating value-in-use through marketing interaction: the exchange logic of relating, communicating and knowing. Mark Theory 6(3):335–348

Barbarosoğlu G, Özdamar L, Çevik A (2002) An interactive approach for hierarchical analysis of helicopter logistics in disaster relief operations. Eur J Oper Res 140(1):118–133

Berger P, Luckmann T (1967) The social construction of reality: a treatise in the sociology of knowledge. Penguin Publishers, London

Besiou M, Stapleton O, Van Wassenhove LN (2011) System dynamics for humanitarian operations. J Humanitarian Logist Supply Chain Manag 1(1):78–103

Carney D (2002) Sustainable livelihood approaches: progress and possibilities for change. DFID Department for International Development, Toronto

Edvardsson B, Tronvoll B, Gruber T (2011) Expanding understanding of service exchange and value co-creation: a social construction approach. J Acad Mark Sci 39(2):327–339

Esper TL, Jensen TD, Turnipseed FL, Burton S (2003) The last mile: an examination of effects of online retail delivery strategies on consumers. J Bus Logist 24(2):177–203

Giddens A (1984) The constitution of society: outline of the theory of structuration. University of California Press, Berkeley

Grönroos C (1979) An applied theory for marketing industrial services. Ind Mark Manag 8 (1):45–50

Grönroos C, Ravald A (2011) Service as business logic: implications for value creation and marketing. J Serv Manag 22(1):5–22

Guha-Sapir D, Vos F, Below R, Ponserre S (2012) Annual disaster statistical review 2011: the numbers and trends. Ciaco Imprimerie, Louvain-la-Neuve

Gupta AK (2008) Linking vertical and horizontal markets for innovations at grassroots: sustainability imperative. Future of logistics conference. Indian Institute of Management Ahmedabad, Hannover

Holguín-Veras J, Jaller M, Van Wassenhove LN, Pérez N, Wachtendorf T (2012) On the unique features of post-disaster humanitarian logistics. J Oper Manag 30(7/8):494–506

Kar K, Datta TK (2009) An overview of mobility and safety issues related to highway transportation in India. ITE J 79(8):40–45

Kilimann S (2011) Carsharing: Jeder will jetzt teilen. Available at: http://www.zeit.de/auto/2011-06/carsharing-konkurrenz. Accessed 15 June 2013

Kovács G, Spens K (2007) Humanitarian logistics in disaster relief operations. Int J Phys Distrib Logist Manag 37(2):99–114

Kovács G, Spens K (2011) Trends and developments in humanitarian logistics – a gap analysis. Int J Phys Distrib Logist Manag 41(1):32–45

Kunz N, Reiner G (2012) A meta-analysis of humanitarian logistics research. J Humanitarian Logist Supply Chain Manag 2(2):116–147

Lovelock C, Gummesson E (2004) Whither services marketing?: In search of a new paradigm and fresh perspectives. J Serv Res 7(1):20–41

Moeller S, Wittkowski K (2010) The burdens of ownership: reasons for preferring renting. Manag Serv Qual 20(2):176–191

Oloruntoba R, Gray R (2006) Humanitarian aid: an agile supply chain? Supply Chain Manag 11 (2):115–120

Pedraza Martinez AJ, Van Wassenhove LN (2013) Vehicle replacement in the international committee of the red cross. Prod Oper Manag 22(2):365–376

Pedraza Martinez AJ, Stapleton O, Van Wassenhove LN (2011) Field vehicle fleet management in humanitarian operations: a case-based approach. J Oper Manag 29(5):404–421

Pettit S, Beresford A (2009) Critical success factors in the context of humanitarian aid supply chains. Int J Phys Distrib Logist Manag 39(6):450–468

Ramachandran J, Pant A, Pani SK (2012) Building the BoP producer ecosystem: the evolving engagement of Fabindia with Indian handloom artisans. J Prod Innov Manag 29(1):33–51

Schaefers T, Moser R (2011) Non-ownership mobility services in rural India: a consumer-preference study. Strategic Management Society – Special Conference, San Diego

Scoones I (1998) Working paper 72: sustainable rural livelihoods: a framework for analysis. Institute for Development Studies, Brighton

Smith L, Maull R, Ng ICL (2011) Servitization and operations management: a service dominant logic approach. The University of Exeter Business School Discussion Papers in Management. The University of Exeter Business School, Exeter

TERI (2008) Mobility for development: Bangalore, India. The Energy and Resources Institute (TERI) & World Business Council for Sustainable Development, New Delhi

Thomas A, Kopczak L (2005) From logistics to supply chain management: the path forward for the humanitarian sector. The Fritz Institute, San Francisco. Available at: www.fritzinstitute.org/PDFs/WhitePaper/FromLogisticsto.pdf. Accessed 04 Jan 2013

Van Wassenhove LN (2006) Humanitarian aid logistics: supply chain management in high gear. J Oper Res Soc 57(5):475–489

Van Wassenhove LN, Pedraza Martinez AJ (2012) Using OR to adapt supply chain management best practices to humanitarian logistics. Int Trans Oper Res 19(1/2):307–322

Vargo SL, Lusch RF (2004) Evolving to a new dominant logic for marketing. J Mark 68(1):1–17

Vargo SL, Lusch RF (2008a) From goods to service(s): divergences and convergences of logics. Ind Mark Manag 37(3):254–259

Vargo SL, Lusch RF (2008b) Service-dominant logic: continuing the evolution. J Acad Mark Sci 36(1):1–10

Chapter 5
Modeling the Barriers of Humanitarian Supply Chain Management in India

Lijo John and A. Ramesh

5.1 Introduction

In the last four decades, the world has witnessed more than 6,500 disasters (including both natural and man-made disasters), which have affected more than five billion people across the globe. The Centre for Research on the Epidemiology of the Disasters (CRED) has reported that the combined loss of all the disasters has crossed the USD 150 trillion mark, leaving more than 180 million people homeless. The earthquakes in Gujarat (2001), Iran (2003), Sumatra (2004), Pakistan (2005), China (2008), Haiti (2010), and Japan (2011) were the major earthquakes in the last decade (de la Torre et al. 2011). The magnitude of the impact of the natural disasters has brought the humanitarian activities into the spotlight in the past. Due to the rapid urbanization, climate changes, and environmental degradation, the impact of the disasters has increased in the past, especially in the less-developed countries (Fink and Redaelli 2011). The World Conference in Disaster Management (2005) called for the better preparedness for a disaster. The preparedness helps to tackle a disaster better and helps in mitigating the risk and alleviating the pain caused by the disaster (Van Wassenhove 2006).

In any humanitarian aid program, the major part (about 80 %) of the entire activity consists of the logistics (Trunick 2005). In any emergency, the logistics management deals with procuring and managing the food, medicines, clothes, and gifts in kind (solicited and unsolicited) from various donors. It includes monitoring

L. John (✉)
Quantiative Methods and Operations Management, Indian Institute of Management
Kozhikode, Kozhikode, Kerala, India
e-mail: lijoj06fpm@iimk.ac.in

A. Ramesh
Assistant Professor, Department of Management Studies, IIT Roorkee,
Roorkee, Uttarakhand, India
e-mail: ram77fdm@iitr.ac.in

© Springer India 2016
B.S. Sahay et al. (eds.), *Managing Humanitarian Logistics*, Springer Proceedings
in Business and Economics, DOI 10.1007/978-81-322-2416-7_5

the commodity, finance, and information along the relief aid flow (Lee and Zbinden 2003). The logistical coordination in the humanitarian aid management brings together the people with expertise, experience, and capabilities in various fields to the disaster-affected area so that their collaborative efforts help to reduce the suffering of the affected people (Dolinskaya et al. 2011). Jahre (2009) mention the importance of forming clusters for the supply chain collaboration and the collaboration between the clusters. Thus, it becomes very important to understand the various factors affecting the humanitarian aid programs, the drivers and barriers of the supply chain of the essential commodities, and the critical success factors. This forms the basis of our study. In view of these, the main objectives of this chapter are:

(i)   To identify and rank the barriers of humanitarian supply chain management (HSCM) in India
(ii) To establish relationships among the identified barriers
(iii) To discuss the managerial implications of this research

The rest of the paper is organized as follows. In Sect. 5.2, we identify the barriers of HSCM. In Sect. 5.3, we discuss the interpretive structural modeling (ISM), and finally we discuss the results and the managerial implications in Sects. 5.4 and 5.5.

5.2   Identification of the HSCM Barriers

In this chapter, to identify the barriers of HSCM and to establish mutual relationships, we followed the methodology suggested by Ramesh et al. (2010). The brainstorming sessions were conducted to reach a consensus. Therefore, the moderator was chosen from the group to facilitate the discussions. The group of experts had a heterogeneous cross section. A total of 12 experts took part in the brainstorming sessions, of which 5 were from academia, 5 from the industry, and one each from NGO and government. All the experts had more than 10 years of experience in their respective domains. Various literatures, reports, and statistics related to the humanitarian aid programs were circulated among the experts beforehand. The first brainstorming session was conducted to identify the variables of the HSCM. After the brainstorming sessions, the experts identified 14 most influencing barriers and outcomes of HSCM. In the second session, the focus was to identify the relationships between the various barriers and the outcomes. To identify the relationship (or influence) between one variable and the other, the experts were asked to individually identify the relationships between the variables and then reach to a consensus as a group. In the third session, the final list of variables and the contextual relationship between the variables were circulated among the experts for their final review and comments. After the final brainstorming session, the final ISM model was circulated among the experts and validated. The final outcomes and barriers are listed below:

- Lack of correct need and damage assessment
- Lack of predictable demand patterns
- Shortage of experienced logisticians
- Lack of bilateral information sharing
- Lack of infrastructure facilities
- Lack of knowledge about customers
- Lack of a central authority
- Lack of knowledge about scale of devastation
- Unpredictable occurrence
- Improper identification of supply sources
- Lack of proper management of aid materials
- Lack of coordination between different actors
- Inadequate procurement of aid materials
- Improper funding

5.2.1 Lack of Correct Need and Damage Assessment

Assessing the damage caused by any disaster is the primary step in planning any of the humanitarian activity. In the initial stages, when the supply chain has to be triggered following the disaster, it is seldom that the damage assessment is done correctly. Therefore, it is based on the previous experiences and any first hand information arriving from the site that is used for the damage assessment. The needs vary from the country to country, within a country from region to region, and within a region from place to place. Under such circumstances, it becomes important to correctly assess the needs of the people and to plan the relief activities. In addition to the relief logistics, it is also important to prevent the outbreak of an epidemic at the disaster site (Granot 1995; Darcy 2005). The next important work to be done is to make sure that the affected communities are safe. The cleaning of the debris and attempts to use the partially destroyed houses and facilities are also important. The match between the demand for the relief (aid) items and the supply has to be achieved, for which a large amount of procurement and logistics activities has to be planned and implemented. Under these circumstances, it becomes quite difficult to assess the damage caused by the disaster and the need arising due to the disaster with high degree of correctness.

5.2.2 Lack of Predictable Demand Patterns

The demands in the HSCM are highly unpredictable, and since there is no referable time series data, which can be used for the prediction, the demand estimation becomes a difficult task. It is very difficult to predict the time and place of occurrence of the demand. Moreover, the demanders (affected people) do not ask for the products or services directly, and the demands received by the distributors are the aggregated demand based on the judgment of the observer. This gives only the aggregated demand and not the disaggregated demand as in the case of the commercial supply chain (Sheu 2007). Furthermore, the demand for the materials is not same throughout the supply chain as it differs in the quantity of the products required and the type of product. The time at which the materials are required also changes throughout the planning horizon (Long and Wood 1995; Balcik et al. 2010; Ergun et al. 2010).

5.2.3 Shortage of Experienced Logisticians

Shortage of the number of experienced logisticians also acts as a barrier. The experienced logistician will have a foresight into the types of the problems that can be expected to arise and how it was tackled in the past. The experienced logistician will be able to make decisions much faster and with pinpoint precision. But, the main issues are that there are very few people working the area of humanitarian logistics who have adequate experience in handling the critical situations (Fritz Institute 2005; Pettit and Beresford 2009). The logisticians working in the humanitarian field are required to have well-developed functional skills compared to the other skills like general management skills, problem-solving skills, and interpersonal skills. The reverse logistics is also one of the areas where the humanitarian logisticians need to focus their attention (Tatham and Kovács 2009). One of the many challenges faced by a humanitarian logistician is to determine which organizations she/he can effectively collaborate with for which purpose. Logisticians are torn between the front-office media exposure of the organization, leading to the requirement to be first on site, which in turn triggers donations to the organization, and the back-office logistical operation that ideally puts the needs of beneficiaries first (Kovacs and Spens 2009).

5.2.4 Lack of Bilateral Information Sharing

Political relationship between the countries of location and countries of distribution also plays a major role in the logistics. It is neither safe nor economically viable to make warehouses in all the countries. Therefore, the international organizations try to strategically place their distribution centers on the globe such that a large area can be accessed easily in the wake of a disaster. But the ease of access is not just limited to the proximity of the distribution center and the crisis-affected zone but also to the political relationship between the countries. This acts as a barrier to the effective flow of information and relief material to the crisis-affected area (Whybark 2007; Balcik et al. 2010). For example, in the case of the Gujarat earthquake in 2001, which ravaged about five district lands left about 20,000 people dead and a lot more injured, managing this scale of devastation was a great challenge. Added to the woes was the fact that the affected area shared the border with Pakistan which could not have been taken lightly. Combined with the lack of bilateral information sharing and the logistics movement, the entire rescue operation was very difficult (Van Wassenhove 2006).

5.2.5 Lack of Infrastructure Facilities

The transportation facilities in the wake of the disaster include the ease of transportation to and from the site of disaster, via various modes of transportation (Kovacs and Spens 2007). It is usually observed that in any case of a disaster, be it anthropogenic in nature or natural, the lack of transportation facilities is the first crisis being faced. Under these circumstances, reaching the affected people in time itself is the biggest challenge. Moreover, most of the time, the political system is not well equipped to handle these kinds of situations. The transportation requirements are often heterogeneous in nature, which compels the aid agencies to even use the vehicles which are not efficient for delivering the goods (Berkoune et al. 2011). The transportation of the affected people from the site of the disaster also depends upon the transportation facilities available. The high uncertainty in the time of impact and nature of disaster lead to the disruption of the transportation facilities which leads even to the loss of life in many situations (Ben-Tal et al. 2010). When information about the specific location of needs began surfacing, the compromised infrastructure significantly increased the difficulty of getting the right supplies to where they were needed. In a post-disaster environment, some information is simply not available, while other information may not make it to the organizations that need it (Whybark et al. 2010).

5.2.6 Lack of Knowledge About Customers

The knowledge about customers (aid recipients) also acts as a barrier in the proper working of the HSC. The term customer has been widely discussed, debated, and understood differently by different people, and they have been viewed and classified into different categories. The knowledge about the customers in the HSCM is very important to understand the way they behave and think and therefore to plan the supply chain. The main difference between the customers in the HSCM and commercial counterpart is that the customers in the commercial supply chain management (CSCM) are the source of money that flows into the supply chain or in other words the customers may be the ultimate end user or the intermediate user; the cash paid by the customers is the source of the income of the supply chain. But, in the case of the HSCM, the end customers (aid recipients) do not usually pay for the services provided (Van Wassenhove 2006). Moreover, the requirement of the aid recipients is rarely known to the suppliers. Most of the requirements are based on the previous experiences and assumptions made by the donors. Kovács and Tatham (2009) identify that gender-insensitive purchasing and gender-specific needs are often neglected due to the lack of knowledge about the requirement of the aid materials. Many a times, the aid materials are purchased without due consideration to the gender. For example, in the case of the Indian Ocean tsunami, only one size of innerwear was available for women (Kovács and Tatham 2009).

5.2.7 Lack of a Central Authority

In most of the disaster management instances, one cannot find any central authority which completely overlooks the entire relief activities. Usually, it is the responsibility of the government of the country where the disaster has occurred to overlook the entire relief operation, but most of the time, the government of the country may be neither experienced nor might be having any expertise to handle such situations which might lead to a lot of confusion and chaos in the entire planning and execution of the relief operation. Under such conditions, there are other autonomous bodies (national or international organizations), which act independently but are obliged to obey the laws of the country. In some cases, the government might lack the experience to handle such critical situations, and under such situations, there might be a lot of confusion and chaos in the entire planning and execution of the relief operation (Seaman 1999; Stephenson 2005). Evidently, the main problem lies in the possible bureaucracy tied to the central strata (the information supply team) and the local strata (humanitarian organizations, local authorities) that confront each other in the realities of the field (Chandes and Pache 2010).

5.2.8 Lack of Knowledge About Scale of Devastation

Estimating the actual number of people affected by the disaster is a very difficult task, and this acts as a challenge in the planning of the relief programs. Sometimes, the cross section of the people affected is homogeneous, or in other words the affected people are from the same geographical area with the same socioeconomic background as usually seen in case of the earthquake. But, sometimes the cross section of people is heterogeneous, as was the case in the 2004 tsunami where a large number of people from different countries were affected. Under such circumstances, the planning of the relief programs is difficult since the socioeconomic fabric differs (Oloruntoba and Gray 2006). The devastation caused by the disaster on the political, economic, social, and infrastructural fabric of the society is very hard to determine. Depending upon the nature and severity of the disaster, there could be massive amounts of debris. This could be blocking roads, obstructing aid supply, or even posing the threat of an epidemic. Thus, it is very important to understand the scale of devastation and the type of losses that are to be dealt with in the post-disaster relief operations (Ergun et al. 2009).

5.2.9 Unpredictable Occurrence

The unpredictability in the nature, the time, the intensity, and the location of the disaster is unknown prior to the occurrence. The population characteristics of the affected areas and the preexisting infrastructure in many disaster-prone areas are not previously available, and it is not possible to predict the extent of post-disaster infrastructural damages prior to the occurrence of the disaster. Due the unpredictability of the occurrence, the post-disaster funding and the supply chain activation also take time (Long and Wood 1995; Balcik et al. 2010).

5.2.10 Improper Identification of Supply Sources

Identification of the supply sources is another important challenge. The humanitarian logistics has two stages of the material transportation, viz., inbound logistics to relief distribution centers (known as the phase of relief supply) and (2) outbound logistics from relief distribution centers to affected areas (known as the phase of relief distribution). Thus, the challenges arise in the identification of the relief supply sources and coordinating the supplied relief to the people who need them the most. The supplies might be procured from the local suppliers in the initial stages of the disaster management, even though the quality and the quantity might be low, but it requires a shorter lead time. In the later stages of the relief activities, the supplies can be procured from the international markets, but still the cost of the entire activities related to the procurement also plays a major role (Balcik et al. 2010). The identification of supply sources is most restricted to the immediate requirement, and a lack of long-term relationship with suppliers as in the commercial supply chains is yet to be seen in the HSCM (Sheu 2007).

5.2.11 Lack of Proper Management of Aid Materials

Reconciling the demand and supply in the pre-disaster and the post-disaster stages is the most difficult of tasks (Lee and Zbinden 2003). This can be attributed to the uncertainty associated with the disaster itself and the lack of the supporting infrastructure to deal with it. Most of the time, the volunteers participating in the relief activities might not have any technical expertise in dealing with such situations. Sometimes the resources may be scarce, and the relief organizations may compete for these resources. This may lead to a lot of problems in the operations and in the collaboration and coordination of the actors in the relief chain management. On the other hand, there might be some resources which might be abundant in the relief chain. This might be the result of the unsolicited donations which might be of no use to the beneficiaries. Under such circumstances, these donations act as a barrier to the smooth functioning of the relief chain. After the 2004 Asian tsunami, more than one third of the donations were lying clogged up in the airports waiting for clearance (Russell 2005; Van Wassenhove 2006; Balcik et al. 2010)

5.2.12   Lack of Coordination Between Different Actors

The coordination between the international and the national agencies, international and national governments, local authorities, and actors who are required for the successful planning, implementation, and coordination of the various relief activities is every important. Intra- and interorganizational coordination is also very important in functions like asset usage, incident management, division of labor for the rescue activities, and public information management, which are a few to name. There must not be any kind of confusion or ambiguity in the definition of roles and activities for each actor in the relief aid programs. The lack of coordination can be traced to number and diversity of actors, donor expectations and funding structure, competition for funding and the effects of the media, unpredictability, resource scarcity/oversupply, and the cost of coordination (Balcik et al. 2010). In addition, humanitarian service providers will have difficulty in equalizing the demand from their customers over time, since most of their services are requested at the same peak times (Schulz and Blacken 2010). In the immediate aftermath of the tsunami, there was considerable interagency "squabbling," and it was not until this was resolved that improved collaboration was achieved. The resolution of such problems precrisis would have ensured that the immediate response was much better. This one example highlights the fact that poor collaboration can have an impact on a number of other success factors including aid material management (Pettit and Beresford 2009).

5.2.13   Inadequate Procurement of Aid Materials

Aid material procurement is another barrier in the area of the humanitarian aid activity. For example, there are a lot of regulations in the food procurement. Every country has its own policies and procedures for the food procurement, and during a crisis situation, this acts as a barrier since a lot of procedures have to be followed and each of which might be time consuming. Due to the preferences of relief agencies for procuring locally and the uncertainties related to disaster occurrences and funding levels, it can often prove difficult to develop strong relationships with suppliers in advance of disasters. This affects the procurement of the supplies on a large-scale basis, and the supply chain does not get the supplies to effectively manage the demand arising due to sudden onset of any disaster. Also, due to the funding constraints, the procurement can be done only through competitive price-based bidding (Bagchi et al. 2011; Balcik et al. 2010).

5.2.14   Improper Funding

The funding also posses another challenge in the HSC. The time taken for the request of the funds to be transferred to the governmental and the nongovernmental organizations and the time taken for the release of these funds affect the stakeholder in the HSCM. The stakeholders who are usually worst hit by these kinds of lags are the aid recipients. Most of the distribution activities do not take place without the funds being allocated. Sometimes, the NGOs function only with the donor funding, and they will be ready to operate in the country only if they are able to get a donor. Moreover, the donors also expect the organizations to function properly, and this makes the donors also a customer of the relief organization. The relief organizations compete for the funding, and this is typically true in the earlier stages of the relief operations. The supply chain agility is also affected by these funding constraints since the organizations are generally required to raise a huge amount of funds in a very short span of time (Seaman 1999; (Hilhorst 2002; Moore et al. 2003; Stephenson and Schnitzer 2006).

5.3   Interpretive Structural Modeling

Interpretive structural modeling (ISM) was first proposed by J. Warfield in 1973 to analyze the complex socioeconomic systems. ISM enables individuals or groups to develop a map of the complex relationships between the many elements involved in a complex situation. Its basic idea is to use experts' practical experience and knowledge to decompose a complicated system into several sub-systems (elements) and construct a multilevel structural model. ISM is often used to provide fundamental understanding of complex situations, as well as to put together a course of action for solving a problem. When the number of variables in the system is too large, indentifying and understanding the relationships between each of these variables is tedious and complex. ISM helps in handling this complexity of the system and comprehending by working out the hierarchical arrangements of the system variables. The model so formed helps in understanding the system or an issue in a carefully designed pattern implying graphics as well as words. ISM methodology helps to impose order and direction on the complexity of relationships among the elements of a system (Ramesh et al. 2010). In this paper, we have adopted ISM methodology to establish the relationship between the barriers/outcomes of humanitarian supply chain management.

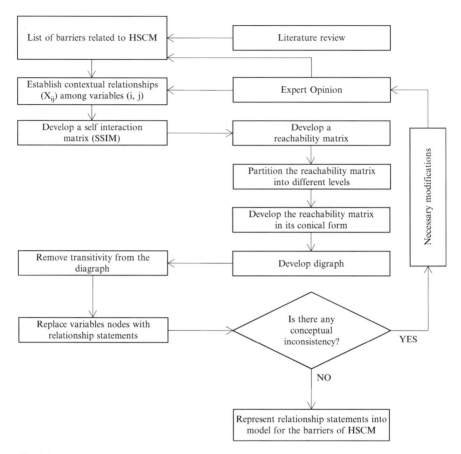

Fig. 5.1 ISM flowchart

ISM is a very helpful tool in understanding the interrelationship between the different variables. It is primarily intended as a group learning process. The method is interpretive since the judgment of the group decides whether and how the variables are related to each other. It is structural since the overall structure is extracted from the complex set of variables. It is a modeling technique as the specific relationships and overall structure are portrayed in a digraph model. Figure 5.1 shows the flow structure of ISM. The various steps in the ISM are summarized below:

(i) Identify the elements, which are relevant to the problem or issues. This could be done by survey or any group problem-solving technique.
(ii) Establish a contextual relationship between elements with respect to which pairs of elements will be examined.
(iii) Develop a structural self-interaction matrix (SSIM) of elements, which indicates pairwise relationship between elements of the system.

(iv) Develop a reachability matrix from the SSIM, and check the matrix for transitivity. Transitivity of the contextual relation is a basic assumption in ISM which states that if element A is related to B and B is related to C, then A is necessarily related to C.
(v) Partition the reachability matrix into different levels.
(vi) Based on the relationships given above in the reachability matrix, draw a directed graph (digraph), and remove transitive links.
(vii) Convert the resultant digraph into an ISM, by replacing element nodes with statements.
(viii) Review the ISM model to check for conceptual inconsistency, and make the necessary modifications.

5.3.1   Structural Self-Interaction Matrix (SSIM)

A total of 15 experts were considered for identifying the contextual relationship between the barriers. ISM suggests that the expert advice (such as brainstorming, nominal group technique, etc.) should be used for obtaining the SSIM, but the questionnaire surveys can also be used to identify the relationship between the variables. In the present work, 15 experts (5 each from academia and industry and 2 each from the NGO and UNDP and 1 member represented the Government of India) were consulted for identifying the relationships between the variables. These experts were well versed in their respective fields and have considerable experience in the humanitarian aid management. Out of the 15 experts consulted, 9 of them had direct involvement in the relief operations post Gujarat earthquake in 2001, and 12 experts had direct involvement in the relief operation post 2004 Indian Ocean tsunami, while 6 experts were involved in both the rescue and relief operations.

In the first stage of the study, the experts were interviewed to identify the specific issues relating to the HSCM activities in India. The interview was based on the set of structured questions drawing form the literature and the issues specific to the Indian context. Each expert was asked to explain about his/her experiences and the barriers that they faced in setting up of the supply chain in the rescue and the relief activities and what efforts were made to overcome them. Based on the interviews, the common barriers faced by the experts were identified. In the second stage, the experts were invited to a common place wherein a moderated brainstorming session was conducted after a small briefing on the ISM methodology and the scope of the present study. At the end of the brainstorming session, the experts were asked to come to a consensus on the SSIM as shown in Table 5.1.

The relationship between two variables (i and j) and the associated direction was also considered. Four symbols were used to identify the direction between the two variables:

- V = barrier "i" influences barrier "j."
- A = barrier "j" influences barrier "i."

Table 5.1 Structural self-interaction matrix (SSIM)

No.	Barrier/outcome	14	13	12	11	10	9	8	7	6	5	4	3	2
1	Lack of proper management of aid materials	A	A	A	A	A	A	A	A	A	A	A	A	A
2	Coordination between different actors	A	A	X	A	A	A	A	A	A	A	A	X	
3	Inadequate procurement of aid materials	A	A	O	A	A	A	A	A	A	X	X		
4	Lack of sufficient funding	A	A	O	A	A	A	A	A	A	X			
5	Identification of supply sources	A	A	O	A	A	A	A	A	A				
6	Lack of correct need and damage assessment	A	A	O	A	A	A	A	A					
7	Lack of predictable demand patterns	A	A	O	A	A	A	A						
8	Shortage of experienced logisticians	O	O	O	V	O	V							
9	Lack of bilateral information sharing	A	A	O	V	A								
10	Lack of infrastructure facilities	A	A	O	V									
11	Lack of knowledge about customers	A	A	O										
12	Lack of a central authority	O	O											
13	Scale of devastation	A												
14	Unpredictable occurrence													

- X = barriers "*i*" and "*j*" influence each other.
- O = barriers "*i*" and "*j*" are unrelated.

For the sake of illustration, the usage of the symbols in SSIM can be explained as follows:

(i) The shortage of the experienced logisticians for managing the HSCM in India leads to poor information sharing between the actors of the supply chain. The importance of the cross-border information sharing is not given much thought. This affects the bilateral information sharing. On the other hand, the bilateral information sharing does not lead to the shortage of the logisticians. Therefore, the relation between them is denoted by "V."

(ii) Improper management of the aid materials (outcome) is influenced by the shortage of experienced logisticians (barrier 8). Thus, the relationship between barrier 1 and barrier 8 is denoted by "A."

(iii) Inadequate procurement of the aid materials (barrier 3) and the improper identification of supply sources (barrier 5) influence each other; thus, the relationship between them is given by "X."

5.3.2 Reachability Matrix

The SSIM has been converted into a binary matrix called the initial reachability matrix by substituting V, A, X, and O by 1 and 0 as per the following rules:

- If the (i, j) entry in the SSIM is "V," the (i, j) entry in the reachability matrix becomes 1 and the (j, i) entry becomes 0.
- If the (i, j) entry in the SSIM is "A," the (i, j) entry in the reachability matrix becomes 0 and the (j, i) entry becomes 1.
- If the (i, j) entry in the SSIM is "X," the (i, j) entry in the reachability matrix becomes 1 and the (j, i) entry also becomes 1.
- If the (i, j) entry in the SSIM is "O," the (i, j) entry in the reachability matrix becomes 0, and the (j, i) entry also becomes 0.

Based on abovementioned rules, the final reachability matrix is given in Table 5.2. The transitivities, as mentioned in the step 3, also incorporated into the final reachability matrix given in Table 5.3. The driving power and the dependence power of each variable are also calculated. The driving power of a variable is the total number of variables (including itself) which may influence the outcome. The dependence power of the variable is the total number of variable (including itself) which might be influenced by the other variables. Based on the driving and dependence power, the variables can be classified into autonomous, dependent, linkage, and independent (driver) barriers.

5.3.3 Level Partitions

The reachability set and the antecedent set for each of the variables is found from the reachability matrix. The former set is a set of barrier being influenced by the barrier including itself, whereas the later set is a set of barrier influencing a barrier including itself. Then the intersection set is derived which in turn is the intersection of the reachability set and the antecedent set. The variable for which the reachability set and the intersection set are the same is given the highest priority and placed at the top of the ISM model. It implies that this variable will not help achieve any other variable above its own level. After identifying the top-level variable, it is discarded from the analysis, and the same procedure is repeated till all the levels and the variable in those levels are identified. It can be observed from the Table 5.3 that the lack of proper management of the aid materials (outcome variable) is at level 1. Thus, it will be placed at the topmost level of the ISM-based model. The iterative procedure is continued till the levels associated with the entire variable are being identified and are summarized in Table 5.3 given below.

74   L. John and A. Ramesh

Table 5.2 Reachability matrix

Barrier/outcome	1	2	3	4	5	6	7	8	9	10	11	12	13	14	Driving Power
1. Lack of proper management of aid materials	1	0	0	0	0	0	0	0	0	0	0	0	0	0	1
2. Coordination between different actors	1	1	0	0	0	0	0	0	0	0	0	1	0	0	3
3. Inadequate procurement of aid materials	1	1	1	1	1	0	0	0	0	0	0	0	0	0	5
4. Lack of sufficient funding	1	1	1	1	1	0	0	0	0	0	0	0	0	0	5
5. Identification of supply sources	1	1	1	1	1	0	0	0	0	0	0	0	0	0	5
6. Lack of correct need and damage assessment	1	1	1	1	1	1	0	0	0	0	0	0	0	0	6
7. Unpredictable demand	1	1	1	1	1	1	1	0	0	0	0	0	0	0	7
8. Shortage of experienced logisticians	1	1	1	1	1	1	1	1	1	0	1	0	0	0	10
9. Lack of bilateral information sharing	1	1	1	1	1	1	1	0	1	0	1	0	0	0	9
10. Inadequate access and transportation facilities	1	1	1	1	1	1	1	0	1	1	1	0	0	0	10
11. Lack of knowledge about customers	1	1	1	1	1	1	1	0	0	0	1	0	0	0	8
12. Lack of a central authority	1	1	0	0	0	0	0	0	0	0	0	1	0	0	3
13. Scale of devastation	1	1	1	1	1	1	1	1	1	1	1	0	1	0	11
14. Unpredictable occurrence	1	1	1	1	1	1	1	0	1	1	1	0	1	1	12
Dependence power	14	13	11	11	11	8	7	1	5	3	6	2	2	1	

Table 5.3 Iteration results

Outcome/barrier	Reachability set	Antecedent set	Intersection set	Level
1	1	1,2,3,4,5,6,7,8,9,10,11,12,13,14	1	I
2	1,2	2,3,4,5,6,7,8,9,10,11,12,13,14	2	II
3	1,2,3,4,5	3,4,5,6,7,8,9,10,11,12,13,14	3,4,5	III
4	1,2,3,4,5	3,4,5,6,7,8,9,10,11,12,13,14	3,4,5	III
5	1,2,3,4,5	3,4,5,6,7,8,9,10,11,12,13,14	3,4,5	III
6	1,2,3,4,5,6	6,7,8,9,10,11,13,14	6	IV
7	1,2,3,4,5,6,7	7,8,9,10,11,13,14	7	V
8	1,2,3,4,5,6,7,8,9,11	8	8	VII
9	1,2,3,4,5,6,7,9,11	9,10,11,13,14	9,11	VI
10	1,2,3,4,5,6,7,9,10,11	10,13,14	10	VII
11	1,2,3,4,5,6,7,11	11,13,14	11	VI
12	1,2,12	2,12	2,12	II
13	1,2,3,4,5,6,7,9,10,11,13	13,14	13	VIII
14	1,2,3,4,5,6,7,9,10,11,13,14	14	14	IX

5.4 Discussion

It can be observed from Fig. 5.2 that the unpredictable occurrence of the demand for the aid materials (barrier 14) is the basic barrier for the functioning of the HSCM, and thus, it forms the base of the ISM model. Evidently it is one of the most difficult tasks for any humanitarian logistician to predict the time, place, and intensity with which the disaster may strike. Moreover it is equally difficult, if not more, to predict the amount of destruction prior to the occurrence of the disaster. The lack of proper management of the aid materials (barrier 1) is the final effect (outcome) of the improper management of the aid materials. The entire HSCM activity revolves

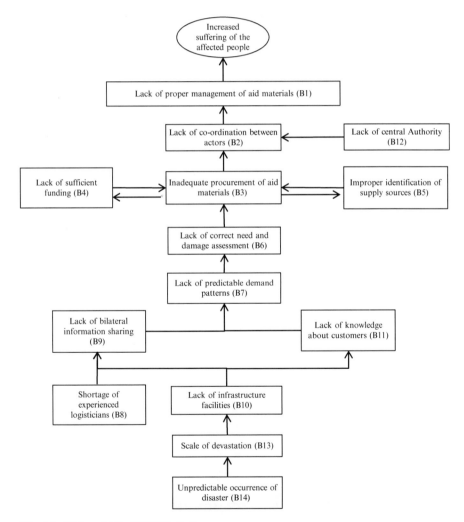

Fig. 5.2 ISM model for HSCM in India

around the effective and efficient management of the aid materials for the beneficiaries to reduce the impact of the disaster in their lives.

The inability to predict the occurrence of the disaster and to forecast the place, time, or impact of the same is the biggest impediment for the functioning of the HSCM in India. The extent of the damages caused by any disaster depends upon the magnitude, nature, and place of occurrence. Predicting the scale of the devastation prior to any disaster with any acceptable level of accuracy is practically impossible. The impact of the disaster on the infrastructure facilities makes the task of setting up of the HSCM quite a challenging task. The lack of pre-disaster preparedness and myopic view on the disaster mitigation activities leaves the authorities with little or no experience to deal with a disaster. Moreover, the lack of strategic intent for developing a supply chain prior to the disaster means there is a lack of experienced logisticians. The lack expertise of the logisticians in India in dealing with the uncertainties arising in the wake of the disaster becomes detrimental for the functioning of the HSCM. The HSCM performs under the bleak availability of the valid and useful information. With a disaster, the level of information generated is usually very high. However, the utility of all the information available is debatable. Under such conditions, the shortage of the experienced logisticians translates into loss of focus from the supply chain goal. The importance of the information sharing is not always appreciated, and therefore, any cross-border or bilateral information is usually not available for the supply chain members. The lack of bilateral information sharing essentially means that the knowledge about the aid recipients is not always available to the supply chain. The combined effect of the lack of information sharing and lack of the knowledge about the need of the aid recipients leaves the supply chain to depend upon previous experiences or speculations.

For a supply chain, which is highly immature, the prospects of the availability of the documented data of prior efforts are austere. The dependence on the previous data and the lack of any predictable demand patterns from the available data essentially leave much to the speculation and the assumption for the supply chain managers. The need or damage assessment made under the dearth of the dependable information is nothing but the expectation of the supply chain managers. Based on this speculated information about the need of the aid recipients, the aid materials are procured. The sources for the financial funding required for the aid material procurement are generally never preplanned. This leads to the backing out of the donors or receiving lesser amount of funds than expected. The lack of the sufficient funds along with the improper identification of the supply sources complicates the problem to a greater extent. The supply sources can be primary supply sources, i.e., suppliers of the aid materials or the secondary supply sources like the warehouses. The suppliers may not be able to supply for the sudden needs arising due to the disaster since the demand is highly unpredictable both on the ends of quantity and the time of requirement unless any long-term agreement or alternative sourcing options are explored prior to the disaster. The secondary sources may not always hold the required quantity, quality, or mix of the aid materials since the holding cost is high and also the obsolescence risk also runs very high owing to the unpredictable nature of the demand.

With all the inherent complexities of setting up of the HSCM, the number of stakeholders is overwhelmingly high. They include the affected people, the government of the state and province, the military, and NGOs, both national and international, to name a few. The major coordination issues arise between these stakeholders since they have conflicting requirements and also tend to compete with each other for the limited resources like aid materials, transportation facilities, volunteers, etc. The lack of coordination and the conflicting requirements lead to the lack of proper management of the resources available. The aid material being the scarcest becomes the most mismanaged in the initial stages of the supply chain formation. As the supply chain stabilizes as the recovery and the rehabilitation activities progress, the excess arrival of the aid material may again create issues as the need for the aid material may not arise.

The impact of the variables is not analyzed by the direct interrelationships rather by the indirect interrelationships. The MICMAC analysis tries to identify the driving power and the dependence power of the variables (Faisal et al. 2006). The variables are classified into four clusters as shown in Fig. 5.3.

The driving power and the dependence power of the variables are shown in Fig. 5.3. The driving power and dependence power can be obtained from Table 5.2 (reachability matrix). For example, the barrier 5 has a driving power of 5 and dependence power of 11, which is placed accordingly in Fig. 5.3, which coincides with the point (5, 11). The four clusters into which the variables are being divided are autonomous variables, dependent variables, linking variables, and independent variables. The autonomous variables (cluster A) are those variables which have

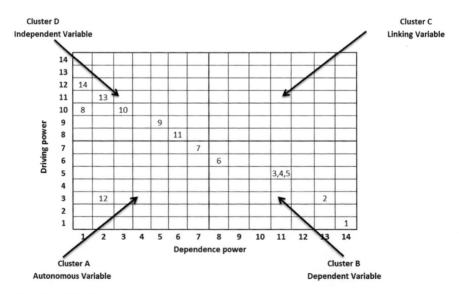

Fig. 5.3 MICMAC analysis

both weak driving power and dependence power. The barriers 12 (lack of central authority) and 7 (lack of predictable demand patterns) are autonomous in this case. Intuitively, the importance of the autonomous variables, particularly their exogenous nature, makes them an integral part of the HSCM in India. The lack of central authority for managing the aid materials in the post-disaster recovery and restoration phase leads to the lack of a strategic view in mitigation and the pre-disaster preparation phase. The lack of strategic intent and the unpreparedness combined with a large number of stakeholders, often competing for the limited resources, leads to the breakdown of the HSCM activities. The lack of central authority and hence the breakdown of the supply chain lead to poor post-disaster review of the effectiveness of supply chain activities. With the loss of the valuable data during the setting up of the supply chain activities, functioning and the final dissolution of the supply chain are lost, thereby leading to a loss of valuable intelligence for the future planning. This loss of intelligence eventually leads to the lack of any predictable demand patterns for pre-disaster preparation and the operation phase of the supply chain. The dependent barriers (variables 1, 2, 3, 4, 5, and 6) are those variables with high dependence power and low driving power. The dependence power of the barrier 6 (lack of correct need and damage assessment) is lower when compared to the other barriers in the same cluster. The need and the damage assessment is one of the most primary data required for the supply chain to react. The HSCM is triggered by any disaster making it essentially a pull supply chain to start off. However, once the supply chain is in place, it transforms in to a push supply chain, not waiting for the actual demand to arrive. The aid material requirement decisions are made based on the previous experiences of the logisticians and the initial speculation of the need and damage. Under this condition, the "responsiveness lag" of the supply chain is magnified by its dependence on the need for the information on the aid requirements. Therefore, the responsiveness of the supply chain is measured by its dependence on the requirement for correct need and damage assessment (barrier 6) making the barrier 6 an impediment for a immature or a nonexistent supply chain, whereas the barrier 6 may not be as important as a barrier for mature supply chain for the humanitarian aid. Thus, in Indian context the barrier 6 plays a major role for the HSCM. The driving barriers (variables 8, 9, 10, 11, 13, and 14) have high driving power and low dependence power.

5.5 Conclusion

The ISM model proposed in this research helps in identifying the links between the barriers and how they affect the working of the HSCM in a combined fashion. The ISM models identify that the logisticians in the supply chain form the very important link between the effective relief program and the managing of the crisis situation. The importance of trained and experienced logisticians is very important for the effective management of most of the activities in the HSCM. Secondly, the ISM model helps in understanding the life cycle of the supply chain and the various intricately affecting issues in the real-time management of the relief activities. Furthermore, the ISM model helps in indentifying and understanding the complex challenges in the HSCM, thereby helping in forming strategic plans and defining the operational goals. Finally, this model helps in highlighting the implications as well as the importance of the coordination between the actors of the HSCM.

The barriers/outcome variables identified in this research can serve as a road map to implementing HSCM. The barriers hindering the proper planning and implementation of HSCM pose challenges for both managers and strategists in the humanitarian aid management. The major barriers have been highlighted and framed into an ISM model to analyze the interactions between barriers. These barriers need to be overcome for successful HSCM. The driving power-dependence diagram (Fig. 5.3) provides valuable insights to the managers of humanitarian aid management to act proactively in dealing with these barriers.

From the ISM model (Fig. 5.2), the managers can identify that the lack of central authority is at the bottom of the model, which leads to a chaotic situation. Thus, the managers should try to train the government of a country to deal with the uncertainties associated with any disaster, since the government of the country will be able to act as a central coordinator of the entire relief activity. The coordination between the actors of the supply chain is also very important, and managers should devise new coordination mechanisms between them so as to optimize the usage of the scarce resources as well as to reduce the suffering of the beneficiaries.

The importance of developing reliable sources of information so as to predict the occurrence of a disaster is also very important. The development of early warning system has to be looked into more specifically. The long-term relationship with the suppliers and pre-positioning of the warehouses as well as training the professional to deal with the conditions forming the environment of HSCM has to be planned strategically. The model discussed and developed in this research is essentially based on the focused group discussions. A larger sample can be used for a better understanding of the situation pertaining to the HSCM activities. The ISM model suggested in this research can be validated by statistical techniques like structural equation modeling (SEM). This can be done with the help of statistical packages like AMOS, LISREL, etc.

References

Bagchi A, Paul AJ, Maloni M (2011) Improving bid efficiency for humanitarian food aid procurement. Int J Prod Econ. doi:10.1016/j.ijpe.2011.07.004

Balcik B, Beamon BM, Krejci CC, Muramatsu KM, Ramirez M (2010) Coordination in humanitarian relief chains: practices, challenges and opportunities. Int J Prod Econ 126(1):22–34

Ben-Tal A, Chung BD, Mandala SR, Yao T (2010) Robust optimization for emergency logistics planning: risk mitigation in humanitarian relief supply chains. Transportation Res B. doi:10.1016/j.trb.2010.09.002

Berkoune D, Renaud J, Rekik M, Ruiz A (2011) Transportation in disaster response operations. Socio-Econ Plann Sci. doi:10.1016/j.seps.2011.05.002

Chandes J, Pache G (2010) Investigating humanitarian logistics issues: from operations management to strategic action. J Manuf Technol Manag 21(3):320

Darcy J (2005) The Indian ocean tsunami crisis: humanitarian dimensions. Available at: www.odi. org.uk/hpg/Tsunami.html. Accessed 13 Aug 2011

de la Torre LE, Dolinskaya IS, Shimolitz KR (2011) Disaster relief routing: integrating research and practice. Socio-Econ Plann Sci. doi:10.1016/j.seps.2011.06.001

Dolinskaya IS, Shi ZE, Smilowitz KR (2011) Decentralized approaches to logistics coordination in humanitarian relief. In: Proceedings of the 2011 industrial engineering research conference. Reno, Nevada, US

Ergun O, Karakus G, Keskinocak P, SwannJ, Villarreal M (2009) Humanitarian supply chain management-an overview. In: Models and algorithms for optimization in logistics Dagstuhl seminar proceedings, vol 10

Ergun O et al (2010) Operations research to improve disaster supply chain management. In: Wiley encyclopedia of operations research and management science

Faisal MN, Banwet DK, Shankar R (2006) Supply chain risk mitigation: modeling the enablers. Bus Process Manag J 12(4):535–552

Fink G, Redaelli S (2011) Determinants of international emergency aid—humanitarian need only? World Dev 39(5):741–757

Fritz Institute (2005) Logistics and the effective delivery of humanitarian relief. Fritz Institute, San Francisco, p 12

Granot H (1995) Proposed scaling of the communal consequences of disaster. Disaster Prev Manag 4(3):5–13

Hilhorst D (2002) Being good at doing good? Quality and accountability of humanitarian NGOs. Disasters 26(3):193–212

Jahre M (2009) Supply chain design and coordination in humanitarian logistics through clusters. Doctoral dissertation, Norwegian School of Management

Kovacs G, Spens KM (2007) Humanitarian logistics in disaster relief operations. Int J Phys Distrib Logist Manag 37(2):99–114

Kovacs G, Spens K (2009) Identifying challenges in humanitarian logistics. Int J Phys Distrib Logist Manag 39(6):506–528

Kovács G, Tatham P (2009) Humanitarian logistics performance in the light of gender. Int J Productivity Perform Manag 58(2):174–187

Lee HW, Zbinden M (2003) Marrying logistics and technology for effective relief. Forced Migr Rev 18:34–35

Long DC, Wood DF (1995) The logistics of famine relief. J Bus Logist 16(1):213–39

Moore S, Eng E, Daniel M (2003) International NGOs and the role of network centrality in humanitarian aid operations: a case study of coordination during the 2000 Mozambique floods. Disasters 27(4):305–318

Oloruntoba R, Gray R (2006) Humanitarian aid: an agile supply chain? Supply Chain Manag Int J 11(2):115–120

Pettit S, Beresford A (2009) Critical success factors in the context of humanitarian aid and supply chains. Int J Phys Distrib Logist Manag 39(6):450–468

Ramesh A, Banwet D, Shankar R (2010) Modelling the barriers of supply chain collaboration. J Model Manag 5(2):176–193

Russell TE (2005) The humanitarian relief supply chain: analysis of the 2004 South East Asia earthquake and tsunami. MLog Thesis, MIT

Schulz SF, Blecken A (2010) Horizontal cooperation in disaster relief logistics. Int J Phys Distr Log Manag 40(8/9):636–656

Seaman J (1999) Malnutrition in emergencies: how can we do better and where do the responsibilities lie? Disasters 23(4):306–315

Sheu JB (2007) Challenges of emergency logistics management. Transportation Res E 43(6): 655–659

Stephenson M Jr (2005) Making humanitarian relief networks more effective: operational coordination, trust and sense making. Disasters 29(4):337–350

Stephenson M, Schnitzer MH (2006) Inter-organizational trust, boundary spanning, and humanitarian relief coordination. Nonprofit Manag Leadersh 17(2):211–232

Tatham PH, Kovács G (2009) Logistics skills and performance in the "for profit" and "not for profit" sectors". In: Proceedings of the logistics research network (LRN) conference, Cardiff, 9–11 Sep 2009

Trunick PA (2005) Special report: delivering relief to tsunami victims. Logist Today 46(2):1–3

Van Wassenhove LN (2006) Humanitarian aid logistics: supply chain management in high gear. J Oper Res Soc 57(5):475–89

Whybark DC (2007) Issues in managing disaster relief inventories. Int J Prod Econ 108:228–235

Whybark DC, Melnyk SA, Day J, Davis E (2010) Disaster relief supply chain management: new realities, management challenges, emerging opportunities. Decision Line, May, pp 4–7

Part II
Humanitarian Logistics Strategies

Even though each disaster situation is distinct, it touches upon common logistical elements like planning, preparedness, design, procurement, transportation, inventory, warehousing, distribution, execution and implementation consisting of various actors, agencies (government, private, and NGOs) and recipients. Formulation of strategies during the preparedness stage is essential for effective and efficient response and recovery from a disaster. Using technology is one of the means to improve the logistics response to a disaster. Particularly, an effective and efficient use of information technology can be an important driver in successful humanitarian relief efforts. Three papers in this section discuss the use of technology for developing framework towards improved preparedness and response to a disaster. The first paper presents a conceptual model for the use of ICTs for effective coordination and management of disasters and an IT-enabled relief network model for effective disaster management and recovery. The second paper attempts to identify the challenges in implementation of information technology in humanitarian relief organisations. The third paper discusses the use of RFID technology to improve collaboration among organisation in disaster supply chains. Increasing complexity of supply chains due to globalisation efforts have led to organisations having difficulties with both collaboration, as well as agility in getting aid to individuals in need. A discussion on various supply chain configurations for disaster management that analyses humanitarian logistics issues and for suggesting a model for incorporating humanitarian logistics into supply chain models has also been presented in this section. Finally, a discussion on using collective capacity as a strategy for improving disaster response and recovery has been presented in this paper.

Chapter 6
Relief Network Model for Efficient Disaster Management and Disaster Recovery

Sumeet Gupta, B.S. Sahay, and Parikshit Charan

6.1 Introduction

The world has witnessed a large number of natural disasters in the last decade. The earthquake in Indonesia, floods in Uttarkashi in India, cyclone in Tamil Nadu, hurricane in Maine, and tsunami in Japan to name a few have been on the news for quite a while in terms of the massive destruction brought about by them. Such disasters not only clog the government machinery and drain its resources but also mar the progressive efforts toward the development of a region. With the Bhuj earthquake in 2001, the Government of India took steps to develop a comprehensive disaster management program in India. In the year 2005, the Disaster Management Act[1] was passed defining various preventive measures for dealing with disasters as well as outlining steps for disaster recovery. The responsibility for disaster management was placed on the state government. A number of disaster management authorities were created in each state directly under the Ministry of Home Affairs. Disaster management faculties were also opened in the state-run training institutes. However, in spite of such effort, the Government of Uttarakhand was left wonderstruck with the cloudbursts of Uttarakhand in 2013 that caused massive destruction. It was least prepared to deal with such disaster although the ominous effect of their efforts of building a dam on River Kedarnath was well

---

[1] http://www.unisdr.org/2005/mdgs-drr/national-reports/India-report.pdf

S. Gupta (✉) • B.S. Sahay
Department of Operations and Systems, Indian Institute of Management Raipur,
Raipur, Chhattisgarh, India
e-mail: sumeetgupta@iimraipur.ac.in; bssahay@iimraipur.ac.in

P. Charan
Department of Management Studies, IIT Delhi, New Delhi, India

Department of Operations and Systems, Indian Institute of Management Raipur,
Raipur, Chhattisgarh, India

© Springer India 2016
B.S. Sahay et al. (eds.), *Managing Humanitarian Logistics*, Springer Proceedings
in Business and Economics, DOI 10.1007/978-81-322-2416-7_6

predicted by locals as well as environmentalists. The supplies were disrupted, and a number of voluntary organizations started their relief efforts, but for 3 days no relief reached the affected people.

The first visible effect of disaster management in India was observed only during the recent Phailin cyclone that struck the coasts of Odisha state at Gopalpur on 13 October 2013. Before the cyclone could show its strong face, around 900,000 people were evacuated and relocated. The cyclone did prove to be massively disastrous for the livestock and natural resources on the coast, although, only a few fatalities were reported as an aftermath of the disaster. The cyclone resulted in the River Phalgu of Jharkhand getting filled with water, which usually ran dry for years. It was considered a benefit in disguise due to floods. The water gates were opened, but this resulted in floods and destruction in five districts of Bengal, which claimed around 9 lives[2]. Thus, while the Government of Odisha and the state government were prepared for dealing with Phailin, they did not estimate that Phailin would result in floods in Bengal. The cyclone was supposed to pass through the states of Jharkhand, Andhra, and Chhattisgarh. However, situation in these states remained calm. In other words the estimated effect of the cyclone remained unpredicted, although their efforts to deal with it in the state of Odisha were commendable.

The above two cases hint at the need for development of a model whereby greater capacity building is needed for dealing with major disaster calling for not only awareness but also participation from private firms, NGOs, and other organizations. While help may be available in abundance, what is required is a well-coordinated and selfless effort from various organizations. Different organizations voice their concern differently, and such concerns can have a debilitating effect on disaster management and recovery efforts of the government and other relief agencies. Building buildings from ruins is the business for many. Different people view natural disasters differently and try to benefit from the disaster. Unless a well-coordinated effort is launched by the government to deal with such disasters, the attempt to benefit from such disasters in some way or another will continue. This gives rise to agency relationships whereby different ostensible beneficiaries of disasters attempt to thwart each other's efforts in the name of helping people. The result is complete chaos, choking of logistics and delaying recovery efforts. In order to achieve proper coordination, it is important to understand the outlook of different stakeholders in a disaster.

Scientists attempt to prophesize their theories such as viewing it as a result of subterrestrial movements or the movement of winds. The Japanese tsunami, for example, was attributed to the earthquake deep within the sea that propagated seawaters to inundate Japanese coasts and caused other significant damages. Similarly, the India Meteorological Department estimated and forewarned the approaching Phailin, and the disaster management efforts were conducted well before Phailin could significantly damage human lives. The forecasting was done

---

[2] http://www.firstpost.com/india/phailin-effect-in-bengal-nine-people-lose-their-lives-in-floods-1178323.html

by the Joint Typhoon Warning Center and other US forecasters who estimated Phailin having a peak intensity at Category 5 level although the India Meteorological Department was less conservative in predicting its intensity.

Religious protagonists viewed it as a wrath of demigods, indicating that something is not right with the way people are approaching life. For example, Uttarakhand floods were attributed to playing with Dhari Devi temple by the Government of Uttarakhand. The wrath took away the lives of thousands of people leaving behind the historic temple of Amarnath. A number of people turn to God during such disasters. Environmentalists view such disasters as the wrath of nature on people. Again the floods in Uttarakhand were viewed as a result of disturbing the ecosystem by building dams and other projects in the otherwise calm atmosphere of Uttarakhand. The similar thing happened when the Government of India tried to break Rama Setu in Rameshwaram in India. The machinery was drowned in the sea. Scientific circles may argue against religionists view, but such views should not be overlooked. The general mass doesn't understand scientific terminologies and, therefore, during the disaster turn to some higher authority which is beyond the control of the federal government.

A number of organizations view such disasters ostensibly as a means of CSR activity. Google, for example, provided helpline and people location service through its people finder service during Uttarakhand floods and Phailin's endemic. We do not have the estimate of help provided by Google's service, but the recent note on its website indicates the data collected by this service could be subjected to misuse. Their people finder website[3] for Uttarakhand reports that Google has deleted the data entered in people finder's website, but such data may be available with active Person Finder sites and that Google does not review or verify the accuracy of data available with them.

Some other firms view it as a means of brand promotion. A number of organizations sprung up with large banners of their philanthropic activity only to grace their corporate magazines with such relief effort to garner public image. The *Times of India*, for example, noted on its website that it was the most read newspaper during the Uttarakhand disaster. It also noted the same during the Taj Hotel bombing by Pakistani militants in the year 2009. Many such firms gather money from the public to provide relief to the affected people. But it is never clear to the donors whether such money ever reaches the intended people. Even if it does, whether the form in which it reaches is correct or not is difficult to ascertain, and perhaps most people are least bothered to ascertain. They are happy thinking that they did their bit in providing relief to the people, knowing little that their bit might not have reached the intended recipient.

There are still others that use such disasters as a dumping ground for useless or unacceptable products. Consider the case of South African Development Community (SDCA), which experienced worst food crisis in over a decade during 2002. The United Nations under its World Food Programme (WFP) in collaboration with

---

[3] http://google.org/personfinder/2013-uttrakhand-floods/

the US Department of Agriculture (USDA) provided 0.9 million tons of genetically modified whole maize. However, Zambia and Zimbabwe both banned imports of such unmilled maize in entering the country as such maize could adversely affect the already poor agricultural economy of these nations. While the UN and WFP may have had good reasons for providing such relief effort, the fact is that genetically modified product has not been received so well not only in the world but in the USA itself. Monsanto has been lobbying the federal government of the USA to provide shelter to its seed in the name of improved variety and quality of seeds. Monsanto claims that genetically modified seeds are superior in quality and pest resistant. However, genetically modified seeds have received severe criticism all over the world. In the USA a number of eatables contain genetically modified ingredients. However, Russia and the European Union have categorically banned genetically modified vegetables and eatables. In India, Monsanto attempted to enter with its subsidiary Mahyco and tried to bring in biotech brinjal and biotech cotton. However, the Government of India has established moratorium over these products considering that as of now genetically modified products are not a necessity. Many view that Monsanto wishes to become the sole supplier and thus create monopoly for the genetically modified seed market. Genetically modified food lack taste and its pest resistant capabilities will make people eat chemicals and thus giving rise to another vicious cycle.

A number of organizations send unsolicited items during such disasters. For example, during the 2004 tsunami, which struck South Asia, Sri Lanka's Colombo airport reported that within 2 weeks of the tsunami, 288 freighter flights had arrived without airway bills to drop off humanitarian cargo (Thomas and Fritz 2006). A large number of ostensibly humanitarian supplies were inappropriate items such as used Western clothes, baked beans, and carbonated beverages which piled up at the airport, clogged warehouses, and remained unclaimed for months. Worse yet, these flights used the fuel available at the airport for returning, leaving the airport out of fuel for the scheduled flights.

During disasters many people try to turn their fortunes. For example, in the recent Uttarakhand disaster, there were cases where affected people were looted for whatever they had in their possession. Cases of organizations dumping nonstandard drugs in the name of relief efforts have also been heard of (Thomas and Fritz 2006). Moreover, the substandard practices of storage of relief items in godowns can eventually lead to dissemination of substandard food products to the recipients in natural disasters.

Not only natural but man-made disasters also complicate the situation. Consider the massive exodus of Assamese from their homes because of hate messages in Facebook and Twitter. Facebook and Twitter are available to everyone but if used improperly can potentially negatively influence a number of people and their lives. Even scientific advices may influence relief efforts. Many people (and even in scientific circles) tend to speculate about the reasons behind disasters, which may influence relief efforts. Not only that, improper estimate of an impending disaster may influence relief efforts. Governments may end up overspending or underspending. For example, the possible effect of impending Phailin cyclone in the coast of Odisha, India, was overestimated by US disaster agencies although the India Meteorological Department stuck to its less conservative estimates and did not feel that Phailin would remain violent for days. And Phailin actually subsided in a day or two, although it damaged the coast of Odisha extensively.

Thus, different people have different agency relationships and outlook toward disaster, which may delay the recovery efforts. Most researchers (e.g., Kovacs and Spens 2007; Balcik et al. 2010) argue that effective coordination is essential for effective disaster management. To achieve effective coordination humanitarian researchers have proposed several approaches, the prominent ones being the cluster approach, chain coordinator approach, development of open networks, engagement of local population, and civil contingencies approach. However, effective coordination in a humanitarian relief chain has remained only a rare commodity.

ICT has been recorded to enhance the coordination efforts, such as that used during recent disasters in Thailand and India (Uttarakhand). This paper looks into the need of a disaster management organization and presents IT-enabled relief network model for efficient disaster management and recovery. Efficient disaster management requires assessment and capacity building before a disaster strikes so that the disaster recovery work goes on smoothly; otherwise, the entire logistics channel gets clogged. The development of relief network is based on the discussion by Thomas and Fritz (2006) on establishing partnerships and draws from the strength of various coordination approaches proposed by researches and combs them with the effective implementation of ICT for improved coordination.

6.2   Literature Review

6.2.1   Humanitarian Relief Supply Chain

To understand this model we first understand a humanitarian supply chain as well as the needs of a relief agency during the disaster. A typical humanitarian supply chain is shown in Fig. 6.1.

In a humanitarian supply chain, there are financial flow and physical flow of goods from owners/government and partners to the relief agency which supplies them to the affected people. When suppliers ask money for the goods supplied by them to the relief agency, there is financial flow from relief agency to the suppliers also. The information flow moves backward.

The second thing we need to understand is the needs of a relief agency. Different disasters have different impact as well as different requirements. Only a proper impact measurement can help estimate the requirement of a disaster. However, a few aspects are usually common to any disaster be it floods, droughts, famine, earthquake, tsunami, cyclone, plague, or massive killings/bombings. The immediate effect of a disaster is usually dislocation of people and disruption of supplies. People are left without shelter, food, or water, cash strapped, and needed medicines.

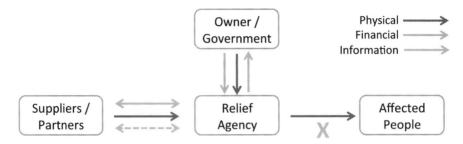

Fig. 6.1 A typical humanitarian supply chain

Moreover, there are chances of emergence of an endemic or an epidemic in the disaster-affected area. So, in other words, what is needed during a disaster is the supply of first aid and basic amenities like clothes, shelter, and food. Moreover, volunteers are required for recovery effort as the relief organizations may fall short of manpower for their relief effort. And the more manpower trained, the better as there are chances of the volunteers of relief efforts themselves falling sick or catching disease. The Indian Army carries out most of the relief operations in India as it has the most trained personnel to carry out such relief efforts. Although the basic requirements are few, but they may take various forms, most of which may not be useful for the recipients. The already discussed example of providing carbonated beverages to the 2004 tsumani-affected people is a case in point. Therefore, a coordinated effort is mandatory for both disaster management and disaster recovery. And the most important thing that is required is the establishment of a communication link between the affected people and their relatives/friends. The panic caused during disasters makes it difficult to establish contact between people and the resource-stripped relief agency. Therefore, a proper IT setup would help establish such a communication link between various parties involved in a disaster.

6.2.2   Need for a Coordinated Effort

The international supply network of humanitarian assistance for managing disaster comprises donors, aid agencies, nongovernmental organizations (NGOs), logistics providers, and governments (Kovacs and Spens 2007). Several researchers have argued for proper coordination among these participants in the supply network of humanitarian assistance for an effective and efficient management of a disaster situation. Nilsson et al. (2010), for example, argue that the prospect of handling disaster and crisis-like events depends on flexible and well-functioning response system at various hierarchical levels. According to Granot (1999), disasters are increasingly viewed as a shared responsibility (Trim 2004), and inter-organizational cooperation is required in order to meet unusual needs. Akhtar et al. (2012) argue that coordination among organizations is a necessity in such circumstances because it is almost impossible for a single organization to fulfill the needs of people affected or rebuild the infrastructure. Hence, different organizations come together to react to these disasters and provide food, water, tarps, shelters, medicines, and other supplies to the affected people. They also assist in the reconstruction of the damaged infrastructure. Balcik et al. (2010) define the term coordination as "the relationships and interactions among different actors operating within the relief environment." In commercial chains, Spekman et al. (1998) and Cao et al. (2008) believe that the coordination system brings together the sequential-interdependent activities of organizations such as suppliers and retailers. These organizations coordinate tangible and intangible assets such as organizational processes, people, management skills, and experiences. They align existing resources with these coordinated assets as well as equally share benefits and risks to manage globally scattered chains. In humanitarian relief chains, this mechanism occurs among different organizations such as among international relief actors, among international relief actors and local organizations, and among relief (both local and international) actors and private or government organizations (Balcik et al. 2010).

Collaboration becomes difficult especially when one is working across political boundaries and/or coordination across organizational boundaries (Connelly 2007). Many factors contribute to coordination difficulties in disaster relief, such as the inherently chaotic post-disaster relief environment, the large number and variety of actors involved in disaster relief, and the lack of sufficient resources (Balcik et al 2010). Lack of coordination among chain members has been shown to increase inventory costs, lengthen delivery times, and compromise customer service (Simatupang et al. 2002). Since logistics accounts for 80 % of relief operations (Van Wassenhove 2006), relief chain coordination is key to improving relief chain performance.

Kovacs and Spens (2007) argue that the preparedness phase is the one in which the physical network, IT systems, and the bases for collaboration are developed so as to shorten the total response time for a disaster. During the preparedness phase, connection to feasible donors, suppliers, other NGOs, and other partners are created but not activated until a catastrophic event takes place. The network so formed comes handy during the immediate response phase where agile response is essential and when coordination and collaboration among all the actors involved in humanitarian response deserve great attention (Balcik and Beamon 2008; Kovacs and Spens 2009; 2007; Maon et al. 2009; Tomasini and Van Wassenhove 2009).

The need for proper coordination is also deeply felt because a disaster situation requires prompt and effective response as time saved means lives saved (Cozzolino et al. 2012). In several academic works, the agile principle has been linked to emergency and humanitarian operations according to the urgent effectiveness objective of the disaster relief logistics (e.g., Charles et al. 2010; Scholten et al. 2010; Kovacs and Spens 2009; Pettit and Beresford 2009; Taylor and Pettit 2009; Oloruntoba and Gray 2006; Towill and Christopher 2002). The agile response requires communication about the situation to partners, creation of a net with suppliers, construction of a dependable logistics system through the creation of a stable net with 3PLs, and formation of a team to implement the emergency plan (Christopher 2005). As can be inferred, coordination among participants is the backbone for agile response.

However, researchers argue that humanitarians face greater challenges in collaboration as compared to their business counterparts (Kovacs and Spens 2007). Coordination of many different aid agencies, suppliers, and local and regional actors, all with their own operating methods, can be very challenging. For humanitarians, this is particularly true, because there is no profit motive, there is no clear command and control, and the priorities are also rapidly changing. Descriptions of relief operations frequently criticize aid agencies for lack of collaboration and duplication of effort (Kovacs and Spens 2007).

6.2.3   Coordination Models and Frameworks

A number of studies have proposed approaches for coordination for disaster response and humanitarian aid. While some of these approaches are generic, a few others have been borrowed from the existing practices either in civil society or military or from supply chains. A few authors (e.g., Burkle and Hayden 2001; Dynes 1994; Kelly 1996) have argued against transferring research knowledge from the military field to civil defense system although military assistance has been taken for dealing with disasters. Among the civilian response organizations, NGOs and international relief and development organizations operating on a global level are primarily examined to develop a contingency approach to dealing with disasters (Foreman 2008; McEntire and Fuller 2002; Shaluf et al. 2003; Trim 2004). They are also supplemented with the approaches developed by national disaster agents and communities or public utilities in relation to national and regional or local strategic and operational disaster planning (Kouzmin et al. 1995; Trim 2004; Quarantelli 1985).

6.2.3.1   Coordination Through Clusters

Cluster thinking has been suggested as a solution to the lack of coordinated disaster response. Clusters for diverse functions, including sheltering, logistics, and water and sanitation, can be viewed as an effort to achieve functional coordination. Jahre and Jenses (2010) discuss the potential of cluster concepts using supply chain coordination and intercluster coordination. Cluster concept is a means of coordination to be carried out in a number of areas. The cluster concept is defined functionally in terms of areas of activity, such as water and sanitation, health, shelter, and nutrition – which typically reflects the important and somewhat separate areas of relief work, often referred to as sectors (Inter-agency Standing Committee 2006). The idea behind cluster approach is to combine various operative bodies that specialize in areas like camp management, medical care, or water and sanitation

(Jahre and Spens 2007) but are largely independent and have their own funding and systems. When these organizations combine, they can face a series of problems related to coordination (Jahre and Jenses 2010). The cluster concept involves organizing humanitarian relief according to a number of sectors with a predefined leadership. According to OCHA (2007), clusters were introduced to improve efficiency in developing sufficient global capacity to meet current and future emergencies; predictable leadership at a global and local level; strengthened partnerships between UN bodies, NGOs, and local authorities; accountability, both for the response and vis-a-vis beneficiaries; and strategic field-level coordination and prioritization. Currently there are 11 clusters, namely, agriculture, camp coordination and management, early recovery, education, emergency shelter, emergency telecommunications, health, logistics, nutrition, protection, and water/sanitation and hygiene.

The benefit of cluster approach is the combined strength and the amenability to mobilization. However, once mobilized the clusters must cooperate with each other; otherwise, the lack of intercluster coordination itself will reduce the effectiveness of disaster management. Many NGOs feel that clusters are overly compartmentalized and there is no need for so many (ActionAid 2007, p. 5). Stoddard et al. (2007) asserted that the inadequate information management and analysis leads to weak intercluster coordination.

6.2.3.2 Chain Coordinators

The chain-coordination mechanism is defined as "a set of methods used to manage interdependencies among organizations" (Xu and Beamon 2006). Although there is no standard definition, Akhtar et al. (2012) define chain coordination as a process whereby the activities of interdependent organizations are brought together to achieve certain objectives. Chain coordination could be horizontal or vertical. Vertical coordination is where organizations coordinate with upstream and downstream activities, such as an NGO coordinating with transport companies to complete certain objectives. It is an arrangement between buyer and seller, entered into freely, to facilitate a mutually satisfying exchange over time, which leaves the operation and control of the two businesses substantially independent (Hughes 1994). Horizontal coordination takes place within a part of chain (Fearne 1998). In the horizontal coordination, different organizations coordinate with each other and manage interdependencies at the same level. A case of the horizontal coordination would be if one NGO coordinates with a second NGO (Balcik et al. 2010). Each chain must be coordinated by a chain coordinator. Such coordinators are the key players who are involved in major decision making, leading and controlling the main coordination activities (Mehta et al. 2003; Akhtar et al. 2010). The coordinators provide a leadership to the network of organizations and manage a portfolio of customers, customer priorities, and customer centricity and resolve conflicts and help manage and build infrastructure, information systems, training programs, and communication (Galbraith 2001). In humanitarian relief chains, the coordinators are often central to the success of coordinating organizations because they lead a number of pivotal activities such as recruiting and retaining paid workers or volunteers, managing and developing staff, managing communication and information, allocating resources, managing accounts and funds, guiding senior managers, and building effective working relationships with relevant decision makers of involved parties like the government or other NGOs.

Research on chain coordinators (Akhtar et al. 2012) has revealed that chain coordinators often are not fully in control of chain-coordination processes. This is one of the main reasons most of collaborative efforts among NGOs have failed to achieve their expected objectives. In fact the good leadership of umbrella organization, coordination, and cluster approach is not enough to guarantee success. Organizations may face problems such as cultural conflicts, structural differences, increasing coordination costs, unnecessary coordination meetings, limited funding, language barriers, lack of cooperation from the host government, shortage of skilled workers, and suitable suppliers (Akhtar et al. 2012).

6.2.3.3   Open Network of Humanitarian Firms

Humanitarian supply chains share some common drivers with their business counterparts. It is critical to get the most out of scarce resources and limited budgets. It is also important to reach more beneficiaries in need and serve them more quickly. However, humanitarian supply chains have their share of unique drivers, such as increasing awareness, becoming better prepared for the next disaster, gaining more rapid access to accurate information about what is needed, and providing better security in the field. If two or more organizations can save more lives or ease more suffering by working together, they should seriously consider it (McLachlin and Larson 2011).

In choosing partners it is important to focus on their complementary capabilities and compatibility or "like-mindedness" (McLachlin et al. 2009). According to Lambert and Knemeyer (2004), compatibility of corporate cultures, compatibility of management philosophy and techniques, strong sense of mutuality, and symmetry between the parties are four fundamental facilitators or environmental factors that enhance partnership growth. Tatham and Kovács (2010) also discuss trust as a critical element in hastily formed humanitarian networks. Trust is more of the norm in disaster relief humanitarian supply chains. During rapid-onset disasters, "swift trust" among logisticians from a variety of organizations could spur improvement of relief operations. Hastily formed networks bring people from different communities together for planning and execution toward fulfillment of a large, urgent mission.

The governance of such loosely held collaborative relationships can be done in the form of hierarchies, markets, or networks (Seybolt 2009). Hierarchies are centralized, with formal rules and patterns for communication. While they can effectively coordinate units in a stable environment, they are slow to respond in environments of rapid change, as in humanitarian crises. Markets are adaptive to environmental changes by enabling independent decision making by individual units. Seybolt (2009) suggests that the humanitarian system combines some negative aspects of both hierarchies (e.g., UN agencies) and markets (e.g., NGOs not cooperating with each other because they compete for funding). Seybolt (2009) further argue that a network approach could give the humanitarian system a useful combination of market and hierarchical governance. Networks are like markets in facilitating horizontal communication and independent decision making by individual organizations. They are also like hierarchies in attempting to reduce conflicts within the system and preserve individual organizations. Network members tend to work collaboratively to plan, implement, and evaluate their activities. This could lead to better coordination of humanitarian organizations (Seybolt 2009).

6.2.3.4   Engagement of Local Population

Humanitarian agencies generally suffer from a heavy turnover of field logistics staff (Van Wassenhove 2006), and this could be as high as 80 % annually (Thomas 2003; Thomas and Kopczak 2005). As a result, a number of agencies struggle to maintain sufficient suitably trained and experienced personnel to be able to respond effectively to natural disasters. An answer to this problem is to increase the involvement of the local populations. Using the case of Typhoon Ondoy (Ketsana) in the Philippines in 2009, Sheppard et al. (2013) explored how local populations can enhance their capacity to respond effectively to natural disasters, particularly at the municipal and village levels, with an emphasis on the final logistics stage – the last mile of delivery –when disaster relief is provided directly to the beneficiaries by local agencies. The main focus of humanitarian agencies during the post-disaster (response) phase in natural disasters is the planning and provision of the right kind of assistance, at the right time, and in the right quantities to meet uncertain demand. McLachlin and Larson (2011) argue that having local partners who have similar views could provide several advantages for coordination and collaboration for dealing with disasters. Such partners have deeper connections with local communities and local authorities. They also have a better understanding of the local culture and value system.

Tomasini and Van Wassenhove (2009) recommended that the greater involvement of the local private sector organizations in the preparedness phase and between disasters is a solution to the lack of indigenous capacity. In areas beset with a significant number and range of natural disasters, a semipermanent response supply network could be established, with private sector organizations being involved as partners in donating money, goods, and expertise to the local population both in improving levels of preparedness and during the actual response phase. The private sector has a clear interest in staying in business and surviving during and after natural disasters such as typhoons, which do not discriminate but impact all levels of society including the commercial organizations themselves. Hence, greater involvement of private sector organizations, particularly in the preparedness phase, would be of significant mutual benefit (Van Wassenhove et al. 2007; APEC

2010). The model for engagement of local population proposed by Sheppard et al. (2013) takes care of centralized control, but that centralized control is now given to the local disaster management authority, and the control at the national level is only for more strategic aspects. The local disaster risk reduction authority would develop and operate logistics clusters with membership including representatives from local government organizations, NGOs, utility suppliers, emergency services, and others. To avoid duplication specific functions would be allocated to cluster members based on their particular areas of expertise.

6.2.3.5 Civil Contingencies Agency Management System

Nilsson et al. (2010) present the civil contingencies agency management system for disaster management. This approach is borrowed from the practices of Swedish Rescue Services Agency (SRSA) that as part of its normal duties also executes humanitarian aid and rescue operations. This approach is different from the approaches followed by NGOs or other relief organizations. The important point to note about the approach of SRSA is its ability to scan its register or operative personnel and place specific competences at a mandatory organization's disposal. The operative workforce is employed for specific operations and a limited time period, during which they are on leave from their regular workplaces (Nilsson et al. 2010).

SRSA's approach is developed with two main underlying rationales: efficiency and humanity. Efficiency applies to optimal goal fulfillment, and humanity comprises a respectful and sympathetic attitude toward those who suffer and toward the organizations' own people as well as those from other organizations. When the efficiency aspect is directed toward person-related qualities of the operation, the emphasis is on a high level of professional task-related knowledge, both concerning the personnel of the management system and the operative workforce. This would mean having the required support (staff) units in terms of competences/experiences, being able to detect which operations are viable in terms of political intentions and financial opportunities, having operative personnel with the skills requested by mandatory organizations, being confident that operative personnel meet high standards, and being able to sell one's own competences to potential mandatory organizations (Nilsson et al. 2010). When efficiency aspect is applied to administration and logistics, the emphasis is on the availability and quality of required resources during different phases of an operation. In such situations procurement laws are not considered, as the requirements are very urgent.

Similarly, when the humane aspect is directed toward the person-related qualities of the operation, the management relies on the staff to have good social/cultural competences. Such attitudes are imbued among the personnel before the operation needs to be carried on. This is important as personnel need to work in different cultures and an understanding of these cultures is required to provide humanitarian aid to the affected people. When the humane aspect is directed toward administration and logistics, the sociocultural atmosphere of the operational environment should be taken into consideration. A humane environment is the one in which the needs of the help recipients and the helpers take priority over fixed routines. It is also an environment with a convivial atmosphere.

Finally, an effective management system of operative personnel both during normal period and during disaster is essential to provide humanitarian aid effectively in this system.

6.3   Conceptual Framework

As discussed the various approaches for coordination during disaster are beset with some issues. However, a common factor among all these approaches is the need for a centralized agency that can coordinate all the activities. Even in cluster approach, which recommends independent clusters for various sectors, the need for a coordinate organization is felt deeply. Thomas and Fritz (2006) propose a framework, which discusses about various kinds of partnerships that a nodal relief organization may enter into for efficient management of disasters. Since disaster relief efforts are clogged mostly by unsolicited supplies, establishing partnerships can help resolve such issues to a large extent. Figure 6.2 summarizes their partnership approaches.

As shown in Fig. 6.2, the four types of approaches are single-company philanthropic partnership, multicompany integrative partnership, single-company integrative partnership, and multicompany integrative partnership. The approaches are based on the number of companies partnering for an alliance with relief agency and the level at which they participate. The level of participation can be considered as a spectrum, one end of which is where companies collaborate to provide cash, goods, and services during the disaster and the other end of the spectrum comprises where companies collaborate to benefit from each other's core competencies. When a single-company allies with a relief agency at a philanthropic level, such partnership is termed as a single-company philanthropic partnership. An example of such an alliance would be the partnership between World Vision and 3M whereby 3M provides first aid supplies, stethoscopes, and respirators. Similarly, Abbott laboratories have partnered with the American Red Cross to provide a variety of products from antibiotics to baby food in the event of a disaster. The problem such partnerships face is that a single company may not be able to fulfill the requirements of a relief agency.

This gives rise to multicompany philanthropic partnerships, whereby a number of companies can join together to form a consortium that could fulfill the requirements of a relief agency. The disaster resource network (DRN), a creation of the World Economic Forum, is a good example of such partnership. DRN facilitates corporate donations during a disaster by matching the resources of company donors with the needs of humanitarian agencies with which its individual members have relationships. DRN helped solicit assistance from its member companies to provide required donations during the Hurricane Ivan, which left 60,000 people homeless on the Island of Grenada in 2004. The challenge in such partnerships lie in verifying

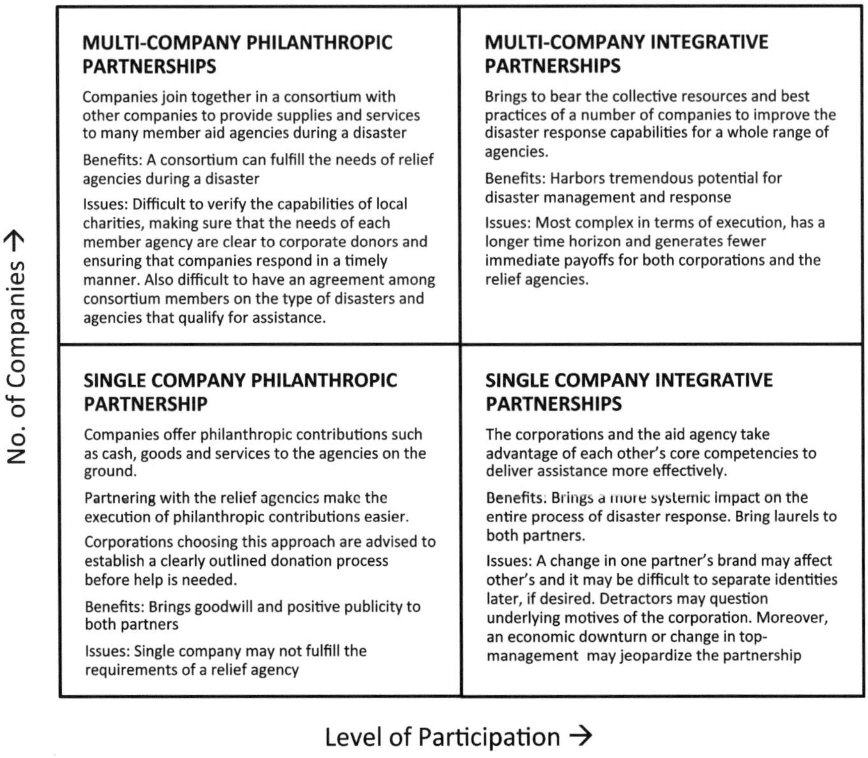

No. of Companies ↑

MULTI-COMPANY PHILANTHROPIC PARTNERSHIPS	**MULTI-COMPANY INTEGRATIVE PARTNERSHIPS**
Companies join together in a consortium with other companies to provide supplies and services to many member aid agencies during a disaster	Brings to bear the collective resources and best practices of a number of companies to improve the disaster response capabilities for a whole range of agencies.
Benefits: A consortium can fulfill the needs of relief agencies during a disaster	Benefits: Harbors tremendous potential for disaster management and response
Issues: Difficult to verify the capabilities of local charities, making sure that the needs of each member agency are clear to corporate donors and ensuring that companies respond in a timely manner. Also difficult to have an agreement among consortium members on the type of disasters and agencies that qualify for assistance.	Issues: Most complex in terms of execution, has a longer time horizon and generates fewer immediate payoffs for both corporations and the relief agencies.
SINGLE COMPANY PHILANTHROPIC PARTNERSHIP	**SINGLE COMPANY INTEGRATIVE PARTNERSHIPS**
Companies offer philanthropic contributions such as cash, goods and services to the agencies on the ground.	The corporations and the aid agency take advantage of each other's core competencies to deliver assistance more effectively.
Partnering with the relief agencies make the execution of philanthropic contributions easier.	Benefits: Brings a more systemic impact on the entire process of disaster response. Bring laurels to both partners.
Corporations choosing this approach are advised to establish a clearly outlined donation process before help is needed.	Issues: A change in one partner's brand may affect other's and it may be difficult to separate identities later, if desired. Detractors may question underlying motives of the corporation. Moreover, an economic downturn or change in top-management may jeopardize the partnership
Benefits: Brings goodwill and positive publicity to both partners	
Issues: Single company may not fulfill the requirements of a relief agency	

Level of Participation →

Fig. 6.2 Partnerships for efficient disaster management

the capabilities of local charities, making sure the needs of each member agency are clear to the corporate donors, and ensuring that the companies respond in a timely manner. Moreover, consortium members must all agree on the types of disasters and establish a method of prioritizing the many requests for aid when an emergency occurs. Moreover, a large number of staff members are required to coordinate the same.

To address the systemic needs of a relief agency and not just the immediate concerns as in the philanthropic partnerships, integrative partnerships are formed whereby companies benefit from each other's core competencies. When a single company forms an integrative partnership with the relief agency, such a partnership mode is termed as single-company integrative partnership. The partnership between Dutch logistics giant TNT and the World Food Programme (WFP) is a good example of such partnership. Their partnership focuses on emergency response, joint logistics supply chain, transparency and accountability, school feeding support, and private sector fund-raising. The integrative partnership between TNT and WFP allowed TNT to use its existing infrastructure to get involved immediately and deeply in the relief efforts during the 2004 tsunami. The integrative alliance brought great laurels to both the organizations. The problem with such an alliance, however, is that it may not work during economic downturns or changes in the structure of the top management. Moreover, people may question the motives of the single organization.

In the last form, a number of companies bring to bear their collective resources and best practices to improve the disaster response capabilities for a whole range of agencies. In terms of execution, it is the most difficult, but in terms of disaster management, it is the most rewarding. An example of such a partnership would be that of Partnership for Quality Medical Donations (PQMD), which was incorporated in 1999 to develop, disseminate, and encourage high standards in the delivery of pharmaceuticals and medical supplies for humanitarian purposes. PQMD provided relief efforts in terms of medicinal supplies in 2004 tsunami, and none of their relief efforts were found to be inappropriate by Pharmaciens Sans Frontieres in a 2005 investigation sponsored by the World Health Organization. The problem lies in terms of forging such partnerships as well as their execution.

All the above models have their pros and cons, although multicompany integrative partnerships yield the highest advantages in terms of disaster management and response. In what follows, we present an IT-based approach to forge such partnerships with a nodal firm that takes care of the disadvantages of the abovementioned approaches.

6.4 IT-Enabled Relief Network Model

Information sharing is at the core of coordination, and ICT has been widely used for facilitating information sharing within the network. Seybolt (2009) argues that information sharing can help overcome the three major obstacles of constraints on network development, namely, the sudden, massive workload following a crisis, the need for trust among the partners, and the political interests of certain actors. The United Nations World Food Programme, for example, utilizes an information and communication technology-sharing network that is based on SAP's commercially available enterprise resource planning software and that permits the global real-time connection of actors in the chain at different levels to share information that is relevant to ongoing projects and current situations. The information and communication technology-sharing network involves a telephone network (FoodSat) that permits free remote calls from any WFP office in the world and a radio network that is used to contact staff in the field (Cozzolino et al. 2012).

Based on the discussion of various types of approaches to coordination and the conceptual framework, we present the IT-enabled relief network model as shown in Fig. 6.3. The IT-enabled relief network model is based on collaborative partnerships where partners are supplying cash and other goods as necessary to the relief organization, which may use that money to purchase goods from suppliers. This approach uses ICT for coordination and uses the advantages of various approaches to coordination. This approach is similar to the civil contingency agency management system as practiced by SRSA except that ICT is used extensively for coordinating across various stakeholders and partners in the network.

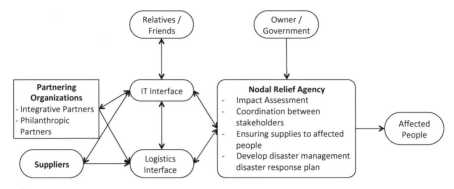

Fig. 6.3 IT-enabled relief network model

To understand this model, we must first establish the underlying principles. These principles are as follows:

(i) Relief efforts call for a selfless approach and are not meant for promotion or brand building by any organization, although in providing such efforts, companies may generate goodwill.

(ii) The nodal relief agency must be an authorized agency, preferably a government agency, and all the relief work should be done through such agency. This is similar to the concept of chain coordinator (Akhtar et al. 2012).

(iii) The government establishes such nodal agencies for prespecified areas prone to disaster. The authority/decision making for each area is vested with the local government who also takes responsibility for training the local population for dealing with disaster.

The IT-enabled relief network model takes advantage of various approaches to coordination and can be described as a multicompany integrative partnerships in terms of the framework proposed by Thomas and Fritz (2006) as summarized in Fig. 6.2.

This model takes advantage of various approaches and blends them together using an IT interface. The model requires integrative partnerships between various corporations interested in participating in disaster management and recovery and the nodal relief agency as authorized by the federal government of the country. The relief agencies are appointed for various areas (as in cluster approach) under the prespecified jurisdiction, and when a disaster falls in the border of various relief agencies, the underlying principle of selfless approach is called forth. These relief agencies then coordinate during disaster recovery. The problem of coordination between various corporations and the relief agency is addressed by having an IT system that helps collaboration between these organizations. The nodal relief agency raises its requirements which are displayed on its IT interface, and various corporations present their interest in either helping as an integrative partner in forging long-term partnerships or helping in a philanthropic manner by providing basic amenities as needed by the nodal relief agency. The interested parties need to register themselves with the nodal agency through their IT interface. The agreements describing the extent of help are also established online. Thus, both philanthropic and integrative partners can express their interest online. An IT interface can be provided by another integrative partner, who is willing to provide its expertise during disaster management and recovery. For example, Google may consider integrating its people finder service in the IT interface of the disaster management organizations. The data thus remains with the government itself and is less prone to misuse by third parties.

The provision of help provided by philanthropic and integrative partners is done through logistics interface. Like the IT interface, the logistics interface may itself be developed by an integrative partner, who takes care of all logistical needs during the disaster because of its expertise. The logistics interface helps in streamlining the flow of necessary goods to the disaster-affected areas. Since the donating organizations are required to register with the nodal relief agency through its IT interface, only the necessary and solicited goods enter into the logistics channel of the relief network thus preventing the logistics channel from clogging. The streamlined flow ensures smooth disaster recovery operations.

The nodal relief agency through its major integrative partners carries out the relief operations beginning with the impact assessment, followed by establishing logistics and communication channels. The IT interface provides a basic assessment of the needs and supplies required for relief operations as well as information about the loss of lives, animal stock, property, etc., due to disasters. A tentative approach to relief management is also provided through the IT interface so that people do not panic. Since, the period for disaster recovery is very short, an IT interface which could be customized for various disaster recovery effort must be kept ready with trained personnel who regularly update the interface. An authorized interface will provide authentic up-to-date information to the concerned people. The philanthropic partners are then called forth through the IT interface for providing necessary supplies (in terms of cash, food, medicine, clothes, and other supplies as needed by the relief agency). Various supplies can be called forth using cluster approach whereby integrative partners who deal in a particular supply form a cluster to supply the requisite quantity during disaster. The nodal relief agency remains the chain coordinator or cluster coordinator for improved coordination in the chain. The integrative partners or the registered philanthropic partners may provide necessary relief as and when needed, and this would prevent the delays that occur in government procurement. The well-established network of supplies, which supplies goods on payment, also provides quick replenishment of supplies provided the rate contracts are already established with them.

The inherent issues with various coordination approaches are taken cared of using the IT-enabled relief network model. The nodal agency is the chain coordinator as well as the cluster coordinator. The nodal agency makes sure through its IT and logistics partner that only the requisite goods enter the disaster-affected area thus preventing problem of choking of supply chain due to unnecessary goods arriving into the disaster-affected area. The nodal agency also ensures the training of the local population for dealing with disasters and developing local capacity for dealing with disasters.

6.5 Conclusion

This paper presents an IT-enabled relief network model to address the problems of disaster management and recovery. The model represents the multicompany integrative partnerships in Thomas and Fritz's (2006) framework, which carries the maximum potential for disaster response. The biggest problem of coordination in such partnerships is addressed by using ICT, which also helps in coordinating with the friends and relatives of those affected by the disaster. The model ensures that only requisite products reach the beneficiaries and also prevents taking undue advantage by firms during a disaster situation. One problem that could be foreseen in such a model is of the ineffective, bureaucratic, and corrupt government machinery itself slowing down the process if the nodal agency happens to be the government. Still, we propose the local/federal government to be the nodal agency as private firms are driven by hidden motivations in their approach which need not necessarily be philanthropic.

The IT-enabled relief network model attempts to address the problem of coordination using IT interface and ensures a streamlined flow of supplies to the affected people. A well-established IT-enabled relief network would address the problem of coordination and allows philanthropic and integrative partners to provide support during relief operations. The model also allows sufficient time for nodal relief agencies to assess the competencies of its partners and work with them for capacity building in critical areas of disaster management. A number of people/organizations try to build business from ruins. The IT-enabled relief model provides equal opportunity to all organizations willing to participate in the relief effort as well as ensures that the participants get their due reward in terms of goodwill/recognition without clogging the logistics channel of the relief network. The government may consider this model for developing their disaster management strategy for the good of all the stakeholders concerned.

The IT-enabled relief network model is conceptual in nature and needs to be validated with its actual implementation or through cases of such management. Future studies can examine various cases of ICT-enabled relief management and integrate it with this model. Rudiments of such approach can be found in the international disaster management organizations such as the American Red Cross, which has developed capabilities in disaster management and recovery efforts.

References

ActionAid (2007) The evolving UN cluster approach in the aftermath of the Pakistan earthquake: an NGO perspective. ActionAid International, Surrey

Akhtar P, Fischer C, Marr N (2010) Improving the effectiveness of food chain coordinators: a conceptual model. In: Paper presented at the third international symposium: improving the performance of supply chains in the transitional economies, Kuala Lumpur, 4–8 July

Akhtar P, Marr NE, Garnevska EV (2012) Coordination in humanitarian relief chains: chain coordinators. J Humanitarian Logist Supply Chain Manag 2(1):85–103

APEC (2010) Public-private partnerships and disaster resilience. Report from APEC workshop on public-private partnerships and disaster resilience, Bangkok, 24–29 Aug

Balcik B, Beamon BM (2008) Facility location in humanitarian relief. Int J Logist Res Appl 11(2):101–122

Balcik B, Beamon B, Krejci C, Muramatsu K, Ramirez M (2010) Coordination in humanitarian relief chains: practices, challenges and opportunities. Int J Prod Econ 126(1):22–34

Burkle FM, Hayden R (2001) The concept of assisted management of large-scale disasters by horizontal organizations. Prehosp Disaster Med 16(3):87–96

Cao N, Zhang Z, Man To K, Po Ng K (2008) How are supply chains coordinated? An empirical observation in textile-apparel businesses. J Fashion Market Manag 12(3):384–397

Charles A, Lauras M, VanWassenhove L (2010) A model to define and assess the agility of supply chains: building on humanitarian experience. Int J Phys Distrib Logist Manag 40(8/9):722–741

Christopher M (2005) Logistics and supply chain management. Creating value adding networks. Prentice Hall, London

Connelly DR (2007) Leadership in the collaborative inter-organizational domain. Int J Public Adm 30:1231–1262

Cozzolino A, Rossi S, Conforti A (2012) Agile and lean principles in the humanitarian supply chain: the case of the United Nations World Food Programme. J Humanitarian Logist Supply Chain Manag 2(1):16–33

Dynes RR (1994) Community emergency planning: false assumptions and inappropriate analogies. Int J Mass Emerg Disasters 12(2):141–158

Fearne A (1998) The evolution of partnerships in the meat supply chain: insights from the British beef industry. Supply Chain Manag Int J 3(4):1–12

Foreman K (2008) Evolving global structures and the challenges facing international relief and development organizations. Nonprofit Volunt Sect Q 28(4):178–197

Galbraith J (2001) Building organizations around the global customer. Ivey Bus J 66(1):17–25

Granot H (1999) Emergency inter-organizational relationships. Disaster Prev Manag 8(1):21–26

Hughes D (1994) Breaking with tradition. Wye College Press, London, pp 5–10

IASC (2006) Guidance note on using the cluster concept to strengthen humanitarian response. Inter-agency Standing Committee. Available at: www.humanitarianreform.org/Default.aspx?tabid=420

Jahre M, Jenses L-M (2010) Coordination in humanitarian logistics through clusters. Int J Phys Distrib Logist Manag 40(8/9):657–674

Jahre M, Spens K (2007) Buy global or go local – that's the question! In: Proceedings of the 1st conference of humanitarian logistics, CHLI, UK, November

Kelly C (1996) Limitations to the use of military resources for foreign disaster assistance. Disaster Prev Manag 5(1):22–299

Kouzmin A, Jarman AMG, Rosenthal U (1995) Inter-organisational policy processes in disaster management. Disaster Prev Manag 4(2):20–37

Kovacs G, Spens KM (2007) Humanitarian logistics in disaster relief operations. Int J Phys Distrib Logist Manag 37(2):99–114

Kovacs G, Spens KM (2009) Identifying challenges in humanitarian logistics. Int J Phys Distrib Logist Manag 39(6):506–528

Lambert DM, Knemeyer MA (2004) We're in this together. Harv Bus Rev 82(12):2–9

Maon F, Lindgreen A, Vanhamme J (2009) Developing supply chains in disaster relief operations through cross-sector socially oriented collaborations: a theoretical model. Supply Chain Manag Int J 14(2):149–164

McEntire DA, Fuller C (2002) The need for a holistic approach: an examination from the El Nino disaster in Peru. Disaster Prev Manag 11(2):128–140

McLachlin R, Larson PD (2011) Building humanitarian supply chain relationships: lessons from leading practitioners. J Humanitarian Logist Supply Chain Manag 1(1):32–49

McLachlin R, Larson PD, Khan S (2009) Not-for-profit supply chains in interrupted environments: the case of a faith-based humanitarian relief organisation. Manag Res News 32(11):1050–1064

Mehta R, Dubinsky A, Anderson R (2003) Leadership style, motivation and performance in international marketing channels. Eur J Mark 37(1/2):50–85

Nilsson S, Sjoberg M, Larsson G (2010) A civil contingencies agency management system for disaster aid: a theoretical model. Int J Organ Anal 18(4):412–429

OCHA (2007) Appeal for building global humanitarian response capacity. Office for the Coordination of Humanitarian Affairs, New York. Available at: http://ochaonline.un.org/HUMANITARIANAPPEAL/webpage.asp?Page=1566

Oloruntoba R, Gray R (2006) Humanitarian aid: an agile supply chain? Supply Chain Manag Int J 11(2):115–120

Pettit SJ, Beresford AKC (2009) Critical success factors in the context of humanitarian aid supply chains. Int J Phys Distrib Logist Manag 39(6):450–468

Quarantelli EL (1985) Organizational behavior in disasters and implications for disaster planning. Federal Management Training Center, Emmitsburg

Scholten K, Scott PS, Fynes B (2010) (Le) agility in humanitarian aid (NGO) supply chains. Int J Phys Distrib Logist Manag 40(8/9):623–635

Seybolt TB (2009) Harmonizing the humanitarian aid network: adaptive change in a complex system. Int Stud Q 53(4):1027–1050

Shaluf IM, Ahmadun F, Said AM (2003) A review of disaster and crisis. Disaster Prev Manag 12(1):24–32

Sheppard A, Tatham P, Fisher R, Gapp R (2013) Humanitarian logistics: enhancing the engagement of local populations. J Humanitarian Logist Supply Chain Manag 3(1):22–36

Simatupang TM, Wright AC, Sridharan R (2002) The knowledge of coordination for supply chain integration. Bus Process Manag J 8(3):289–308

Spekman RE, Kamauff JW Jr, Myhr N (1998) An empirical investigation into supply chain management: a perspective on partnerships. J Supply Chain Manag 3(2):53–67

Stoddard A, Harmer A, Haver K, Salomons D, Wheeler V (2007) Cluster approach evaluation. Humanitarian Policy Group, ODI, London. Available at: www.humanitarianreform.org/Default.aspx?tabid=457

Tatham P, Kovács G (2010) The application of 'swift trust' to humanitarian logistics. Int J Prod Econ 126(1):35–45

Taylor D, Pettit S (2009) A consideration of the relevance of lean supply chain concepts for humanitarian aid provision. Int J Serv Technol Manag 12(4):430–444

Thomas A (2003) Humanitarian logistics: enabling disaster response. Fritz Institute, San Francisco

Thomas AS, Kopczak LR (2005) From logistics to supply chain management: the path forward in the humanitarian sector, vol 15. Fritz Institute, San Francisco, pp 1–15

Thomas A, Fritz L (2006) Disaster relief Inc. Harvard Business Review, pp 1–9

Tomasini R, Van Wassenhove LN (2009) Humanitarian logistics. Palgrave Macmillan, Basingstoke

Towill D, Christopher M (2002) The supply chain strategy conundrum: to be lean or agile or to be lean and agile? Int J Logist Res Appl 5(3):299–309

Trim PRJ (2004) An integrative approach to disaster management and planning. Disaster Prev Manag 13(3):218–225

Van Wassenhove LN (2006) Humanitarian aid logistics: supply chain management in high gear. J Oper Res Soc 57(5):475

Van Wassenhove LN, Tomasini R, Stapleton O (2007) Corporate responses to humanitarian disasters. The mutual benefits of private-humanitarian Cooperation. Research report no. R01415-08-WG, The Conference Board INSEAD, Paris

Xu L, Beamon BM (2006) Supply chain coordination and cooperation mechanisms: an attribute-based approach. J Supply Chain Manag 42(1):4–12

Chapter 7
Exploring the Challenges in Implementation of Information Technology in Humanitarian Relief Organisations in India: A Qualitative Study

Gaurav Kabra and A. Ramesh

7.1 Introduction

The unique geo-climatic condition of India makes it one of the most disaster-prone countries in the world (Ministry of Home Affairs India (MHA) 2011). The occurrence of floods, droughts, cyclones, earthquakes, and landslides are common in India. The rise in the occurrence of disastrous events is a major hurdle for the overall development of the country.

India has witnessed several devastating natural disasters in the past like supercyclones in Orissa in the year 1999, an earthquake in the Gujarat in the year 2001, and the tsunami in coastal state in 2004. Humanitarian logistics has received enormous attention from the research point of view, after the occurrence of tsunami disaster in 2004.

Humanitarian supply chain management (HSCM) comes into the picture immediately after the occurrence of disaster with the aim to save lives, alleviate suffering and maintain human dignity (Costa et al. 2012). HSCM involves the effective and efficient management of different elements in the system, i.e. available information, goods and materials, human resource, available infrastructure, etc. to reduce the impact of a disaster on the disaster-affected people (Lijo and Ramesh 2012).

A typical humanitarian supply chain (HSC) is explained in Fig. 7.1 starting from government donor to consumers. Information technology (IT) has proved to be an important driver in the success of commercial supply chain management (CSCM)

G. Kabra (✉)
Research Scholar, Department of Management Studies, IIT Roorkee, Roorkee, Uttarakhand, India
e-mail: kabraddm@iitr.ac.in

A. Ramesh
Assistant Professor, Department of Management Studies, IIT Roorkee, Roorkee, Uttarakhand, India
e-mail: ram77fdm@iitr.ac.in

© Springer India 2016
B.S. Sahay et al. (eds.), *Managing Humanitarian Logistics*, Springer Proceedings in Business and Economics, DOI 10.1007/978-81-322-2416-7_7

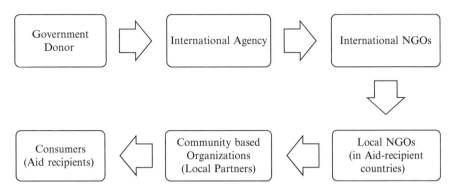

Fig. 7.1 A typical humanitarian supply chain (Source: Oloruntoba and Gray 2006)

and IT utilisation can also improve the efficiency to a very great extent in humanitarian supply chain management (HSCM). Information technology includes intranet and extranets, electronic data interchange, videoconferencing, mobile phones and radios used for communication, etc.

The structure of humanitarian relief organisations (HROs) is very complex, and challenges occur not only within their own organisations but also among various other organisations that support them in the time of the disaster for providing help to the disaster-affected peoples.

The objective of this study is to explore the barriers to the implementation of IT in HSCM; particularly within the context of India.

The remainder of the paper is organised in five sections. The next (second) section begins with a brief review of previous research in this area. The third section provides a brief description of the research methodology employed in this study. Barriers in IT implementation of HSCM in India are explained in the fourth section. In the fifth section, the paper concludes with a discussion, and finally in the last (sixth) section limitations of the study and related future work were discussed.

7.2 Literature Review

Humanitarian supply chains (HSC) are experts in managing large-scale risks, and commercial supply chain (CSC) is also interested in their effective and efficient management, as a disaster anywhere on the globe can disrupt supplies or destroy markets (Wallace and Webber 2004). The global relevance of HSC can be seen by that the governments of all countries are being involved in humanitarian aid as either donors or recipients (Kovács and Spens 2007).

In recent years there has been strong emphasis to improve the whole structure and efficiency of humanitarian aid (Steets et al. 2010), and there has been an increase in the numbers of stakeholders in disaster management. This not only includes the national and international HROs but also governments of different countries, military, media, individuals, private organisations, etc. Management of humanitarian relief activities also becomes complex due to increase in the number of stakeholders. Moreover, due to the increase in the frequency of occurrence of the disaster, the HROs are not getting enough time for improving their efficiency by analysing strategies used in relief activities (Besiou et al. 2011).

The significance of the information highlighted the researchers is "In modern supply chains, the information replaces the inventory" (Simchi-Levi et al. 2010). Information management helps to make a critical decision related to placement of a distribution system, the mode of transport to be used to reach the far-flung area and the category of specialised staff required for different disaster-affected areas. Thus, relief activities mainly depend on the information and clarity of the situation (Lijo and Ramesh 2012). There is a substantial amount of literature available highlighting the importance of information and management of information in disaster management (Simchi-Levi et al. 2010; Perry 2007; Long and Wood 1995).

Information can come from virtually anywhere, for example, media, blogs, past experiences, books, articles, expert suggestion to name a few, but the most important is the availability of reliable information with minimum time. Erroneous and sometimes inappropriate information leads to wrong and misleading decision (Balcik et al. 2010). Advanced IT systems have the capability to effectively utilise the available information at the time of disaster. For example, IT systems that are designed appropriately could allow decision makers at the field level to directly access the required information rather than depending on other for pushing the information to them.

IT has the potential to play a very important role in disaster management by providing assistance in the integration of various activities and provides useful information for effective functioning of the system (Roh et al. 2008; Pettit and Beresford 2009). IT has long been acknowledged to be very important for the support of relief activities. Specific decision support systems, communications and information systems are considered as most important in managing relief operations (Pettit and Beresford 2009). Power (2005) also demonstrated that the decision support system can provide help in the better decision making during a disaster.

Chan et al. (2004) demonstrated that advanced technologies have the capability to improve acute medical care during mass casualty incidents and disaster from the site to the hospital in the future by highlighting the importance of integrated information and telecommunications network system. The Community Disaster Information System (CDIS) was developed using information technology for enhancing community-based disaster preparedness (Troy et al. 2008). Such systems can assist in disaster management to reduce the suffering of the disaster victims.

There has been significant growth in the use of geographic information systems (GISs), global positioning systems (GPSs) and modelling and simulation techniques. All these systems are found to be very useful in effective management of scarce resources (Board on Natural Disasters, National Research Council, Washington (1999)).

IT is also found to be very helpful in coordinating the relief activities during different phases of a disaster. For example, it serves as a communication tool and provides enhanced access to past experiences (Telleen and Martin 2002; Jefferson 2006; Stephenson and Anderson 1997; Chan et al. 2004; National Research Council Washington 1999). Communication systems are found to be most useful in timely passing the warning signals in the probable disaster area and evacuating the people from that area and thus reducing the effect of these disasters on the people residing in that area (Whybark 2010). The Hurricane Katrina response also emphasised that there is a strong need to enhance the information and communication technology capabilities (Shannon 2006; Arnone 2005).

Thus, it becomes very important to understand the various factors affecting the humanitarian aid programmes. This forms the basis of our study. Lack of awareness about the existence of barriers in IT implementation hinders the proper establishment and functioning of HSCM.

7.3 Methodology

The challenges were derived in this study by in-depth semi-structured interviews with different ten humanitarian actors consisting of HRO members, academic experts, etc. All the experts had more than 6 years of experience in their respective domains. Various literature, published reports and information related to the programmes run for disaster victims were circulated among the experts beforehand.

The information recorded during the interview was sent to the respective interviewees to ensure the reliability of information. The comparison of this data with the literature and key findings in the report provided a source of validity of the common themes that emerged.

To avoid any kind of biasness, semi-structured interviews with middle management of HROs were conducted. Semi-structured interviews and published reports were the main source of data in identifying the challenges due to their flexibility, adaptability and diversity in probing.

Many researchers argue that using a sampling method makes possible a higher overall accuracy than a census (Saunders et al. 2007). HROs have to be purposefully selected. The goal of purposive sampling was to get a detail and a practical description of the phenomena by those who experience it rather than get generalised findings. Generalisations were drawn from interviews after a rigorous search for themes and patterns.

The present study adheres to the principles of voluntary participation and informed consent. To guarantee privacy and security, we assured the interviewees confidentiality and secrecy when requested.

7.4 Identification of Barriers in IT Implementation in HSCM

The major problem highlighted by academicians and practitioners in disaster preparedness measures is the behaviour of donors. Donors do not like funding logistics infrastructure despite its importance for coordination (Whiting and Ayala-Öström 2009). It is evident that may HROs have incompatible information technology systems in the field. Information still kept in silos which limits the use of many humanitarian logistics operation metrics (Maspero and Itmann 2008). An effective logistics information system (like Helios) is therefore required to centrally collect data on humanitarian logistics actor effectiveness (Chikolo 2006). Apart from these challenges, there are many others that also exist, which are faced by humanitarian relief organisations in the implementation of information technology in India.

7.4.1 Low Level of Investment for Implementation of IT

The use of IT is very low in the disaster relief supply chain as compared to the commercial supply chain. One reason for low use of IT can be considered as lack of awareness about how a technology-assisted response could help in managing the situation better. Prior awareness and training are required to tap into such technology, but the task is challenging, due to involvement of many actors in the humanitarian supply chain (HSC) and low investment in IT.

7.4.2 Lack of Strategic Planning

There is strong need for the integration of disaster mitigation and preparedness in development programmes; long-term development plans and use of IT are required for India. The key to an effective disaster response is increasing awareness in the mind of local peoples so that they can learn to help themselves. It is needed to train local teams to better prepare and respond to local disasters and address the frequent issue of a limited pool of trained staff. Proper strategic planning for implementation of IT is required to cope up with the other interdependent barriers.

7.4.3 Lack of Management-Level SCM Professionals

Majority of HRO leaders are not having corporate experience; their background is mainly social science or law (Gustavsson 2003). The CSC involves the activities such as procurement, warehousing, transportation, inventory management and accountability (Thomas, 2003). These activities are also common in HSC, but the presence of experts for each activity is not sure in contrast to CSC.

7.4.4 Low Level of IT Awareness

This is the most important barrier in the implementation of IT in HSC. The volunteers of the relief organizations are not aware about the efficiency of IT for HSC such as ease the process of string and transferring of data, so that the right kind of help could be available at the right place with minimum delay.

7.4.5 Decentralised Organisation Structure

HROs generally have a decentralised organisational structure in which field workers do not care about top management. The main advantage of a decentralised organisational structure is that field workers can develop better understanding of the local situation, needs of the people, etc. where disaster has occurred. This in-depth understanding of the situation helps HROs to respond in a quick, effective and efficient manner. But the disadvantage of decentralised structure comes into the picture when field officers work according to their wish, and they choose separate software or not to use them at all; this complicates the process of information sharing which is considered essential for the effective and efficient management of relief activities (Maiers et al. 2005).

7.4.6 Resistive to Change to IT Enable

Resistance to change is one of the most important challenges in the implementation of IT in relief organisations. IT often represents completely new for many people working in the HROs. The perception of an employee that advanced technologies represent a daunting curve and possible chances that they can lose their job introduces fear into their mind about IT and creates significant resistance to change (Beaumaster 2002).

7.4.7 Low Priority by Management

The implementation of IT requires the commitment and support from the top management of the concerned organization. The fund, efforts and time are prerequisite for the successful implementation of IT. This requires the support and commitment from the top management, not at some particular stage, but starting from the initial planning stage through complete implementation. But the top management in HRO views implementation of information technology as an overhead cost.

7.4.8 Lack of Common Language

Language is one of the major barriers in implementing IT, as the most widely spoken language is Hindi or any other regional language. The use of computers and the Internet facilities mainly depends on English. Almost all softwares use English language for their functioning. But if disaster occurs in a place where field workers are not comfortable with the English language, then it is difficult to use IT at that place. Lack of common language is also a barrier in the training process.

7.5 Discussion and Conclusion

The barriers to IT implementation in HSCM in India identified in this study can serve as a road map to facilitate the implementation of IT in HSCM. The barriers resisting the process of adoption of IT in HSCM possess challenges for both, HROs and strategist involve in the relief supply chain. These barriers need to be overcome for successful IT implementation in HSCM. The coordination between the actors of the supply chain is also very important, and they should device new coordination mechanisms between them so as to optimise the usage of scarce resources as well as to reduce the suffering of the beneficiaries. The importance of developing reliable sources of information so as to predict the occurrence of a disaster with the help of IT is also very important. The development of an early warning system has to be looked into more specifically. The long-term relationship with the suppliers and prepositioning of the warehouses as well as training the professional to deal with the conditions forming the environment of HSCM has to be planned strategically.

7.6 Limitations and Suggestion for Further Studies

The study reveals that the HROs are not able to implement IT due to existing barriers. It is hoped that this study can serve as a road map for further studies in the field of IT. Despite these contributions the present study is also not free from limitations. One of the most complex issues in the study was in the methodology, and this was related to the population for the study. It was difficult to confirm the level of involvement of organizations in the past relief operations. Hence, the similar weight-age was given for each organizations. As such the population chosen for the study was easily reachable. If all organisations were to be considered, maybe the result would have been different.

Further study can be done to make a hierarchy-based model in order to identify the relationships among the existing barriers and classifying them into the driver and dependent categories to understand how these barriers are influencing each other, so that the decision makers can focus on overcoming these barriers and successfully implement IT in HROs.

References

Arnone M (2005) IT crucial for FEMA reform. FCW. COM. http://www.fcw.com/article91161-10-19-05-Web. Accessed 25 May 2013

Balcik BB, Krejci BM, Muramatsu CC, Ramirez KM (2010) Coordination in humanitarian relief chains: practices, challenges and opportunities. Int J Prod Econ 126:22–34

Beaumaster S (2002) Local government IT implementation issues: a challenge for public administration. In: 35th Hawaii international conference on system sciences, 2002, Hawaii

Besiou M, Stapleton O, Van Wassenhove LN (2011) System dynamics for humanitarian operations. J Humanitarian Logist Supply Chain Manag 1(1):78–103

Boin A, Kelle P, Whybark DC (2010) Resilient supply chains for extreme situations: outlining a new field of study. Int J Product Econ 126(1):1–6

Chan TC, Killeen J, Griswold W, Lenert L (2004) Information technology and emergency medical care during disasters. Acad Emerg Med 11:1229–1236

Chikolo I (2006) Role of logistics in humanitarian relief operation. CILT World 14:7

Costa SRA, Campos VBG, de Mello Bandeira RA (2012) Supply chains in humanitarian operations: cases and analysis. Proc Soc Beh Sci 54:598–607

Gustavsson L (2003) Humanitarian logistics: context and challenges. Forced Migration Rev 18:6–8

Jefferson TL (2006) Using the internet to communicate during a crisis. VINE J Inf Knowledge Manag Syst 36(2):139–142

Kehoe D, Boughton N (2001) Internet based supply chain management: a classification of approaches to manufacturing planning and control. Int J Oper Prod Manag 21(4):516–524

Kovács G, Spens KM (2007) Humanitarian logistics in disaster relief operations. Int J Phys Distrib Logist Manag 37(2):99–114

Lijo J, Ramesh A (2012) Humanitarian supply chain management in India: a SAP-LAP framework. J Adv Manag Res 9(2):217–235

Long DC, Wood DF (1995) The logistics of famine relief. J Bus Logist 16(1):213–239

Maiers C, Reynolds M, Haselkorn M (2005) Challenges to effective information and communication systems in humanitarian relief organizations. IEEE International Professional Communication Conference Proceedings

Maspero EL, Itmann HW (2008) The rise of humanitarian logistics. In: 27th Southern African transport conference, Pretoria, 7–9 July

Ministry of Home Affairs India (2011) Disaster management in India. Available in: www.ndmindia.nic.in. Accessed 28 June 2013

National Research Council (1999) Reducing disaster losses through better information. National Academy Press, Washington, DC, pp 1–61

Oloruntoba R, Gray R (2006) Humanitarian aid: an agile supply chain? J Supply Chain Manag 11(2):115–120

Perry M (2007) Natural disaster management planning. Int J Phys Distrib Logist Manag 37(5): 409–433

Pettit SJ, Beresford AKC (2005) Emergency relief logistics: an evaluation of military, non-military, and composite response models. Int J Logist Res Appl 8(4):313–31

Pettit S, Beresford A (2009) Critical success factors in the context of humanitarian aid and supply chains. Int J Phys Distrib Logist Manag 39(6):450–468

Power D (2005) DSS for crisis planning, response and management. 2nd ISCRAM Conference, Brussels. Available at: http://www.iscram.org/index.php?option¼content&taskview& id¼693&Itemid¼2. Accessed 16 Sept 2012

Roh S, Pettit SJ, Beresford AKC (2008) Humanitarian aid logistics: response depot networks. Abstract proceedings of the NOFOMA conference, June, Helsinki

Saunders M, Lewis P, Thornhill A (2007) Research method for business students. Prentice Hall/ Financial Times, Essex

Shannon MM (2006) The network of life. Commun ACM 49(1):29–32

Simchi-Levi D, Philip K, Simchi-Levi E, Shanker R (2010) Designing and managing the supply chain: concepts, strategies, and case studies. Tata McGraw-Hill Education Private Limited, New Delhi

Steets J, Grünewald F, Binder A, Geoffroy VD, Kauffmann D, Krüger S, Meier C, Sokpoh B (2010) Cluster approach evaluation 2 synthesis report. IASC Cluster Approach Evaluation 2nd Phase. Groupe URD and the Global Public Policy Institute. Reinhardtstraße, Berlin, Germany

Stephenson R, Anderson PS (1997) Disasters and the information technology revolution. Disasters 21(4):305–334

Telleen S, Martin E (2002) Improving information access for public health professionals. J Med Syst 26(6):529–542

Troy DA, Carson A, Vanderbeek J, Hutton A (2008) Enhancing community-based disaster preparedness with information technology. Disasters 32(1):149–165

Wallace M, Webber L (2004) The disaster recovery handbook. AMACOM, New York

Whiting MC, Ayala-Öström BE (2009) Advocacy to promote logistics in humanitarian aid. Manag Res News 32(11):1081–9

Whybark DC (2007) Issues in managing disaster relief inventories. Int J Product Econ 108(1):228–235

Chapter 8
Managing Disaster Supply Chains with RFID for Humanitarian Logistics

Joy Mukhopadhyay and Sancharan Roy

8.1 Introduction

> Logistics is the part [of any disaster relief] that can mean the difference between a successful or failed operation (Van Wassenhove 2006).

The management of the supply chain in disaster relief operations is considered an essential element in the resolution of a crisis since the tsunami in Southeast Asia (December 26, 2004), the Katrina Hurricane (August 2005) and the Himalayan Tsunami (June, 2013) in Uttarakhand, India. The scale of these disasters is huge both in geographical size and in severity. The Katrina Hurricane affected 92,000 square miles of land, and hundreds of thousands of people were displaced from their homes. Over 40 countries and 700 nongovernmental organisations (NGOs) provided humanitarian assistance. Usually, the term 'disaster' refers to a 'disruption that physically affects a system as a whole and threatens its priorities and goals' (Van Wassenhove 2006). With respect to cause, it is possible to distinguish between a natural and a man-made disaster; with respect to predictability and speed of occurrence, it is possible to distinguish between a sudden-onset and a slow-onset disaster (Van Wassenhove 2006). Taking into account also the different impact in terms of required logistic effort (from higher to lower), it is possible to identify four types of disaster:

(i) Calamities, characterised by natural causes and sudden-onset occurrences (e.g. earthquakes, hurricanes, tornadoes)

J. Mukhopadhyay (✉)
Department of Management, International School of Business Research, Bangalore, Karnataka, India
e-mail: joymukh@yahoo.com

S. Roy
Department of Management, New Horizon College of Engineering, Bangalore, Karnataka, India

© Springer India 2016
B.S. Sahay et al. (eds.), *Managing Humanitarian Logistics*, Springer Proceedings in Business and Economics, DOI 10.1007/978-81-322-2416-7_8

(ii) Destructive actions, characterised by man-made causes and sudden-onset occurrences (e.g. terrorist attacks, coups d'état, industrial accidents)
(iii) Plagues, characterised by natural causes and slow-onset occurrence (e.g. famines, droughts, poverty)
(iv) Crises, characterised by man-made causes and slow-onset occurrence (e.g. political and refugee crises)

Different types of disasters need to be managed in different ways: the aid provided to assist in a region's development is distinct from that given to deal with famine and drought; running refugee camps is very different to providing the kind of aid that is needed after a sudden-onset natural disaster or a nuclear accident. Humanitarian efforts are organised along two broad lines (Kovács and Spens 2007):

(i) Disaster relief
(ii) Continuous aid work

Logistics is the most important element in any disaster relief effort, and it is the one that makes the difference between a successful and a failed operation (Van Wassenhove 2006). But it is also the most expensive part of any disaster relief: it has been estimated that logistics accounts for about 80 % of the total costs in disaster relief (Van Wassenhove 2006). And given that the overall annual expenditure of aid agencies is of the order of $20 billion, the resultant logistic spending is around $15 billion (Christopher and Tatham 2011).

8.1.1 Humanitarian Logistics and Stages in the Emergency Supply Chain

A successful response to a disaster is not improvised. The better one is prepared the more effective the response. (Van Wassenhove 2006)

Since disaster relief efforts are characterised by considerable uncertainty and complexity, they need to be properly managed in order to address and implement better responses. Thus, disaster management is a key factor that drives successful execution of relief efforts, and it begins with strategic process design (Tomasini and Van Wassenhove 2009a, b).

Disaster management is often described as a process composed of several stages, even though there is disagreement among authors as to the structure and nomenclature of the stages (Kovács and Spens 2007; Altay and Green 2006; Pettit and Beresford 2005; Van Wassenhove 2006; Lee and Zbinden 2003; Thomas 2003; Cottrill 2002; Long 1997). However, for the most part, the literature concurs on the existence of the four phases, namely, mitigation, preparation, response and reconstruction.

These four phases (Miller et al. 2006) constitute the disaster management cycle. With the focus on logistic and supply chain management, the process that involves logisticians mainly concerns the preparation, response and reconstruction; together these constitute humanitarian logistic stream.

(i) Mitigation, which includes the activities needed to prevent natural disaster, reduce its impact and minimise ensuing losses and damages. For example, the geometry of a hillside may be artificially modified to reduce the risk of avalanches, or snow fences are placed in the most critical areas.

(ii) Preparedness, which has the objective to prepare the resources or facilities for a response. This includes the identification of threats, determination of the capabilities of organisations if a disaster strikes, definition of scenarios for training purposes, identification of main partners like suppliers, identification of critical assets and so on.

(iii) Response, which includes those immediate actions taken to deal with a disaster or an emergency. Response activities should have the purpose of mobilising emergency responders, resources and services for the affected region. In this phase, the coordination among the relief actors is an essential activity.

(iv) Recovery, whose objective is to try to restore the disaster area to the state before the crisis. Recovery is a stabilisation phase, which may be conducted for the long term.

Supply chain management may be present in all the four phases of disaster management described above for different reasons and with different roles. In the prevention and the preparedness phase, supply chains are used to stockpile and maintain disaster supplies and equipment, which may be used in disaster management. In these phases, the management of the supply chain is relatively easy as the location of the stockpiling facilities and inventories is well known and the transfer of the materials is planned in advance. In the response phase, supply chains are an essential element in the resolution of the crisis. Depending on the features of the disasters described earlier, supply chain management can become extremely complex as there are many different players, large quantity of materials to be distributed and degraded infrastructures. Furthermore, there are severe time constraints as people may die if goods (e.g. medicines, food) are not distributed in time. In the recovery phase, relief chains are used to provide support to the rebuilding of destroyed property and the repair of critical infrastructures.

8.2 RFID in Disaster Supply Chain Management

8.2.1 Role of Technology in Disaster Supply Chain Management

Technology can be essential in improving disaster supply chain management and in providing more capabilities to the partners involved in the resolution of the crisis.

Long (1997) highlights the importance of information technology to improve the resolution of a disaster. A number of technologies have been presented in literature for disaster management. They include decision support systems, fast deployable communications, sensor networks, remote sensing and tools to support warehousing and supply chain management.

One of the basic ingredients of supply chain management is information. Supply chain managers need to know what is the demand of the goods, where they are located at any time, when and where they will be shipped and so on. These tasks are already complex in a generic commercial supply chain, but in disaster supply chain management, they become even more difficult.

An essential element is the proper identification of the goods and the distribution of this information to all the involved partners. In natural disasters, goods may come from any types of sources, because aid agencies are sometimes not equipped to tag the material in the proper way. Autier et al. (1990) discuss the case of drug supplies, after the 1988 Armenian earthquake, when at least 5,000 t of drugs were sent by international relief operations but only one-third was usable because it was properly identified, relevant for the emergency situation and distributed in time. One-fifth of the supplies had to be destroyed at the end of 1989.

8.2.2 Security

Security is one important requirement for the technologies used in disaster management. Sensitive data may be distributed among the coordinators of the relief operations. Criminal entities may take advantage of the chaotic conditions to steal or redirect goods to the wrong destination. The information present in the supply chain management systems must be secured and protected so that it cannot be used for criminal purposes. Technology can improve the secure access and distribution of information in a number of ways.

One technology, which has recently gained wide acceptance in supply chain management, is RFID. There is already an extensive literature on the use of RFID in commercial supply chains. Sarac et al. (2010) provide a recent overview of the application of RFID in commercial supply chains. There are a very limited number of papers which propose the application of RFID technology for relief chains or support to disaster management. A recent paper is Yang et al. (2010), which describes the design of hybrid RFID sensor network architecture for humanitarian logistic centre management. The current design provides important features for humanitarian logistics including improved resilience, fast deployment and low power consumption, but the paper does not address security issues.

Secure RFID in disaster supply chains: Tags, a reader/writer and a host system compose a typical RFID system. An RFID tag is usually of very small-sized and low-cost device, so that it can be easily implanted on a physical object like a product, a box or even an animal or a person. An RFID tag is composed by tiny electronic circuits able to store and process a limited amount of data (from several bits to several kilobytes) and by a miniature antenna for short-range wireless communication.

RFID tags are classified as passive or active. Passive tags work by taking the energy received from the reader through the tag antenna and using that energy to transmit stored data back to the reader. Passive tags are less expensive than active tags, which include their own power supply, usually a battery, to transmit information directly to a reader. The battery can also be used to power or improve the interaction with other devices. For example, a company shipping perishable goods may want to use active tags that integrate with thermometers to ensure the goods are kept at an acceptable temperature.

Portable readers or fixed readers are connected to the control centre, respectively, through wireless or fixed communications.

RFID provides better data security in comparison to traditional barcode technology, and it can be a powerful enabler to improve the operational efficiency of supply chain management (Tajima 2007; Lin 2009).

8.2.3 System Architecture

Fig. 8.1 describes the workflow of RFID in humanitarian logistics.

8.3 Literature Review

8.3.1 RFID Use and Collaboration

Since collaboration typically involves consistent communication and alignment of incentives, RFID's ability to offer instant scalability in service, pricing options and media, according to an organisation's and the supply chain partner's needs, will enhance alignment in terms of communication and incentives received from RFID use. Further, RFID offers mobile interactivity and the ability to share information with supply chain partners using a variety of different media (Iyer and Henderson 2010). This is dissimilar to web-based EDI applications, which still require a common platform on either end. Additionally, RFID offers the ability for users to analyse terabytes of data in a period of minutes, which is a substantial increase in speed of information flow over traditional information technologies.

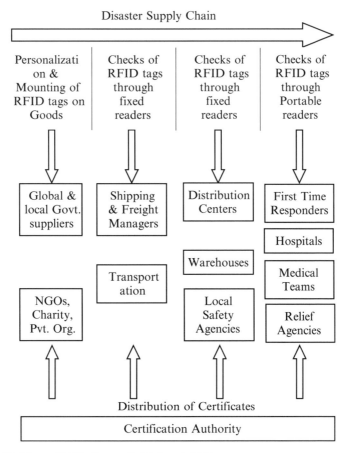

Fig. 8.1 Workflow of RFID (Source: Baldini et al. 2012)

8.3.2 Inter-organisational Trust

Inter-organisational trust is vital in supply chain management especially in humanitarian logistics where multiple agencies are involved. There should be smooth communication flow between different members particularly between government agencies, defence services, NGOs and media.

There are various definitions of inter-organisational trust with dimensions including credibility, goodwill, honesty, integrity, benevolence, etc. Inter-organisational trust is one party's confidence and belief in the credibility and goodwill of an object of trust (Zhang et al. 2011). Further, both dimensions take into account the importance of dependability, reliability and acting in the best interests of one another. Dependable and reliable supply chain partners are vital for several reasons. First, organisations are increasingly demanding accountability, transparency and value in return for sponsorship. This expectation is also influencing companies to become more professional in their approach to managing operations. Agile supply chains require reduced security risks, while at the same time delivering speed and efficiency that can prove difficult with complex supply chains involving various actors. A transparent supply chain provides timely and accurate exchange of information. This greater transparency is also likely to lead to improved systems' processes. In the majority of empirical studies, inter-organisational trust is seen as a main effect that leads to positive attitudes, higher levels of cooperation and higher levels of performance (Dirks and Ferrin 2001). Various studies have examined the direct effect of trust on workplace attitudes and performance (Jones and George 1998). Trust overall is identified as critical for effective collaboration in a supply chain (Ke and Wei 2006).

8.3.3 Collaboration and Agility

Perhaps even more vital than the relationships between RFID use, inter-organisational trust and collaboration is the ultimate impact on agility. Agility has several definitions, including a supply chain's ability to respond to customers' unforeseen changes (Sheffi 2004), responding rapidly to short-term changes in demand and market turbulence (Swafford et al. 2006), and ability to thrive in constant and unpredictable change, being centred on customer responsiveness and focused on market turbulence. All of these definitions have one commonality: responding quickly to unforeseen changes. It also requires higher levels of respon-siveness and effectiveness in delivering the correct products to the right place, at the right quantity and during the right time period (Charles et al. 2010).

8.4 Theoretical Background and Model

8.4.1 Resource-Based View (RBV)

The connection between information technology and collaboration is not new in literature and has a strong background in RBV (Bharadwaj 2000). RBV mentions that firms compete using unique resources that are valuable, rare, difficult to imitate and nonsubstitutable by other resources (Schulze 1992). These resources in turn can be used for competitive advantage. While resources are vital, it is more critical how the firm utilises them to maximise competitive potential. It has been considered in this research that RFID to be a valuable, rare and difficult to imitate resource if firms utilise and scale it according to their own and their partner's needs. Since collaboration requires mutual incentives (Hendricks and Singhal 2003), RFID can optimise it through massively scalable services that perpetuate greater collaborative relationships between supply chain partners.

8.4.2 Social Capital Theory/Agency Theory

Social capital theory suggests that benefits derived from relationships between entities can generate intangible and tangible benefits, including those that are social, psychological, emotional and economic in the short and long term (Lin 2000). Social capital is comprised of seven dimensions, including: group characteristics, generalised norms, togetherness, everyday sociability, neighbourhood connections, volunteerism and trust, which help to develop both short- and long-term benefits (Narayan and Cassidy 2001).

This theory helps define the relationship between collaboration and agility and the moderating impact of inter-organisational trust on the relationship. Collaboration typically involves both continuous communication and an effective platform to collaborate on (Oke and Idiagbon-Oke 2010). When communication and platforms are present, other types of social capital develop, including generalised norms, togetherness, sociability and established connections, which according to social capital theory, can lead to a variety of benefits, including agility.

Trust is also considered a vital social capital that can lead to a variety of internal and external benefits. Trust is known to offset risks associated with behaviours underlying competitiveness, thereby allowing greater benefits of knowledge transfer, joint learning and sharing of risks associated with exploiting opportunities in collaboration. Given the recency of RFID and associated security concerns, an adequate amount of inter-organisational trust can provide a foundation for using RFID to perpetuate greater collaboration. Both RBV and social capital theory can be used to explain the intricate relationships depicted in Fig. 8.2, which presents our conceptual model that we will analyse using partial least squares analysis.

8.5 Research Methodology

The quantitative approach is adopted as the research methodology for this research. A quantitative survey is considered to be the most feasible and adequate research strategy for this research as it is beneficial to deal with the questions of 'what' the important factors are and 'how much' strength these factors have. To increase the

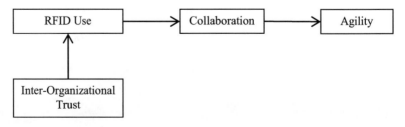

Fig. 8.2 Conceptual model of RFID in humanitarian logistics

sample size of the survey, two approaches are adopted. First, an invitation letter and e-mail are sent to directors and senior executive managers of various major humanitarian logistic companies in Bangalore, Delhi, Mumbai, Kolkata, Chennai, Pune, Coimbatore and Mysore in India. Then questionnaire surveys are distributed by e-mail or post to those directors or managers accepting the survey invitation. The respondents are invited to distribute the questionnaires to their industry partners or practitioners that they know to have rich experiences in SCM development in India. A total of 90 questionnaires are despatched via both e-mail and post, and 29 returns are usable for the analysis—giving a net usable response rate of 32 %. The questionnaire consists of two sections. The first section serves to introduce the objectives and scope of the survey. This section is also used to collect demographic data regarding the respondents' previous experience and general knowledge in the area. In the second section, participants are invited to provide their opinions on the importance of proposed factors that influence RFID in SCM on a seven-point Likert scale (1'not important at all' to 7'most important'). In order to guarantee that the respondents are knowledgeable about the topic of the research, a survey has been conducted directly associated with information technology or supply chain management activities in the organisations. Titles included information officers, directors of supply, chief and head of operations, etc.

8.6   Findings and Discussions: Summary of the Survey Results

The Pearson correlation coefficient has been adopted to test the relationship among all factors. In Table 8.1, it is found that the inter-organisational trust, collaboration and agility are all significantly and positively correlated to RFID use.

Descriptive statistics for all survey items appear in Table 8.2. Our model was assessed and validated (Hulland 1999). Individual item reliability is assessed by looking at the loadings of each item with their construct. The minimum level threshold for item loadings is 0.7 (Henseler et al. 2009). As seen in Table 8.2, all items in the research analysis are well above the 0.7, thus providing results for individual reliability. Convergent validity suggests that a number of items represent one and only one underlying construct. To assess convergent validity, each of the composite reliabilities is assessed for each construct, all of which has a minimum value of 0.7.

Table 8.1 Pearson correlation

Variable	1	2	3	4
RFID use	1.00			
Inter-org trust	0.26**	1.00		
Collaboration	0.25**	0.36***	1.00	
Agility	0.08	0.23**	0.34***	1.00

Notes: $*p < 0.01$, $**p < 0.05$, $***p < 0.001$

Table 8.2 Descriptive statistics: mean, SD and factor loadings

Factors	Mean, SD	Loading
RFID use		
Use of RFID technology relative to industry standard	4.48, 1.55	0.739
Extent to which our organisation uses RFID to integrate with our supply chain partners	4.02, 1.54	0.868
Reliance on RFID technology in conducting business processes	3.73, 1.46	0.815
Reliance on RFID technology in conducting business with our supply chain partners	5.07, 1.33	0.829
Inter-organisational trust		
Our organisation feels that it is important not to use any proprietary information to our supply chain partner's disadvantage	3.89, 1.45	0.913
A characteristic of the relationship between our organisation and its supply chain partners is that neither supply chain partner is expected to make demands that might be damaging to the other	5.05, 1.26	0.849
Our organisation feels that our supply chain partner will not attempt to get its way when it negatively impacts our organisation	4.81, 1.33	0.762
Our organisation has strong confidence in our supply chain partner	4.93, 1.31	0.737
Our organisation can always rely on another supply chain partner when it counts	3.75, 1.78	0.709
Our organisation believes that our supply chain partner will work hard in the future to maintain a close relationship with us	3.74, 1.65	0.823
Collaboration		
Our organisation and supply chain partners exchange timely information	3.90, 1.63	0.851
Our organisation and supply chain partners exchange accurate information	4.24, 1.48	0.811
Our organisation and supply chain partners exchange complete information	4.12, 1.59	0.823
Our organisation and supply chain partners have agreement on the goals of the supply chain	3.83, 1.65	0.792
Our organisation and supply chain partners have agreement on the importance of collaboration across the supply chain	3.64, 1.44	0.856
Our organisation and supply chain partners share benefits (e.g. saving costs)	3.80, 1.50	0.76
Our organisation and supply chain partners share any risks that can occur in the supply chain	4.07, 1.59	0.793
Our organisation and supply chain partners share benefits for providing to our end user	3.70, 1.55	0.828
Our organisation and supply chain partners have frequent contact on a regular basis	4.40, 1.48	0.738
Our organisation and supply chain partners have open and two-way communication	4.48, 1.47	0.765

(continued)

Table 8.2 (continued)

Factors	Mean, SD	Loading
Our organisation and supply chain partners influence each other's decisions through discussion	4.60, 1.38	0.823
Our organisation and supply chain partners jointly search and acquire new and relevant knowledge	4.22, 1.44	0.814
Our organisation and supply chain partners jointly identify end user needs	4.35, 1.54	0.817
Agility		
Our supply chain is able to respond to changes in demand	4.73, 1.35	0.735
Our supply chain is able to leverage the competencies of our partners to respond to demand	4.93, 1.18	0.786
Joint planning in our supply chain is important	4.20, 1.45	0.741
Our organisation works with our suppliers to seamlessly integrate our inter-organisation processes	4.90, 1.33	0.841
Improving our organisation's level of service is a high priority	5.51, 1.22	0.745
Improving our organisation's delivery reliability is a higher priority	4.48, 1.54	0.719
Improving our organisation's responsiveness is a high priority	4.23, 1.61	0.75
Demand is accessible throughout our organisation's supply chain	4.67, 1.77	0.713
Inventory levels are visible throughout our organisation's supply chain	4.21, 1.61	0.742

Notes: All items were measured on a seven-point Likert scale. All factor loadings are significant at $p < 0.001$

8.7 Conclusions and Future Work

Increasing complexity of supply chains due to globalisation efforts has led to organisations having difficulties with both collaboration and agility in getting aid to individuals in need. RBV is used to clarify the positive association between RFID use and collaboration among organisations and their suppliers. Social capital theory and its ability are also discussed to demonstrate the association of inter-organisational trust and its moderating role in the relationship between RFID use and collaboration as well as collaboration and its positive association with agility.

A conceptual model of RFID has been provided that is both theoretically and empirically supported through the use of RBV, social capital theory and partial least squares analysis. Research provides empirical support for the positive association between RFID use and collaboration among organisations and their suppliers as well as the ultimate positive impact on agility. This, in turn, creates a framework for supply chain management scholars to examine agility and how it may be impacted by information technology such as RFID.

References

Altay N, Green WG (2006) OR/MS research in disaster operations management. Eur J Oper Res 175(1):475–493

Autier P, Ferir MC, Hairapetien A, Alexanian A, Agoudjian V, Schmets G, Dallemagne G, Leva MN, Pinel J (1990) Drug supply in the aftermath of the 1988 Armenian earthquake. Lancet 335(8702):1388–1390

Baldini G et al (2012) Securing disaster supply chains with cryptography enhanced RFID. Disaster Prev Manag 21(1):51–70

Bharadwaj A (2000) A resource-based perspective on information technology capability and firm performance: an empirical investigation. MIS Q 24:169–196

Charles A, Lauras M, Wassenhove LV (2010) A model to define and assess the agility of supply chains: building on humanitarian experience. Int J Phys Distrib Logist Manag 40(8/9):722–741

Christopher M, Tatham P (2011) Introduction. In: Christopher M, Tatham P (eds) Humanitarian logistics. Meeting the challenge of preparing for and responding to disasters. Kogan Page, London, pp 1–14

Cottrill K (2002) Preparing for the worst. Traffic World 266(40):15

Dirks KT, Ferrin DL (2001) The role of trust in organizational settings. Organ Sci 12(4):450–467

Henseler J, Ringle CM, Sinkovics RR (2009) The use of partial least squares path modeling in international marketing. In: Sinkovics RR, Ghauri PN (eds) Advances in international marketing (AIM), vol 20. Emerald, Bingley, pp 277–320

Hulland J (1999) Use of partial least squares (PLS) in strategic management research: a review of four recent studies. Strateg Manag J 20(2):195–204

Iyer B, Henderson J (2010) Preparing for the future: understanding the seven capabilities of RFID. MIS Q Exec 9:117–131

Jones GR, George JM (1998) The experience and evolution of trust: implications for cooperation and teamwork. Acad Manag Rev 23(3):531–546

Ke W, Wei KK (2006) Factors affecting trading partners' knowledge sharing using the lens of transaction cost economics and socio-political theories. Electron Commerce Res Appl 21(2):133–143

Kovács G, Spens KM (2007) Humanitarian logistics in disaster relief operations. Int J Phys Distrib Logist Manag 37(2):99–114

Lee HW, Zbinden M (2003) Marrying logistics and technology for effective relief. Forced Migration Rev 18:34–35

Lin N (2000) Inequality in social capital. Contemp Sociol 29:785–795

Lin LC (2009) An integrated framework for the development of radio frequency identification technology in the logistics and supply chain management. Comp Ind Eng 57(3):832–842

Long D (1997) Logistics for disaster relief: engineering on the run. IIE Solut 29(6):26–29

Miller HE, Engemann KJ, Yager RR (2006) Disaster planning and management. Commun Int Inf Manag Assoc 6(2):25–36

Narayan D, Cassidy MF (2001) A dimensional approach to measuring social capital: development and validation of a social capital inventory. Curr Sociol 49:59–102

Oke A, Idiagbon-Oke M (2010) Communication channels, innovation tasks and NPD project outcomes in innovation-driven horizontal networks. J Oper Manag 28(5):442–453

Pettit SJ, Beresford AKC (2005) Emergency relief logistics: an evaluation of military, non-military, and composite response models. Int J Logist Res Appl 8(4):313–331

Sarac A, Absi N, Dauzere-Peres S (2010) A literature review on the impact of RFID technologies on supply chain management. Int J Prod Econ 128(1):77–95

Schulze W (1992) The two schools of thought in resource-based theory: definitions and implications for research. In: Academy of management 1992 proceedings, Las Vegas. Available at: http://proceedings.aom.org/content/1992/1/37.short

Sheffi Y (2004) Combinatorial auctions in the procurement of transportation services. Interfaces 34(4):245–252

Swafford PM, Ghosh S, Murphy NN (2006) The antecedents of supply chain agility of a firm: scale development and model testing. J Oper Manag 24(2):170–188

Tajima M (2007) Strategic value of RFID in supply chain management. J Purch Supply Manag 13(4):261–273

Thomas A (2003) Why logistics? Forced Migration Rev 18:4

Tomasini R, Van Wassenhove LN (2009a) From preparedness to partnerships: case study research on humanitarian logistics. Int Trans Oper Res 16(5):549–559

Tomasini R, Van Wassenhove LN (2009b) Humanitarian logistics. Palgrave Macmillan, London

Van Wassenhove LN (2006) Blackett memorial lecture. Humanitarian aid logistics: supply chain management in high gear. J Oper Res Soc 57(5):475–489

Yang H, Yang L, Yang S (2010) Hybrid Zigbee RFID sensor network for humanitarian logistics centre management. J Netw Comp Appl 34(3):938–948

Zhang C, Viswanathan S, Henke JW Jr (2011) The boundary spanning capabilities of purchasing agents in buyer-supplier trust development. J Oper Manag 29:318–328

Chapter 9
An Agile and Flexible Supply Chain for Efficient Humanitarian Logistics in a Disaster Management System

B.R. Raghukumar, Ashish Agarwal, and Milind Kumar Sharma

9.1 Introduction

The term "disaster" is usually applied to a breakdown in the normal functioning of a community that has a significant adverse impact on people, their works, and their environment, overwhelming local response capacity. Alexander (1993) defines natural disaster as some rapid, instantaneous, or profound impact of the natural environment upon the socioeconomic system. He also recommends Turner's (1976) definition of natural disaster as "an event, concentrated in time and space, which threatens a society or subdivision of a society with major unwanted consequences as a result of the collapse of precautions which had previously been culturally accepted as adequate." There were 6,637 natural disasters between 1974 and 2003 worldwide, with more than 5.1 billion affected people, more than 182 million homeless, and more than 2 million deaths and with a reported damage of 1.38 trillion USD (Centre for Research on the Epidemiology of the Disasters – CRED 2004). The September 11 attacks (2001), tsunami in South Asia (2004), Hurricane Katrina (2005), earthquakes in Pakistan (2005) and Java (2006), and cloudbursts in Leh (2010) and Uttarakhand (2013) are just some examples of the deadliest disasters witnessed by humankind in the past few years. As per data of WHO Collaborating Centre for Research on the Epidemiology of Disasters (CRED 2004), in the year 2011 more than 30,770 people were killed, 244.7 million people were affected, and the economic loss was US$ 366.1 billion due to natural disasters. The

B.R. Raghukumar (✉)
Indian Armed Forces, SOET, IGNOU, New Delhi, India

A. Agarwal
School of Engineering and Technology, IGNOU, New Delhi, India

M.K. Sharma
Department of Production and Industrial Engineering, Faculty of Engineering and Architecture, M.B.M. Engineering College, J.N.V. University, Jodhpur, Rajasthan, India
e-mail: milindksharma@rediffmail.com

© Springer India 2016
B.S. Sahay et al. (eds.), *Managing Humanitarian Logistics*, Springer Proceedings in Business and Economics, DOI 10.1007/978-81-322-2416-7_9

Table 9.1 Disaster categorization and examples

	Man-made	Natural
Slow onset	Political crisis, refugee crisis	Famine, drought
Sudden onset	Terrorist attacks, chemical leaks	Hurricanes, floods, earthquakes, tsunamis

Source: Adapted from Ergun et al. (2011)

consequences of these events are colossal even if one considers only human lives and destroyed homes and families. But when the entire situation is studied in holistic manner, taking into account the havoc wreaked on the states, the socioeconomic impact becomes unfathomable. Disasters can be grouped into two main categories: natural and man-made disasters (CRED 2004). Natural disasters are the consequences of natural hazards that affect people, whereas man-made disasters are caused by human actions. Though no disaster can be avoided entirely (especially natural ones), the mitigation of the situation is possible with an emergency team and suitable planning. Disaster response supply chain is a function of the geographical location where disaster takes place, nature of disaster, suppliers, actual need of the community, organizations who are working there, available information, government policies, local culture, etc. (Dash et al. 2013). It can be seen easily that the management of disaster relief and the logistics requires different techniques at different levels. In disaster relief the eventual purpose of the emergency supply chain is to deliver the right products and services to the right people or destination at the right time. Cost and information confidentiality are both secondary. This makes the quick setup and quick response of an emergency SC possible (Douglas et al. 2005). The establishment of a SC in any disaster is characterized always by two factors. Firstly, this task is going to be at a short notice with minimum of resources: man, material, transportation, location, and power/communications (Table 9.1).

Secondly, the cost implications of the type of SC will play a major role in affecting all SC strategies irrespective of the availability of the resources. In the past, firm performance on disaster preparedness was poor, as noted by Helferich and Cook (2002). No matter the type of disaster, the management of these events typically follows four sequential stages (CRED 2004): mitigation, preparedness, response, and recovery. The various stages of the disaster are as shown below in Table 9.2. SCs link the sources of "supply" (suppliers) to the owners of "demand" (end customers) (CRED 2004). In a typical humanitarian SC, governments and NGOs are the primary parties involved. After the primary phase in the secondary phase, which may be from few days to several weeks, other agencies such as military, local donors, international agencies, media, industries, and private volunteer agencies are typically involved.

The military agencies are an entity which in an Indian scenario forms the backbone of the entire SC network. The affected parties become the customers in the disaster SC parlance in comparison with a traditional SC. The elements of the SC's main responsibility thus become "the fastest and accurate means of ensuring the supplies reach the affected parties or customers."

Table 9.2 Disaster timeline and operations

Pre-disaster	Disaster	Post-disaster
Mitigation and preparedness	*Response*	*Recovery*
Assessment	Relief operations	1. Debris cleaning
1. Risk factors	1. First phase	2. Infrastructure rebuilding
2. Vulnerability	Medics, food, shelter	3. Reestablishing communities
Planning	Second phase	Measure the effects of:
1. Infrastructure	(a) Housing	1. Infrastructure
2. Policy making	(b) Food, supply chain building	2. Planning
3. Capacity building		3. Short- and long-term response
4. Pre-positioning resources		
Training/education	Logistics stages	Lessons learned, feedback to logistics, and response
	1. Mobilization and procurement	
	2. Long haul	
	3. The last mile	

Adapted from Ergun et al. (2011)

9.2 Logistic Necessities in Disaster Management

The Yokohama message emanating from the international decade for natural disaster reduction in May 1994 underlined the need for an emphatic shift in the strategy for disaster mitigation (Yokohama 1994). The Yokohama Strategy also emphasized that disaster prevention, mitigation, and preparedness are better than disaster response in achieving the goals and objectives of vulnerability reduction. Disaster response alone is not sufficient as it yields only temporary results at a very high cost. Much of the research in the disaster management field is targeted to public servants, government agencies, and insurance firms charged with responding in times of crisis and has traditionally focused on crises such as hurricanes, earthquakes, flooding, and fires (Iakovou and Douligeris 2001; Witt 1997; Warwick 1995; McHugh 1995; Hale and Moberg 2005). Drabek and McEntire conducted a literature review to evaluate the impact of emergent phenomena in disasters and the coordination of multiple organizations responding to crises (Drabek and McEntire 2003). Research has found that humans behave in a compassionate manner during disasters without much panic or antisocial behavior immediately after the crisis (Fischer 2002). The Columbia-Wharton/Penn Roundtable on "Risk Management Strategies in an Uncertain World" took place in April 2002 (Hale and Moberg 2005). With the support of the Council of Logistics Management, Helferich and Cook (2002) and Hale and Moberg (2005) completed perhaps the most comprehensive review of supply chain security in the aftermath of September 11. One valuable part of their management report is an annotated bibliography of disaster planning and emergency response research and articles from the previous 25–30 years (Hale and Moberg 2005).

The vast majority of articles in this comprehensive bibliography come from the business trade press, research in the disaster planning and management literature, and guidelines developed by government agencies such as FEMA. Federal Emergency Management Agency (FEMA) is the primary organization for preparedness and response to federal-level disasters in the United States. The resulting white paper and research report provides managers with a thorough review of current research, offers a detailed process for development of a disaster management plan for the supply chain, and includes detailed information on resources, web pages, and government reports that can be used by managers while implementing disaster management plans (Hale and Moberg 2005). The above research notwithstanding, there is still felt a requirement for more research in the areas of the SC management in terms of warehousing, SC risk mitigation, SC flexibility and agility, etc., which are only some of the areas which immediately demand concern.

9.3 Existing Literary Resources

Logistics typically refers to activities that occur within the boundaries of a single organization, and SCs refer to networks of companies that work together and coordinate their actions to deliver a product to market. In this context a disaster response SC model can be visualized as given in the Fig. 9.1.

Any disaster management SC has uncertainty as inherent part of the organization. This uncertainty removal process consists of various compartmentalization of the processes as shown in Fig. 9.1. However it is pertinent to note that the reasoning of the disaster response chain to the causes of the disaster is less important than the response itself while addressing the gargantuan issues as posed by any disaster. This shall be addressed later in this paper, where structural changes to the present organizational tree are discussed as a proposed model.

9.3.1 Secure Site Location Decision Process

The secure site location decision process proposed by Hale and Moberg (2005) combines the recommendations from disaster management agencies, service expectations within the supply chain, and location science into one process. The resulting model will lead to the selection of a minimum number of emergency resource locations that provide logistics managers with quick access to critical resources while minimizing the total costs spent by the supply chain preparing

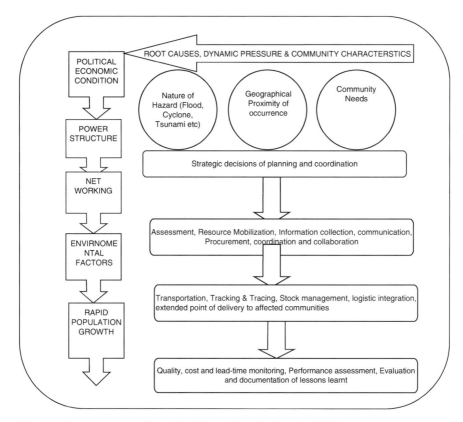

Fig. 9.1 Disaster response SC model (Adapted from Dash et al. (2013))

for future crises. This model consists of the following steps (Hale and Moberg 2005):

Step 1: Identify the emergency resources needed at each secure location.

- Helferich and Cook noted that critical documents, such as contact lists of key managers, government agencies, and nonprofit organizations, area maps, and other essential checklists for managers, should be stored in a safe and secure location (Helferich and Cook 2002). In addition, FEMA's Disaster Management Guide for Business outlines other critical items, such as medical supplies, generators, water, and backup communications that should be available during emergencies.

Step 2: Identify all critical facilities within the supply chain.

- The second step in the process is to identify the locations within the supply chain that will need access to emergency resources.

Step 3: Set maximum response time goals for access to emergency resources and minimum distances to secure site storage areas from supply chain facilities.

- Because the storage of emergency resources will be off-site and because each secure location may service multiple facilities, a decision must be made about the maximum time it should take any facility in the supply chain to gain access to emergency resources.
- Here, logistics managers must also set minimum and maximum distance constraints to ensure the safety of materials but also provide reasonable response times during disasters.

Step 4: Use the proposed decision model to identify the number and approximate location of emergency resource storage facilities.

9.3.2 Logistics and Process Analysis Tool (LPAT)

Argonne National Laboratory (a US Department of Energy laboratory managed by UChicago Argonne, LLC) has developed a portfolio of modeling tools to simplify the process of SC at the macro- and the microlevels. LPAT, under development at Argonne, combines the capabilities of two existing discrete modeling tools – ELIST *(Enhanced Logistics Intra-theater Support Tool)* and PAT *(Process Analysis Tool)* – into one comprehensive analysis system. When used individually, ELIST and PAT are powerful tools for analyzing the multi-scale impact of SC operations. By integrating these two models into a SC system (Logistics and Process Analysis Tool), the *emergency management or public health professional* gains the ability to test, analyze, and understand how the interaction between individual parts of the supply chain influences each other. The benefits for emergency management and public healthcare professionals can be listed as below:

- Answer real-world questions about actual situations.
- Test and evaluate logistic issues before an incident and evaluate response alternatives after an event.
- Use as a planning tool to prepare for an incident of local, state, or national significance.
- Master connections among strategic, tactical, and operational levels of deployment.
- Assess hazard impacts, such as damage to housing, hospitals, and utilities, and analyze the assets required for response/recovery, such as trucks, power generators, staff, and supplies.
- LPAT's combination of transportation and processing analysis can function as a useful platform within and across many domains:

  - Epidemiologic Modeling
  - Emergency Management and Public Health Deployment
  - Multimode Transportation Analyses
  - Evacuation

A long-term, strategic coordination and management of disaster response SC has challenging problems. The supply network is remote and complicated with numerous players (donors, NGOs, government, military, and suppliers), and it is difficult to coordinate all of them along with all the items that need to be delivered. However, collaboration, coordination, professionalism, and accountability are important factors on which the performance of the SC relies on. Based on the above principles, the model in Fig. 9.2 is suggested instead of conventional function-based system.

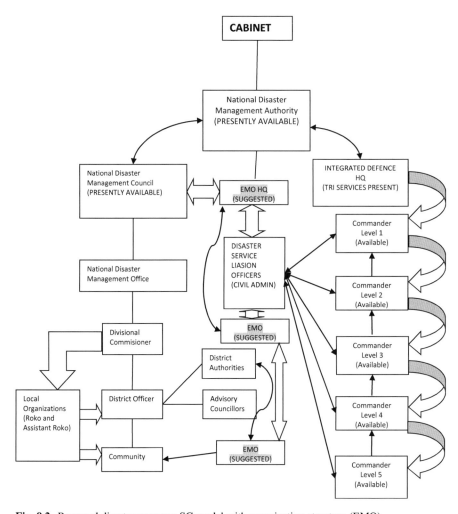

Fig. 9.2 Proposed disaster response SC model with organization structure (EMO)

9.4   Discussions on Suggested Model

The models referred in Fig. 9.1 and other such models discussed above have all ingredients of a good SC model; however, it is evident from the model that it discusses all issues that are technically inherent to a SC model except that there are no humanitarian logistic issues explicitly addressed. This trend can be seen generally in all such models, which is basically due to the fact that these models are built on the SC principles that have roots in commercial SC. This approach may make a model for humanitarian logistics deficient as is evident from excerpts ". . .. disaster relief supply chains are treated as a subset of humanitarian supply chains. . ..; .. there are important differences between the situation encountered by a humanitarian supply chain and those met by disaster relief supply chains. . ." Whybark et al. (2010).

The humanitarian SC requirement is evident from the statement "The specific organizations that are assembled for any particular disaster is a function of severity, location, the nature of the disaster, availability of potential participants, anticipated needs and prescribed procedures" Whybark et al. (2010).

The present organization within the Indian National Disaster Management Authority is studied for the purpose of developing a new model to cater for the humanitarian logistic aspects as discussed. The structure presently available for the functionaries of the disaster management system is available at http://ndma.gov.in/ndma/dmstructure.html. However, the system is another reflection of the government machinery rather than being a flexible SC to cater for flow of both the decision matters and goods. It seems at times the system heavily relies on the military and paramilitary forces for the execution of the disaster management activities. The community is entirely surrounded by the state functionaries, but at execution point it is exasperating for the community to communicate with the functionaries as there are no single window solutions for the ground-level problems.

The suggested graphical representation of the model is as shown in the Fig. 9.2. The inputs considered at the international level for the use of military capabilities beyond certain limits are mixed. There is a view that the military has a primary role of guarding the country, and the frequent exposure to the administrative roles may erode their competitiveness at times of war. However, the capabilities of the military to assist at times of disaster can never be overlooked. The alternative to direct deployment of the military is to have a mechanism within the precincts of the civilian organizational structure akin to military establishment and who are trained under the aegis of the military establishment in handling such disasters. The discipline and training combined with suitable resources can help establish such a system over a period of time which can independently handle disasters up to some extent, so that the military is not deployed at the drop of the hat. The military deployment can then be regulated as per a format of deciding how severe a disaster is and what resources are required. The military resources are quite expensive and precious; its mindless deployment is only going to erode such resources as is the habit now.

It will be much better utilization of the available resources in case such a plan can materialize which will help a parallel deployment of a force which can be smaller in magnitude than the military but with much more teeth in terms of required resources which are more disaster specific.

The model suggested in the figure reflects the direction of flow of instructions and orders. At times military commanders have often been ordered by civilian authorities to supplement or replace civilian emergency management and response agencies when the latter have struggled or failed in the performance of their mandated duties to the public, as occurred during Hurricane Katrina in the United States (Lester and Krejci 2007; White 2006). The same is true for the Indian democracy also.

9.4.1 The Emergency Management Organization (EMO)

The establishment of an organization called Emergency Management Organization (EMO) will obviate the requirement of the entire gamut of government departments to be associated with the entire gamut of military, paramilitary, police, fire, home guards, scouts, etc. Instead the state and central government machinery can concentrate on the strategic issues rather than on the tactical and operational issues as happening now. The EMO is expected to have all resources as required by its deployment locale. For example, an EMO unit deployed in Uttarakhand (mountainous terrain) will naturally have different resources as compared to an EMO unit deployed in Haryana and Punjab (planes). This obviates the requirement of movement of resources as it is happening now from one place to another, thus saving enormous time in becoming operational, which is of utmost importance in disasters. The advantages of an independent organization are:

- The strained relations do not interfere in inter-organizational cooperation.
- High uncertainty levels exist at all levels regarding decisions; thus, delays get generally obviated when an organization like EMO with an agenda of helping a community foremost on its responsibility exists with readily available resources.
- The resources and its procurement can be independently collaborated with specialists on its charter and its maintenance at all times can be organized.
- Training of men and collaboration with the community with inter alia relations with other organizations which may be handy during disasters can be streamlined.
- The military and paramilitary forces can concentrate on their primary responsibilities.

9.5 Conclusion

It may be extremely clear by now that the SC which operates in a disaster management environment is substantially different from the commercial SC. The proposed model in the discussion above has the flexibility and required agility to act at the shortest notice and is in possession of the wherewithal to operate at times of disaster. This has a well-integrated humanitarian logistic element being closely knit with the local community and adept at maintaining focus on the task at all times. This organization has also the advantage of being accessible by one and all at all times, thus making it very efficient in handling its responsibilities. It is also required at times to mandate with training of the manpower as to whom it may become associated at times of action. Although there has not been a great amount of research on humanitarian and other "nontraditional" supply chains, interest is increasing and more is being published now. This is an effort which is expected to provide a direction for such future SC which may obviate some of the problems faced now in disaster management situations, thus making them more flexible and agile at all situations.

References

Alexander DE (1993) Natural disasters. UCL Press, London

Beamon B (2004) Humanitarian relief chains: issues and challenges. In Proceedings of the 34th international conference on computers and industrial engineering, San Francisco

Centre for Research on the Epidemiology of Disasters (2004) Thirty years of natural disasters 1974–2003: the numbers. UCL Press, Brussels. http://www.emdat.be/Documents/Publications/publication_2004_emdat.pdf. Accessed 15 Jan 2009

Dash SR, Mishra US, Mishra P (2013) Emerging issues and opportunities in disaster response SC management. Int. J Sup. Chain. Mgt 2(1):55–61. March 2013

Douglas P, Gail K, Michel D (2005) Exploring the Complexity of social and ecological resilience to hazards. In: Paton D, Johnston D (eds) Disaster resilience: an integrated approach. Charles C. Thomas Publisher, Springfield, Ill, USA, pp 190–212

Drabek TE, McEntire DA (2003) Emergent phenomena and the sociology of disaster: lessons, trends, and opportunities from the research literature. Disaster Prev Manag 12(2):97–112

Ergun O, Karakus G, Keskinocak P, Swann J, Villarreal M (2011) Operations research to improve disaster supply chain management. H. Milton Stewart School of Industrial and Systems Engineering, Georgia Institute of Technology, Atlanta

Fischer HW (2002) Terrorism and 11 September 2001: does the 'behavioral response to disaster' model fit? Disaster Prev Manag 17(2):123–7

Hale T, Moberg CR (2005) Improving supply chain disaster preparedness: A decision process for secure site location. Int J Phys Distrib Logist Manag 35(3):195–207

Helferich OK, Cook RL (2002) Securing the SC: management report. CLM Publications, Oak Brook

Iakovou E, Douligeris C (2001) An information management system for the emergency management of hurricane disasters. Int J Risk Assess Manag 2(3/4):243–62

Lester W, Krejci D (2007) Business 'not' as usual: the national incident management system, federalism, and leadership. Public Adm Rev 67(1):84–93. December 2007

McHugh CP (1995) Preparing public safety organizations for disaster response: a study of Tucson, Arizona's response to flooding. Disaster Prev Manag 4(5):25–36

Warwick M (1995) Painful lessons in crisis mismanagement. Commun Int 22(2):4–5

White House (2006) The federal response to Hurricane Katrina, Lessons Learned Washington. http://www.whitehouse.gov/reports/katrina-lessonslearned.pdf

Whybark DC, Melnyk SA, Day J, Davis ED (2010) Disaster relief supply chain management: new realities, management challenges, emerging opportunities. Decis Line, pp 4–7. http://ejournal. narotama.ac.id/files/Disaster%20relief%20supply%20chain%20management.pdf

Witt JL (1997) Creating the disaster-resistant community. Am City County 112(1):23–31

Yokohama strategy and plan of action for a safer world-guidelines for natural disaster prevention, preparedness and mitigation (1994) World Conference on Natural Disaster Reduction Yokohama, Japan. http://www.ndmindia.nic.in/Mitigation/mitigationhome.html

Chapter 10
A "Collective Impact Framework" to Improve Output and Outcomes in Disaster Reconstruction Programs

Debashish Naik

10.1 Introduction

The occurrence of large-scale disasters such as super cyclones, hurricanes, tsunamis, and earthquakes are increasing day by day. Though the world is advancing in technology and in its ability to respond to the pre- and post-disaster operations, still it is beyond the capacity to control its occurrence. The impacts of these disasters are huge. The tasks of reconstruction post disaster remain a great challenge and require a coordinated effort of all participants for effective and efficient delivery of outputs and outcomes. It requires a high level of coordination and management program to manage the reconstruction activities (Le Masurier et al. 2006). The affected people need support not only in the form of funding but also from the NGOs and agencies who get engaged in reconstruction activities. The donor support is decreasing due to present economic conditions across the world and the increase in occurrence in the number of disasters. In many countries though the government takes care of the reconstruction but still there is dependency on donors.

10.2 Background to the Paper

As a part of an international agency, the author was involved in rehabilitation and reconstruction activities during the post super cyclone in 1999–2000 in Odisha. From his experience, his observation of rehabilitation and reconstruction work and interaction with the organizations involved in such work including the community, he has understood that large-scale rehabilitation and reconstruction require broad

D. Naik (✉)
Management Consultant at Mevocon, Bangalore, Karnataka, India
e-mail: debanaik7@gmail.com

© Springer India 2016   141
B.S. Sahay et al. (eds.), *Managing Humanitarian Logistics*, Springer Proceedings in Business and Economics, DOI 10.1007/978-81-322-2416-7_10

cross-sector coordination. But he has seen that many of such organizations in the social sector remain focused on the isolated intervention of their individual organizations. People may say that the effort put by different organizations is a collective effort to rehabilitate the affected people, but a careful observation would reveal that each organization is still driven by their individual agendas.

The author has seen the ground-level reality in rehabilitation and reconstruction work and appreciates the efforts by many local NGOs, international NGOs, international agencies, government and public sectors, and the community. It has also been seen that these agencies collaborate to a certain extent to deliver their services. But at the same time he also has felt that the organizations always have tried to isolate their individual contribution for various reasons such as to showcase their individual capability, creating a differentiation to compete for funding, and most importantly to communicate on what they have contributed. Though this is the reality, the author strongly believes that the output and outcomes from this way of working can further be improved a lot through collective impact approach or process. This belief is built upon the experience gained by working in leading companies in the world and the way they collaborate to develop products and deliver services. The study of academic literature also provided input through proven examples and approach to make this belief of collective impact stronger.

From a practitioner's point of view, the author has tried to communicate a "Collective Impact Framework" blending his experience in super cyclone projects in Odisha and his experience in the development sector and in the corporate.

10.3   Collective Impact

Collective impact is the commitment of a group of important actors or stakeholders from different sectors to a common agenda for solving a specific social problem (Kania and Kramer 2011). Collaboration is nothing new. The social sector is filled with examples of partnerships, networks, and other types of joint efforts. But collective impact initiatives (Kania and Kramer 2011) are distinctly different. Unlike most collaboration, collective impact approach involves a centralized infrastructure, a dedicated staff, and a structured process that leads to a common agenda, shared measurement, continuous communication, and mutually reinforcing activities among all participants (Kania and Kramer 2011).

One of the examples of collective impact in the social sector is in 1993; Marjorie Mayfield Jackson helped found the Elizabeth River Project with a mission of cleaning up the Elizabeth River in southeastern Virginia. For decades the river was a dumping ground for industrial waste. More than 100 stakeholders, including the city governments of Chesapeake, Norfolk, Portsmouth, and Virginia Beach, the Virginia Department of Environmental Quality, the US Environmental Protection Agency (EPA), the US Navy, and dozens of local businesses, schools, community groups, environmental organizations, and universities, were engaged in developing an 18-point plan to restore the watershed. It was a great success and 15 years later, more than 1,000 acres of watershed land have been conserved or restored. Pollution has been reduced by more than 215 million pounds, concentrations of the most severe carcinogen have been cut sixfold, and water quality has significantly improved. Much remains to be done before the river is fully restored, but already 27 species of fish and oysters are thriving in the restored wetlands, and bald eagles have returned to nest on the shores.

Another example is of a citywide effort to reduce and prevent childhood obesity in elementary school children in Somerville, Massachusetts. Led by Christina Economos, an associate professor at Tufts University's Gerald J. and Dorothy R. Friedman School of Nutrition Science and Policy, and funded by the Centers for Disease Control and Prevention, the Robert Wood Johnson Foundation, Blue Cross Blue Shield of Massachusetts, and the United Way of Massachusetts Bay and Merrimack Valley, the program engaged government officials, educators, businesses, nonprofits, and citizens in collectively defining wellness and weight gain prevention practices. Schools agreed to offer healthier foods, teach nutrition, and promote physical activity. Local restaurants received a certification if they served low-fat, high nutritional food. The city organized a farmers' market and provided healthy lifestyle incentives such as reduced-price gym memberships for city employees. Even sidewalks were modified and crosswalks repainted to encourage more children to walk to school. The result was a statistically significant decrease in body mass index among the community's young children between 2002 and 2005.

The author's interaction and study of "Karuna Trust," a not-for-profit organization in India, managing around 70 PHCs (primary health centers) in a PPP mode, also indicates the benefit of collective impact process. Engaged with the government and the community, the organization is providing healthcare services in rural areas. The impact in terms of output and outcome is higher than the output delivered by government PHCs.

These varied examples all have a common theme: that large-scale social change comes from better cross-sector coordination rather than from the isolated intervention of individual organizations. Evidence of the effectiveness of this approach is still limited, but these examples suggest that substantially greater progress could be made if nonprofits, governments, businesses, and the public were brought together around a common agenda to create collective impact. Generally this process is not practiced because it is very difficult to manage the participating organizations together and bind them, but because it is so rarely attempted. Funders and the organizations involved in execution overlook the potential for collective impact because they are used to focusing on independent action as the primary vehicle for social change.

10.4   Isolated Impact

Many international agencies, international NGO, government bodies, and local NGOs were involved in rehabilitation and reconstruction activities. Though it was looking like all the organizations were working together, it was not a collective impact and the degree of collaboration was low.

To undertake reconstruction or social programs, various small and large NGOs (grantees) apply to the large funders and the international agencies. The funders and the international agencies choose a few grantees from many. While granting the funders evaluate the organizations based on their capability of execution and past records of development and reconstruction work. To get grant the organizations emphasize how their individual activities have produced the greatest impact. During evaluation of impact each organization tries to focus on its contribution and the impact of their effort. In the process they downplay the advantage gained due to collaboration with other organizations. This approach or behavior is termed as isolated impact. The ground-level experience and observation indicates that the isolated impact of these individual organizations fails to identify the potential benefits of getting engaged with other organizations having expertise in different fields. As a result they are not able to leverage the benefits of cross-sector coalitions that engage other organizations including those outside the nonprofit sector. If we see in the field of education, even the most highly respected nonprofits—such as the Harlem Children's Zone, Teach For America, and the Knowledge Is Power Program (KIPP)—have taken decades to reach tens of thousands of children, a remarkable achievement that deserves praise, but one that is three orders of magnitude short of the tens of millions of US children that need help. It is not that all social problems or all reconstruction programs follow collective impact. In fact, some social problems are best solved by individual organizations.

When the organizations with different expertise work toward a common goal and through an integrated approach of where each is supported by a centralized infrastructure, governance and management system deliver higher output and outcomes. Adopting the Collective Impact Framework is not just encouraging more collaboration or public-private partnerships. It is a systemic approach that focuses on the relationships between organizations and the progress toward shared objectives. It requires the creation of a new set of nonprofit management organizations that have the skills and resources to assemble and coordinate the specific elements necessary for collective action to succeed.

10.5   Collective Impact Framework

Successful collective impact initiatives typically have five conditions that together produce true alignment and lead to powerful results: a common agenda, shared measurement systems, mutually reinforcing activities, continuous communication,

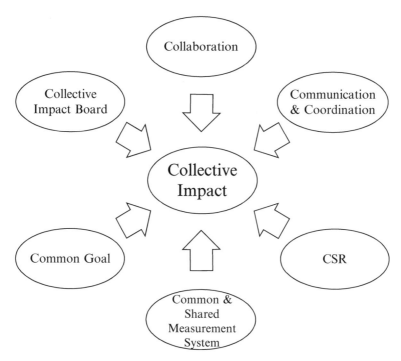

Fig. 10.1 Collective Impact Framework

and backbone support organizations (*collective impact*). Corporate social responsibility (CSR) is being added as a component to these elements from India's point of view. CSR activities are becoming mandatory for big companies in India. The author believes that CSR as a component can be added where companies can directly contribute their expertise in rehabilitation and reconstruction programs that will have greater effects.

The five conditions as success factors along with CSR are the six components of the Collective Impact Framework. Each component has a specific purpose and aligned to the overall goal. Each component brings an added advantage and overall this framework can deliver superior results over isolated impact (Fig. 10.1).

10.5.1   Common Goal

All the contributing organizations including the community are aligned to a shared vision or a common goal. This includes a joint approach to reconstruction programs. All the participants in development understand their part of contribution which is aligned to their expertise. Every organization understands that when they perform better, it ensures higher outputs in the reconstruction programs. For example, in a housing construction program, a construction company becomes a member and takes care of construction. The company understands the overall goal and aligns itself to optimize, quality, cost and time using its expertise of construction and project management. As a result the program delivers more output with the same resources which is higher than the result of isolated impact. The community management NGO who has expertise in mobilizing people and able to resolve any community-related issues does it better as it is their expertise.

Each organization may have a slightly different definition of the ultimate goal. These differences are easily ignored when organizations work independently on isolated initiatives. As part of the common goal of the Collective Impact Framework, it is expected that these differences be discussed and resolved. The Collective Impact Board plays an important role in resolving the conflicts and ensuring the delivery of higher results. Funding agencies also play a major role to create harmony in the system.

10.5.2 Common and Shared Measurement System

Common and shared measurement system is a necessary condition to achieve the goal of collective impact initiative. When a common goal is established, the measurement system aligned to the goal becomes a common driving factor for all participants. Participants work together as an overall system prospective that just has local impact with respect to their specific role and activities. It guides all the participants on where to focus, where to subordinate, and most importantly how to support each other to achieve the common goal of the reconstruction program.

The common and shared measurement system ensures that all efforts remain aligned to the result. It creates harmony in the system that enables participants to learn from each other's success and failures and also to hold each other accountable without creating conflict. This approach increases efficiency and effectiveness. It results into reduction in cost, reduction in program lead time, and improve in quality.

The common goal and the common and shared measurement system not only help in bringing clarity in roles and responsibility of the diverse group of participants but also help in removing the confusion in terms of accountability.

10.5.3 Collaboration

Collaboration as a component of Collective Impact Framework is basically the mutually reinforcing activities by the diverse group of organizations engaged in development through the collective impact initiative. In this system when the diverse groups of stakeholders work together, they not necessarily do the same thing. They focus on their expertise and are encouraged to take up activities at which they are good at. The most important thing is that each other's activities are well coordinated with the activities of others.

The result of collective impact initiative is higher than the isolated impact, not because of the number of participants but because of the coordination of their differentiated expertise and activities. Each participant does their best on the specific role in the overall coordinated rehabilitation and reconstruction activities. Taking the example of housing reconstruction, a group having expertise in mobilizing a community would ensure to resolve community-level conflicts, and the construction organization would focus on better project management to reduce cost and reduce the lead time of construction without affecting the quality. The organization having expertise in information technology (IT) would focus on how IT can enable other participants in better coordination and access to information.

In collective impact initiative the reconstruction programs are aimed to deliver results in a holistic way than in isolated result. This works beyond collaboration. The following example can explain how the impact is holistic. When a school building is constructed, other than the construction, the other participants who are having expertise in developing teachers, counseling students, IT system, etc. also participate. As a result they are able to deliver better methodology to deliver a program, establishing a library, providing equipments and IT-enabled system for program delivery. At the end the reconstruction of school results in an ideal school that can boost the morale of the students and their parents and can help them to forget the trauma due to the disaster.

10.5.4   Corporate Social Responsibility (CSR)

Many corporations allocate certain amount from their profit for the development of the society. In this context of Collective Impact Framework, CSR is considered just not in terms of funding but with a focus in participating in the reconstruction program and performing the specific activities or role based on their expertise. The expertise can bring benefit in terms of maximizing value of delivery to the cost of delivery and also doing more with less compared to others who have less expertise. A participant having expertise in logistics and supply chain can add more value in terms of cost, time, and quality compared to a company working in the form of an isolated impact.

10.5.5   Communication and Coordination

Communication and coordination is another necessary condition to achieve the goal of the collective impact initiative. When there are many participants working together, it is bound to have issues and challenges due to communication and coordination. A strong system for communication and coordination ensures that the collective efforts are channelized in the right direction and aligned to the common goal.

With the advancement of information technology, it is easy to design an effective system for communication and coordination. IT-enabled communication and coordination system together with strong governance can help the participants to deliver their best without getting stuck due to dependence activities of other participants.

With a common goal and measurement, a well-structured communication and coordination system can reduce the lead time of reconstruction program. Most importantly it would reduce the confusion due to dependent activities by the divers group of participants. Good governance with well coordination helps to appreciate and motivate each other.

They need time to see that their own interests will be treated fairly and that decisions will be made on the basis of objective evidence and the best possible solution to the problem, not to favor the priorities of one organization over another.

10.5.6   Collective Impact Board

The Collective Impact Board is the backbone of the collective impact initiative. The board consists of senior management and the execution managers from each participating organization. It provides a structure, a system, and governance to establish a common goal, measurement system, oversee the execution, and most importantly resolve any conflict that arises among the participants in the reconstruction programs. The most important thing it does is it establishes the priority of reconstruction program's deliverables. It does so by involving closely the participants including the beneficiary community. As a result not only do the process of need identification and its prioritization based on the fund available become robust but they also deliver better output and outcomes.

It provides good governance and ensures that each participant is treated fairly and fulfills its own interest without compromising the objective and deliverables of programs. It facilitates a healthy and harmonious environment to resolve conflicts and to take decision based on objective evidence without favoring one over others. Most importantly the board brings together all the participants to solve bigger problems in the reconstruction programs. Due to togetherness the board gets power to negotiate appropriate support from the government and at the same time gain confidence from the donor that their respective fund is appropriately used.

The Collective Impact Board provides a common and shared infrastructure, dedicated staffs for common support activities, logistical support, and technology to improve productivity of each participant. This arrangement not only reduces the cost for many participants but also provides services to many which the participants might not have been able to afford. While working together on the shared services, the collective board can learn from different participants and can infuse the best practices in terms of tools, techniques, and processes for managing these shared service activities effectively. The review board consists of member from each participant, it brings transparency in terms of work, increase accountability in terms of delivery, and gives opportunity for cross-learning of success and failures.

10.6 The Challenges

From a strategic point of view, the biggest challenge for adopting the collective impact approach is overcoming the mindset of both funding and executing organizations, i.e., moving from an isolated impact perspective to collective impact approach.

Once there is an agreement to join together through collective impact approach, the next challenge is working together and resolving the conflict of fulfilling every participant's interest and at the same time achieving the goal of the reconstruction programs.

There are also other obstacles that the participants have to overcome while executing the reconstruction programs through collective impact approach. Expertise and money are needed in setting up a collective board that offers a shared infrastructure and various other services. It needs a dedicated specialized team who would build up the skills and systems that can be easily replicated or reused without adding much cost and at a lesser time.

10.7 Overcoming the Challenges

This requires a fundamental change in thinking. The large funding agencies, the international agencies, and the large national and multinational NGOs engaged in reconstruction programs need to seat together and elaborate on the ultimate benefits to the beneficiaries or the community by adopting the collective impact approach.

Once they are able to establish the common goal and able to measure how the collective impact approach delivers more output and outcomes compared to isolated impact approach, they can overcome the mindset of isolated impact approach and move to the collective impact approach. This is the biggest challenge. The next challenge of execution needs ownership and investment from large organizations involved in reconstruction programs. After a few executions the concern organization can develop a sustainable and replicated system including various assets such as IT applications, processes, and the management system. The developed system can be adopted with very less time and less cost in other reconstruction programs where many agencies and NGOs are getting engaged in reconstruction developmental work after a high-impact disaster.

10.8 Conclusion

The isolated impact approach predominantly dominates the social sector. There is always a need of fund to fulfill the reconstruction requirements in a large-scale disaster. To overcome such challenge or gap, one of the strategies is to optimize the output and outcomes from the utilization of fund. Though isolated impact approach has been delivering good results, a move into collective approach can increase further in the output and outcomes. Considering the limitation and challenges in getting resources, the need of the hour is to achieve more output and outcomes with the available resource.

A change in traditional thinking, pilot of the Collective Impact Framework, and development of the reusable system can further strengthen the acceptance of Collective Impact Framework.

References

Alexander O, Yves P (2009) Business model generation. Osterwalder Alexander and Pigneur Yves (Self-published), Amsterdam. ISBN 978-2-8399-0580-0

Burns LR, DeGraaff RA, Danzon PM, Kimberly JR, Kissick WL, Pauly MV (2002) The Wharton school study of the health care value chain. In: Burns LR (ed) The health care value chain: producers, purchasers, and providers. Wiley Jossey-Bass, San Francisco, pp 3–26. ISBN 978-0-7879-6021-6

Chia S, Zalzala A, Zalzala L, Karimi A (2013) Towards intelligent technologies for a self-sustainable, RFID-based, decentralized rural e-Health system. IEEE Technol Soc Mag 32(1): 36–43, IEEE, Spring 2013

Jack W, Suri T (2010) The Economics of M-PESA. http://www.mit.edu/~tavneet/M-PESA.pdf

Kania J, Kramer M (2011) Collective Impact. Stanford Soc Innov Rev. http://www.ssireview.org/articles/entry/collective_impact

Le Masurier J, Rotimi JOB, Wilkinson S (2006) A comparison between routine construction and post-disaster reconstruction with case studies from New Zealand. In: Boyd D (ed) Proceedings of 22nd annual ARCOM conference, 4–6 September 2006, Birmingham, UK, Association of Researchers in Construction Management, pp 523–530

McGuinness E (2011) Can health micro-insurance protect the poor. Microfinance Opportunities, Washington, DC

Peters DH, Garg A, Bloom G, Walker DG, Brieger WR, Rahman MH (2008) Poverty and access to health care in developing countries. Ann N Y Acad Sci 1136:161–171

Sinead B, Helen S, Lesley G (2008) Small-scale evaluation in health: a practical guide. SAGE, Los Angeles. ISBN 978-1-4129-3006-2

Part III
Humanitarian Logistics Modelling

Humanitarian logistics modelling includes integrative, analytical, conceptual, inter or multi-disciplinary approaches and methods of dealing with the logistics, transport and supply chain management and emergency, crisis and disaster preparedness, response and management. The models and approaches form the backbone for the decision support systems in logistics operations. The first paper in this section discusses the developing of a comprehensive model to find the optimal location of suppliers and to assist planners during the design of the logistics efforts for humanitarian relief that mitigates and reduces the risk of a disruption in the humanitarian aid. Part of modelling is to model human elements of the supply chain. The second paper uses theory of constraints to model the human elements, namely, donors and frontline staff involved in delivering humanitarian aid for efficient relief operations. The third paper discusses business modelling for the sustainability of a successful humanitarian effort of an existing rural healthcare system deployed in an Ahmedabad slum community. Modelling of supplies is also important for efficient relief operations. The transportation of supplies and relief personnel must be done quickly and efficiently to maximise the survival rate of the affected population and minimise the cost of such operations. The fourth paper discusses the modelling of supplies using p-median approach by developing a mathematical model that describes the integrated supply chain operations in response to disasters. One of the problems during disaster relief operations is to select the right suppliers who would be able to supply right relief items immediately. The fifth paper in this section presents a hybrid algorithm for multi-period demand allocation in humanitarian supply chain. This hybrid algorithm prioritises the suppliers and then allocates the multi-period demand among the suppliers. This model is useful for maximising the total value of procurement taking into consideration multi-period demand condition, budget constraint, delivery lead-time and multi-period supplier capacity. Most studies lose focus of the recovery aspect of disaster management. Sustainability is the key as the number of disasters is on the rise. The sixth paper in this section discusses the modelling of reverse supply chain so that the direct benefits, such as reduction of cost, reclaiming value of used products, profits in secondary markets and indirect benefits such as gaining customer confidence, enhancing the green image of the organisation, compliance of regulations, etc., can be appropriated. The last paper in this section also discusses post-disaster humanitarian logistics structure and presents an analytical hierarchy process-based model. It evaluates the three such structures, namely, Agency Centric Efforts (ACEs), Partially Integrated Efforts (PIEs) and Collaborative Aid Networks (CANs) with respect to the important determinants for these structures.

Chapter 11
An Approach of Modeling for Humanitarian Supplies

Devendra Kumar Dewangan, Rajat Agrawal, and Vinay Sharma

11.1 Introduction

In today's scenario, disasters seem to be prominent in all corners of the globe; the importance of disaster management is undeniable. A large amount of human losses and unnecessary demolition of infrastructure can be avoided with more foresight and specific forecast. Disaster management or emergency management is the discipline of avoiding risks and dealing with risks. No country and no community are protected from the risk of disasters. Disaster management or emergency management is a discipline that involves preparing for disaster before it happens, responding to disasters instantaneously, as well as sustaining and rebuilding societies after the natural or human-made disasters have occurred because disaster management is a continuous process. It is necessary to have comprehensive emergency plans and estimate and improve the plans constantly. The related activities are usually classified as four phases of preparedness, response, recovery, and mitigation. Appropriate actions at each phase in the cycle lead to greater preparedness, better warnings, reduced susceptibility, or the prevention of disasters during the next iteration of the cycle. When an expanse is struck by a severe disaster, humanitarian supplies must be provided to victims/evacuees efficiently throughout the entire disaster periods. The delivery of emergency packages like food, water, sanitation supplies, medicine, medical equipment, etc. from suppliers to shelters must be done within certain time limits.

D.K. Dewangan (✉)
Research Scholar, Department of Management Studies, Indian Institute of Technology Roorkee, Roorkee, Uttarakhand, India
e-mail: devenddm@iitr.ernet.in; deva.iitr@gmail.com

R. Agrawal • V. Sharma
Assistant Professor, Department of Management Studies, Indian Institute of Technology Roorkee, Roorkee, Uttarakhand, India
e-mail: rajatfdm@iitr.ac.in; vinayfdm@iitr.ac.in

© Springer India 2016
B.S. Sahay et al. (eds.), *Managing Humanitarian Logistics*, Springer Proceedings in Business and Economics, DOI 10.1007/978-81-322-2416-7_11

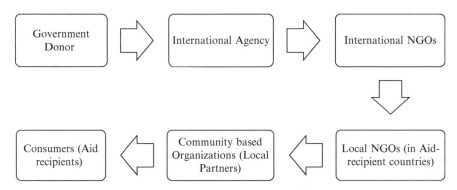

Fig. 11.1 A typical humanitarian supply chain (Source: Richard et al. 2006)

11.2 The Humanitarian Supply Chain

There is no solitary form of humanitarian supply chain, although a typical supply chain could follow the sequence in Fig. 11.1 which shows a typical humanitarian supply chain multilateral approach through international agencies and NGOs, although aid is often given on a mutual country-to-country basis and delivered in a number of ways. Unlike most business supply chains, the humanitarian aid supply chain is often unbalanced. The purpose of this paper is that we shall make certain assumptions about good practice in supply chain management.

11.3 Literature Review

In this section, the literature related to pre-positioning supplies and disaster planning in humanitarian supply chains is reviewed. We will also briefly converse several streams of research that are indirectly related to this problems.

11.3.1 Supply Chain Management and Humanitarian Aid

The parameters of supply chain management are a subject of some debate (e.g., Mentzer et al. 2001; Cooper et al. 1997; Croom et al. 2000), but for the purposes of this paper, we shall make certain assumptions about good practice in supply chain management. They are that there should be a planned approach, that a longer-term, strategic perspective is adopted, and that it is important to coordinate functions. If we attempt to apply such concepts from the "business model" to the humanitarian aid supply chain, we find many parallels but also important differences.

11.3.2 Disaster Planning

As expected, most of the educational research on disaster management and emergency preparedness can be found outside the logistics and supply chain ground. Much of the research in the disaster management field is targeted to public servants, government agencies, and insurance firms charged with responding in times of crisis and has traditionally focused on crises such as hurricanes, earthquakes, flooding, and fires (e.g., Iakovou and Douligeris 2001;Witt 1997; Warwick 1995; McHugh 1995). Several researches in the disaster literature offer models, guidelines, and planning actions for the development of effectual disaster plans. A representative, but not complete, review of relevant research in this area for logistics managers includes a study by Joseph and Couturier (1993) where seven management activities are proposed as necessary to support effective disaster planning. These activities included arranging in advance with outside organizations necessary agreements and developing contingency plans for each part of the disaster process. In a survey of local and city governments, Kartez and Lindell (1987) found a positive relationship between the amount of disaster preparedness meetings by city officials and the adoption of sound disaster practices. Dalhammer and D'Souza (1997) identified the keystones of disaster preparedness for businesses. And finally, several recent efforts have looked at the interactions between disasters and disaster response groups (e.g., Harrald et al. 2002; Webb et al. 2000).

11.3.3 Objective Functions Under Disaster Relief Operations

The main objective functions during disaster relief operation are to:

11.3.3.1 Minimize Total Response Time

The main objective is to minimize the total arrival time or total transportation time of delivering humanitarian supplies to all beneficiaries. In the total response time, the location-routing problems play a crucial role during disaster relief operation. Since there is a tremendous type of literature on facility location problems, we only focus on facility location or location-routing problems directly pertinent to the humanitarian operations after disasters, i.e., the facility location problems with crowded facilities.

Such models are commonly used in placing ambulances, fire stations, and other emergency services like medical aids, foods, clothes, etc. They attempt to assure adequate service either by requiring superfluous coverage or by explicitly considering the queuing aspect of the problem.

11.3.3.2 Minimize Latest Arrival

The objective minimizes the latest arrival of goods to a group of beneficiaries.

11.3.3.3 Maximize Travel Reliability

The main objective is to maximize the reliability of vehicles, such as the probability of vehicles arriving to their proposed destinations.

11.3.3.4 Minimize Cost

The main objective is to minimize costs, which may be travel or inventory costs or a combination. If the location routing is more effective and efficient, then the movement of goods from origin to disaster areas (destination) is more convenient. So, by this we can minimize the total cost in terms of fuel consumptions, vehicle maintenance cost, salary of driver and other staff based on hourly basis.

11.3.3.5 Goods

- Stochastic supply: the quantity of goods available for distribution is uncertain.
- Stochastic demand: the amount of need at final destinations is uncertain.
- Multi-commodity: multiple types of goods are transported, each having different quantities of demand and weight or volume taken up on vehicles.

11.3.3.6 Routing

- Multiple depots: vehicle routes begin and end at one of many designed depots.
- Single depot: vehicle routes begin and end at a single depot.
- No depot: vehicles do not have specific routes beginning and ending at depots.
- Heterogeneous vehicles: vehicles can differ in transportation capacity, speed, fuel consumption, or roads and beneficiaries that are accessible to them.
- Stochastic travel time: vehicle travel time can be uncertain.

11.3.4 Reliable Transportation During Disaster

11.3.4.1 Relief Operations

Planning for humanitarian supplies and response operations have largely been the concern of emergency management agencies. Under the disaster situation, deficiency in the flow of supplies may have direct consequences. As per the recent research, the humanitarian relief and development have put great prominence on issues providing a more reliable, efficient logistic and information infrastructure that are best addressed through increased interagency collaboration. A recent research is focused on the preparation and planning of disaster evacuation and mitigation, and little attention has been put on humanitarian response problem during and after disasters. Humanitarian response is the process in which the relief aids are delivered by agencies according to preset humanitarian principles. These agencies consist of government agencies as well as local and international non-government organizations. Humanitarian supplies can be categorized to urgent/immediate distribution, low priority distribution, and non-priority items. For each supply priority and each agency, corresponding response strategies is needed.

11.3.4.2 Location-Routing Problems

This category explores the dynamics of environmental facility location with respect to cost and service. It uses facility location models to identify optimal locations for stocks. The reader is referred to the surveys by Daskin et al. (1988) and Berman and Krass (2002) for thorough discussions of these models. A related branch of literature considers models in which the facilities may be unable to provide service due to facility disruptions (see Snyder 2006; Daskin et al. 2002; Snyder and Daskin 2006). The pre-positioning problem in humanitarian supply chains and disaster relief under facility location approach has been addressed by Akkihal (2006). His work focuses on identifying locations that optimize worldwide humanitarian operations. Additional literature related to the problem includes the work in harmful transportation.

11.3.4.3 Location-Routing Model

The traditional facility location problem considers that the deliveries are direct and independent. According to Daskin (1995) or Mirchandani and Francis (1990) under the assumption that the delivery is done under full-truck load (FTL) which means that the truck is filled with supplies for just one customer. However, there are situations in which clients are visited along a specific route. Moreover, most of the deliveries are done under less-than-truck load (LTL) where the truck contains supplies for different clients who are visited through a route.

In this paper, our focus is on situations where the routing problem has to be solved together with the facility location problem trying to minimize the total cost by selecting a set of facilities and constructing delivery routes with constraints such as:

- Customer demands.
- Vehicle and facility capacities.

- Number of vehicles.
- Route lengths or route durations (specified time limit).
- Tour constraint: each vehicle has to start and end at the same facility.

The incapacitated LRP version of the problem, in which there is no facility and vehicle constraints, was defined by Berger et al. (2007) as follows:

Let S be a set of client locations and L be the set of candidate facility locations. We can define a graph $G = (N, E)$ where $N = S \cup L$ or $L \subseteq S$ the set of nodes and $E = N \times N$ is the set of edges. We can also define, r as a feasible route that starts at facility i visits a subgroup of nodes and returns to facility i and F_r the set of feasible routes for facility, i. With this notation (and the notation defined previously), Perl (1983) formulates the following integrated location routing problem:

The Integer Programming formulation of the problem is

Minimize

$$\sum_{i \in L} f_i x_i + \sum_{i \in L} \sum_{r \in F_r} c_r y_{ir}$$

Subject to:

$$\sum_i \sum_r a_{vir} y_{ir} = 1, \quad \forall v \tag{11.1}$$

$$X_i \geq Y_{ir}, \quad \forall i, \forall r \tag{11.2}$$

$$x_i, y_{ir} = \{0, 1\}$$

Where:

F_i = cost of fixed facility i.
c_{ir} = cost of route r associated with facility i.
$x_i = 1$ if facility i is selected, 0 otherwise.
$y_{ir} = 1$ if route r associated with facility i is selected, 0 otherwise.
$a_{vir} = 1$ if route r associated with facility i visits client v, 0 otherwise.

This objective function minimizes both the fixed costs and the routing costs whenever each client is served by one facility (Constraint 11.1) and assuring that only routes of selected facilities are selected (Constraint 11.2). As mentioned in Sect. 11.2, Berger et al. (2007) solved this problem with a branch and price algorithm which uses Desrosiers et al. (1984) column generation approach.

11.3.4.4 Integrated Location-Routing Models

In the integer programming formulation model, we can consider two types of cost, i.e., fixed cost and routing cost. Here, we consider integrated location-routing problems combine three components of supply chain design:

- Facility location
- Customer allocation to facilities
- Vehicle routing

There are different locations/routing problems that have been described in the literature, and they tend to be very complicated to solve since they merge two NP hard problems:

- Facility location
- Vehicle routing

It has been observed that many of the authors and researchers have worked on location-routing problems. Laporte et al. (1988) summarized the various types of formulations, solution algorithms, and computational results of work published prior to 1988. In general, three-layer problems include flows from plants to distribution centers to customers, whereas two-layer problems focus on flows from distribution centers to customers.

An example of a three-layer location-routing problem is the formulation of Perl (1983) and Perl and Daskin (1985); their model extends the model of Geoffrion and Graves to include multiple stop tours serving the customer nodes, but it is limited to a single commodity. We define the following additional notations:

Notations

P_s = set of points = I $\cup$ J.
N_d = distance between node i$\in P_s$ and j$\in P_s$.
Vc_j = variable cost per unit processed by a facility at candidate facility site j$\in$J.
T_j = maximum throughput for a facility at candidate facility site j$\in$J.
S = set of supply points (analogous to plants in the Geoffrion and Graves model), indexed by s.
Cs_j = unit cost of shipping from supply point s$\in$S to candidate facility site j$\in$J.
V = set of candidate vehicles, indexed by v.
σ_v = capacity of vehicle v$\in$V.
τ_v = maximum allowable length of a route served by vehicle v$\in$V.
α_v = cost per unit distance for delivery on route v$\in$V.

Decision variables

$$Z_{ijv} = \left\{ 1, \text{ if vehicle } v \in V \text{ goes directly from} \atop \text{point j} \in P_s. \atop 0, \text{ if not} \right\}$$

Q_{sj} = quantity shipped from supply source s $\in$ S to facility site j $\in$ J.

With this notation we incorporate all the following: facility location, customer allocation to facilities, and vehicle routing.

Minimize

$$\sum_{j\in J} f_j X_j + \sum_{s\in S}\left[\sum_{j\in J} C_{sj}\cdot Q_{sj}\right] + \sum_{j\in J} V_{cj}\cdot\left[\sum_{i\in I} h_i\cdot Y_{ij}\right] + \sum_{v\in V}\sigma_v\cdot\left[\sum_{j\in P_s}\sum_{i\in P_s} N_d Z_{ijv}\right]$$

(11.3)

$$\sum_{i\in I} h_i\cdot\left[\sum_{j\in P_s} Z_{ijv}\right] \le \sigma_v, \quad \forall v\in V$$

Subjected to:

$$\sum_{v\in V}\sum_{j\in P_s} Z_{ijv} = 1, \quad \forall i\in I \tag{11.4}$$

$$\sum_{i\in I} h_i\cdot\left[\sum_{j\in P_s} Z_{ijv}\right] \le \sigma_v, \quad \forall v\in V \tag{11.5}$$

$$\sum_{j\in P_s}\sum_{i\in P_s} N_d Z_{ijv} \le \tau_v, \quad \forall v\in V \tag{11.6}$$

$$\sum_{j\in P_s} Z_{ijv} - \sum_{j\in P_s} Z_{ijv} = 0 \quad \forall i\in P_s; \forall v\in V \tag{11.7}$$

$$\sum_{j\in J}\sum_{i\in I} Z_{ijv} \le 1 \quad \forall v\in V \tag{11.8}$$

$$\sum_{s\in S} Q_{sj} - \sum_{i\in I} h_i\cdot Y_{ij} = 0 \quad \forall j\in J \tag{11.9}$$

$$\sum_{m\in P_s} Z_{imr} + \sum_{h\in P_s} Z_{jhv} - Y_{ij} \le 1, \quad \forall j\in J; \forall i\in I; \forall v\in V \tag{11.10}$$

$$X_{j\in\{0,1\}}, \quad \forall j\in J \tag{11.11}$$

$$Y_{ij\in\{0,1\}}, \quad \forall i\in I; \forall j\in J \tag{11.12}$$

$$Z_{ijv\in\{0,1\}}, \quad \forall i\in P_s; \forall j\in P_s; \forall v\in V \tag{11.13}$$

$$Q_{sj} \ge 0, \quad \forall s\in S; \forall j\in J \tag{11.14}$$

Here, the objective function (11.3) minimizes the sum of the fixed facility location costs, the shipment costs from the origin points (plants) to the facilities, and the variable facility throughput costs and the routing costs to the customers. Constraint (11.4) requires each customer to be on exactly one route. Constraint (11.5) imposes a capacity restriction for each vehicle, whereas constraint (11.6) limits the length of each route. Constraint (11.7) states that enter and exit route node is same. Constraint (11.8) states that a route can operate out of only one facility. Constraint (11.9) implies the flow into a facility from the origin points in terms of the total order or demand that is served by the facility. Constraint (11.10) shows that if route k∈K leaves customer node i∈I and also leaves facility j∈J, then customer i∈I must be assigned to facility j∈J. This constraint associates the vehicle routing variables (Z_{ijv}) and the assignment variables (Y_{ij}). Constraints (11.11, 11.12, 11.13, and 11.14) are standard integrality and nonnegativity constraints.

So, integrated location-routing models are more effective and efficient as compared to integer programming formulation model because in integrated location-routing (ILR) models, we consider more constraints as compared to ILR. Hence, integrated location-routing models are more appropriate, accurate, and most reliable paths in solving the location-routing problems.

11.3.4.5 Location Choosing for Pre-position Inventory

All the assumtions are summarized below which are used in formulating model:

1. All demand points are candidates to pre-position supplies.
2. All demand points have to be covered by at least one facility.
3. All services of the network can fail.
4. We do not account for the capacity of the pre-positioning facility or the distribution vehicles.
5. We assume that all facilities are disruptions.

With the following assumptions, our main goal is to choose the locations to pre-position inventory under a possible disaster operation such that the probability of the inventory to reach all the demand or destination points is maximized.

We use the same notation as the location-routing problem; our proposed formulation under these assumptions is

Minimization

$$-\sum_{i\in L}\sum_{r\in F_r}R_{ir}y_{ir}(1 - p_i)$$

Subject to

$$\sum_{i}\sum_{r}a_{vir}y_{ir} = 1, \quad \forall v \tag{11.15}$$

$$X_i \geq y_{ir}, \quad \forall i; \forall r \tag{11.16}$$

$$\sum_{i\in L}f_ix_i \leq B \quad \forall i \tag{11.17}$$

$$x_i, y_{ir} = \{0, 1\}$$

Constraints (11.3) and (11.4) are similar to Berger's formulation and show that each customer (affected zone or demand point) v is served by one facility (in this situation by a pre-position location) and that only routes from preferred facilities are used. Finally, constraint (11.5) is the budget constraint where B is the maximum budget (supply point) available for opening the facilities to preposition the supplies.

11.4 Conclusions

In this paper, we focused on a methodology that incorporates the idea of the most trustworthy path in a facility location problem or location-routing problems which is used for solving the inventory pre-positioning problem for humanitarian supply chains. This model arose from the realization that the network can be susceptible to disruptions and the selection of locations to pre-position inventories must fundamentally account for these disruptions. Hence, it is important that the location-routing problems and facilities chosen for inventory pre-positioning must be reliable and also assure the highest approachability to the remaining affected zones.

We formulate the model combining the solution of the most reliable paths in an IP formulation based on the location-routing problem (LRP). Hence, using only the most reliable paths in solving the IP, we device a technique to select the routes with the lowest probability of collapse.

References

Akkihal AR (2006) Pre-positioning for humanitarian operations. MS thesis, Massachusetts Institute of Technology

Berger RT, Coullard CR, Daskin MS (2007) Location-routing problems with distance constraints. Transp Sci 41(1):29–43

Berman O, Krass D (2002) Chapter 11: Facility location problems with stochastic demands and congestion. In: Facility location: applications and theory. Springer, Berlin, p 329

Cooper MC, Lambert DM, Pagh JD (1997) Supply chain management: more than a new name for logistics. Int J Log Manage 8(1):1–14

Croom S, Romano P, Giannakis M (2000) Supply chain management: an analytical framework for critical literature review. Eur J Purch Supply Manage 6(1):67–83

Dahlhamer J, D'Souza M (1997) Determinants of business disaster preparedness. Int J Mass Emerg Disasters 15(2):265–268

Daskin MS (1995) Network and discrete location: models, algorithms, and applications. Wiley Interscience, New York

Daskin MS, Coullard CR, Shen ZJM (2002) An inventory-location model: formulation, solution algorithm and computational results. Ann Oper Res 110(1–4):83–106

Daskin MS, Hogan K, ReVelle C (1988) Integration of multiple, excess, backup, and expected covering models. Environ Plann B 15(1):15–35

Desrosiers J, Soumis F, Desrochers M (1984) Routing with time windows by column generation. Networks 14(4):545–565

Geoffrion AM, Graves GW (1974) Multicommodity distribution system design by benders decomposition. Manage Sci 20(5):822–844

Harrald JR, Barbera J, Renda-Tanali I, Coppola D, Shaw GL (2002) Observing and documenting the Iinter-organizational response to the September 11th Attack on the Pentagon, NSF Report. National Science Foundation, Arlington

Iakovou E, Douligeris C (2001) An information management system for the emergency management of hurricane disasters. Int J Risk Assess Manage 2(3–4):243–262

Joseph GW, Couturier GW (1993) Essential management activities to support effective disaster planning. Int J Inform Manage 13(5):315–325

Kartez J, Lindell MK (1987) Planning for uncertainty. Am Plan Assoc J 53:487–498

Laporte G, Nobert Y, Taillefer S (1988) Solving a family of multi-depot vehicle routing and location-routing problems. Transport Sci 22:161–172

McHugh CP (1995) Preparing public safety organizations for disaster response: a study of Tucson, Arizona's response to flooding. Disaster Prev Manage 4(5):25–36

Mentzer JT, DeWitt W, Keebler JS, Min S, Nix NW, Smith CD, Zacharia ZG (2001) Defining supply chain management. J Bus Log 22(2):1–25

Mirchandani PB, Francis RL (1990) Discrete location theory. Wiley, New York

Oloruntoba R, Gray R (2006) Humanitarian aid: an agile supply chain? Supply Chain Manage 11(2):115–120

Perl J, (1983) A unified warehouse location-routing analysis. Ph.D. Dissertation, Department of Civil Engineering, Northwestern University, Evanston

Perl J, Daskin MS (1985) A warehouse location-routing problem. Trans Res Part B Methodol 19(5):381–396

Snyder LV (2006) Facility location under uncertainty: a review. IIE Trans 38(7):547–564

Snyder LV, Daskin MS (2006) Stochastic p-robust location problems. IIE Trans 38(11):971–985

Warwick M (1995) Painful lessons in crisis mismanagement. Commun Int 22(2):4–5

Webb G, Tierney K, Dahlhamer J (2000) Businesses and disasters: empirical patterns and unanswered questions. Natural Hazards Rev 1(1):83–90

Witt JL (1997) National mitigation strategy: partnerships for building safer communities. Diane Publishing, Washington

Chapter 12
Reinforcing the Human Elements in Downstream Supply Chain in TOC Way

Kuldeep Malik and Sheelan Mishra

12.1 Introduction

The concept of "flow" always remains important in a typical supply chain. The flow determines the success of a supply chain, which requires efficient and effective movement of goods and services across a supply chain. The flow also ensures that the right products are made available in the right place, at the right time (Brown et al. 2005).

Commercial supply chains and the humanitarian supply chains have a common problem – frequent stockouts and excess stock situations. This issue results in reduction in business volume for a commercial supply chain and, however, the same in humanitarian supply chains as well, which results in failures of relief operations.

Generally, commercial supply chains have been keen to undertake various initiatives to improve supply chain responsiveness by improving processes, networks, and the integration (van Hoek 2001). However, humanitarian supply chains have paid less attention to undertake various initiatives to improve their supply chains.

K. Malik (✉)
Department of Commerce & Management, Jain University, Bangalore, Karnataka, India
e-mail: kuldeepmalik2007@rediffmail.com

S. Mishra
Department of Management Studies, Center for Innovation and Entrepreneurship,
New Horizon College of Engineering, Bangalore, Karnataka, India

© Springer India 2016
B.S. Sahay et al. (eds.), *Managing Humanitarian Logistics*, Springer Proceedings in Business and Economics, DOI 10.1007/978-81-322-2416-7_12

12.2 Conceptual Framework

Theory of constraints (TOC) is a major change initiative, which has helped several commercial supply chains to achieve significant improvements in supply chain. Humanitarian supply chain involves high interactions and interdependencies among supply chain members, processes, and resources, and TOC is well suited in such cases (Min and Zhou 2002). TOC can be applied in humanitarian supply chains to achieve higher ROI of humanitarian aid initiatives.

12.3 Theory of Constraints (TOC)

Managing the TOC way is synonymous with handling four key questions about change: what to change, what to change to, how to cause the change, and how to establish continuous improvement (Fedurko 2013).

12.4 Research Objective

The objective of this study is to describe how TOC concepts, which are a popular mechanism to improve commercial supply chain performance, can be applied in humanitarian supply chain management.

12.5 Literature Review

12.5.1 What to Change?

Many firms undertake various supply chain initiates to improve flow in supply chain; however, most of them fail to achieve the desired results. The main issue faced by the commercial as well as the humanitarian supply chains is the uncertainty of future demand. Consequently, demand forecasts do often fail, resulting in mismatch of inventory in the upstream and the downstream supply chain. The level of inventory typically held at the upstream supply chain is often quite different from what is demanded at the downstream side (Poirier and Reiter 1996). Keeping temporary buffers also does not help much as beyond a certain limit; additional buffers fail to take care of forecast errors and major spikes in demand. As a result, frequent stockouts and excess stock situations become common problems. The supply chain managers and sales and operations staff react badly in such a scenario. The decision makers in organizations try to correct the situation by revamping the process and procedures and/or exert performance pressure on sales force, operations personnel, and upstream and downstream supply chain members. But the results often remain the same despite the steps taken up by firms such as declaring performance-linked variable remuneration (PLVR) to encourage sales force to exert higher level of selling efforts. Though many firms also consider opinion of sales force in planning for future need of inventory. But, in the event of forecasts failures, sales force is often under increased pressure to exert extra efforts by achieving higher sales quota in the subsequent months.

Quality and performance usually suffer in time-pressured environments. People or groups of people usually underperform under time pressure. It has been often mentioned in the decision-making literature that time pressure decreases the accuracy of human judgment and performance (Hwang 1994; Svenson and Maule 1993).

Time pressure has damaging impact on relational exchange primarily due to the response and effect it may invoke. Social exchange theory, which was introduced in the 1960s by George Homans, also supports the argument that firms try to achieve desirable results in social interactions by maximizing rewards and minimizing costs (McDonald 1981; Thibaut and Kelley 1959), and the norm of reciprocity believes that actors in exchange relationships will reciprocate the actions of others and respond to each other in similar fashions (Gouldner 1960). Time pressure may lead to substandard work, acceptance of inappropriate audit evidence, premature sign-off, and reduced audit quality (Kelley and Margheim 1990). In totality, time pressure can reduce performance results.

It can be safely assumed that an improper inventory practice in supply chain management has greater chances of stockouts and surpluses, which often manifests in the form of time pressure, underperformance of sales force in case of commercial supply chains, and frontline operations personnel in humanitarian supply chains. In the context of humanitarian supply chain management, it must be ensured that working conditions for staff (frontline operations personnel) across the supply chain are safe, that supply chain members are treated with utmost respect and dignity, and that operations are in full compliance with the laws, rules, and regulations of the countries of relief operations. However, the poor performance of supply chain let the pressure be on sales force/frontline operations personnel, which in itself is not humanitarian.

Another issue that plagues a traditional inventory management model (in both the cases of commercial as well as humanitarian supply chains) is the excessive focus on getting results based on available inventory in downstream supply chain at a given point of time. This situation often ignores measuring the extent of stockouts at item levels, and hence, it becomes difficult to quantify the unmet demand or loss of sale due to stockouts in a given period (Dai and Jerath 2002).

Higher level of inventory in the system leads to increase in total investment and reduction in return on investment (ROI). In order to liquidate excess stock, commercial supply chains often roll out a higher-powered incentive scheme for sales force. Interestingly, increasing demand uncertainty leads to a higher-powered contract for the salesperson (Dai and Jerath 2002). In other words, as the cost of inventory increases due to surpluses, the firm may pay the sales force a larger reward for liquidating a higher level of inventory, which eventually puts tremendous pressure environments on sales force.

12.5.2 What to Change to?

The humanitarian supply chain needs to be highly efficient because inability to achieve efficiency for them means inability to save many lives as well as wasting of scarce resources of donors collected by humanitarian organizations (Oloruntoba and Grey 2006). It is being observed that performance pressure on various stakeholders involving humanitarian supply chains may increase in the future (Roh et al. 2008; Perry 2007). Going forward, the disasters resulting from "act of God" and "act of men" would require increased flow of goods and services across extended supply chain suppliers' suppliers, suppliers, upstream supply chain members, downstream supply chain members, customers, and customers' customers (Power et al. 2001). The only way out is to have an agile supply chain and to develop operational capabilities to set up distribution networks in quick time.

12.5.3 How to Cause the Change?

The inability of humanitarian firms/NGO to accurately estimate future demand (Long and Wood 1995), the uncertainty of the timing and place of occurrence of a disaster and substandard infrastructure in underdeveloped regions, and joint operations of humanitarian supply chain personnel with defense forces make delivering results very difficult (Van Wassenhove 2006).

Implementing theory of constraints (ToC) mechanism of dynamic buffer management (DBM) makes it easy to find out what level of inventory is to be replenished by upstream supply chain link to the downstream supply chain links in humanitarian supply chain. The buffer size, which is a single number, is divided in three colors. The top third is called the green zone, the middle third is called the yellow zone, and the bottom third is called the red zone.

The proposed TOC way of managing humanitarian supply chain begins with computation of a "norm" or target level of inventory to be maintained based on maximum anticipated consumption in replenishment time factored for variability of the replenishment time. The supply of humanitarian items from parent location to a child location is made as per consumption at child location. The mechanism of ordering daily and replenishing frequently (ODRF) is followed to reduce order lead time and to provide near-real-time visibility to all stakeholders into the stock situation, which fulfill the need of knowing how much inventory must be supplied by parent location to child location. DBM system monitors replenishment cycle and adjustments by following the following rules:

(i) Too much penetration in the green zone: If an item is in the green zone on three consecutive replenishment cycles, it is suggested to reduce the buffer size by one-third.
(ii) Too much penetration in the red zone: If an item is in the red zone on two consecutive replenishment cycles, it is suggested to increase the buffer size by one-third.

DBM lets each supply chain members (including frontline staff) to have a proper visibility of items that are unavailable, items in transit, and level of buffer penetration in the three zones which indirectly supports the views of Hoek (2001) which states that in order to achieve market sensitivity, an organization, its suppliers, and its customers must share information and knowledge across common systems.

The norm provides a "lock" to prevent oversupplies, thus eliminating the possibility of surplus inventory. The three-color mechanism (GYR) provides a robust prioritization mechanism for ensuring timely supplies to maintain high availability by reacting to actual stock situation, thus eliminating shortages. This allows the supply chain to channel inventory to locations where it is required most while deferring supplies to locations where it may not be required urgently; thus, using aggregation, the supply chain can operate at low levels of inventory. The dynamic buffer management (DBM) mechanism of TOC protects the system against variability in demand. The application of DBM to handle variability in demand in humanitarian supply chain can serve the purpose of establishing robust standards to achieve economic efficiency in humanitarian supply chain management.

12.6 Research Methodology

This study involves a narrative literature review summarizing different primary studies from which conclusions have been drawn into a holistic interpretation contributed by the authors' professional expertise and experience, existing theories, and models. The study uses meta-ethnography as a research method to synthesize research findings and to generate an interpretative synthesis from a variety of sources.

12.7 Reinforcing the Human Elements in Downstream Supply Chain with TOC

TOC solutions help downstream supply chain members ensure higher availability at low level of inventory. Hence, downstream supply chain members begin to play the role of "sales ennoblers." Supply chain helps the salespeople of commercial supply chain and frontline operational staff of humanitarian supply chain to achieve a higher level of overall performance with reduced stress, which in turn establishes humanitarian elements by bringing in respect and dignity for salespeople and frontline operational staff of humanitarian supply chains. Subsequently, it becomes relatively easy for commercial supply chains to expand their market reach and range through partnership programs involving collaboration of downstream supply chain members. Now firms do not have to struggle in successful implementation of their partnership programs as humanitarian elements or the people issues get proper attention as stress or time pressure gets eliminated by having an agile supply chain (Dion et al. 1995).

Various studies reveal that the sales force is often dissatisfied with the performance of its downstream supply chain members. Quite often, sales force complain of the poor performance of supply chains by labeling their supply chain staff being as "sales disablers" (Reuben 2004). Nevertheless, complains of sales force increase significantly when instances of stockouts increase. It is mentioning that with a traditional forecast-based replenishment system, the downstream supply chain of a firm is bound to have stockouts of certain items and excess stock of others, which are primarily a by-product of forecast errors. The excess stocks often attract quantity purchase schemes (QPS) or turnover discount (TOD) schemes for a retailer, which creates "time pressure" on everyone involved including the sales force. In other words, certainly, the pressure becomes to achieve higher sales targets; necessitates that the excess stock is quickly sold or liquidated.

This pressure on sales force is damaging as it leads to many undesirable effects (UDEs), in the form of emotional disturbances and undesirable negative cognitive and affective responses. For instance, decision makers (in this case, sales force) may feel anxiety and lack of confidence, when put under time pressure. The poor performance, in turn, might encourage indirectly punitive actions on salespeople. For instance, forecast error leads to stockouts of certain items, when these items are in great need, which results in a salesperson failing to achieve his or her sales quota and a higher probability that a relatively higher sales quota would be required to be achieved in the subsequent months to cover the shortfall of the previous month. This pressure would create a loop of one undesirable effect leading to another undesirable effect and so on.

12.8   Conclusions

The humanitarian view in downstream supply chain and logistics, in this context, means that the downstream supply chain function must support salespeople in a way that the performance of sales force is maximized, which, in turn, would lead to salespeople getting the well-deserved respect and dignity (humanitarian approach). This would be possible only if there is a sound supply chain strategy to respond to the challenges of how to respond to high uncertainty in quantum, timing of demand, and location of demand. TOC helps in establishing humanitarian treatment to sales force as downstream supply chain can maintain high availability of the right products, at the right time and at the right location, thereby becoming "sales enablers."

12.9   Discussion

The task of creation of more responsive supply chain requires often exchange flows under time pressure (Thomas 2003). The TOC solution in humanitarian supply chain makes supply chain agile, and the time pressures are taken away from supply chain members, sales force (in commercial supply chains), and donors and frontline personnel (in humanitarian supply chains).

References

Brown JR, Dant RP, Ingene CA, Kaufmann PJ (2005) Supply chain management and the evolution of the "Big Middle". J Retail 81(2):97–105

Dai T, Jerath K (2002) Salesforce compensation with inventory considerations. Available at: http://ssrn.com/abstract=2193376. Accessed on 15 Aug 2013

Dion P, Easterling D, Miller S (1995) What is really necessary in successful buyer/seller relationships. Ind Mark Manage 24:1–9

Fedurko J (2013) TOC thinkers writing and thinking from TOC thinkers and experts in Goldratt's Theory of Constraints. Hosted by Clarke Ching. Available at: http://www.tocthinkers.com/jelena-fedurko/. Accessed on 15 Aug 2013

Gouldner AW (1960) The norm of reciprocity: a preliminary statement. Am Sociol Rev 25(2):161–178

Hwang MI (1994) Decision making under time pressure: a model for information systems research. Inf Manage 27:197–203

Kelley T, Margheim L (1990) The impact of time budget pressure, personality, and leadership variables on dysfunctional auditor behavior. Auditing 9(2):21–42

Long DC, Wood DF (1995) The logistics of famine relief. J Bus Log 16:213–229

McDonald GW (1981) Structural exchange and marital interaction. J Marriage Family 825–839

Min H, Zhou G (2002) Supply chain modeling: past, present and future. Comput Ind Eng 43:231–249

Oloruntoba R, Grey R (2006) Humanitarian aid: an agile supply chain? Supply Chain Management: An International Journal 11:115–120

Perry M (2007) Natural disaster management planning: a study of logistics managers responding to the tsunami. Int J Phys Distrib Log Manage 37:409–433

Poirier CC, Reiter SE (1996) Supply chain optimization. Business Book Review Library 13(4):1

Power D, Sohal A, Rahman S (2001) Critical success factors in agile supply chain management. Int J Phys Distrib Log 31:247–265

Roh S, Pettit SJ, Beresford AKC (2008) Humanitarian aid logistics: response depot Networks. Abstract proceedings of the NOFOMA conference, Helsinki

Slone RE (2004) Leading a supply chain turnaround. Harvard Business Review

Svenson O, John Maule A (1993) Time pressure and stress in human judgement and decision making. Plenum, New York

Thibaut J, Kelley H (1959) The social psychology of groups. Wiley, New York

Thomas AS (2003) Why logistics? Forced Migration Review 18:4

Thomas RW (2008) Exploring relational aspects of time-based competition. Int J Phys Distrib Log Manage 38(7):540–545

van Hoek R (2001) The rediscovery of postponement a literature review and directions for research. J Oper Manage 19(2):161–184

Van Wassenhove LN (2006) Blackett Memorial Lecture Humanitarian aid logistics: supply chain management in high gear. J Oper Res Soc 57:475–489

Chapter 13
Business Modeling for the Sustainability of Humanitarian Projects

Darshan Suresh Rathi and Ali M.S. Zalzala

13.1 Background

An RFID Individual Tracking and Records Management Solution (RFID-ITRM) has already been implemented in 2011 in the slums of Ahmedabad, India, at a very low cost and is proving to be very effective among the poor people (Chia et al. 2013).

The system has highly scalable properties and may create a great impact on the communities if used at large scale. However, larger-scale deployment and everlasting impact on the community need the solution to be self-sustainable on the long run. The initial costs of the project may be borne by public or private donations, but running over a longer period a sustainable business model is needed.

13.2 Field Location

Ramapir No Tekro, also known as the Tekro, is the largest slum area in Ahmedabad, located across the street from the Gandhi Ashram, and managed by the NGO Manav Sadhna. Home to approximately 150,000 residents, the slum consists mainly of people falling under the classification of *scheduled caste* who are originally from villages around Gujarat or potter families from Rajasthan. The entire development is considered an encroachment because the land is owned by the

D.S. Rathi
Finance and Banking, Institute of Management Technology, Ghaziabad, Uttar Pradesh, India

A.M.S. Zalzala (✉)
Institute of Management Technology, UAE
e-mail: zalzala@communitytracks.org

© Springer India 2016   173
B.S. Sahay et al. (eds.), *Managing Humanitarian Logistics*, Springer Proceedings
in Business and Economics, DOI 10.1007/978-81-322-2416-7_13

government and is therefore temporary, although people have been living in the Tekro for over 50 years. Today, through government attention, most of this slum area has electricity, water, sidewalks, and a gutter system. However, due to problems with addiction, health issues, superstitions, high-interest loans, and illiteracy, many slum dwellers continue to live in the same cycle of despair and poverty. They earn their incomes by driving rickshaws, rag picking, cleaning homes, shining shoes, and working as potters or day laborers.

After analysis during the initial stages of administering the education project with the community members, Manav Sadhna came to know about a need for quality and cost-effective healthcare facilities for the members. And thus, with the help of the local community, a medical clinic was set up in certain parts of a local temple near the community center.

13.3   The Business Model

A business model describes the rationale of how an organization creates, delivers, and captures value. It is composed of nine different building blocks which describe the way value is created along the different processes of a system: customer segments, value propositions, channels, customer relationships, revenue streams, key activities, key resources, key partnerships, and cost structure (Figs. 13.1, 13.2, and 13.3).

13.3.1   Customer Segments

Different customer groups can be segmented depending on the severity of their illness: the greater the severity of the illness, the more follow-up costs and additional care are required for that customer. Different patients are broadly categorized into five customer segments.

Normal Illness (clinic): People having normal illness may visit the clinic directly. They may directly get treated and would at the most visit twice or thrice. They would not have any association with the community health care worker (Raman) unless they show symptoms of some major illness and have to be referred to some hospital for further treatment. This is the most profitable segment in monetary terms, and if proper diagnosis and treatment is done at this segment, it prevents patients in this segment from entering the other segment (however, there is a 10 % probability of patients in this segment entering the other two segments). The monthly average of patients with normal illness is around 250 (source: clinic helper).

Severe Illness: People who are diagnosed with certain noncommunicable chronic diseases like malaria, diarrhea, jaundice, etc. These diseases require adhering to the treatment schedule strictly and hence also need regular follow-up by the

Fig. 13.1 An alley in the Tekro

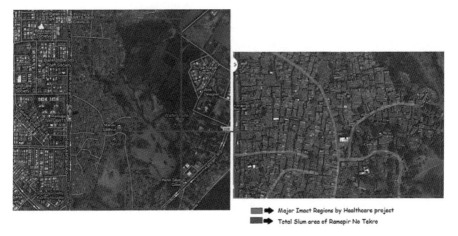

Major Imact Regions by Healthcare project
Total Slum area of Ramapir No Tekro

Fig. 13.2 Google map of the Tekro showing the current impact area of the healthcare solution

community health care worker. People usually don't complete the entire course of their medication; once they feel better by taking initial treatment, they stop taking medicines and necessary precautions. Thus, regular follow-up over the entire

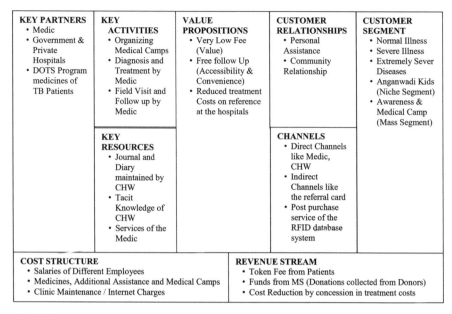

KEY PARTNERS	KEY ACTIVITIES	VALUE PROPOSITIONS	CUSTOMER RELATIONSHIPS	CUSTOMER SEGMENT
• Medic • Government & Private Hospitals • DOTS Program medicines of TB Patients	• Organizing Medical Camps • Diagnosis and Treatment by Medic • Field Visit and Follow up by Medic	• Very Low Fee (Value) • Free follow Up (Accessibility & Convenience) • Reduced treatment Costs on reference at the hospitals	• Personal Assistance • Community Relationship	• Normal Illness • Severe Illness • Extremely Sever Diseases • Anganwadi Kids (Niche Segment) • Awareness & Medical Camp (Mass Segment)
	KEY RESOURCES • Journal and Diary maintained by CHW • Tacit Knowledge of CHW • Services of the Medic		CHANNELS • Direct Channels like Medic, CHW • Indirect Channels like the referral card • Post purchase service of the RFID database system	
COST STRUCTURE • Salaries of Different Employees • Medicines, Additional Assistance and Medical Camps • Clinic Maintenance / Internet Charges			REVENUE STREAM • Token Fee from Patients • Funds from MS (Donations collected from Donors) • Cost Reduction by concession in treatment costs	

Fig. 13.3 A business model for the healthcare solution

treatment period is required by the community health care worker. Also such patients may need additional help with regard to some tests which need to be conducted like blood sample, urine tests, etc. which are needed to further diagnose the disease. Such patients need to be referred to external nursing homes and pathology labs, either government owned or privately funded. Hence, a direct referral system is being executed for the same. These patients need to carry a referral letter from the community health care worker or the doctor at the clinic, and most of the time, their treatment at the external institute is done free of cost. Treatment cycle lasts for around 3 weeks. The average number of patients covered under this segment by the community health care worker are as follows:

- Direct referral: 25 per month
- Follow-up: 15 per month
- Number of patients who don't adhere to their medication cycle: 5 per month
- Patients who usually enter the extremely severe disease segment as they don't follow their medication regime: 2 per month (Fig. 13.4)

Extremely Severe Diseases: Patients who are diagnosed with extremely severe chronic diseases like cancer, HIV, tuberculosis, etc. who need extreme care and regular follow-up by the community health care worker for their treatment. Such patients usually don't continue their treatment after specific period; hence, regular follow-up by the community health care worker is required. They also need to visit the hospital for treatment on a regular basis, the community health care worker usually accompanies them on their visits and helps them with their queries if any

Fig. 13.4   Patients queuing in the clinic

regarding the treatment; if the treatment costs are too high and the patients can't afford it, he tries to convince the authorities over there to give some concession and thus tries to reduce the treatment costs. In certain cases, if the need arises, Manav Sadhna arranges for the funds from its account. Number of patients in this segment covered by the community health care worker are as follows:

- Patients who need regular follow-up: 15 per month
- Number of visits to the hospital by the community health care worker: 24 per month
- Patients who need special concession for their treatment expenses: 30 per annum
- Number of patients for whom funds are arranged by Manav Sadhna: amount more than Rs. 10,000, 2 per year, and amount less than Rs. 10,000, 12 per year

Anganwadi Kids (Niche Segment): The community health care worker also visits the various Anganwadis on a monthly basis and checks for malnourished kids and follows up with their parents to find out the cause for the same. He also advises the parents on different aspects in which they can provide nourishment to their kids and what the ill effects of malnourishment are and how it affects the health of the child. He advises them on the different cost-effective ways in which they can provide healthy foodstuff to their kids.

- Number of Anganwadis covered under this scheme: 6 per week, 25 per month
- Number of kids who are malnourished and need follow-up with their parents: 10 per month
- Number of kids in these 25 Anganwadis: 750

13.3.2 Awareness Program and Medical Camps (Mass Market Customer Segment)

Awareness Program: Every year during the onset of monsoon, some volunteers from the Indian Red Cross Society visit this community and cover each and every home and check for the cleanliness and hygiene which is maintained in their houses. They are provided with a certain checklist to be filled by them after performing a hygiene audit and also some information pamphlets and chlorine tablets. They distribute these pamphlets and advise on different causes for the spread of malaria and other water-borne diseases. They also check the family members in the house for any symptoms of malaria and advise them to take necessary precautions and also initial treatment in case certain patients show signs of the disease. They are also assisted by staff members and few volunteers from Manav Sadhna:

- Number of homes covered by the team: 3,000
- Number of households covered per volunteer per day: 20
- Number of people who usually have symptoms of malaria: 55 per week

Further scope for awareness program needs to be conducted about the different precautionary measures to be taken before the start of summer.

Medical Camps: Manav Sadhna also conducts around 3–5 medical camps every year in association with the different hospitals in the region; each medical camp covers different organs of the body. Patients who are diagnosed with different diseases or illness during these camps and who need further treatment at the hospital are treated free of costs throughout their medication cycle, and these camps also act as awareness program for various sanitation and hygiene habits.

- Average number of patients examined/treated during each medical camp: 400
- Average number of patients who need further treatment at the hospital: 25 (Figs. 13.5 and 13.6)

13.3.3 Value Propositions

The major value propositions which create value for the customers can be characterized as follows:

- *Very low fee (price):* For the patients to be examined and get medication at the clinic, Manav Sadhna charges only a token fee of Rs. 3 per patient per visit. Hence this makes up a very important value proposition for the patients.
- *Free follow-up and field visits by the healthcare worker (accessibility and convenience):* The community health care worker frequently visits the different sections of the community and enquires the patients about their treatment and also informs them to keep up with their medication cycle. He is also approached

Fig. 13.5 Anganwadi children

Fig. 13.6 Medical camp

by people who seek his advice even for normal illness. He is trusted and respected by the entire community.

- *Medical camp (accessibility and cost reduction):* Manav Sadhna organizes regular medical camp in association with various hospitals where a number of people get examined and treated for various illnesses. Also some patients need further treatment at the hospital for their illness; all the costs for these treatments are borne by the hospital on reference of the senior staff members of Manav Sadhna.

13.3.4 Channels

There are three major channels acting as points of contact for the customer to avail access to the healthcare facility.

There are direct channels like the doctor at the clinic and the community health care worker. The doctor (medic) treats the patients at the clinic and acts as the direct channel for them and the central medical facility. Similarly the CHW acts as the direct channel between the hospitals and the patients. He also acts as the direct link between some patients and the central medical facility.

There are also indirect channels like the referral card which is provided to the patients before going to the hospital. These referral cards are for those patients who can afford to go to the hospital on their own and have someone to accompany them. For other patients the CHW acts as the direct referral link between the patient and the hospital.

The current system being implemented under the RFID-based system tries to integrate the processes under the two direct channels, and this results in efficient tracking of diseases. Also the way of delivery of the service and maintaining history (post-purchase service) by the RFID system has streamlined the entire system.

13.3.5 Customer Relationships

There are two major kinds of relationships which exist between the patients and the healthcare system.

The first is the personal assistance relationship of treatment and follow-up provided by the clinic doctor and the community health care worker. There is direct interaction between the patients and the employees. This is also the costliest relationship in case of the community health care worker as he has to give personal assistance to each and every patient and it narrows down his scope and reach of operations. There is some scope for improvement and substitution in this type of relationship which will increase the accessibility of the CHW in the community by deploying certain mobile value-added services. However, it may result in additional costs to the customer not in monetary terms but during knowledge transfer.

The second type of relationship which occurs is the community relationship between the patients (customers) of the medical camps and the awareness programs. This is kind of a promotional service under the healthcare program which makes more and more patients integrate into the system, and it increases the coverage area of the system. Issuing RFID cards to these patients and making them an integral part of the system will be a major step in covering the entire community in a faster and efficient manner.

13.3.6 Revenue Streams

There are two major sources of revenue in this existing system:

• Patients pay for every visit to the clinic. However, this forms only a small portion of the revenue which is needed to fund the project (6 %).
• The other major source of revenue is the funds which are supplied by Manav Sadhna. Manav Sadhna receives these funds from various donors throughout the world. Hence the project as of now is totally dependent on the donors of Manav Sadhna.

Also a major source of revenue stream (cost reduction) in the system can be the concession which is provided by the government and private hospitals to the patients on reference of Manav Sadhna. Although it can't be formally categorized as a revenue stream, it provides the same functionality of a revenue stream.

13.3.7 Alternate Sources for Revenue

SMS and telemarketing are two of the major media of marketing over the mobile platform. An advertising agency charges almost 15 paises per SMS to a corporate organization while conducting SMS marketing on their behalf. Also it charges around 2 rupees per call for every IVRS call it does to potential customers on behalf of corporates. Now some of the activities like follow-up for patients in the severe illness segment and medication reminders can be sent over these advertising messages and calls.

This gives a wider customer base to the ad agency/corporate. As also this program may integrate with their CSR activities. Also it creates a new value proposition to the existing system of integrating mobile technology at the customer level (Fig. 13.7).

Setting up own server and GSM module:

• Cost of the GSM device and related software: Rs. 2,500
• Cost for sending SMS: 1 paise per SMS @ 500 SMS per day

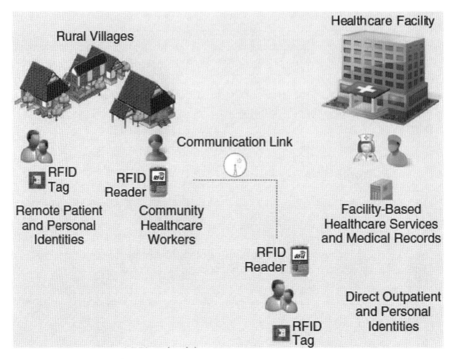

Fig. 13.7 RFID e-health system

- Revenue which may be generated by implementing this scheme: 14 p per SMS, Rs. 70 per day for every 500 SMS
- However, a database of all the mobile numbers in the community is the most essential requirement of this system.

13.3.8 Key Resources

A journal and diary maintained by the community health care worker is one of the most essential resources of the system; he maintains all his appointments and reports and field visit data in that journal. This key resource plays a major role in the activities performed by the community worker as a communication channel.

This journal can be substituted by the mobile device which is connected to the database at the clinic. The database is a more organized and efficient way of storing this data in a redundant manner. Also, due to the high security level and multiple physical locations of the database, the threat of loss of data is almost eliminated.

Tacit knowledge of the community health care worker is also an important resource in the system. The community health care worker has acquired a good knowledge about some of the basic illnesses and also the major symptoms of some chronic diseases. During his field visits, he is approached by many people for advice if they feel sick. He advises them on the ways they can get treated and directs them to the clinic or to the hospital depending on the severity of their illness.

This can be supported by a knowledge-based decision support intelligent system hosted on the database server as a separate entity. In this manner the CWH has to feed in the symptoms into the mobile device and which will advise him on the possible diseases and the path of action in the treatment process.

13.3.9 Key Activities

- Diagnosing the illness of the patients by the doctor at the clinic and advising on necessary treatment and medication is the most important activity at the clinic and the most essential requirement for successful execution of the system.
- Procuring medicines which need to be distributed at the clinic on the advice of the doctor in bulk quantity (so as to obtain discounts) is also an important activity.
- Meeting up with government/private hospital dean or head and requesting them to organize medical camps in community area.
- Also in certain cases reducing the cost of treatment for some patients who could not afford the treatment, by meeting up with various doctors in other private hospitals and clinic if the treatment cannot be done at government hospitals.
- Following up on patients and going on regular field visit are the important activities undertaken by the community health care worker.
- Also organizing and planning out the different requirements and scheduling of the medical camps are an important activity in this system (Fig. 13.8).

13.3.10 Key Partnerships

Medic: The medic who provides his services under the program by diagnosing and treating the patients for their illness is one of the most important partners in the system.

After implementation of this new system under the RFID project, he was not too flexible of adapting to this system as it meant additional work for him. And he being the most important component of the system must be totally flexible for any change in the system. Thus to keep him integrated with the system, there has to be some minor changes in the system specially as regards to the interface of this RFID system. A special touch panel GUI-based interface would be a welcome move for the medic.

Government and Private Hospitals: All the patients with severe illnesses are referred to the government and private hospitals for further treatment and tests. Hence a strong partnership and bond had to be established with these entities. Also

Fig. 13.8 Student volunteers interacting with staff of Manav Sadhna

specific tie-ups with these hospitals and inviting them to conduct medical camps are also an essential part of the system. It helps in obtaining economies of scale for treatment of a number of patients simultaneously and also integrating more patients (prospective customers) in the system.

The DOTS program holds biweekly meetings with TB patients and provides advice on medication and precautions at the clinic. Encouraging other such successful government/privately funded projects for chronic diseases will help in reaching out to more number of patients with chronic diseases and easy tracking of their medication. Thus their dependence on hospitals will be reduced. Also, it will reduce their opportunity costs of visiting the hospital and increased productivity.

13.3.11 Cost Structure

The different cost structures in the system can be categorized into three major headings:

- Salaries of the different employees in the system
- Medicines, additional assistance, and medical camp/awareness program
- Clinic maintenance and Internet charges (Fig. 13.9).

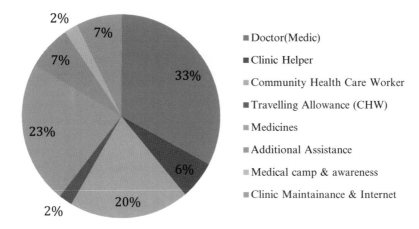

Fig. 13.9 Breakup of different annual variable costs

13.3.12 Scope for Improvement

The salary of the community health care worker is Rs. 5,000 per month. He works on an 8-h shift for 25 days in a month. Thus he is paid Rs. 25 for every hour of his service. His weekly breakup of time allocated to various activities covered under different sections includes:

- Field visits (including hospital visits with patients): 8 h week
- Follow-up on patients: 4–6 h per week
- Visiting Anganwadi and following up the parents of malnourished kids: 6–8 h per week

The World Bank stipulates that around 2.1 % of rural population in the developing countries needing constant access to healthcare facilities, i.e., around 2,100 people in the community with population of 100,000. Obviously this entire population cannot be covered by only one community health care worker; he needs more subordinates like him. Also integrating different technological channels in this system can be used and understood by various actors in the existing system without much hardship. These technologies will supplement the existing processes and also create new value propositions. This can be achieved by adding some mobile value-added services to the existing system.

Increasing the number of clinic and running them in multiple shifts of 2 h each, thus even though it would increase the fixed costs and variable costs of the system, it will increase the accessibility of the system to a wider customer (patient) base. Thus for certain illness and disease if properly cured in the initial stage would prevent them from becoming fatal. Thus in the long run, it would reduce the medical costs of the entire system including the community members.

13.4   Incorporation of Microinsurance

Microinsurance is the protection of low-income people against specific perils in exchange for regular premium payment proportionate to the likelihood and cost of the risks involved.

One of the greatest challenges for microinsurance is the actual delivery to clients. Methods and models for doing so vary depending on the organization, institution, and provider involved. In general, there are four main methods for offering microinsurance: the partner-agent model, the provider-driven model, the full-service model, and the community-based model. Each of these models has their own advantages and disadvantages.

By considering the demographic profile of the community people and the proximity to members of a community-based microinsurance model, it will be most feasible for them.

13.4.1   Community-Based Model

In India health expenses are mostly funded by out-of-pocket spending (OOPS). Thus, spending on healthcare makes up a large chunk of the resource poor households. Hence, access to a microinsurance is the need of the hour.

Now, to provide people with access to microinsurance, a proper delivery model has to be implemented. For number of people insured less than 100,000 and belonging to the same geographic region, a community-based microinsurance model is most feasible as can be seen in case of Uplift India, a Pune-based NGO. This model can be basically mapped to four different actors:

- Insurance policy holder
- Members of the community belonging to different subcultures (CHALI's) nominated as representatives of the community
- NGO/government/private organizations
- Private clinics/hospitals/labs

The work of the model can be summarized as follows:

- In the initial stages, the NGO along with some support from the government and private donors creates an insurance fund.
- Then it nominates intellectual sound-minded people from different sectors/ regions of the community to the board of the microinsurance company (for handling funds).
- These board members perform the task of fixing the initial premium amt and schedule of payment. They along with support from the members of the NGO also educate other people from the community regarding the benefits of microinsurance and how they can use it.
- This committee also connects with private hospitals and clinics and persuades them to give special discounts to holders of this scheme by committing for long-term associations.

- The committee also decides on the settlement of claims and subsequent premiums in the next year for such customers/members.
- The major advantage of such a committee and the diversity associated with it is that they know the severity of the situation and sanction the claims accordingly.

13.5 Discussions

In the business model of the existing processes, each building block of the model has been carefully analyzed. The findings indicate an advantage for revenue generation in the cost structure by collaborating with private players such as advertising agencies for the intended SMS/IVRS value-added service module.

After examining the existing system under the savings program and studying the existing successful practices in microinsurance delivery in similar circumstances, a community-based microinsurance delivery model was suggested.

As can be seen above, the existing system is not used extensively by the medic, and the intended impact cannot be observed. Thus some changes have to be done to the existing system for it to work effortlessly.

The system can be integrated with point of sale kind of display system for the medic as can be seen at some chains of fast food restaurants. Thus the medic has to only touch the display panel and enter the details of the customer without typing anything. This will reduce the workload on the medic and may substantially reduce the time required to diagnose each patient from the existing 4.5 min (Fig. 13.10).

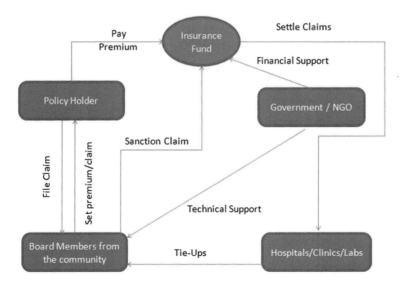

Fig. 13.10 Community-based microinsurance model

Acknowledgments This work was carried out during an internship as part of the Postgraduate Diploma in Management (Dual Country) Program. The authors are grateful for the support and facilities provided by the Institute of Management Technology in Dubai and Ghaziabad in the course of conducting the project. This work was partly supported by a grant from the Vodafone Americas Foundation. The cooperation and support of staff from Manav Sadhna is gratefully acknowledged.

References

Alexander O, Yves P (2009) Business model generation. Osterwalder Alexander and Pigneur Yves (Self-published), Amsterdam. ISBN 978-2-8399-0580-0

Burns LR, DeGraaff RA, Danzon PM, Kimberly JR, Kissick WL, Pauly MV (2002) The Wharton School Study of the health care value chain. In: Burns LR (ed) The health care value chain: producers, purchasers, and providers. Wiley, Jossey-Bass, San Francisco, pp 3–26, ISBN 978-0-7879-6021-6

Chia S, Zalzala A, Zalzala L, Karimi A (2013) Towards intelligent technologies for a self-sustainable, RFID-based, decentralized rural e-Health system. IEEE Technol Soc Mag 32(1):36–43, IEEE, Spring

Jack W, Suri T (2010) The economics of M-PESA. http://www.mit.edu/~tavneet/M-PESA.pdf

McGuinness E (2011) Can health micro-insurance protect the poor. Microfinance Opportunities, Washington, DC

Peters DH, Garg A, Bloom G, Walker DG, Brieger WR, Rahman MH (2008) Poverty and access to health care in developing countries. Ann N Y Acad Sci 1136:161–171

Sinead B, Helen S, Lesley G (2008) Small-scale evaluation in health: a practical guide. SAGE, Los Angeles. ISBN 978-1-4129-3006-2

William J, and Suri T (2010), "The Economics of M-PESA." http://www.mit.edu/~tavneet/M-PESA.pdf

Chapter 14
Supplier Selection and Multi-period Demand Allocation in a Humanitarian Supply Chain

Amol Singh

14.1 Introduction

Humanitarian supply chain management, the process of planning, implementing, and controlling the efficient and cost-effective flow of goods of humanitarian SCM network, includes procurement of goods, storage of goods, and distribution of goods from point of origin to the point of consumption in such a way that it alleviates the suffering of the vulnerable people as efficiently as possible. Humanitarian supply chain management and humanitarian logistics are used interchangeably in the literature. Purchasing is an important function of humanitarian supply chain management. The literature in this context significantly focused on choosing the right suppliers and allocating the appropriate demand of goods to these suppliers. In an increasingly competitive environment, firms are paying more attention to selecting the right suppliers for procurement of raw materials and component parts for their products. Choi and Hartley (1996) reported that supplier evaluation and selection together has an important role in the supply chain process and is crucial to the success of a firm. Similarly, procurement activity in the humanitarian supply chain is very important owing to demand that is generated from random events that are unpredictable in terms of timing, type, and size. As a result, the opportunities in this research area include determining the number of suppliers, managing changing buyer-supplier relationship, sourcing strategies, and outsourcing decisions for humanitarian supply chains. The present research work focuses on this issue of humanitarian supply chain management. The main objective of the study is to address the problem of optimal allocation of demand of items among candidate suppliers in order to maximize the purchase value of items. The purchase value of the items directly relate to cost and quality of raw materials purchased from the

A. Singh (✉)
Department of Operations Management, Indian Institute of Management, Rohtak, Rohtak, Haryana, India
e-mail: amol.singh@iimrohtak.ac.in

© Springer India 2016   189
B.S. Sahay et al. (eds.), *Managing Humanitarian Logistics*, Springer Proceedings in Business and Economics, DOI 10.1007/978-81-322-2416-7_14

supplier. Supplier selection problem is a multi-criteria decision-making problem involving both qualitative and quantitative performance measures. Usually, several conflicting criteria make the supplier selection problem a complex problem. It is often desirable to make a compromise among the conflicting criteria.

In this study, a new hybrid algorithm has been developed to solve the problem of multi-period customer demand allocation among more suppliers under multi-period demand condition, budget, delivery lead time, and multi-period supplier capacity constraints. The remainder of the paper comprises six sections. Section 14.2 provides the review of literature on supplier selection, identifies the research issues, which form the basis for problem formulation, and then presents the objective of the study. Section 14.4 discusses the proposed hybrid algorithm to solve the multi-criteria demand allocation problem. Section 14.5 reports the case study and the findings of the computational experiments. Section 14.6 concludes the study along with future research directions.

14.2 Review of the Literature

Supplier selection is one of the growing research areas. Studies show that supplier selection is a complex process involving several criteria such as procurement cost, material quality, delivery lead time, reliability of the supplier, etc. These criteria can be defined variously as buyers take into account numerous conflicting factors. Illustratively, low price can offset poor quality or delivery lead time. Dickson (1966) identified 23 criteria in his study of various supplier selection problems. He reported that quality, delivery, and performance history are the three most important criteria. Similarly, Weber et al. (1991) in a review of 74 articles obtained similar results pertaining to the multi-criteria nature of supplier selection problem. From a generalized perspective, alternative approaches suggested in the literature may be grouped into three categories: linear weighting models, mathematical programming approaches, and probabilistic approaches. However, their study identified very few articles based on the mathematical programming approach for supplier selection. Bhutta (2003) provided a review of 154 supplier selection research articles and alternative methods/techniques adopted. Although most buyers still consider cost to be their primary concern, new more interactive and interdependent selection criteria are increasingly being used. Table 14.1 provides a summary of various criteria used by researchers.

The literature shows a variety of methodologies and approaches used for the supplier selection problem. Traditionally, linear weighting models, total cost approach, multiple attribute utility theory, and total cost ownership are used for supplier selection. None of these approaches have received significant support in literature or in practice for their limitation to address the issues of real supplier selection environment. In the last one decade, researchers focused on optimization techniques, multi-objective programming, analytic hierarchy process, data envelopment analysis, artificial intelligence, and hybrid approaches. The brief

Table 14.1 Criteria used in literature for supplier selection

No.	Criteria	No.	Criteria
1.	Green competencies	21.	Relationship
2.	Product quality	22.	Technological capability
3.	Price (cost)	23.	Financial performance
4.	Purchasing cost	24.	Quality of service
5.	Age and position in the market	25.	Competitive priority
6.	Top management support	26.	Strategic purchasing
7.	Environmental engagement	27.	Demand
8.	On-time delivery	28.	Management and organization
9.	Delivery capability	29.	Attitude
10.	Customer focus	30.	Labor relation
11.	Consistency	31.	Training aids
12.	After-sale service	32.	Communication system
13.	Warranty and claim	33.	Production capability
14.	Research and development	34.	Packaging capability
15.	Information technology	35.	Operational control
16.	Service innovation	36.	Amount of past business
17.	Location	37.	Reciprocal arrangements
18.	Political and economical stability	38.	Impression
19.	Flexibility	39.	Business attempt
20.	Reliability	40.	Maintainability

description of alternative approaches in terms of general application, features, and limitations is as follows.

14.2.1 Optimization Techniques

The popular techniques are dynamic programming (Masella and Rangone 2000), linear programming (Ghodsypour and O'Brien 1998), and multi-objective programming (Weber and Ellram 1993). Zhang and Zhang (2011) used the MILP approach to solve the supplier selection problem under stochastic demand. They selected the suppliers and allocated the ordering quantity properly among the selected suppliers to minimize the total cost including selection, purchasing, holding, and shortage costs. Sawik (2011) also applied the MILP approach to study the problem of order allocation of parts among the suppliers in a customer-driven supply chain. The study suggested that future research could consider supplier selection in the customer-driven supply chain taking into account risk and dynamic multi-period demand. Osman and Demirli (2010) addressed the supplier selection problem related to an aerospace company and tried to optimize its outsourcing strategies in order to meet the expected demand and customer satisfaction requirements under delivery dates and approved budget. They used the goal-programming approach to achieve the company's objectives. The optimization approaches suffer from some drawbacks in that they are unable to accommodate the qualitative measures of supplier selection problems.

14.2.2 Multi-objective Programming

Multi-objective programming approach considers several criteria simultaneously and makes the trade-off among the key supplier selection criteria. This approach is especially suitable to just-in-time scenarios (Weber and Ellram 1993). An additional flexibility of this approach is that it allows a varying number of suppliers into consideration and offers suggested volume allocation to the supplier. Ho et al. (2009) provide a literature review on multi-criteria decision-making approaches for supplier evaluation and selection. The objective of their survey was to determine which approaches are used widely in the literature, which evaluating criteria received more attention, and whether there was any inadequacy of the approaches. They found the individual approach (58.97 %) more popular than the integrated approach (41.03 %). In the individual approach, the most popular approach is DEA followed by mathematical programming, AHP, CBR, ANP, fuzzy set theory, and genetic algorithm. DEA attracted researchers mainly because of its robustness. The wide applicability of individual approach was due to its simplicity, ease of use, and flexibility (Ho et al. 2009). In the supplier selection problem, besides the rating of suppliers, the decision makers also need to consider the resource limitations (budget of buyer and capability of supplier). In this situation, goal programming can be preferred to AHP/ANP/TOPSIS techniques. The decision-making process facilitates when AHP/ANP/TOPSIS and GP are integrated. They suggested that the voice of stakeholders should be considered and the evaluating criteria should be derived from the requirements of stakeholders using a series of house of quality. As far as the evaluating criteria for supplier selection is concerned, they reported that 87.18 % of buyers considered quality in the supplier selection. The second most popular criteria (82.05 %) was delivery, and the third most popular criteria (80.77 %) was price or cost.

Choi and Hartley (1996) studied the supplier selection practice in US auto industries and concluded that quality, delivery, and consistency were the key factors. However, price turned out to be the least important factor in supplier selection. These facts indicate that the traditional single criterion approach based on lowest cost bidding is no longer supportive in supply chain management. In the last decade, numerous studies have focused on supplier selection process using alternative approaches such as single-objective technique, i.e., cost ratio method, linear or mixed integer programming, and multi-objective techniques, i.e., goal programming (Ghodsypour and O'Brien 1998; Yan et al. 2003; Oliveria and Lourenco 2002). Despite their usefulness, the optimization methods suffer from certain drawbacks associated with their implementation. Of particular interest, the major shortcoming is the exclusion of qualitative criteria, considered important in supplier selection problem in both the single and multi-objective programming.

14.2.3   Analytic Hierarchy Process (AHP)

Analytic hierarchy process (AHP) developed by Saaty (1980) is a mathematical procedure to assign weights to several alternatives using a scheme of pairwise comparison. The model has witnessed applications to a wide variety of decision-making areas including research and development, project selection, supplier selection, evaluating alternatives, etc. This method allows the decision maker to convert the complex problems in the form of a hierarchy or a set of integrated levels. The advantage of the hierarchical structure is that it allows the systematic decomposition of the overall problem into its fundamental components and inter-dependencies with a large degree of flexibility. This is the main reason for choosing the AHP for tackling the supplier selection problem, which involves many intangible factors (Nydick and Hill 1992). Generally, the hierarchy has at least three levels, namely, the goal, the criteria, and the alternatives. For the supplier selection problem, the goal is to select the best overall supplier; the criteria could be quality, on-time delivery, price, etc.; and the alternatives are the different proposals supplied by the suppliers. Bruno et al. (2012) reported that in a corporate environment, AHP is one of the most prominent methodologies for supplier evaluation. They also reported the strength and weakness of AHP methodology in supplier evaluation process. The suitability of AHP to supplier selection problem derives from four distinctive characteristics: (1) ability to handle both tangible and intangible attributes, (2) ability to structure the problems in a hierarchical manner, (3) ability to monitor the consistency with which a decision maker makes a judgment, and (4) ability to provide a synthetic score for each supplier. As regards the drawbacks, its use is not straightforward for practitioners. A consensus is required for aggregating individual judgments for the pairwise comparison matrices. There cannot be single hierarchy for most of the supplier selection problems. The reliability of the outcome depends not only on the quality of the data but also on the knowledge and judgments of decision makers (Chan and Chan 2004).

14.2.4   Data Envelopment Analysis

Data envelopment analysis (DEA) postulates the concept of the efficiency of a decision alternative. The benefit criteria (output) and the cost criteria (input) determine the decision alternative, i.e., the supplier. The ratio of the weighted sum of outputs (i.e., the performance of the supplier) to the weighted sum of inputs (i.e., the costs of using the supplier) determines the efficiency of a supplier. For each supplier, the DEA method finds the most favorable set of weights, i.e., the set of weights that maximizes the supplier's efficiency without making its own or any other supplier's efficiency greater than one. In this way, DEA helps the buyer in classifying the suppliers into two categories: efficient suppliers (efficient frontier) and inefficient suppliers. Weber (1996) reported the efficacy of DEA approach in supplier selection problems especially when multiple and conflicting criteria are considered. Toloo and Nalchigar (2011) proposed an integrated data envelopment analysis (DEA) model to evaluate the overall performance of the suppliers in the presence of cardinal as well as ordinal data. They considered three evaluating factors including total cost of shipment, supplier reputation, and bill received from the supplier without error. They emphasized on the simultaneous consideration of cardinal and ordinal data in supplier selection process neglected by previous studies.

14.2.5 Artificial Intelligence

The literature provides evidence of researchers using various advanced techniques: neural network (Luo et al. 2009; Aksoy and Ozturk 2011), genetic algorithm, analytic network process (ANP), fuzzy set theory (Ozkok and Tiryaki 2011; Yucel and Guneri 2011), and hybrid approach for supplier selection. In the real supplier selection environment, the modeling of many situations may not be sufficient or exact, as the available data are inexact, vague, imprecise, and uncertain by nature (Ozkok and Tiryaki 2011; Yucel and Guneri 2011). The decision-making processes that take place in such situations have to contend with uncertain or imprecise information. For managing the vagueness and uncertainty of the problems, the fuzzy set theory can prove an effective method (Chen et al. 2006). In order to model such situations, the fuzzy set theory represents the uncertainty in terms of linguistic variable converted into fuzzy numbers. Most of the fuzzy multi-criteria supplier selection models defuzzify into a crisp one in the initial stage, thereby defeating the very purpose of collecting fuzzy data pertaining to different opinions of decision makers.

14.2.6 Hybrid Approaches

Recognizing the fact that no particular technique can provide a generalized perspective on the supplier selection problems, researchers have been encouraged to develop the hybrid approaches. Within the framework of hybrid approaches, alternative supplier selection models are integrated for achieving a richer model based on a combination of advantages of different techniques. Ha and Krishna (2008) reported a hybrid approach using multiple techniques in order to evaluate the competitive suppliers in a supply chain. Amid et al. (2009) used the fuzzy set theory and MILP techniques for demand allocation to suppliers. During their investigation, they considered three objective functions encompassing minimization of the cost, the rejected items, and the late deliveries, under the capacity and demand requirement constraints. Bhattacharya et al. (2010) used analytic hierarchy process (AHP) and quality function deployment (QFD) in combination with cost factor measure to rank the suppliers. For evaluating the suppliers, they considered several criteria, namely, delivery, quality, responsiveness, management discipline, financial position, facility, and technical capability. Liao and Kao (2011) developed a hybrid methodology using fuzzy set theory, TOPSIS, and goal programming to measure the comparative rating of the suppliers. This integrated approach allows the decision makers to set multiple aspiration levels for supplier selection problems. Zouggari and Benyoucef (2012) proposed a hybrid approach combining fuzzy set theory, ANP, and TOPSIS for prioritizing the suppliers. Chen (2011) proposed a structured methodology for supplier selection and evaluation based on a combination of DEA and TOPSIS approaches. The major drawback of this model is that it does not capture the uncertainties of supplier selection environment. Vinodh et al. (2011) used a hybrid model, which integrated AHP with fuzzy set theory. The AHP methodology enabled crisp value of numerical judgments at the initial stage rather than at final stage, which could have been beneficial for addressing the problem of fuzzification in supplier selection model.

From a critical perspective, most of the studies reviewed in the above share some common features. Firstly, single supplier selection problem constitutes the focus for most studies. However, there may be instances in humanitarian supply chain when the single supplier does not have the capacity to fulfill the demand of the buyer company. The supplier may also be incapable to supply the quantity of desirable items due to some unexpected events. In these circumstances, a pool of suppliers could satisfy the demand of the buyer company. Secondly, in real supplier selection process, most input information can be known imprecisely. In this context, researchers rely on hybrid models involving fuzzy sets theory for handling uncertainty. However, hybrid models also suffer from drawbacks. Moreover, hybrid approaches are scarce (Sevkli et al. 2008). Research in this area can be useful to develop efficient hybrid methodologies, which can improve the efficacy of the input information due to the uncertainty of the supplier evaluation environment and optimal allocation of multi-period demand among suppliers.

14.3   Research Issues and Objective of the Study

A critical review of literature brings to the fore some crucial issues for research. Firstly, humanitarian supply chain deals with a pool of supplier rather than a single supplier for meeting the demand of the goods. This situation creates a new scenario in the supplier selection problem. Secondly, supplier selection is a multi-criteria decision-making problem, encompassing risk and uncertainties. Existing studies have not devoted much attention to this aspect of supplier selection environment. Thirdly, supplier selection models based on fuzzy set theory adopt the practice of data defuzzified into a crisp one in the initial stage. This approach undermines the advantage of collecting the fuzzy data (opinion of all decision makers). Fourthly, in the literature, multi-period demand aspect of the supplier evaluation process has not received much attention. Taking cues from the critical research issues identified in the literature review, the study aims at addressing the following tasks:

- A complex problem of multi-period customer demand allocation in a humanitarian supply chain is considered, and the rating of the suppliers is integrated with the MILP process in order to maximize the value of procurement.
- Qualitative and quantitative criteria apply in the computation of the supplier rating.
- A hybrid fuzzy TOPSIS algorithm tackles the risk of supplier selection environment. It defuzzifies the fuzzy data in the final step of the ranking process.
- The hybrid fuzzy TOPSIS algorithm is integrated with the MILP process for optimal multi-period demand allocation among suppliers.

In the present research work, by considering the above task, a hybrid algorithm, combining fuzzy set theory, TOPSIS (Hwang & Yoon 1981) and MILP methodologies, is developed to solve the problem of multi-period demand allocation among candidate suppliers under the uncertainties of supplier selection environment. The detailed methodology is explained below:

14.4 Hybrid Fuzzy, TOPSIS, and MILP Methodology

In fuzzy multi-criteria decision-making problems, fuzzy numbers usually characterize scores of suppliers with respect to the criteria. Similarly, the weight assigned to each criterion represents a fuzzy number. A fuzzy number is a convex fuzzy set with a membership value between 0 and 1. In this study, scores of suppliers with respect to the criteria and weight of each criterion are considered as linguistic variables. These linguistic variables are converted into fuzzy number as shown in Tables 14.2 and 14.3.

In multi-criteria supplier evaluation problem, each decision maker assigns fuzzy score to the supplier against a criterion and similarly assigns the fuzzy score to each criterion. These fuzzy scores are expressed in the fuzzy matrix format.

Suppose $X = [x_{ij}]_{m \times n}$ is a fuzzy decision matrix in which $A_1, A_2 \ldots A_m$ are m possible suppliers and $C_1, C_2, \ldots C_n$ are n possible criteria. The performance of supplier A_i with respect to criteria C_j is expressed by x_{ij}, and the weight of criterion C_j is expressed by w_j, where x_{ij} and w_j are represented by triangular fuzzy scores. A triangular fuzzy score is represented as $x = [(x_1, x_1'); x_2; (x_3 \ x_3')]$. The steps of hybrid fuzzy TOPSIS methodology are explained below:

Step 1: A group of k decision makers is identified, and this group defines a set of relevant criteria for supplier evaluation. It may be noted that the interval value

Table 14.2 Linguistic variables for the rating of the suppliers

Very poor (VP)	[(0, 0); 0; (1, 1.5)]
Poor (P)	[(0, 0.5); 1; (2.5, 3.5)]
Moderately poor (MP)	[(0, 1.5); 3; (4.5, 5.5)]
Fair (F)	[(2.5, 3.5); 5; (6.5, 7.5)]
Moderately good (MG)	[(4.5, 5.5); 7; (8, 9.5)]
Good (G)	[(5.5, 7.5); 9; (9.5, 10)]
Very good (VG)	[(8.5, 9.5); 10; (10, 10)]

Table 14.3 Linguistic variables for the importance of the criterion

Very low (VL)	[(0, 0); 0; (.1, .15)]
Low (L)	[(0, 0.05); 0.1; (0.25, 0.35)]
Medium low (ML)	[(0, 0.15); 0.3; (0.45, 0.55)]
Medium (M)	[(0.25, 0.35); 0.5; (0.65, 0.75)]
Medium high (MH)	[(0.45, 0.55); 0.7; (0.8, 0.95)]
High (H)	[(0.55, 0.75); 0.9; (0.95, 1)]
Very high (VH)	[(0.85, 0.95); 1; (1, 1)]

allows the decision maker to define the lower bound and upper bound values for matrix element and for the weight of each criterion.

Step 2: Determine the score of the considered suppliers with respect to each criterion and similarly the score of each chosen criterion.

Step 3: Compute average score of each supplier with respect to a criterion and average weight of each criterion. For instance, if in the decision-making group there are K decision makers and each assigns their own score to each supplier with respect to a criterion and similarly to each criterion, the average scores of each supplier with respect to a criterion and importance of each criterion are computed by using the following relations:

$$x_{ij} = \frac{1}{k}\left[x_{ij}^1 + x_{ij}^2 + \cdots\cdots\cdots\cdots x_{ij}^k \right] \qquad (14.1)$$

$$w_{ij} = \frac{1}{k}\left[w_{ij}^1 + w_{ij}^2 + \cdots\cdots\cdots\cdots w_{ij}^k \right] \qquad (14.2)$$

Step 4: The fuzzy scores computed in step 3 are in different units; hence, these scores are normalized by converting them into nondimensional ratio for comparison. Fuzzy scores $x_{ij} = [(a_{ij}, a'_{ij}); b_{ij}; (c_{ij}\ c'_{ij})]$ computed in step 3 are converted into nondimensional ratio by using the following equations:

$$r_{ij} = \left[\left(\frac{a_{ij}}{c_j}, \frac{a'_{ij}}{c_j} \right); \frac{b_{ij}}{c_j}; \left(\frac{c'_{ij}}{c_j}, \frac{c_{ij}}{c_j} \right) \right], i = 1, 2\ldots\ldots\ldots m, \ j \in \Omega_b \qquad (14.3)$$

$$r_{ij} = \left[\left(\frac{a_j^-}{a'_{jj}}, \frac{a_j^-}{a_{ij}} \right); \frac{a_j^-}{b_{ij}}; \left(\frac{a_j^-}{c_{ij}}, \frac{a_j^-}{c'_{ij}} \right) \right], \quad i = 1, 2 \ldots\ldots m, \; j \in \Omega_c \qquad (14.4)$$

where

$$c_j^+ = \max(c_{ij}), \; j \varepsilon \Omega_b$$

$$a_j^- = \min(a'_{ij}), \; j \varepsilon \Omega_c$$

Step 5: Convert the normalized fuzzy decision matrix computed in step 4 into weightage normalized fuzzy decision matrix $(v = [v_{ij}]_{n \times m}, \text{ where } v_{ij} = r_{ij} \times w_j)$ by using the following relation:

$$v_{ij} = \left[\left(r_{1ij} \times w_{1ij}, r_{1ij} \times w'_{1j} \right); r_{2j}, \times w'_{2j},; \left(r_{3ij} \times w'_{3j}, r_{3ij} \times w_{3j} \right) \right]$$
$$= \left[\left(g_{ij}, g'_{ij} \right); h_{ij}; \left(l_{ij}, l'_{ij} \right) \right] \qquad (14.5)$$

Step 6: Determine positive ideal $(A+)$ and negative ideal $(A-)$ solutions by using the following equations:

$$A^+ = [(1, 1); 1; (1, 1)] \quad \text{for } j \varepsilon \Omega_b \qquad (14.6)$$
$$A^- = [(0, 0); 0; (0, 0)] \quad \text{for } j \varepsilon \Omega_c \qquad (14.7)$$

Step 7: Compute the separation measures (Euclidean distances) of each supplier from the positive ideal $(A+)$ and negative ideal $(A-)$ solutions by using the following relations:

$$D^-(N, M) = \sqrt{\frac{1}{3} \sum_{i=1}^{i=3} \left[\left(N_{xi}^- - M_{yi}^- \right)^2 \right]} \qquad (14.8)$$

$$D^+(N, M) = \sqrt{\frac{1}{3} \sum_{i=1}^{i=3} \left[\left(N_{xi}^+ - M_{yi}^+ \right)^2 \right]} \qquad (14.9)$$

where $D^-(N, M)$ and $D^+(N, M)$ are the primary and secondary separation measures; hence, the separation measure of each supplier $(D^+{}_{i1}, D^+{}_{i2})$ from the positive ideal solution is computed by using the following equations:

$$D_{i1}^+ = \sum_{j=1}^{n} \sqrt{\frac{1}{3} \left[\left(g_{ij} - 1 \right)^2 + \left(h_{ij} - 1 \right)^2 + \left(l_{ij} - 1 \right)^2 \right]} \qquad (14.10)$$

$$D_{i2}^{+} = \sum_{j=1}^{n} \sqrt{\frac{1}{3}\left[\left(g_{ij}' - 1\right)^2 + \left(h_{ij}' - 1\right)^2 + \left(l_{ij}' - 1\right)^2\right]} \qquad (14.11)$$

Similarly, the separation measure of each supplier (D_{i1}^{-}, D_{i2}^{-}) from the negative ideal solution is computed by using the following relations:

$$D_{i1}^{-} = \sum_{j=1}^{n} \sqrt{\frac{1}{3}\left[\left(g_{ij} - 0\right)^2 + \left(h_{ij} - 0\right)^2 + \left(l_{ij} - 0\right)^2\right]} \qquad (14.12)$$

$$D_{i2}^{-} = \sum_{j=1}^{n} \sqrt{\frac{1}{3}\left[\left(g_{ij}' - 0\right)^2 + \left(h_{ij}' - 0\right)^2 + \left(l_{ij}' - 0\right)^2\right]} \qquad (14.13)$$

Step 8: Compute the fuzzy relative closeness of each supplier by using each pair of separation measure as computed in step 7. The fuzzy relative closeness of supplier A_i is computed by using the following equations:

$$RC_1 = \frac{D_{i2}^{-}}{D_{i2}^{+} + D_{i2}^{-}} \quad \text{and} \quad RC_2 = \frac{D_{i1}^{-}}{D_{i1}^{+} + D_{i1}^{-}} \qquad (14.14)$$

Step 9: Compute crisp value of fuzzy relative closeness as computed in step 8 of each supplier by using the following relation:

$$RC_i^{*} = \frac{RC_1 + RC_2}{2} \qquad (14.15)$$

Step 10: Finally, the output of fuzzy TOPSIS model as computed in step 9 is integrated with MILP. The multi-period optimal demand allocation model is formulated by using the following equations:

$$MaxZ = \sum_{i=1}^{n} RC_i \times Q_{ij} \quad \text{for } i = 1 \text{ to } n\text{th supplier and } j = 1 \text{ to 4th quarter} \qquad (14.16)$$

The objective function maximizes the total purchase value of items subject to the following constraints:

- Budget constraint

$$\sum_{i=1}^{i=n} P_i \times Q_{ij} \leq (B)_{max} \quad (\text{for } j = 1 \text{ to 4th quarter}) \qquad (14.17)$$

$$\sum_{i=1}^{i=n} P_i \times Q_{ij} \geq (B)_{\min} \quad (\text{for } j = 1 \text{ to 4th quarter}) \tag{14.18}$$

- Demand constraint

$$\sum_{i=1}^{i=n} Q_{ij} = (D_j) \quad (j = 1 \text{ to 4th quarter}) \tag{14.19}$$

- Delivery lead time constraint

$$\sum_{i=1}^{i=n} L_i Q_{ij} \leq \text{LT} \quad (j = 1 \text{ to 4th quarter}) \tag{14.20}$$

- Supplier capacity constraint

$$Q_i \leq C_{ij} \quad \text{for } i = 1 \text{ to } n\text{th supplier and } j = 1 \text{ to 4th quarter} \tag{14.21}$$

where Q_{ij} is the number of unit purchase from ith supplier in the jth quarter, P_i is sales price of ith supplier, $(B_{\max}, B_{\min})$ are the maximum and minimum budget limit for purchasing items, D_j is the total demand of the items in jth quarter, L_i is the delivery lead time of ith supplier, LT is the average delivery time required as per the policy of the company, and C_{ij} is the capacity of ith supplier in jth quarter. The efficacy of the hybrid algorithm is demonstrated with the help of a case study in Sect. 14.6.

14.5 Case Study

A logistics company devises its procurement plan and updates it quarterly. The company has candidate suppliers to allocate the demand of goods to candidate suppliers, namely, S_1, S_2, S_3, and S_4. These four suppliers are evaluated by four decision makers, namely, M_1, M_2, M_3, and M_4 based on four criteria, namely, quality (C_1), price (C_2), on-time delivery (C_3), and consistency (C_4). Here, consistency means how the supplier will ensure that it consistently provides high-quality goods. Each decision maker gives his assessment based on linguistic variable as given in Tables 14.4 and 14.5 respectively. The interval value is computed by using the Eqs. 14.1 and 14.2. The calculated interval values are given in Table 14.6. Further, decision values given in Table 14.6 are normalized by using Eqs. 14.3 and 14.4. The normalized values are given in Table 14.7. Each criterion has linguistics weights; hence, these weights are applied to the normalized values, and weighted normalized values are calculated by using Eq. 14.5. The weighted normalized values are shown in Table 14.8. Separation measures from ideal and negative

Table 14.4 Rating of decision makers on importance of criterion

Criteria	M_1	M_2	M_3	M_4
C_1	M	MH	M	ML
C_2	VH	H	H	VH
C_3	VH	H	H	H
C_4	MH	H	MH	MH

Table 14.5 Assessment of suppliers based on each criterion

		Decision makers			
Criterion	Suppliers	M1	M2	M3	M4
C_1	S1	MG	VG	G	G
	S2	VG	G	VG	VG
	S3	MG	G	G	G
	S4	MG	G	VG	G
C_2	S1	VG	F	F	MG
	S2	VG	G	MG	MG
	S3	MG	VG	VG	VG
	S4	F	MG	VG	G
C_3	S1	MG	F	MG	G
	S2	VG	MG	G	G
	S3	VG	VG	VG	G
	S4	G	G	G	MG
C_4	S1	F	G	MG	VG
	S2	MG	G	G	F
	S3	VG	VG	VG	VG
	S4	F	F	VG	VG

Table 14.6 Interval value of supplier assessments and weights

	Decision makers			
Suppliers	C_1	C_2	C_3	C_4
S1	[(6, 7.5), 8.75, (9.25, 9.87)]	[(4.5, 5.5), 6.75, (7.75, 8.63)]	[(4.25, 5.5), 7.0, (8.0, 9.12)]	[(5.25, 6.5), 7.75, (8.5, 9.25)]
S2	[(7.75, 9.0), 9.75, (9.87, 10.0)]	[(5.75, 7.0), 8.25, (8.87, 9.75)]	[(6, 7.5), 8.75, (9.25, 9.87)]	[(4.5, 6.0), 7.5, (8.37, 9.25)]
S3	[(5.25, 7.0), 8.5, (9.13, 9.87)]	[(7.5, 8.5), 9.25, (9.5, 9.87)]	[(7.75, 9.0), 9.75, (9.87, 10.0)]	[(8.5, 9.5), 10.0, (10.0, 10.0)]
S4	[(6, 7.5), 8.75, (9.25, 9.87)]	[(5.25, 6.5), 7.75, (8.5, 9.25)]	[(5.25, 7.0), 8.5, (9.13, 9.87)]	[(5.5, 6.5), 7.5, (8.25, 8.75)]
Weights	[(0.24, 0.35), 0.5, (0.64, 0.73)]	[(0.70, 0.85), 0.95, (0.98, 1.0)]	[(0.63, 0.8), 0.93, (0.96, 1.0)]	[(0.48, 0.6), 0.75, (0.84, 0.96)]

ideal solution are computed by using Eqs. 14.6, 14.7, 14.8, 14.9, 14.10, 14.11, 14.12, and 14.13 respectively. These separation measures are presented in Table 14.9. The relative closeness from ideal and negative ideal solution would be as an interval, and this interval is computed by using Eq. 14.14. Finally, with the

Table 14.7 Normalized decision matrix

Suppliers	Decision makers			
	C_1	C_2	C_3	C_4
S1	[(0.6, 0.75), 0.88, (0.93, 0.99)]	[(0.82, 1.0), 0.67, (0.58, 0.52)]	[(0.43, 0.55), 0.7, (0.8, 0.91)]	[(0.53, 0.65), 0.78, (0.85, 0.93)]
S2	[(0.78, 0.9), 0.98, (0.99, 1.0)]	[(0.64, 0.78), 0.55, (0.51, 0.46)]	[(0.6, 0.75),0.88, (0.93, 0.99)]	[(0.5, 0.6), 0.75, (0.84, 0.93)]
S3	[(0.53, 0.7), 0.85, (0.92, 0.99)]	[(0.53, 0.6), 0.49, (0.47, 0.46)]	[(0.78, 0.90), 0.98, (0.98, 1.0)]	[(0.85, 0.95), 1.0, (1.0, 1.0)]
S4	[(0.6, 0.75), 0.88, (0.93, 0.99)]	[(0.69, 0.86), 0.58, (0.53, 0.49)]	[(0.53, 0.7), 0.85, (0.91, 0.99)]	[(0.55, 0.65), 0.75, (0.83, 0.88)]

Table 14.8 Weighted normalized decision matrix

Suppliers	Decision makers			
	C_1	C_2	C_3	C_4
S1	[(0.14, 0.26), 0.44, (0.60, 0.72)]	[(0.57, 0.85), 0.64, (0.57, 0.52)]	[(0.27, 0.44), 0.65, (0.77, 0.91)]	[(0.25, 0.39), 0.59, (0.71, 0.89)]
S2	[(0.19, 0.32), 0.49, (0.63, .73)]	[(0.45, 0.66), 0.52, (0.5, 0.46)]	[(0.38, 0.60),0.82, (0.89, 0.99)]	[(0.24, 0.36), 0.56, (0.71, 0.89)]
S3	[(0.13, 0.25), 0.43, (0.59, 0.72)]	[(0.37, 0.51), 0.47, (0.46, 0.46)]	[(0.49, 0.72), 0.91, (0.94, 1.0)]	[(0.41, 0.57), 0.75, (0.84, 0.96)]
S4	[(0.14, 0.26), 0.44, (0.60, 0.72)]	[(0.48, 0.73), 0.55, (0.52, 0.49)]	[(0.33, 0.56), 0.79, (0.87, 0.99)]	[(0.26, 0.39), 0.56, (0.70, 0.84)]

Table 14.9 Separation measures from ideal and negative ideal solutions

Suppliers	(D_{i1}^{+}, D_{i2}^{+})	(D_{i1}^{-}, D_{i2}^{-})
S1	(2.05, 1.73)	(2.11, 2.54)
S2	(2.02, 1.68)	(2.24, 2.55)
S3	(1.9, 1.55)	(2.36, 2.65)
S4	(2.06, 1.71)	(2.2, 2.53)

Table 14.10 Interval value of relative closeness and the final relative closeness of each supplier

Suppliers	Interval of relative closeness	Final score of suppliers (Rc^{*})
S1	(0.51, 0.59)	.551
S2	(0.53, 0.60)	.564
S3	(0.55, 0.63)	.592
S4	(0.52, 0.60)	.557

help of Eq. 14.15, the relative closeness of each supplier is computed. The interval value of relative closeness and final relative closeness is given in Table 14.10.

Let the expected demand, available capacity of suppliers, their lead times, and cost for the next 4 quarters be as follows: Company wants to purchase at least 5,000 but less than 5,500 units of an item in each quarter. The unit material cost for supplier S_1, S_2, S_3, and S_4 are \$9, \$8, \$10, \$12 respectively, and the quarterly capacity of candidate suppliers are 3,000, 3,500, 2,500, and 3,200 units, respectively. The annual budget for purchasing the items is \$200,000. The quarterly delivery times of suppliers are 2, 4, 6, and 3 days, respectively. According to company's policy, average delivery time should not be more than 4 days.

The output of fuzzy TOPSIS algorithm as given in Table 14.10 is integrated with MILP approach. In this context, the optimization model is developed by using the Eqs. 14.16, 14.17, 14.18, 14.19, 14.20, and 14.21 as given in Sect. 14.4. The objective function and constraints of the formulated model are given below:

Total procurement value

$$
\begin{aligned}
\text{Max } Z = {} & [0.551 \times (Q_{11} + Q_{12} + Q_{13} + Q_{14})] \\
& + [0.564 \times (Q_{21} + Q_{22} + Q_{23} + Q_{24})] \\
& + [0.592 \times (Q_{31} + Q_{32} + Q_{33} + Q_{34})] \\
& + [0.557 \times (Q_{41} + Q_{42} + Q_{43} + Q_{44})]
\end{aligned}
$$

Quarterly demand constraint

$$
\begin{aligned}
Q_{11} + Q_{21} + Q_{31} + Q_{41} &\geq 5,000 \,(\text{First quarter demand}) \\
Q_{11} + Q_{21} + Q_{31} + Q_{41} &\leq 5,500 \,(\text{First quarter demand}) \\
Q_{12} + Q_{22} + Q_{32} + Q_{42} &\geq 5,000 \,(\text{Second quarter demand}) \\
Q_{12} + Q_{22} + Q_{32} + Q_{42} &\leq 5,500 \,(\text{Second quarter demand}) \\
Q_{13} + Q_{23} + Q_{33} + Q_{43} &\geq 5,000 \,(\text{Third quarter demand}) \\
Q_{13} + Q_{23} + Q_{33} + Q_{43} &\leq 5,500 \,(\text{Third quarter demand}) \\
Q_{14} + Q_{24} + Q_{34} + Q_{44} &\geq 5,000 \,(\text{Fourth quarter demand}) \\
Q_{14} + Q_{24} + Q_{34} + Q_{44} &\leq 5,500 \,(\text{Fourth quarter demand})
\end{aligned}
$$

Budget constraint

$$
\begin{aligned}
& [9 \times (Q_{11} + Q_{12} + Q_{13} + Q_{14})] + [8 \times (Q_{21} + Q_{22} + Q_{23} + Q_{24})] \\
& + [10 \times (Q_{31} + Q_{32} + Q_{33} + Q_{34})] + [12 \times (Q_{41} + Q_{42} + Q_{43} + Q_{44})] \\
& \leq 200,000
\end{aligned}
$$

Average delivery time constraint

$$
\begin{aligned}
& ([2 \times (Q_{11} + Q_{12} + Q_{13} + Q_{14})] + [4 \times (Q_{21} + Q_{22} + Q_{23} + Q_{24})] \\
& + [6 \times (Q_{31} + Q_{32} + Q_{33} + Q_{34})] \\
& + [3 \times (Q_{41} + Q_{42} + Q_{43} + Q_{44})])/(4 \times 5,500) \leq 4
\end{aligned}
$$

Supplier capacity constraint

$Q_{11} \leq 3,000 X_{11}, Q_{12} \leq 3,000 X_{12}, Q_{13} \leq 3,000 X_{13}, Q_{14} \leq 3,000 X_{14}$ (capacity of supplier S_1)
$Q_{21} \leq 3,500 X_{21}, Q_{22} \leq 3,500 X_{22}, Q_{23} \leq 3,500 X_{23}, Q_{24} \leq 3,500 X_{24}$ (capacity of supplier S_2)
$Q_{31} \leq 2,500 X_{31}, Q_{32} \leq 2,500 X_{32}, Q_{13} \leq 2,500 X_{33}, Q_{34} \leq 2,500 X_{34}$ (capacity of supplier S_3)
$Q_{41} \leq 3,200 X_{41}, Q_{42} \leq 3,200 X_{42}, Q_{43} \leq 3,200 X_{43}, Q_{44} \leq 3,200 X_{44}$ (capacity of supplier S_4)

$X_{11}, X_{12}, X_{13}, X_{14}, = 1,$ if supplier S_1 is selected for quarter 1, 2, 3, or 4. 0, otherwise
$X_{21}, X_{22}, X_{23}, X_{24}, = 1,$ if supplier S_2 is selected for quarter 1, 2, 3, or 4. 0, otherwise
$X_{31}, X_{32}, X_{33}, X_{34}, = 1,$ if supplier S_3 is selected for quarter 1, 2, 3, or 4. 0, otherwise
$X_{41}, X_{42}, X_{43}, X_{44}, = 1,$ if supplier S_4 is selected for quarter 1, 2, 3, or 4. 0, otherwise

where O_{ij} denotes the demand allocated to ith supplier in jth quarter, and $Xij = i$th supplier is selected for jth quarter. This problem is solved by using the Lindo software to obtain optimal solution. The demand allocation to the suppliers and their optimum values calculated by the Lindo software are $Q_{11} = 2,667$, $Q_{12} = 2,898$, $Q_{13} = 0$, $Q_{14} = 2,435$, $Q_{21} = 333$, $Q_{22} = 530$, $Q_{23} = 3,000$, $Q_{24} = 2,137$, $Q_{31} = 2,500$, $Q_{32} = 2,072$, $Q_{33} = 2,500$, $Q_{34} = 928$, $Q_{41} = 0$, $Q_{42} = 0$, $Q_{43} = 0$, and $Q_{44} = 0$. The value of the binary variables are $X_{11} = 1$, $X_{12} = 1$, $X_{13} = 0$, $X_{14} = 1$, $X_{21} = 1$, $X_{22} = 1$, $X_{23} = 1$, $X_{24} = 1$, $X_{31} = 1$, $X_{32} = 1$, $X_{33} = 0$, $X_{34} = 1$, $X_{41} = 0$, $X_{42} = 0$, $X_{43} = 0$, and $X_{44} = 0$. Total purchase value $Z = 12,528$. According to the relative closeness computed by single approach (i.e., TOPSIS), supplier S_3 is the best supplier. However, a total of 8,000, 6,000, 8,000, and 0 units are assigned to suppliers S_1, S_2, S_3, and S_4 by using the hybrid algorithm, which maximize the total value of the procurement. The maximum units are assigned to supplier S_1 and S_3, 8,000 to each. This allocation of the units maximizes the value of procurement. On the contrary, the individual approach (i.e., TOPSIS) assigns the lowest rating to the supplier S_1. In this context, it may be concluded that the hybrid approach improves the efficacy of the individual approaches. However, the wide applicability of individual approach in literature is due to its simplicity, ease of use, and great flexibility. These observations support the literature findings to develop more hybrid approaches for the supplier selection problems.

14.6   Conclusion and Future Research Directions

The present research work is aimed at providing a new scenario to the supplier selection problem pertinent to the humanitarian supply chain management. Rating of the suppliers was computed and the demand allocated optimally among the suppliers. In this scenario, the buyer company did not depend upon the single supplier. This should be encouraging to the humanitarian SCM managers interested in improving the reliability of the suppliers as well as quality of the items by creating the competition among the suppliers, maximizing their value of procurement, and switching over to the demand from one supplier to another supplier when the first supplier is not capable of supplying the items due to unavoidable circumstances. Further, a rated group of suppliers can help the humanitarian SCM managers in operating their supply chain smoothly without any breakdown due to the nonavailability of the goods not supplied by one of the suppliers. The present research work will be helpful for the humanitarian SCM managers who are interested in reconfiguring their supply chain under the failure of any supply chain partner or in a changing business environment.

In a scenario, if a supplier declines to supply the units in a particular quarter, then the proposed model is supportive for the managers as they can adjust the value of variables in the model as per their choices and determine the optimal quantity for allocation among the rest of the suppliers. The model provides flexibility to the managers for evaluation of the different available alternatives in order to take a decision of optimal demand allocation among the suppliers.

The proposed hybrid model to the supplier selection problem derives from four distinctive characteristics: (1) its ability to capture qualitative as well as quantitative criteria consistent with the real supplier selection environment, (2) its ability to not only assign the rating of the suppliers but also assess the status of all possible suppliers, (3) its ability to capture the subjective estimates of the decision makers in terms of linguistic variables, and (4) its ability to optimally allocate the demand among suppliers. Significantly, the proposed hybrid (fuzzy, TOPSIS, and MILP) model provides more objective information for supplier evaluation and demand allocation among suppliers in supply chain. The managers can use the proposed model to the analysis of other management decision-making problems.

The supply chain network is witnessing a changing business environment due to government policies aimed at promoting new small manufacturing enterprises (SMEs) for intermediate parts and components. Hence, the managers have an option to select the new group of suppliers and allocate the optimal multi-period demand among new group of suppliers in order to maximize their purchase value. In this context, the proposed hybrid model would be beneficial for the managers to operate their supply chain effectively and efficiently.

Continuous research for improvement in the existing system/practice has been the basic nature of human beings. Supplier evaluation and selection has always remained as an interesting area for research and has received worldwide attention over the past few decades. Diversified problems encountered by the real-time manufacturing systems and the complex nature of the problem in itself pursued to be achieved have been the sources of motivation in supplier evaluation and selection research. The study on supplier evaluation and multi-period demand allocation among suppliers presented in this research paper could be extended in various ways. Firstly, more case studies on manufacturing systems engaged in diversified operations could underline the practical usefulness of the hybrid methodology as derived from the experimental results. Secondly, future research could consider the transportation cost during demand allocation among suppliers. Thirdly, uncertainty of multi-period demand instead of fixed multi-period demand in supplier selection problem could be taken up. Finally, research can be extended by developing more hybrid approaches for uncertain multi-period demand allocation among suppliers.

References

Aksoy A, Ozturk N (2011) Supplier selection and performance evaluation in just in time production environment. Expert Syst Appl 38:6351–6359

Amid A, Ghodsypour SH, O'Brien C (2009) A weighted additive fuzzy multiobjective model for the supplier selection problem under price breaks in a supply chain. Int J Prod Econ 121:323–332

Bhattacharya A, Geraghty J, Young P (2010) Supplier selection paradigm: an integrated hierarchical QFD methodology under multi-criteria environment. Appl Soft Comput 10:1013–1027

Bhutta MKS (2003) Supplier selection problem: methodology literature review. J Int Technol Info Manag 12(2):53–72

Bruno G, Espositoa E, Genovesea A, Passaroc R (2012) AHP-based approaches for supplier evaluation: problems and perspectives. J Purch Supply Manag 18(3):159–172

Chan FTS, Chan HK (2004) Development of the supplier selection model: a case study in the advanced technology industry. Proc Inst Mech Eng Part B 218:1807–1824

Chen YJ (2011) Structured methodology for supplier selection and evaluation in a supply chain. Inf Sci 181:1651–1670

Chen CT, Lin CT, Huang SF (2006) A fuzzy approach for supplier evaluation and selection in supply chain management. Int J Prod Econ 102:289–301

Choi TY, Hartley JL (1996) An exploration of supplier selection practices across the supply chain. J Oper Manag 14:333–345

Dickson GW (1966) An analysis of supplier selection system and decision. J Purch 2(1):5–17

Ghodsypour SH, O'Brien C (1998) A decision support system for supplier selection using an integrated analytic hierarchy process and linear programming. Int J Prod Econ 56:199–212

Ha SH, Krishna R (2008) A hybrid approach to supplier selection for the maintenance of a competitive supply chain. Expert Syst Appl 34:1303–1311

Ho W, Xu X, Dey PK (2009) Multi criteria decision making approaches for supplier evaluation and selection: a literature review. Eur J Oper Res 202:16–24

Hwang CL, Yoon K (1981) Multiple attributes decision making methods and applications. Springer, Berlin/Heidelberg

Liao CN, Kao HP (2011) An integrated fuzzy TOPSIS and MCGP approach to supplier selection in supply chain management. Expert Syst Appl 38:10803–10811

Luo X, Wu C, Rosenberg D, Barnes D (2009) Supplier selection in Agile Supply chain: an information processing model and an illustration. J Purch Supply Manag 15:249–262

Masella C, Rangone A (2000) A contingent approach to the design of vendor selection systems for different types of co-operative customer/supplier relationships. Int J Oper Prod Manag 20(1):70–84

Nydick RL, Hill RP (1992) Using AHP to structure the supplier selection procedure. Int J Purch Mater Manag 28(2):31–36

Oliveria RC, Lourenco JC (2002) A multi-criteria model for assigning new orders to service supplier. Eur J Oper Res 139:390–399

Osman H, Demirli K (2010) A bilinear goal programming model and a modified Benders decomposition algorithm for supply chain reconfiguration and supplier selection. Int J Prod Econ 124:97–105

Ozkok BA, Tiryaki F (2011) A compensatory fuzzy approach to multi-objective linear supplier selection problem with multiple item. Expert Syst Appl 38:11363–11368

Saaty (1980) The analytic hierarchy process, New York, McGraw-Hill.

Sawik T (2011) Supplier selection in make-to-order environment with risks. Math Comput Model 53:1670–1679

Sevkli M, Lenny Koh SC, Zaim S, Demirbag M, Tatoglu E (2008) Hybrid analytical hierarchy process model for supplier selection. Ind Manag Data Syst 108(1):122–142

Toloo M, Nalchigar S (2011) A new DEA method for supplier selection in presence of both cardinal and ordinal data. Expert Syst Appl 38:14726–14731

Vinodh S, Ramiya RA, Gautham SG (2011) Application of fuzzy analytic network process for supplier selection in a manufacturing organization. Expert Syst Appl 38:272–280

Weber CA (1996) A data envelopment analysis approach to measuring vendor performance. Supply Chain Manag 1(1):28–39

Weber CA, Ellram LM (1993) Supplier selection using multi-objective programming: a decision support system approach. Int J Phys Distrib Logist Manag 23(2):3–14

Weber CA, Current JR, Benton WC (1991) Vendor selection criteria and methods. Eur J Oper Res 50:2–18

Yan H, Yu Z, Cheng TCE (2003) A strategic model for supply chain design with logical constraints: formulation and solution. Comput Oper Res 30:2135–2155

Yucel A, Guneri AF (2011) A weighted additive fuzzy programming approach for multi criteria supplier selection. Expert Syst Appl 38(5):6281–6286

Zhang JL, Zhang MY (2011) Supplier selection and purchase problem with fixed cost and constrained order quantities under stochastic demand. Int J Prod Econ 129:1–7

Zouggari A, Benyoucef L (2012) Simulation based Fuzzy TOPSIS approach for group multi-criteria supplier selection problem. Engineering. Appl Artif Intell 25(3):507–519

Chapter 15
Hierarchical Decision Modeling Approach for Risks Prioritization in Sustainable Supply Chains

Divya Choudhary and Jitendra Madaan

15.1 Introduction

A thriving increase in the consumption of resources in the past few decades has perilously affected our ecology and has made it inconsistent with the sustainable development, and it is becoming essential to impede this reckless consumption of resources. So to curb the exploitation of natural resources, concepts such as recycle, reuse, remanufacture, etc. are being encouraged nowadays across the globe. In a study (Keong 2008) it has been found that if all the people across the globe who have mobiles brought back just one used device, then 240,000 t of raw materials can be saved which can reduce greenhouse gases to the same effect as taking four million cars off the road. This scenario has brought in fore the concept of reverse supply chain (RSC) which is the backflow of end-of-use products, end-of-life products, obsolete products, and commercial returns from the customers to the manufacturer for retrieving the value of the products through reuse, recycle, and resale or for proper disposal. In reverse supply chain value of previously shipped parts, goods and materials are recaptured.

The reverse flow of products is an extension of traditional supply chains in which used products or materials are returned to the organizations for reprocessing or for proper disposition (Prahinski and Kocabasoglu 2006). Further, a conventional supply chain can be defined as "the combination of the interrelated organizations, resources, and processes that create and deliver products and services to end customers" (Russell and Taylor 2001). Figure 15.1 illustrates the structure of the traditional supply chain (Blackburn et al. 2004).

On the other hand, reverse supply chain refers to "the series of activities necessary to remove dead stock or used products from a customer for the purpose of recycling, remanufacturing, and re-using the product" (Guide and Van wassenhove 2002). This chain is traditionally characterized by backward flow of materials.

D. Choudhary (✉) • J. Madaan
Department of Management Studies, Indian Institute of Technology, Delhi, India
e-mail: divyachoudhary2626@gmail.com

© Springer India 2016
B.S. Sahay et al. (eds.), *Managing Humanitarian Logistics*, Springer Proceedings in Business and Economics, DOI 10.1007/978-81-322-2416-7_15

Fig. 15.1 Supply chain process

Fig. 15.2 Reverse supply chain

Three drivers, namely, economic, regulatory, and consumer pressure, drive product returns worldwide. Concerns about environmental issues, sustainable development, and legal regulations have made organizations responsive to reverse logistics (Srivastava and Srivastava 2006). This emerging area involves the activities in the returned product flow, starting from the end customers upward along the forward commercial supply chain till the manufacturers or suppliers (Harrison and Van Hoek 2008). Prahinski and Kocabasoglu (2006) clarified that the scope of reverse supply chain is slightly broader than the reverse logistics. Reverse logistics involves the activities related to transportation, warehousing, and inventory management, while the reverse supply chain includes the coordination and collaboration with channel partners additionally. The reverse supply chain entails five processes which are explained below (Guide and Van wassenhove 2002; Prahinski and Kocabasoglu 2006):

(i) Product acquisition – It includes product acquirement from the customers.
(ii) Reverse logistics – It refers to the process of recovering the goods from the end users for reclaiming the value or for proper discarding. It includes activities related to transportation, warehousing, distribution, and inventory management.
(iii) Inspection and disposition – In this process all the returned products are examined for their quality and to identify a suitable recovery strategy for each of them.
(iv) Reconditioning – In this step, products are transferred to a reconditioning operation, such as repair, refurbishing, remanufacturing, and recycling, if it is found to be suitable.
(v) Distribution and sales – Creating secondary markets for recovered products.

This complete process of reverse supply chain can be depicted as in Fig. 15.2.

In today's world, where the environment has become a primary concern and legislations are put in place by governments in order to obligate companies to reduce their waste and recycle their damaged, returned and aged products, reverse supply chain has become more important than ever. RSC has numerous advantages such as reducing production costs, increasing customer satisfaction, and enhancing competitive ability of companies along with many environmental benefits (Guo 2012). Another sector linked with RSC that can bring profit to the organizations is the secondary markets where returned products can be sold. However, despite the benefits, companies are still hesitant in incorporating recovery practices due to the huge amount of intricacies and uncertainties involved. Uncertainty is one of the characteristics of reverse supply chain, which is leading to the complex and vibrating operations. Further, due to the various associated ambiguities and complexities, apart from various mentioned remunerations RSC also brings along a large number of risks in an organization.

There has been considerable research related to risks in forward supply chain, but in reverse supply chain, it is relatively unexplored and undeveloped. It is necessary to analyze the various risks associated with the reverse supply chain in order to support the organizations to handle them. This paper attempts to explore the various risks related to reverse supply chain and to study the relationship between them to recognize the most critical risks. The objectives of this paper are (a) to identify the various risks present in reverse supply chain, (b) to analyze the interactions among the identified risks, and (c) to create a framework which can assist the organizations in handling the risk issues. The rest of the paper is arranged as follows: Sect. 15.2 gives an introduction about the risks and identifies the RSC risks, Sect. 15.3 contains the methodology to create the framework of these risks, Sect. 15.4 includes the result, and Sect. 15.5 deals with the conclusion and discussions.

15.2   Risks in Sustainable/Reverse Supply Chain

The word "risk" derives from the early Italian word "risicare, which means to dare" (Bernstein 1996). According to the Association of the Project Managers, risk is defined as an uncertain event or set of circumstances which, should it occur, will have an effect on achievement of one or more objectives (Tuncel and Alpan 2010). According to Taylor (2007) the term "risk" refers to potential problems or issues that may arise and adversely impact the progress or outcome of a project. Risk can be due to the presence of flawed practices and uncertainties within an organization or among the network partners or can be at a higher industry or environment level that affects the outcome of the supply chain (Gaonkar and Viswanadham 2007). According to Tang and Musa (2011), a better definition of risk should refer to (i) events with small probability but may occur abruptly and (ii) these events bring substantial negative consequences to the system.

A typical process of risk management contains four basic steps (Tuncel and Alpan 2010):

(i) Risk identification, which helps in recognizing the potential risks in order to manage these scenarios effectively
(ii) Risk assessment, which refers to the assignment of probabilities to risk-bearing events in the system and identifying the consequences of these risk events defined in the first step

(iii) Risk management, which refers to the implementation of actions for managing the risks

(iv) Risk monitoring, where the system is supervised to detect the risks when they occur

In an expedition to become more agile and lean, organizations are now using more of outside support because of which the various links of supply chain are getting exposed to different types of risks (Faisal et al. 2006). There is a substantial amount of risk involved in the RSC which needs to be explored, and the process of risk management usually begins with a study to identify the potential risks that a project could generate or to which it could be exposed (Gandhi et al. 2012). So, to identify the various risks in the reverse supply chain, the literature related to both forward and reverse supply chain risks is explored.

Juttner (2005) suggested three categories of supply chain risk: environmental risk, demand and supply risk, and process risk. To understand the various types of risks and to know about the tools being used to handle the risks, data was collected with the help of surveys and with discussions with the professionals. He concluded that traditional risk management approaches derived from a single company perspective are not ideally suited to accommodate the requirements in a supply chain context. Faisal et al. (2006) identified 11 enablers of risk mitigation such as information sharing, agility in the supply chain, strategic risk planning, risk sharing in the supply chain, etc. and developed an ISM model to show the interrelation between them. According to Tang and Tomlin (2008), there are at least six major types of supply chain risks that occur regularly: supply risk, demand risk, process risk, intellectual property risk, behavioral risk, and social/political risk. Schoenherr et al. (2008) acknowledged 17 risk factors (such as product quality, product cost, demand risk, order fulfillment risk, wrong partner risk, supplier risk) under three main headings: product characteristics, partner characteristics, and environment characteristics. Manuj and Mentzer (2008) discussed about global supply chain risks and strategies to manage these risks. They recognized 11 global supply chain risks: currency, transit time, forecast, quality, safety, business disruption, survival, inventory and tools ownerships, culture, dependency and opportunism, and oil price increase. Olson and Wu (2010) presented a review of enterprise risk management in the supply chain, and they broadly segregated the risks in two broad categories: internal risks and external risks. External risks include nature, political risks, competitor, and market, whereas internal risks include available capacity, internal operation, and information system. Tuncel and Alpan (2010) divided the risks into four categories: supplier, inbound/outbound logistics, manufacturer, and customer. Tang and Musa (2011) explored the risk issues in the supply chain and explained the various risks in detail. They identified various risk issues under the four categories: material flow risk, financial flow risk, information flow risks, and intellectual property risk. According to Sofyalioglu and Kartal (2012), there are four risk groups in the supply chain: supply risk, operational risks, demand risks, and environmental risks. Gandhi et al. (2012) prioritize the various risks (such as quality, vendor, financial, flexibility, technical, etc.) in the supply chain with the help of various hypotheses and surveys. They found that in several hypotheses, quality has been ranked as one of the primary risks and intellectual property has been consistently sighted as a low risk.

According to Yong et al. (2007), reverse supply chain has the following risks: transportation delays, shipment quantity inaccuracies, culture and language differences, volume and mix requirement changes, cost reduction capability, and information capability. Some of the papers determined the risks in reverse supply chain under the categories macroscopic risk, marketing risk, management risk, business risk, financial risk, and system risk (Huizhe and Donglin 2009). Zhang and Fan (2009) identified the reverse logistics outsourcing risks as decision maker risk, cooperation risk, financial risk, capacity risk, and human resource risk. Ravi and Shankar (2005) analyze the interaction among the barriers of reverse logistics with the help of an ISM model, and the barriers considered were lack of information and technological systems, problems with product quality, company policies, resistance to change to reverse logistics, lack of appropriate performance metrics, lack of training and education, financial constraints, lack of commitment by top management, lack of awareness about reverse logistics, lack of strategic planning, and reluctance of the support of dealers, distributors, and retailers. Mangla et al. (2012) recognized the enablers of the product recovery system as supplier commitment, cost, regulations, environmental issue, industry-specific barriers, market edge, and customer redundancy which will affect the outcomes of product recovery system which are green products, capacity utilization, customer satisfaction, environmental benefits, energy consumption reduction, processing time and productivity, and effectiveness. Based on the literature, the various risks associated with the reverse supply chain are identified and are described in Table 15.1.

After identifying the various risks in reverse supply chain, the next thing an organization requires is to determine the most critical risks which can have a severe impact on the organization functioning. For this it is required to understand the interactions and dependencies among all the risks. ISM is very helpful in such circumstances to deal with the entire maze of risks and to provide a systematic framework. It provides a hierarchy of risks and helps in identifying the most significant risks which act as enablers for the other risks.

15.3 Methodology

Interpretive structural modeling (ISM) is an efficient technique to deal with intricate matters. With the help of ISM, diverse variables affecting the system under consideration directly can be structured in to a comprehensive systematic model (Sohani and Sohani 2011). The ISM assists in the transformation of vague, inadequately articulated mental models of systems into perceptible, precise models helpful for many purposes (Ahuja et al. 2009). It also helps in spotting the interrelationships among the variables. It is an appropriate modeling methodology for evaluating the effect of one variable on other variables (Gupta et al. 2012). The

Table 15.1 Risks in sustainable/reverse supply chain

Risks	Description	References
Supplier risk (R1)	Uncertainty associated with reverse logistics provider activities and in general relationships	Solomon et al. (2012); Tang and Tomlin (2008), Zhang and Fan (2009)
Financial risk (R2)	Inability to complete the project within a given budget and the risk associated with cost of RL processes. It includes bank risk, capital management risk, and down-side risk	Gandhi et al. (2012), Huizhe and Donglin (2009)
Global risk (R3)	Risks associated with the global reverse supply chain such as exchange rate risk, transit time risk, culture differences, and quality standard differences	Sofyalioglu and Kartal (2012), Manuj and Mentzer (2008), Yong et al. (2007)
Transportation risk (R4)	Risks during the transportation of the returned goods, such as delays due to bad weather, traffic density and breakdown, containers going overboard, and truck accidents	Tuncel and Alpan (2010), Harrison and Van Hoek (2008)
Operational disruption risk (R5)	Risk due to operational contingencies, natural disasters, and political instability including terrorism	Tang and Musa (2011), Juttner (2005)
Facility risk (R6)	Risk due to the breakdown of machine and electricity or water failure causing a delay or leading to unavailability of plants, warehouses, and official buildings	Gaonkar and Viswanadham (2007), Gaudenzi and Borghesi (2006)
Information risk (R7)	Failure of information and communication infrastructure due to computer hardware or software failure leading to the inability to coordinate operation and execute transaction. It also includes information accuracy and security risk	Olson and Wu (2010), Zhang and Fan (2009)
Process risk (R8)	Risk of lower-than-expected yields which reduces the plant's effective capacity. It includes recovery rate risk	Tang and Tomlin (2008)
Technical risk (R9)	The inability of the technology to provide the expected performance	Gandhi et al. (2012)
Compliance risk (R10)	The inability of an organization to comply with appropriate regulations (local and global)	Sofyalioglu and Kartal (2012)
Quality risk (R11)	The inability of the end product (manufactured by the recycled raw material) to satisfy customer requirements	Ravi and Shankar (2005)
Schedule risk (R12)	The inability to process the returned products within the originally specified period of time	Zhang and Fan (2009)
Human resource risk (R13)	The risk of unavailability of trained manpower	Huizhe and Donglin (2009)

(continued)

Table 15.1 (continued)

Risks	Description	References
Strategic planning risk (R14)	Risk due to the lack of the understanding and detection of reverse logistics goals and absence of long-term plans for managing them	Tibben-Lembke and Rogers (2002)
Management risk (R15)	Risk due to lack of commitment by top-level management	Srivastava and Srivastava (2006)
Resistance risk (R16)	Risk due the resistance by the employees, stakeholders, etc. for the implementation of RL	Ravi and Shankar (2005)
Forecast risk (R17)	Risk due the inability to predict the time and amount of return products	Tibben-Lembke and Rogers (2002)

basic series of steps followed in ISM methodology are as follows (Govindan and Murugesan, 2011).

15.3.1 Step-by-Step Procedure in the ISM Methodology

Step 1: Attributes for the system under consideration are listed.

Step 2: Contextual relationship is established among attributes with respect to which pairs of attributes would be examined.

Step 3: A structural self-interaction matrix (SSIM) is developed for attributes, which indicates pairwise relationships among attributes of the system under consideration.

Step 4: Reachability matrix is developed from the SSIM and the matrix is checked for transitivity. Transitivity is the basic assumption made in ISM; it states that if an attribute A is related to B and B is related to C, then A is necessarily related to C.

Step 5: The reachability matrix obtained from Step 4 is partitioned into different levels.

Step 6: A digraph graph is drawn and the transitive links are removed based on the relationship given in the above reachability matrix.

Step 7: The resultant digraph is converted into an ISM by replacing attribute nodes with statements.

Step 8: The ISM model developed in Step 7 is reviewed to check for conceptual inconsistency and necessary modifications are made.

Subsequently, based on the above mentioned steps, ISM methodology is applied to obtain a hierarchy of RSC risks in order to prioritize them.

15.3.1.1 Development of Structural Self-Interaction Matrix (SSIM)

Opinions of the experts are used to develop the contextual relationship between the different variables. Four symbols used to denote the direction of relationship between the attributes are given below (i and j):

- V – attribute i will help in achieving attribute j.
- A – attribute i will be achieved by attribute j.
- X – attribute i and j will help to achieve to each other.
- O – attribute i and j are unrelated.

The SSIM constructed for the risks associated with RSC is shown in Table 15.2.

15.3.1.2 Constructing Initial Reachability Matrix

The SSIM is transformed into a binary matrix, called the initial reachability matrix. The rules for the substitution of 1 and 0 are the following:

- If the (i, j) entry in the SSIM is V, then the (i, j) entry in the reachability matrix becomes 1 and the (j, i) entry becomes 0.
- If the (i, j) entry in the SSIM is A, then the (i, j) entry in the reachability matrix becomes 0 and the (j, i) entry becomes 1.
- If the (i, j) entry in the SSIM is X, then the (i, j) entry in the reachability matrix becomes 1 and the (j, i) entry also becomes 1.

Table 15.2 Structural Self Interaction Matrix (SSIM)

RISKS	R17	R16	R15	R14	R13	R12	R11	R10	R9	R8	R7	R6	R5	R4	R3	R2
Supply risk (R1)	A	V	A	A	O	V	V	V	A	V	A	A	A	A	V	V
Financial risk (R2)	A	V	X	A	A	A	A	A	V	A	V	A	A	A	A	
Global Risk (R3)	V	V	A	A	O	V	V	V	O	O	A	O	A	A		
Transportation Risk (R4)	V	V	A	A	O	V	O	O	O	O	A	O	A			
Operational disruption Risk (R5)	V	V	O	O	O	V	O	O	O	O	V	O				
Facility Risk (R6)	O	V	A	A	O	V	O	O	A	V	O					
Information Risk (R7)	V	V	A	A	O	V	O	O	A	O						
Process Risk(R8)	A	V	O	O	A	V	O	A	A							
Technical Risk (R9)	V	V	A	A	O	V	V	V								
Compliance Risk (R10)	O	V	A	A	A	O	O									
Quality Risk (R11)	O	V	O	O	A	O										
Schedule Risk (R12)	A	V	O	A	A											
Human resource Risk (R13)	O	V	A	A												
Strategic planning Risk(R14)	V	V	A													
Management Risk (R15)	O	V														
Resistance Risk (R16)	A															
Forecast Risk (R17)																

- If the (i, j) entry in the SSIM is 0, then the (i, j) entry in the reachability matrix becomes 0 and the (j, i) entry also becomes 0.

The initial reachability matrix derived from SSIM (Table 15.2) is shown in Table 15.3.

15.3.1.3 Constructing Final Reachability Matrix

The final reachability matrix for the attributes is obtained by incorporating the transitivity rule (i.e., if A is related to B and B is related to C, then A is related to C) and is shown in Table 15.4. The values obtained by incorporating the transitivity are represented by "*" in the final reachability matrix i.e. Table 15.4.

15.3.1.4 Level Partitions

With the help of final reachability matrix, the reachability and antecedent sets for each factor are derived. The intersection of corresponding reachability and antecedent sets is the intersection set for each attribute. If the reachability set and the intersection set are the same, then that attribute is considered to be in level I and is given in the top position in the ISM hierarchy. These iterations are repeated until the level of each variable has been decided. The iterations are given in Tables 15.5 and 15.6.

On the basis of the final reachability matrix, the hierarchal model is constructed. The relationship between the risks is depicted with the help of the arrows. The graph generated from these relations is called a digraph. On eliminating transitivity as explained in the ISM methodology, the digraph is finally converted into the ISM model as shown in Fig. 15.3.

15.4 Results

The ISM model assists us in studying the relationships between the various risks and to classify the risks on the basis of their dependence power and driving power. It is observed from the ISM model that the strategic planning risk (R14) and operation disruption risk (R5) are the most critical risks in the reverse supply chain as they form the base of the ISM hierarchy. All the identified risks finally lead to the resistance risk which is at the top of the hierarchy and lead to the opposition against the inclusion of the reverse supply chain in the system. The following points can be derived from the ISM model.

Operational disruption risk (R5) is the most uncertain risk associated with any supply chain as no organization has any control over it and can have severe impact on the functioning of the RSC. It further leads to the disruption of the transportation system (R4) due to the damage or obstruction of the paths. Strategic planning risk (R14) is also a very crucial risk as lack of appropriate planning to implement the

Table 15.3 Initial reachability matrix

Risks	R17	R16	R15	R14	R13	R12	R11	R10	R9	R8	R7	R6	R5	R4	R3	R2	R1
Supply risk (R1)	0	1	0	0	0	1	1	1	0	1	0	0	0	0	1	1	1
Financial risk (R2)	0	1	1	0	0	0	0	0	1	0	1	0	0	0	0	1	0
Global risk (R3)	1	1	0	0	0	1	1	1	0	0	0	0	0	0	1	1	0
Transportation risk (R4)	1	1	0	0	0	1	0	0	0	0	0	0	0	1	1	1	1
Operational disruption risk (R5)	1	1	0	0	0	1	0	0	0	0	1	0	1	1	1	1	1
Facility risk (R6)	0	1	0	0	0	1	0	0	0	1	0	1	0	0	0	1	1
Information risk (R7)	1	1	0	0	0	1	0	0	0	0	1	0	0	1	1	0	1
Process risk (R8)	0	1	0	0	0	1	0	0	0	1	0	0	0	0	0	1	0
Technical risk (R9)	1	1	0	0	0	1	1	1	1	1	0	1	0	0	0	0	1
Compliance risk (R10)	0	1	0	0	0	0	0	1	0	1	0	0	0	0	0	1	0
Quality risk (R11)	0	1	0	0	0	0	1	0	0	0	0	0	0	0	0	1	0
Schedule risk (R12)	0	1	0	0	0	1	0	0	0	0	0	0	0	0	0	1	0
Human resource risk (R13)	0	1	0	0	1	1	1	1	0	1	0	0	0	0	0	1	0
Strategic planning risk (R14)	1	1	0	1	1	1	0	1	1	0	1	1	0	1	1	1	1
Management risk (R15)	0	1	1	1	1	0	0	1	1	0	1	1	0	1	1	1	1
Resistance risk (R16)	0	1	0	0	0	0	0	0	0	0	0	0	0	0	0	0	0
Forecast risk (R17)	1	1	0	0	0	1	0	0	0	1	0	0	0	0	0	1	1

Table 15.4 Final reachability matrix

Risks	R1	R2	R3	R4	R5	R6	R7	R8	R9	R10	R11	R12	R13	R14	R15	R16	R17	Driving power
Supply risk (R1)	1	1	1	0	0	0	1*	1	1*	1	1	1	0	0	1*	1	1*	12
Financial risk (R2)	1*	1	1*	1*	0	1*	1	1*	1	1*	1*	1*	1*	1*	1	1	1*	16
Global risk (R3)	1*	1	1	0	0	0	1*	1*	1*	1	1	1	0	0	1*	1	1	12
Transportation risk (R4)	1	1	1	1	0	0	1*	1*	1*	1*	1*	1	0	0	1*	1	1	13
Operational disruption risk (R5)	1	1	1*	1	1	0	1	1*	1*	1*	1*	1	0	0	1*	1	1	14
Facility risk (R6)	1	1	1*	0	0	1	1*	1	1*	1*	1*	1	0	0	1*	1	0	12
Information risk (R7)	0	1*	0	1	0	0	1	1*	0	1*	1*	1	0	0	0	1	1	11
Process risk (R8)	1	1	0	0	0	0	1*	1	1*	0	0	1	0	0	1*	1	0	7
Technical risk (R9)	0	1*	1*	0	0	1	0	1	1	1	1	1	0	0	0	1	1	11
Compliance risk (R10)	0	1	0	0	0	0	1*	1	1*	1	0	1*	0	0	1*	1	0	8
Quality risk (R11)	0	1	0	0	0	0	1*	0	1*	1	1	0	0	0	1*	1	0	6
Schedule risk (R12)	0	1	0	0	0	0	1*	0	1*	0	0	1*	0	0	1*	1	0	6
Human resource risk (R13)	0	1	0	1	0	0	1*	1	1*	1	1	1	1	1	1*	1	0	10
Strategic planning risk (R14)	1	1	1	1	1	1	1	1	1	1	1	1	1	1	1	1	1	16
Management risk (R15)	1*	1	0	1	0	1	1	1*	1	1	1*	1*	1	1	1	1	1*	16
Resistance risk (R16)	0	0	0	0	0	0	0	0	0	0	0	0	0	0	0	1	0	1
Forecast risk (R17)	1	1	1*	0	0	0	1*	1	1*	1*	1*	1	0	0	1*	1	1	12
Dependence power	10	16	11	6	1	5	15	14	14	13	13	15	4	3	14	17	10	

Table 15.5 Iteration 1

Risks	Reachability set	Antecedent set	Intersection set	Level
R1	R1,R2,R3,R7,R8,R10, R11, R12,R15,R16,R17	R1,R2,R3,R4,R5,R6,R7,R9, R14,R15,R17	R1,R2,R3, R7,R15, R17	
R2	R1,R2,R3,R4,R6,R7,R8, R9,R10,R11,R12,R13, R14,R15,R16,R17	R1,R2,R3,R4,R5,R6,R7,R8,R9, R10,R11,R12,R13,R14,R15,R17	R1,R2,R3, R4,R6,R7, R8,R9,R10, R11,R12, R13,R14, R15,R17	
R3	R1,R2,R3,R7,R8,R9, R10,R11,R12,R15,R16, R17	R1,R2,R3,R4,R5,R6,R7,R9,R14, R15,R17	R1,R2,R3, R7,R9,R15, R17	
R4	R1,R2,R3,R4,R7,R8,R9, R10,R11,R12,R15,R16, R7	R2,R4,R5,R7,R14,R15	R2,R4,R7, R15	
R5	R1,R2,R3,R4,R5,R7,R8, R9,R10,R11,R12,R15, R16, R17	R5	R5	
R6	R1,R2,R3,R6,R7,R8,R9, R10,R11,R12,R15,R16	R2,R6,R9,R14,R15	R2,R6,R9, R15	
R7	R1,R2,R3,R4,R7,R8,R10, R11,R12,R16,R17	R1,R2,R3,R4,R5,R6,R7,R8,R10, R11,R12,R13,R14,R15,R17	R1,R2,R3, R4,R7,R8, R10,R11, R12,R17	
R8	R2,R7,R8,R9,R12,R15, R6	R1,R2,R3,R4,R5,R6,R7,R8,R9, R10,R13,R14,R15,R17	R2,R7,R8, R9,R15	
R9	R1,R2,R3,R6,R8,R9,R10, R11,R12,R16,R17	R1,R2,R3,R4,R5,R6,R8,R9,R10, R11,R12,R13,R14,R15,R17	R1,R2,R3, R6,R8,R9, R10,R11, R12,R17	
R10	R2,R7,R8,R9,R10,R12, R15,R16	R1,R2,R3,R4,R5,R6,R7,R9,R10, R13,R14,R15,R17	R2,R7,R9, R10,R15	
R11	R2,R7,R9,R11,R15,R16	R1,R2,R3,R4,R5,R6,R7,R9, R11,R13,R14,R15,R17	R2,R7,R9, R11,R15	
R12	R2,R7,R9,R12,R15,R16	R1,R2,R3,R4,R5,R6,R7,R8,R9, R10,R12,R13,R14,R15,R17	R2,R7,R9, R12,R15	
R13	R2,R7,R8,R9,R10,R11, R2 R13,R15,R16	R2,R13,R14,R15	R2,R13,R15	
R14	R1,R2,R3,R4,R6,R7,R8, R9,R10,R11,R12,R13, R14,R15 R16,R17	R2,R14,R15	R2,R14,R15	
R15	R1,R2,R3,R4,R6,R7,R8, R9,R10, R11,R12,R13,R14,R15, R16,R17	R1,R2,R3,R4,R5,R6,R8,R10, R11,R12,R13,R14,R15,R17	R1,R2,R3, R4,R6,R8, R10,R11, R12,R13, R14,R15,R17	

(continued)

Table 15.5 (continued)

Risks	Reachability set	Antecedent set	Intersection set	Level
R16	R16	R1,R2,R3,R4,R5,R6,R7,R8, R9R10,R11,R12,R13,R14,R15, R16, R17	R16	I
R17	R1,R2,R3,R7,R8,R9,R10, R11,R12,R15,R16,R17	R1,R2,R3,R4,R5,R7,R9, R14,R15,R17	R1,R2,R3, R7,R9,R15, R17	

Table 15.6 Iteration 2 to 7

Iteration	Risks	Reachability set	Antecedent set	Intersection set	Level
II	R2	R1,R2,R3,R4, R6,R7,R8, R9,R10,R11, R12,R13,R14, R15,R17	R1,R2,R3,R4,R5,R6,R7,R8, R9R10, R11,R12,R13,R14, R15,R17	R1,R2,R3,R4,R6, R7, R8,R9,R10,R11, R12, R13,R14,R15, R17	II
II	R7	R1,R2,R3,R4, R7,R8,R10, R11,R12,R17	R1,R2,R3,R4,R5,R6,R7,R8, R10,R11,R12,R13,R14, R15,R17	R1,R2,R3,R4,R7, R8, R10,R11,R12, R17	II
II	R9	R1,R2,R3,R6, R8,R9,R10, R11,R12, R17	R1,R2,R3,R4,R5,R6,R8,R9, R10,R11,R12,R13,R14, R15, R17	R1,R2,R3,R6,R8, R9, R10,R11,R12, R17	II
II	R11	R2,R7,R9,R11, R15	R1,R2,R3,R4,R5,R6,R7,R9, R11,R13,R14,R15,R17	R2,R7,R9,R11, R15	II
II	R12	R2,R7,R9,R12, R15	R1,R2,R3,R4,R5,R6,R7,R8, R9, R10,R12,R13,R14,R15,R17	R2,R7,R9,R12, R15	II
III	R8	R8,R15	R1,R3,R4,R5,R6,R8, R10,R13,R14,R15,R17	R8,R15	III
III	R15	R1,R3,R4,R6, R8,R10,R13, R14,R15,R17	R1,R3,R4,R5,R6, R8 R10, R13, R14, R15, R17	R1,R3,R4,R6,R8, R10, R13, R14, R15,R17	III
IV	R10	R10	R1,R3,R4,R5,R6, R10,R13, R14,R17	R10	IV
V	R1	R1,R3,R17	R1,R3,R4,R5,R6,R14,R17	R1,R3,R17	V
V	R3	R1,R3,R17	R1,R3,R4,R5,R6,R14,R17	R1,R3,R17	V
V	R13	R13	R13,R14	R13	V
V	R17	R1,R3,R17	R1,R3,R4,R5,R14,R17	R1,R3,R17	V
VI	R4	R4	R4,R5,R14	R4	VI
VI	R6	R6	R6,R9,R14	R6	VI
VII	R5	R5	R5	R5	VII
VII	R14	R14	R14	R14	VII

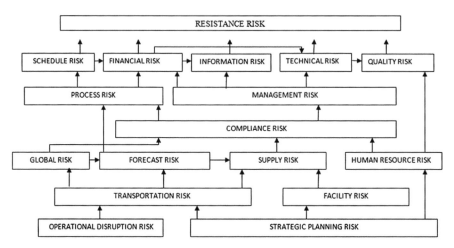

Fig. 15.3 ISM-based risk model for sustainable/reverse supply chains

reverse supply chain can cause the failure of the entire system and will result in the lack of training (R13), absence of proper maintenance of machines (R6), and lack of appropriate transportation system (R4). Facility risk (R6) has vertical interaction with supply risk (R1) as breakdown of machines, unavailability of electricity, etc. can affect the supplier performance. Transportation risk (R4) is related to forecast risk (R17), supply risk (R1), and global risk (R3) as it can cause the delay in delivery of the returned products to organization, and in global supply chains it further increases the uncertainty due the large distances. Also, global risk (R3) has horizontal interaction with forecast risk (R17) as ambiguity associated with the inter-country trade of returned products is even more. Forecast risk (R17) is the most common risk as the amount and time of returns is always vague in RSC, and it further leads to process risk (R8) which in turn directs toward schedule risk (R12) and financial risk (R2) as unavailability of expected amount of reusable products can affect the manufacturing and delivery schedule and can also result in loss of sale. These global (R3), supply (R1), and HR risks (R13) further cause the organization difficulties in complying with the rules and regulations (R10). Next, the compliance risk (R10) has vertical interaction with the management risk (R15) as the presence of so many insecurities in the RSC results in lack of commitment by the top-level management. Then management risk (R15) is related to financial risk (R2) as if management is uninterested in RSC, then availability of capital for initial investment becomes a major issue.

Subsequently, financial risk (R2) is associated with information risk (R7) and technical risk (R9) horizontally because lack of financial resources will avert the arrangement of appropriate information system and technology which are essential for the RSC. The technology risk (R9) can affect the recovery process which in turn can influence the quality of reclaimed material and products (R11). Lastly, all these risks – schedule, financial, information, technical, and quality risk – further lead to the resistance risk (R16).

15.5   Conclusion and Scope

Sustainable/reverse supply chain is becoming a necessity in today's competitive world as it can act as a stepping stone toward success for many organizations and also assist in achieving sustainable development. RSC has many benefits which include direct gains such as reduction of cost, reclaiming value of used products, and profits in secondary markets and indirect gains such as gaining customer confidence, enhancing the green image of the organization, compliance of regulations, etc. Despite these remunerations, organizations across the globe are hesitant in incorporating RSC due to the complexity and ambiguities associated with it. This paper is an attempt to identify these risks associated with RSC and to provide a framework which can prepare the organizations to handle these risks. It can help the organizations in the successful execution of the RSC.

ISM can guide the management in understanding the interactions between the risks and to recognize the critical risks which have the major influence on the RSC functioning and also act as the enablers for other risks. With the help of the literature, seventeen major risks aligned with the RSC are recognized and their hierarchy is created with the help of ISM. From the model it is found that operational disruption risk and strategic planning risk are the most critical risks as they form the base of the hierarchy. So, it can be concluded that proper strategic planning is most essential for the proper functioning of RSC and to mitigate the risks associated with it. Transportation risk and facility risk are the next significant risks. Subsequently, another major requirement of RSC is to have an appropriate transportation system which can handle the randomness associated with the time and quantity of returns efficiently and economically. Proper maintenance of all the machines, facilities, and transportation system is also essential to diminish the risks. Other major crucial risks which need to be focused upon are global risk, forecast risk, human resource risk, and supply risk.

Although some major risks associated with the RSC are identified, the rest of the risks cannot be ignored and should be taken care of. To curb the depletion of resources and to protect our ecology, there is a strong need for the incorporation of the RSC in the existing organization systems and for that it is required to handle these risks associated with it. This paper has provided a base framework to understand the various RSC risks and their interrelationships.

In future this work can be further extended by applying multi-criteria decision analysis techniques such as ELECTRE, TOPSIS, etc. to determine the ranking of risks according to their criticality. Future work can also include the analyses of various ways and strategies to mitigate these risks. Additionally, it can be interesting to explore the application of traditional risk mitigation strategies in RSC.

References

Ahuja V, Yang J, Shankar R (2009) Benefits of collaborative ICT adoption for building project management. Constr Innov 9(3):323–340

Bernstein P (1996) Against the gods: the remarkable story of risk. Wiley, Chichester

Blackburn JD, Guide V, Gilvan CS, Van Wassenhove L (2004) Reverse supply chains for commercial returns. Calif Manage Rev 46:6–22

Faisal M, Banwet DK, Shankar R (2006) Supply chain risk mitigation: modeling the enablers. Bus Process Manag J 12(4):535–552

Gandhi SJ, Gorod A, Sauser B (2012) Prioritization of outsourcing risks from a systemic perspective. Strateg Outsourcing Int J 5(1):39–71

Gaonkar RS, Viswanadham N (2007) Analytical framework for the management of risk in supply chains. IEEE Trans Automat Sci Eng 4(2):265–273

Gaudenzi B, Borghesi A (2006) Managing risks in the supply chain using the AHP method. Int J Logist Manag 17(1):114–136

Ghadge A, Dani S, Kalawsky R (2012) Supply chain risk management: present and future scope. Int J Logist Manag 23(3):313–339

Govindan K, Murugesan P (2011) Selection of third-party reverse logistics provider using fuzzy extent analysis. Benchmarking Int J 18(1):149–167

Guide V, Van Wassenhove L (2002) The reverse supply chain. Harv Bus Rev 80(2):25–26

Guo W (2012) Selection model of third-party reverse logistics service providers under supply chain management. In: Proceedings of 24th Chinese control and decision conference, Beijing, pp 1761–1764

Gupta MP, Mangla S, Madaan J (2012) Multi-objective decision modeling using interpretive structural modeling (ISM) for green supply chains. In: Proceedings of POMS 23rd annual conference, Chicago

Harrison A, Van Hoek R (2008) Logistic management and strategy – competing through the supply chain, 3rd edn. Pearson Education Limited, Harlow

Huizhe Y, Donglin Y (2009) Research on risk assessment of reverse logistics of retailing based on unascertained measurement. In: Proceedings of IEEE, Wuhan, 23–24 May, pp 1–4

Juttner U (2005) Supply chain risk management: understanding the business requirements from a practitioner perspective. Int J Logist Manag 16(1):120–141

Keong LM (2008) Nokia kiosks collect phones for recycling. Available: http://news.cnet.com/8301-11128_3-10045417-54.html, August 2012

Mangla S, Madaan J, Chan FTS (2012) Analysis of performance focused variables for multi-objective flexible decision modeling approach of product recovery systems. Global J Flex Syst Manag 13(2):77–86

Manuj I, Mentzer JT (2008) Global supply chain risk management strategies. Int J Phy Distrib Logist Manag 38(3):192–223

Olson LD, Wu DD (2010) A review of enterprise risk management in supply chain. Kybernetes 39(5):694–706

Prahinski C, Kocabasoglu C (2006) Empirical research opportunities in reverse supply chains. Omega 34:519–532

Ravi V, Shankar R (2005) Analysis of interactions among the barriers of reverse logistics. Technol Forecasting Soc Change 72:1011–1029

Russell R, Taylor B (2001) Operations management, 3rd edn. Prentice Hall, Upper Saddle River

Schoenherr T, Tummala VMR, Harrison TP (2008) Assessing supply chain risks with the analytic hierarchy process: providing decision support for the offshoring decision by a US manufacturing company. J Purch Supply Manag 14:100–111

Sofyalioglu C, Kartal B (2012) The selection of global supply chain risk management strategies by using fuzzy analytical hierarchy process – a case from Turkey. Procedia Soc Behav Sci 58:1448–1457

Sohani N, Sohani N (2011) Developing interpretive structural model for quality framework in higher education: Indian context. J Eng Sci Manag Edu 5(2):495–501

Solomon A, Ketikidis P, Choudhary A (2012) A knowledge based approach for handling supply chain risk management. In: Proceedings of BCI'12, Novi Sad

Srivastava SK, Srivastava RK (2006) Managing product returns for reverse logistics. Int J Phys Distrib Logist Manag 36(7):524–546

Tang O, Musa SN (2011) Identifying risk issues and research advancements in supply chain risk management. Int J Prod Econ 133:25–34

Tang C, Tomlin B (2008) The power of flexibility for mitigating supply chain risks. Int J Prod Econ 116:12–27

Taylor H (2007) Outsourced IT projects from the vendor perspective: different goals, different risks. J Global Info Manag 15(2):1–27

Tibben-Lembke RS, Rogers DS (2002) Differences between forward and reverse logistics in a retail environment. Supply Chain Manag Int J 7(5):271–282

Tuncel G, Alpan G (2010) Risk assessment and management for supply chain networks: a case study. Comput Ind 61:250–259

Yong Z, Lin-jun X, Xu-hong L, Su-fang W (2007) Designing a reverse logistics network considering risk management. In: Proceedings of international conference on wireless communications, networking and mobile computing, IEEE, Shanghai, 21–25 Sept, pp 4636–4639

Zhang W, Fan T (2009) Research on enterprise reverse logistics outsourcing risk evaluation based on fuzzy comprehensive analytic method. In: Proceedings of international conference on information management, innovation management and industrial engineering, IEEE, Xi'an, 26–27 Dec, pp 106–109

Chapter 16
Selection of Post-Disaster Humanitarian Logistics Structure Using AHP Approach

Vivek Roy, Sumit Agarwal, Subhash Kumar, and Parikshit Charan

16.1 Introduction

Humanitarian logistics are in response to extreme catastrophic events. Critical supplies such as water, food and medicine in the impacted area are destroyed or quickly depleted. So the response in the form of external assistance is required to reduce the further loss of life (Van Wassenhove 2006). The process of transporting critical supplies post the disaster is very complex. It is therefore required that the relief operation must be very efficient and appropriate to match the requirements of the situation (Van Wassenhove and Pedraza Martinez 2012). There are three structures of post-disaster humanitarian logistics (PD-HL) operation, namely, Agency Centric Efforts (ACEs), Partially Integrated Efforts (PIEs) and Collaborative Aid Networks (CANs). These structures differ from each other to various extents (Holgin-Veras et al. 2012).

The question arises in the superiority of these structures, one over the other. Thus, it is very important to choose the appropriate post-disaster humanitarian logistics structure. An evaluation framework is required, which should incorporate all the determinants of these structures and is useful to select to most appropriate structure. One such approach, with an application of a systematic analysis technique is presented in this paper. This technique evaluates the various determinants of the mentioned PD-HL structures through an analytic hierarchy process (AHP) model.

V. Roy (✉) • S. Agarwal • S. Kumar
Department of Operations Management, Indian Institute of Management Raipur,
Raipur, Chhattisgarh, India
e-mail: vivekroy.iimraipur@gmail.com

P. Charan
Department of Management Studies, IIT Delhi, New Delhi, India

Department of Operations and Systems, Indian Institute of Management Raipur,
Raipur, Chhattisgarh, India

© Springer India 2016
B.S. Sahay et al. (eds.), *Managing Humanitarian Logistics*, Springer Proceedings in Business and Economics, DOI 10.1007/978-81-322-2416-7_16

There are number of variables which affects the selection of PD-HL structure. Analytical hierarchical process (AHP) is one of the analytical tools, which can be used to handle a multi-criteria decision-making problem (Saaty 1980). The AHP model presented in this paper structures the problem related to selection of a PD-HL structure in a hierarchical form. Identification of the important determinants is very important in this evaluation.

16.2 Determinants of PD-HL Structures

After review of literature and discussion with ten experts, some important PD-HL determinants are identified. These eight determinants are, namely, Speed, Agility, Adaptability, Decentralisation, Resilience, Alignment, Information System and Resource Availability. These are briefly described below.

16.2.1 Speed

The humanitarian aid supply network in disaster relief is characterised both by its speed of inception and execution, as well as their relative impermanence. Furthermore, it serves a common goal (that of alleviating the suffering of those in need), an important characteristic in team formation (Tatham and Kovacs 2010). There has always been a significant increase in the focus on improving the response to rapid onset disasters following any high-profile events.

16.2.2 Agility

Agility is quick response to change. Lee (2004) advocated that agility is critical in any supply chain. As post-catastrophic events, agility is very essential, since nobody knows that what challenges the relief operation is next going to face. So it has to match the requirements of the situation.

16.2.3 Adaptability

As the situation changes, the PD-HL structure must be able to respond to the demand of the situation in the most appropriate way. Lee (2004) advocated that it is not necessary to maintain the status quo in the mode of operation. If the situation demands, then the facilities can be relocated, source of supplies can be changed, and outsourcing can be done if required.

16.2.4 Decentralisation

The impacted area can be severely affected from various locations. So decentralisation is very important to reach those affected locations simultaneously. Many literatures have established that it's quite better to go for decentralisation rather than making the system centralised.

16.2.5 Resilience

A resilient supply chain parts the wide range of risks. It can respond quickly when a problem occurs. As there are risks such as operational risks and functional risks which can arise during the relief operation, so the structure must be resilient enough to respond to ever changing situation.

16.2.6 Alignment

The alignment of interests is very important. Any relief operation is interlinked with various activities and processes. If the goals for the effective relief are not aligned, then any operation cannot work in the desired way.

16.2.7 Information System

Information system plays a vital role in traceability of goods. As the experience in many past disasters has demonstrated, a successful local delivery operation requires not only logistical structure but also information systems, e.g., properly trained individuals well connected to others in the network. Also the real-time information of the current scenario is very essential to ensure the relief operation is going as desired. Information system provides which way now to proceed and what modification in the strategy is now required as per the situation.

16.2.8 Resource Availability

The resource available gets exhausted continuously in any relief operation. So the resources must be checked regularly and replenished as required. The strategy must be very clear regarding the same. If the resources are not available, then ultimately the relief operation will be affected severely.

16.3   Alternatives for Structuring Post-disaster Humanitarian Logistics Operation

After the review of literature and discussion with ten experts, some important structures of PD-HL operations are identified. These alternatives are Agency Centric Efforts (ACEs), Partially Integrated Efforts (PIEs) and Collaborative Aid Networks (CANs). AHP framework is used for the evaluation of these alternatives. The descriptions of these alternatives are discussed below.

16.3.1   Agency Centric Efforts (ACEs)

The operation is based on the internal capacities of the group. This mainly comprises of the individuals and groups who are from the communities affected from disaster. This is based on the internal capacities. The other components in this are the foreign relief groups, but they don't have any relationship to the local people. Thus, knowledge to the local conditions is limited. They are internally strong but have a weak local connection (Holgin-Veras et al. 2012).

16.3.2   Partially Integrated Efforts (PIEs)

Here some group members can be local. The extensiveness depends on the local partnership. This structure is internally strong and could be well connected to the locals. The foreign group along with some locals helps with the local distribution of the supplies. They can comprise of international organisation, N.G.O, that focuses on human assistance (Holgin-Veras et al. 2012).

16.3.3   Collaborative Aid Networks (CANs)

CANs have significant presence inside the impacted area and significant presence in the rest part of the country. They also comprises of social and religious groups. The relationship to local people is very strong, as they are the part of the community. The knowledge of the local conditions is very extensive. The strength of the network is very strong. Extent of local contacts is huge here (Holgin-Veras et al. 2012).

16.4 The Decision Environment

A graphical representation of the AHP model and the decision environment is shown in Fig. 16.1. The overall objective is to select PD-HL structure. The determinants for selection (Speed, Agility, Adaptability, Decentralisation, Resilience, Alignment, Information System and Resource Availability) are described in Sec. 16.2. The various alternatives available to the decision-makers are ACEs, CANs and PIEs.

16.4.1 Analytic Hierarchical Process

AHP (Saaty 1980) is a multi-criteria decision-making technique. It can handle multiple criteria easily. AHP takes both quantitative and qualitative data into account. AHP involves the principles of decomposition, pair-wise comparisons, and priority generation and synthesis. This process is based on the reasoning, knowledge and experience of the experts in the field. Thus, both tangible and intangible attributes are incorporated here, so it can act as a qualitative tool for strategic decision-making problems. This process has certain limitations, such as extensive requirements of brainstorming sessions and discussions. Another limitation is that it requires the careful track of matrices and pair-wise comparisons.

16.4.2 AHP Model for the Selection of PD-HL Structure

The AHP model is applied to analyse the three different post-disaster humanitarian logistic structures (ACEs, PIEs and CANs). This helps in making a comparison between these three structures and to select the best possible alternative among these three.

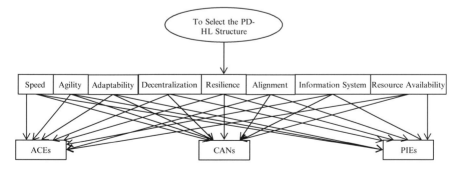

Fig. 16.1 AHP-based framework for selecting the PD-HL structure

16.4.2.1 Step 1: Model Development and Problem Formulation

The relevant determinants and alternatives are chosen on the basis of the review of the literature and discussion with ten experts both from industry and academia. The determinants are structured in the form of a hierarchy. The determinants at the top level in the model are of major significance. The top-level determinants in this model are Speed, Agility, Adaptability, Decentralisation, Resilience, Alignment, Information System and Resource Availability.

The objective of this hierarchy is to select the best possible alternative that will meet the requirements of the post-disaster relief. Figure 16.1 shows the developed AHP model. The alternative the decision-maker wishes to evaluate are shown at the bottom of the model.

The opinion of the experts was sought in comparison of the relative importance of the criteria and the formation of pair-wise comparison matrices to be used in the AHP model. The result of all eight determinants is used in the calculation of the composite score of each alternative.

16.4.2.2 Step 2: Pair-Wise Comparison of Eight Determinants

In this step, experts were asked to respond to a series of pair-wise comparisons where two components at a time are compared with respect to an upper level 'control' criterion. These comparisons are made so as to establish the relative importance of determinants. In such comparisons, a scale of 1–9 is used to compare two options (Saaty 1980). In this a score of 1 indicates that the two options under comparison have equal importance, while a score of 9 indicates the overwhelming dominance of the component under consideration (row component) over the comparison component (column component) in a pair-wise comparison matrix. In case, a component has weaker impact than its comparison component, the range of the scores will be from 1 to 1/9, where 1 indicates indifference and 1/9 represents an overwhelming dominance by a column element over the row element. For the reverse comparison between the components already compared, a reciprocal value is automatically assigned within the matrix, so that in a matrix $a_{ij}a_{ji} = 1$. The matrix showing pair-wise comparison of determinants along with the e-vectors of these determinants is shown in Table 16.1.

The e-vectors (also referred to as local priority vector) are the weighted priorities of the determinants and shown in the last column of the matrix. In this paper, a two-stage algorithm (Saaty 1980) is used for computing e-vector. For the computation of the e-vector, we first add the values in each column of the matrix. Then dividing each entry in each column by the total of that column, the normalised matrix is obtained which permits the meaningful comparison among elements. Finally averaging over the rows is performed to obtain the e-vectors. These e-vectors would be used in Table 16.10 for the calculation of the composite score of the alternatives.

Table 16.1 Pair-wise comparison of determinants [Consistency ratio: 0.07]

Determinants	Speed	Agility	Adaptability	Decentralisation	Resilience	Alignment	Information system	Resource availability	e-vector
Speed	1	1/3	3/1	8/1	5/1	2/1	6/1	4	0.095
Agility	3	1	2/1	6	5	3	4	3	0.219
Adaptability	1/3	1/2	1	5	2	3	4	2	0.158
Decentralisation	1/8	1/6	1/5	1	1/3	1/4	2	1/3	0.087
Resilience	1/5	1/5	1/2	3	1	1/2	3	1/2	0.105
Alignment	1/2	1/3	1/3	4	2	1	3	3	0.136
Information System	1/6	1/4	1/4	1/2	1/3	1/3	1	1/5	0.080
Resource Availability	1/4	1/3	1/2	3	2	1/3	5	1	0.122

16.4.2.3 Step 3: Evaluation of Alternatives

The final set of pair-wise comparisons is made for the relative impact of each of the alternatives [Agency Centric Efforts (ACEs), Collaborative Aid Networks (CANs) and Partially Integrated Efforts (PIEs)] on the determinants. In present case, there are eight determinants, which lead to eight such pair-wise matrices, which are shown in Tables 16.2, 16.3, 16.4, 16.5, 16.6, 16.7, 16.8 and 16.9.

Table 16.2 Matrix for alternatives' impact on determinants Speed [Consistency ratio (CR): 0.03]

Speed	ACE	CAN	PIE	e-vector
ACE	1	1/7	1/4	0.187
CAN	7	1	3	0.516
PIE	4	1/3	1	0.297

Table 16.3 Matrix for alternatives' impact on determinants Agility [CR: 0.02]

Agility	ACE	CAN	PIE	e-vector
ACE	1	1/6	1/3	0.187
CAN	6	1	3	0.490
PIE	3	1/3	1	0.270

Table 16.4 Matrix for alternatives' impact on determinants Adaptability [CR: 0.03]

Adaptability	ACE	CAN	PIE	e-vector
ACE	1	1/7	1/3	0.187
CAN	7	1	4	0.568
PIE	3	1/4	1	0.270

Table 16.5 Matrix for alternatives' impact on determinants Decentralisation [CR: 0.01]

Decentralisation	ACE	CAN	PIE	e-vector
ACE	1	1/5	1/2	0.187
CAN	5	1	2	0.403
PIE	2	1/2	1	0.236

Table 16.6 Matrix for alternatives' impact on determinants Resilience [CR: 0.03]

Resilience	ACE	CAN	PIE	e-vector
ACE	1	1/9	1/5	0.187
CAN	9	1	3	0.561
PIE	5	1/3	1	0.320

Table 16.7 Matrix for alternatives' impact on determinants Alignment [CR: 0.09]

Alignment	ACE	CAN	PIE	e-vector
ACE	1	1/8	1/5	0.187
CAN	8	1	4	0.594
PIE	5	1/4	1	0.320

Table 16.8 Matrix for alternatives' impact on determinants Information System [CR: 0.07]

Information System	ACE	CAN	PIE	e-vector
ACE	1	7	4	0.568
CAN	1/7	1	1/4	0.187
PIE	1/4	4	1	0.297

Table 16.9 Matrix for alternatives' impact on determinants Resource [CR = 0.09]

Resource	ACE	CAN	PIE	e-vector
ACE	1	8	4	0.594
CAN	1/8	1	1/5	0.187
PIE	1/4	5	1	0.320

16.4.2.4 Step 4: Calculation of the Composite Score for the Alternatives

The composite score for an alternative i is the summation of the products of the relative importance weights of the alternative (A_{ia}) and the relative importance weights of the determinants (D_a).

$$\text{Composite Score} = \sum A_{ia} D_a$$

For example, the composite score for CANs is calculated as

$$\begin{aligned}
\text{Composite Score}_{\text{CANs}} = & \left[(0.095 \times 0.516) + (0.219 \times 0.490) + (0.158 \times 0.568) \right. \\
& + (0.087 \times 0.403) + (0.105 \times 0.561) + (0.136 \times 0.594) \\
& \left. + (0.080 \times 0.187) + (0.122 \times 0.187)\right] = 0.59913
\end{aligned}$$

The final results are shown in Table 16.10.

It is observed from Table 16.10 that CANs are the most-suited alternative as a post-disaster relief humanitarian logistics structure. PIEs and ACEs follow this alternative. It is observed from Table 16.1 that agility is the most important determinant which any humanitarian logistic structure should be able to attain.

16.5 Result and Discussion

The major contribution of this research lies in the development of a comprehensive model, which incorporates diversified issues for selecting the appropriate post-disaster humanitarian logistics structure. The proposed model in this paper not only guides the decision-makers in the selection of the appropriate humanitarian logistics structure but also enables them to visualise the impact of various criteria in the arrival of final solution.

The result (Table 16.10) indicates that CANs must be the first choice to structure any post-disaster humanitarian logistics system. PIEs and ACEs follow CANs. The superiority of CANs can be attributed to its significant presence in the affected area

Table 16.10 Weightages of determinants for the alternatives

	e-vectors	ACEs	CANs	PIEs
Speed	0.095	0.079	0.659	0.263
Agility	0.219	0.095	0.655	0.25
Adaptability	0.158	0.084	0.705	0.211
Decentralisation	0.087	0.128	0.595	0.276
Resilience	0.105	0.063	0.672	0.265
Alignment	0.136	0.064	0.699	0.237
Information System	0.080	0.696	0.075	0.229
Resource Availability	0.122	0.699	0.064	0.237
Composite score		*0.15442*	*0.59913*	*0.245659*

and outside of it. Also the presence of large components of CANs outside the affected area and significant manpower capacity (supported by religious and social networks) gives it an upper hand. From Table 16.1, it is seen that Agility (0.219) is the most important criteria in the selection of any post-disaster humanitarian logistic structure. Adaptability (0.158), Alignment (0.136), Resource Availability (0.122), Resilience (0.105), Speed (0.095), Decentralisation (0.087) and Information System (0.080) follow it. So agility must be taken special care of in any humanitarian logistic operation.

Though the proposed AHP model is based on a sound algorithm for systematic decision-making, care must be taken in its application, since any relief operation can be affected by the externalities outside the scope of the model.

16.6 Conclusion

After any disaster, the prime priority is to save the human lives. How to structure the relief operation and which structure to select is the prime question. The AHP model presented in this paper structured the problem of selection of the structure for post-disaster humanitarian logistic operation. The model has also linked the important determinants associated. Thus, this AHP model integrates both quantitative and qualitative aspects and aids the decision-makers in arriving at the best possible solution.

The model developed has certain limitations as well. The formation of pair-wise comparison matrices and data acquisition is a tedious and time consuming task. Also, more importantly, the results reported in this research are based on the opinion of the experts. So user's knowledge and familiarity are the prime issue of concern. So the aspect of biasing might have influenced the results. Although we have tried to minimise this by checking the consistency of comparison using the method of consistency ratio as suggested by Saaty (1980). The consistency ratio is calculated for all pair-wise comparisons to check the inconsistency in decision-making. In the proposed model, the consistency ratio varies from 0.001 to 0.11, which is in the tolerable limit (Saaty and Kearns 1985).

References

Tatham P, Kovács G (2010) The application of "swift trust" to humanitarian logistics. Int J Product Econ 126(1):35–45

Holguín Veras J, Jaller M, Wachtendorf T (2012) Comparative performance of alternative humanitarian logistic structures after the Port au Prince earthquake: ACEs, PIEs, and CANs. Transportation research part A: policy and practice 46(10):1623–1640

Lee HL (2004) The triple-A supply chain. Harvard business review 82(10):102–113

Saaty TL (1980) The analytic hierarchy process. McGraw-Hill, New York

Saaty TL, Kearns KP (1985) Analytical planning. Pergamon Press, Oxford

Van Wassenhove LN (2006) Humanitarian aid logistics: supply chain management in high gear. J Oper Res Soc 57(5):475–489

Van Wassenhove LN, Pedraza Martinez AJ (2012) Using OR to adapt supply chain management best practices to humanitarian logistics. Int Trans Oper Res 19(1–2):307–322

Part IV
Relief Supply Chain for Disaster Management

With the ever-growing natural and manmade disasters reaching epic proportion, the need for nodal agencies with appropriately trained manpower, know-how and machinery to reduce, avoid and hedge the uncertainty is paramount. Knowing what to do before, during and after the disaster is an essential part of preparedness and disaster relief operations. During necessary chaos, when every second is crucial in saving life and material property, capacity building, although costly, is the only differentiating factor in ensuring the safety and security before, during and after the disaster. Furthermore, the role that the stakeholders play in improvising, learning, unlearning and relearning from the disaster experience would lead to a better response in the humanitarian circumstances. What needs to be explored is how the stakeholder's behaviour impacts the operational and executional capability. The first paper in this section discusses the importance of developing trained manpower for disaster readiness so as find out new vistas for dealing with disaster situations. The second paper in this section examines human resource management related challenges in managing the relief supply chain through the lens of international human resource management practices. The third paper discusses the unique features of disaster management situation in a high-altitude area. As the high-altitude environment degrades the functional efficiency of both men and machines, plans made for other locations cannot be templated for such areas. The fourth paper deals with the most simplistic logistics that is usually applied or can be applied to ensure proper relief and rescue operation during a disaster, be it natural or man-made. Finally, the last paper presents the least researched issue of dealing with human remains after disasters. Vulnerable people affected by disaster include family members and community of the deceased in the aftermath of a disaster. After a mass-fatality disaster if the human remains are not recovered, not preserved, not communicated to the community, not identified, and/or not dispositioned according to the tradition, culture, and religious practices, it leaves a Zeigarnik effect on the community and the surviving family members. The paper discusses humanitarian logistics from the perspective of humanitarian remains and defines it as recovery of human remains, preservation of human remains, communication about human remains, identification of human remains, and disposition of human remains after a disaster involving mass fatalities.

Chapter 17
Supply Chain for Disaster Management: An Empirical Study

Ashwini Sharma, Dixit Garg, and Ashish Agarwal

17.1 Introduction

Indian education system has always been the source of curiosity across the world. The tradition of gurukul and world renowned university, i.e., Takshashila and Nalanda, had attracted many of the scholars and knowledge seekers from all the countries. Somehow after a long duration of invasion and ruling, education has been affected the most among the other areas. It is not what has been the original system which apart from the core education included practicing moral and ethical values. Engineering education is not the exception to it. Today it is said that out of the all engineers passing out from engineering, merely 30 % of them are employable, i.e., of required quality. In any crisis situation, for example, flood, drought, earthquake, or war, the activities connected with providing humanitarian aid (HA) to those requiring it will often be treated as a series of discrete activities disconnected from each other (UNDP 1993).

Usually, the term "disaster" refers to a "disruption that physically affects a system as a whole and threatens its priorities and goals" (Van Wassenhove 2006). With respect to cause, it is possible to distinguish between a natural and a man-made disaster; with respect to predictability and speed of occurrence, it is possible to distinguish between a sudden-onset and a slow-onset disaster. Taking

A. Sharma (✉)
Department of Mechanical Engineering, ITM University, Gurgaon, Haryana, India
e-mail: asharma87@hotmail.com

D. Garg
Mechanical Engineering Department, National Institute of Technology Kurukshetra, Kurukshetra, Haryana, India

A. Agarwal
School of Engineering and Technology, IGNOU, New Delhi, India

© Springer India 2016
B.S. Sahay et al. (eds.), *Managing Humanitarian Logistics*, Springer Proceedings in Business and Economics, DOI 10.1007/978-81-322-2416-7_17

241

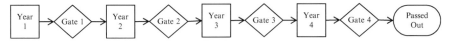

Fig. 17.1 Stage gate process for present engineering system

into account also the different impact in terms of required logistic effort (from higher to lower), it is possible to identify four types of disasters (Cozzolino 2012): (1) calamities, characterized by natural causes and sudden-onset occurrences (e.g., earthquakes, hurricanes, tornadoes); (2) destructive actions, characterized by man-made causes and sudden-onset occurrences (e.g., terrorist attacks, coups d'état, industrial accidents); (3) plagues, characterized by natural causes and slow-onset occurrence (e.g., famines, droughts, poverty); and (4) crises, characterized by man-made causes and slow-onsets occurrence (e.g., political and refugee crises).

Considering the situation, something can be done in order to improve the quality of education in engineering which should not be superficial and which will help the students to develop process and systems to fight disaster at the time of need.

As shown in Fig. 17.1, the students take admission in year 1 having two semesters and two exams. If the minimum criterion (which is different for different institutes) is met, then gate 1is crossed; otherwise, he/she has to prepare till gate 1 is crossed. In the same manner, the other gates are to be crossed till the student is passed out from the institute. The value added in all the 4 years that get accumulated should reflect at the time of crossing each gate.

In the present system, the stage gate process as shown above does not hold good for the readiness of students in different disaster situations; therefore, it is needed to rethink the whole of the process to find out the missing link.

17.2 Literature Review

Engineering education system in India is going through a high degree of transition from quite sometimes. A good engineering education system is supposed to be one which equips the student with a sense of responsibility toward the society apart from the technical know-how of the specialization in respective branch. At present in the engineering system where the trained manpower is needed to cater for the disaster management and humanitarian logistics, very few initiatives have been taken by the universities especially in the engineering field. It gives a clear-cut impression that there is something missing in the delivery of knowledge, research in the field, or learning by the student.

Emergency logistics is often the largest and most complex element of relief operations (UNDP 1993), and in order for successful supply chains to be effective, there is a requirement for a clear understanding of the problems and issues involved.

India is vulnerable, in varying degrees, to a large number of natural as well as man-made disasters. 58.6 % of the landmass is prone to earthquakes of moderate to very high intensity; over 40 million hectares (12 % of land) is prone to floods and river erosion; of the 7,516 km long coastline, close to 5,700 km is prone to cyclones and tsunamis; 68 % of the cultivable area is vulnerable to drought, and hilly areas are at risk from landslides and avalanches.

Lu et al. (2006) identified the factors which are most important to humanitarian aid and emergency relief organizations in providing an effective response in crisis situations and, secondly, the variables which contribute to the effectiveness of each. From desk and field research, the extent to which CSFs are recognized and understood within aid agencies is assessed. They demonstrated how such factors can assist agencies in developing improvements in both strategy and response and contribute more generally to the development of an assessment tool for humanitarian aid supply chains.

Factors such as global warming, environmental degradation, and increasing urbanization expose a greater number of people to the threat of natural disasters. In the last three decades, the rate of disasters has risen from 50 to 400 per year (Kovacs and Spens 2007), and it is still expected to increase five times more on the next 50 years (Thomas and Kopczack 2007). In 2010, 207 million people suffered from disasters, which caused 296,800 deaths and losses of 109 billion dollars (Sapir 2011). In the last decade, Brazil has suffered, on average, six natural disasters per year (UN 2011), and, in 2008, it was the thirteenth country most affected by natural disasters, having two million victims affected mainly by floods or landslides (Lima et al. 2011).

The first four objectives of the national policy on disaster management in India are (1) promoting a culture of prevention, preparedness, and resilience at all levels through knowledge, innovation, and education; (2) encouraging mitigation measures based on technology, traditional wisdom, and environmental sustainability; (3) mainstreaming disaster management into the developmental planning process; and (4) establishing institutional and techno-legal frameworks to create an enabling regulatory environment and a compliance regime. It shows that there is an immediate need for promoting the need for managing the disaster effectively and efficiently by educating the students at all level of their education. (Khanduja et al. 2009) stated that education is a social process, and the form of education is a product of society-education dialectics. In this context, quality of education assumes an added importance and becomes the primary concern of all the stakeholders in education. In current market turbulence, a focus on entrepreneurship has a special strategic significance for engineering education as it reflects a growing perception that new graduates need the technical and behavioral attributes of an entrepreneur for a successful professional life. In response to this inevitable change, educationists must do rethinking on the way the students are educated by infusing creative thinking and innovation in their educational curriculum. With this change in the mind-set and the relative knowledge that entrepreneurs bring forth, in many institutes some courses on entrepreneurship and innovation are being developed and offered to cater to the increasing demand. As engineering institutes meet this demand through a heightened entrepreneurial outlook, the paper discusses their strategic role in generating entrepreneurship which is a potential source of employment generation in a developing nation like India. (Yeomans and Atrens 2001) described a methodology and framework for discipline-specific curriculum development in a local context. They outlined a strategy for the delivery of a centralized curriculum development workshop for academic staff follow-up visits and local curriculum activities with participating universities and the presentation of technical short courses as guidance for such activity in other settings and/or discipline areas. While the paper is a report on curriculum activities in a particular setting, it is written in a manner that allows application of the methodology to other settings. (Walkington 2002) in his paper identified a process, developed in recent research, to provide curriculum leaders and policy-makers with a practical and flexible approach for designing and implementing curriculum. A thorough investigation of the engineering education context, including the analysis of an engineering case study, was carried out to identify issues that impinge on curriculum decision-making, including the consideration of professional engineering needs, the social and economic pressures, institutional parameters, and student factors. The process represents a significant breakthrough in higher education faculties. It directs policy-makers to consider parameters in addition to those traditionally addressed. It recommends a holistic view of curriculum and suggests that there are explicit ramifications for the policies in faculties that govern how curriculum change takes place.

The 2004 earthquake and resulting tsunami in South Asia claimed approximately 230,000 lives and displaced 1.7 million people. Over 40 countries and 700 nongovernmental organizations (NGOs) provided humanitarian assistance. The response in the private sector was unprecedented: for example, US companies alone mobilized more than US$565 million (cash and in kind), and the role of logistics companies (e.g., UPS, FedEx, and DHL)—together with their existing aid agency partners—was also crucial in providing free or subsidized transportation and logistics. The world responded by donating more than $13 billion and initiating the largest relief effort in history (Thomas and Fritz 2006).

Sharma et al. (2012) reported intensive studies based on the work carried out by various researchers in the area of supply chain management. An attempt was made to identify conceptual interlinking between supply chain management and quality management through literature review.

One obvious reason why studying disaster relief supply chains are important is because of the potential to save lives and reduce suffering for those people affected by a disaster. Another, less obvious, reason is that there are lessons to be learned for the private sector. The study of such highly responsive supply chains could help inform other contexts in which a growing importance is placed on customer responsiveness and product innovation, contrasted with cost and efficiency (Whybark et al. 2010). Moreover, increasing the breadth of supply chain research will help in developing classifications, identifying drivers of attributes and uncovering transferable practices that can benefit other sectors.

Considering the literature review as above, there is a serious need to take initiative to innovate in existing curriculum to make aware and to train the students in the area of humanitarian logistics.

17.3 Methodology

The research methodology is based on the interviews taken from the experts from different walks of life and academia. The authors surveyed a number of people to find out their views of what should be included in the survey form. A through survey which included 25 experts from different professions was selected for interview, while academicians were also included to take their views. Based on the interviews, a survey instrument was designed to know the understanding of disaster management among the engineering graduates studying in different years and different branches. Based on the feedback and interviews, the stage gate process in Fig. 17.1 was modified to accommodate suggestions as shown in Fig. 17.2.

Four value added (VA) courses (noncredit but practical oriented) were proposed to the existing syllabus. VA1 was related to increase the communication and presentation ability. VA2 and VA3 were related to the extra inputs in design and manufacturing which included CAD/CAM/CAE, quality, and humanitarian logistics inputs by the professionals. VA 2 and 3 included seven industrial visits, five industrial interactions, and eight expert lectures. In the third year, out of 120 students, 30 students based on their interest and zeal to get in to the engineering world were selected and trained further. VA4 was related to the real-time application of knowledge gained in previous value added courses. Students found VA4 to be highly challenging as well as interesting where all were involved with innovation and team playing. A high-end world class lab was made available for the students to work out the VA1, 2, and 3.

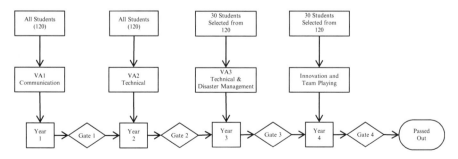

Fig. 17.2 Modified stage gate process

17.4   Results and Discussions

The author focused on the understanding of the supply chain disaster management by the engineering students in order to know the present state. Surprisingly the results as discussed further are not as per the expectation, and authors found out that there is lot of things which needs to be considered on priority. Further there is a huge scope of improvement, which can result in to making a potential difference. As shown in Fig. 17.3 the overall understanding of the students about humanitarian logistics is very poor. As shown in Fig. 17.4, 39 out of 85 students agreed to the fact that they have an idea about how to react in a situation of disaster. This call for

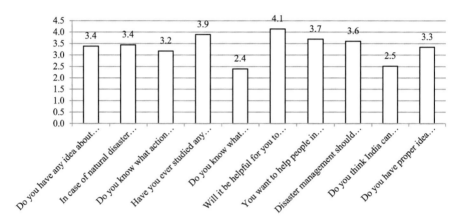

Fig. 17.3 Response of students out of 5 for overall understanding of Supply chain disaster management

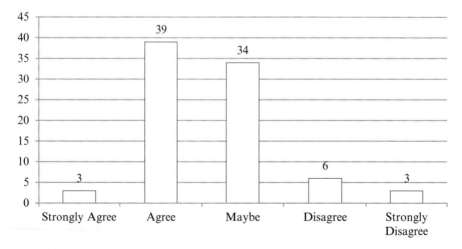

Fig. 17.4 Do you have any idea about how to react to a disaster?

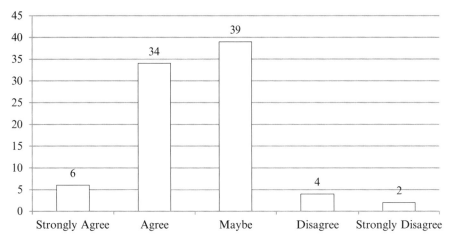

Fig. 17.5 In case of natural disaster will you be able to save yourself?

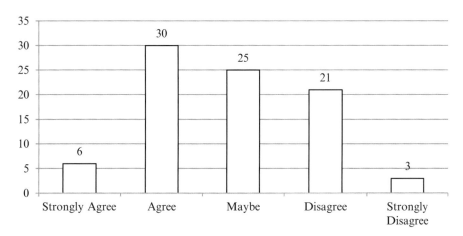

Fig. 17.6 Do you know what action should be taken to save the people In case of natural disaster?

immediate attention as it comes out to be nearly a 50 % engineering graduate does not know what to do in a situation of crisis.

As shown in Fig. 17.5, only 50 % of students agreed that they would be able to save themselves, which again call for immediate action as the sample of students included only male candidates. As shown in Fig. 17.6, only 42 % of students agreed that they know what to do in case of emergency situation.

As shown in Figure 17.7 it is evident that the youth or young India is aware at least of disaster management, but does not give clue as to how much they know about it. The response may be taken as false response as it does not reflect the level of understanding in all the responses taken. This is shown by Fig. 17.8 where 54 %

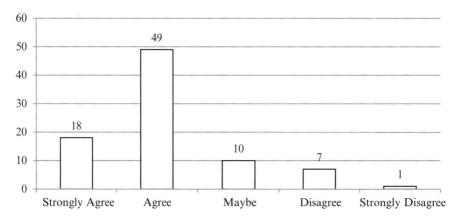

Fig. 17.7 Have you ever studied any literature related to disaster?

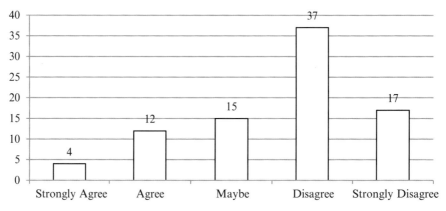

Fig. 17.8 Do you know what humanitarian logistics is?

of the students do not know what humanitarian logistics is. This again indicates the call for action on an immediate basis.

Seventy-five percent of respondents felt that there is a serious need for training in the area of disaster management as shown in Fig. 17.9. This is indicated in Fig. 17.10 in which 81 % of the respondents felt helpless when they want to contribute in time of disaster; they cannot help because they do not know how to help, as reflected in Fig. 17.11 where 70 % of the engineering students responded affirmatively that a course on disaster management is introduced only as an elective subject. As shown in Fig. 17.12, more than 50 % of the respondents have given surprisingly negative answer to the question if India can respond effectively to the emergency situations. More than 50 % of the respondents do not have any idea about the aftereffect of a disaster and how to tackle the same, as shown in Fig. 17.13.

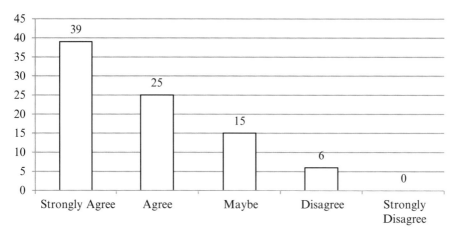

Fig. 17.9 Will it be helpful for you to get trained for 3 days in managing the natural disaster and calamities?

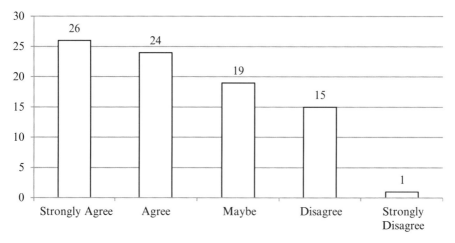

Fig. 17.10 You want to help the people in your capacities in case of disaster but don't know how to help them

With the above results, a clear understanding can be formed easily that there exists an untapped potential in India which can really contribute to emergency situations just so by training them.

17.5 Conclusion

With the above results and discussions, it can be concluded that a good deal of talent as well as potential has not been thought upon to cater to the requirements which arise in emergency situations. Only if this talent is given training of not

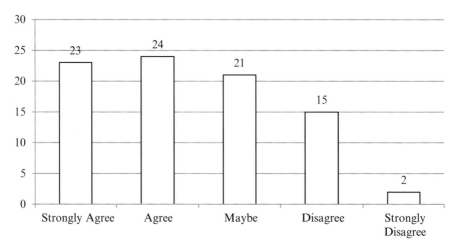

Fig. 17.11 Disaster management Should be taught as one of the elective subject in engineering

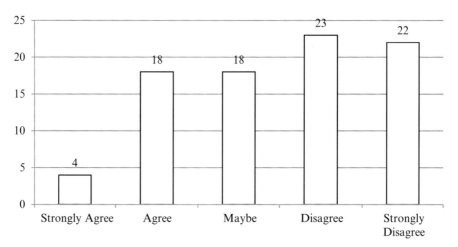

Fig. 17.12 Do you think India can respond in case of disaster effectively in emergency situations?

getting panicked at the time of emergency can create a huge difference as the engineering graduates across the India counts for approximately 20 lakhs. If we see the state of their understanding about humanitarian logistics as in the results, it calls for an immediate action from academicians, curriculum designers, universities, government organizations, and people who have expertise in this area.

The authors have proposed an elective subject to be taught to engineering students related to disaster management which can result into cascading of knowledge. Employment opportunities for students can be another potential aspect as the disaster management field is new and rather less explored by the engineers. The real

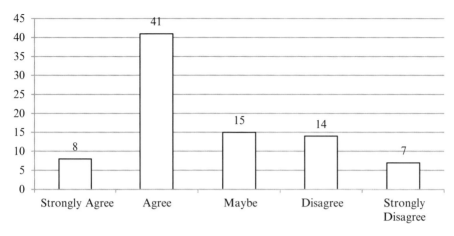

Fig. 17.13 Do you have proper idea about after effects of disaster?

need is training of the students to fight in emergency situations where they can contribute effectively by saving the own lives which may result in to saving the lives of others and the huge amount of losses in times of disasters.

References

Cozzolino A (2012) Humanitarian logistics and supply chain management. Humanitarian logistics: cross-sector cooperation in disaster relief management. Springer, 5–15. http://ndmindia.nic.in/NPDM-101209.pdf. Accessed on 14 July 2013

Khanduja D, Vineet S, Rajdeep S (2009) Entrepreneurial ambience of engineering education in India. Int J Indian Cult Bus Manag 2(4):341–355

Kovacs G, Spens K (2007) Humanitarian logistics in disaster relief operations. Int J Phys Distrib Logist Manag 37(2):99–114

Lima F, Medeiros H, Gonçalves M (2011) Clusters in humanitarian supply chain: the center assembly of the United Nations logistics – UNJLC. XXV ANPET – Congress Research and Education in Transportation, Date 7 to 11, Belo Horizonte – MG, pp 1–12

Lu KD, Pettit S, Beresford A (2006) Critical success factors for emergency relief logistics. WHAMPOA An Interdisciplinary J 51:177–184

Melnyk SA, Davis EW, Spekman RE, Sandor J (2010) Outcome- driven supply chains. Sloan Manage Rev 51(2):33–38

Sapir GD (2011) Disasters in Numbers 2010. CRED, Catholic University of Louvain, Brussels. 24 Jan, Geneva

Sharma A, Garg D, Agarwal A (2012) Quality management in supply chains: the literature review. Int J Qual Res 6(3):193–206

Thomas A, Fritz L (2006) Disaster relief. *Inc*. Harv Bus Rev 84(11):114–126

Thomas A, Kopezak L (2007) Life-saving supply chains: challenges and path forward. In: Lee HL, Lee CY (eds) Building supply chain excellence in emerging economies. Springer Science, New York

UN: desastre naturais atingem 7,5 milhões no Brasil. O Último Segundo [online], 25 janeiro (2011) Brasil. Available at: http://ultimosegundo.ig.com.br/brasil/onu+desastres+naturais +atingem+75+milhoes+no+brasil/n1237967836366.html. Accessed in 15 June 2013

United Nations Development Programme (1993) Logistics, 1st edn. UNDP, Geneva

Van Wassenhove LN (2006) Blackett memorial lecture. Humanitarian aid logistics: supply chain management in high gear. J Oper Res Soc 57(5):475–489

Walkington J (2002) Curriculum change in engineering. Eur J Eng Educ 27(2):133–148

Whybark DC, Melnyk SA, Day J, Davis E (2010) Disaster relief supply chain management: new realities, management challenges, emerging opportunities. Decision Line 41:4–7

Yeomans SR, Atrens A (2001) A methodology for discipline-specific curriculum development. Int J Eng Educ 17(6):518–524

Chapter 18
Role of Humanitarian Supply Chain Management in Various Disaster Situations Across the Globe

Laxhminarayan Das

18.1 Introduction

Natural calamities and disaster are occurring frequently across the globe creating havoc in human civilization. Due to rapid urbanization and environmental degradation, human society is suffering many problems from the nature. Many of such problems are man-made and few are nature based. Recent flood in Uttaranchal has given a clear signal about the human error in the urbanization process and its consequences. Disasters are wreaking havoc on human lives and nations' economies at an alarming and rising rate. The humanitarian approach of the government of India as well as the government of Uttaranchal has somehow made it possible to rescue as well as recover bodies of various people affected by disasters. Whether it is a tsunami in the Pacific or a national event such as Hurricane Katrina, government, nonprofit organizations, and private industries need to be better prepared to respond and recover from disasters, offering timely and necessary aid to those in need through efficient humanitarian supply chains. The way the Indian Air Force has shown their commendable approach for rescuing and saving thousands of lives in the Uttaranchal flood is a clear approach of humanitarian approach in supply chain management. The entire study leads towards the same approach. For this study the data and other vital resources are collected through secondary resources particularly for several research papers published in those areas by several academicians across the globe.

L. Das (✉)
Department of Marketing, Ravenshaw Business School, Ravenshaw University, Cuttack, Odisha, India
e-mail: laxhminarayan@yahoo.com

© Springer India 2016
B.S. Sahay et al. (eds.), *Managing Humanitarian Logistics*, Springer Proceedings in Business and Economics, DOI 10.1007/978-81-322-2416-7_18

18.2   Humanitarian Supply Chain Management

In general businesses, supply chain links the sources of supply (suppliers) to the owners of demand end customers. The ultimate goal of any supply chain is to deliver the right supplies in the right quantities to the right locations at the right time. Supply chains comprise all activities and processes associated with the flow and transformation of goods from the raw material stage through the end user. Similar to commercial supply chain, supplies flow through the relief chain from the donation to the consumers. There is no single form of humanitarian supply chain, but the government and NGOs are the primary parties involved. Governments hold the main power with the control they have over political and economical conditions and directly affect supply chain processes with their decisions. Donors and public and private organizations are the other significant players in the humanitarian supply chains. Donors have become particularly influential in prompting humanitarian organization to think in terms of greater donor accountability and transparency of the whole supply chain. Two-way arrow in the figure represents two-way communications in information, product, and fund flows among the parties in the humanitarian chain.

According to McLachlan, humanitarian supply chains tend to be unstable, prone to political and military influence, and inefficient due to lack of joint planning and interorganizational collaboration. They deal with inadequate logistics infrastructure, along with shifting origins of and/or destinations for relief supplies without warning. Further, donors often request their funds be spent on direct materials and food, and even at a particular disaster location, rather than on crucial but indirect services such as information systems, staff training, and/or disaster preparedness. Therefore, humanitarian supply chain management does not only deal with delivering goods, materials, or information to the point of consumption for the purpose of alleviating the suffering of vulnerable people, but also need to manage value to donors and other stakeholders.

18.3   Challenges to Humanitarian Logistics

There are a few challenges of humanitarian logistics which are enumerated as follows:

High uncertainty in demand

Two earthquakes of similar magnitude may have entirely different outcomes if one hits a high population density area in a developing country, and the other hits a better-prepared city in a developed country. Relief demand is unknown both in size and type, and it is affected by dynamic and hard-to-measure factors such as disaster characteristics, local economy and infrastructure, social and political conditions, etc.

High uncertainty in timing.

In general, it is difficult to predict exactly when a disaster is going to strike. This time frame could be relatively delimited as in a hurricane season or hardly predictable as in an earthquake. Therefore, one needs to be in a constant state of readiness and to plan during an uncertain time, which requires additional flexibility.

High uncertainty in location.

For other disasters such as hurricanes, more information based on historical data and models help to predict the path after it starts, but even a specific storm can change paths. Affected locations might also be dynamic as in the case of a pandemic influenza, so planning should account for this. Location uncertainty imposes additional challenges to preparedness activities such as relief supplies and equipment pre-positioning, infrastructure investment, etc.

High uncertainty and challenges in supply.

Donations may be variable or restricted in their use by donors, while in-kind donations may also be inadequate and unmatched with the demand. Building up relationships with local vendors, usually in a very short period of time, may be a difficult task as well.

Challenges in collaboration among the multiple players and decision-makers in a humanitarian supply chain.

Each of the responders (governments, military, local authorities, etc.) may compete for limited resources to achieve their own goals. Organizations and governments may also have different incentives that impair the effectiveness of collaborations.

The impact of the political, cultural, and socioeconomic conditions of the region.

Responders must have an understanding of the region as they are usually in a highly politicized environment. Unawareness of specific local issues may cause even the best stand-alone plan to fail or become impractical. The human factor is crucial in humanitarian operations, which includes language, customs, political views, etc. Also, every organization involved is under the public eye which puts more stress on the response operation.

The strong dependency of the last mile operations on the location and disaster severity.

Transportation infrastructure might be disrupted, and required equipment may not be locally available, affecting the supply chain responsiveness. This can be aggravated by a limited location access or poor construction.

Limited telecommunications and information infrastructure.

The Internet is still not widely available in some developing countries. Land-based phones and cellular phone communication towers might be down as a result of a disaster. Also, since there might be more than one organization collecting data, it is common to find inconsistencies in the aftermath reports.

Long-term impact of the many activities carried out during humanitarian operations.

This happens as cities are rebuilt, people are relocated, new products and vendors are introduced to the local market, etc. There are trade-offs between short-term effectiveness of the response and a long-term impact on the communities that guarantees their sustainability.

The success of humanitarian operations is hard to measure.

Economic success is the standard performance measure in the pro-profit world. For nonprofit organizations this evaluation is more complex, considering difficult-to-formulate elements such as unmet need fulfilled and more tractable ones like cash flow. Keeping complete track, control, and accountability of the humanitarian programs and their outcomes is challenged by the high urgency and pace of this type of operations, and time for analyzing and recording is usually tight.

18.4   Steps in Humanitarian Supply Chain Management

In HSCM several steps are to be followed to maintain the systematic routes for supply chain during the time of difficulties and emergency. The steps are as follows:

18.4.1   Assessment and Planning

An accurate assessment depends on thorough planning, design, and preparation. Under normal circumstances, the means of collecting the necessary data and information should be established as part of an organization's pre-disaster planning. Planning and assessment are therefore very complementary. Assessments enable logisticians to understand the impact of a disaster on the environment and how the impact affects the population and how the logistics services are to be provided. The findings from logistics assessments are critical in enabling appropriate decision-making, planning, and organization for effective disaster response.

To effectively support a response to the needs in an emergency, it is very important to include a logistics assessment during the general needs assessment exercise. Having a logistics staff on the program needs assessment team ensures that the needs are properly understood by logisticians and therefore adequately provisioned for. Some of the key considerations are (Fig. 18.1):

- Numbers of the affected population
- Distribution plans

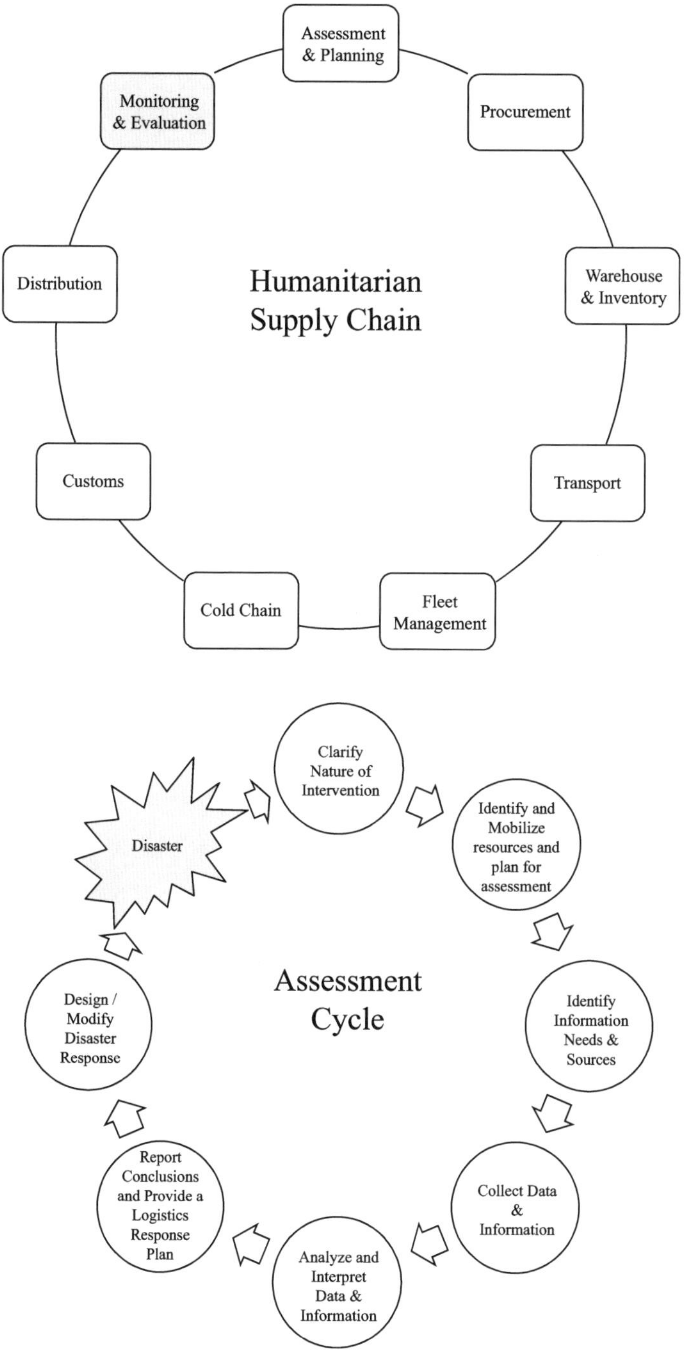

Fig. 18.1 Adapted from UNDMTP/Disaster Assessment (1994)

- Materials required (commodities and supplies)
- Electric power, hydro facilities
- Water/sewage
- Civil aviation, airports, alternative aircraft
- Seaports
- Railroads
- Roads and bridges
- Local trucking capacity
- Transfer points
- Communications
- Coordination capacity
- Warehousing

18.4.2 Planning Process

Planning is largely a decision-making process that involves choosing among alternatives. The seven basic steps of planning are (Fig. 18.2):

- Problem identification – is it flooding, drought, conflict, or a complex disaster?
- Data or information gathering – community needs, response team needs such as relief items, vehicles, environmental assessment
- Choosing among alternative solutions
- Evaluating the alternatives and deciding
- Implementing the solution
- Following up implementation and taking action where changes are required
- Exit strategy

18.4.3 Procurement

Procurement is a key activity in the supply chain. It can significantly influence the overall success of an emergency response depending on how it is managed. In humanitarian supply chains, procurement represents a very large proportion of the total spending and should be managed effectively to achieve optimum value. Procurement works like a pivot in the internal supply chain process turning around requests into actual products/commodities or services to fulfill the needs. It serves three levels of users:

 (i) The internal customer
 (ii) Programs in response to emergencies and ongoing programs
(iii) Prepositioning of stocks, for both internal customers and program needs

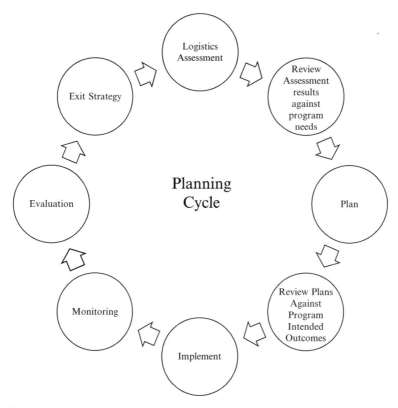

Fig. 18.2 Steps in planning

In collaboration with the warehouse function, products/commodities are mobilized and delivered. Procurement is a large subject area and bridges the fulfillment of identified needs (Fig. 18.3).

18.4.3.1   Procurement in the Humanitarian Context

The three important principles of humanitarian logistics procurement are:

- Transparency – all phases in the procurement process are fair and accurately documented.
- Accountability – accountability to donors who may require certain rules to be followed when using the money they have provided.
- Efficiency and cost-effectiveness – meeting the six rights of supply: price, right time, right quantity, quality services, delivery to the required places, and from the most cost-effective source.

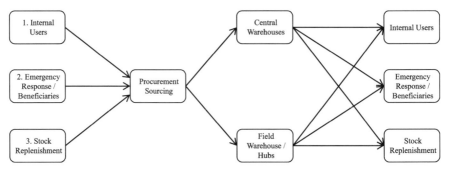

Fig. 18.3 The role of procurement

The principles and their importance stem from three key facts:

- That the resources utilized are usually funded by donor
- That transparency contributes to the establishment of sound and reliable business relations with suppliers
- That efficiency and cost-effectiveness have a direct impact on operations and ultimately on beneficiaries

The procurement function must guard and mitigate against risk, understand the market, build relationships with suppliers, meet needs in a timely manner, and constantly monitor performance to improve service provision, hence the need for an organization to have clearly defined policies that are well understood.

18.4.4 Warehousing and Inventory Management

A simple definition of a warehouse is: "a warehouse is a planned space for the storage and handling of goods and material." In general, warehouses are focal points for product and information flow between sources of supply and beneficiaries. However, in humanitarian supply chains, warehouses vary greatly in terms of their role and their characteristics.

18.4.4.1 Policies

The policies contain hard and fast rules and regulations that define the general conduct of the warehouse operation. Examples of the types of policies that organizations will define are as follows:

- Organizational specific
- Health and safety
- Human resources management
- Security

- Pest control
- Warehouse maintenance and cleaning
- Quality control
- Record keeping and reporting
- Reverse logistics – return of goods and exit strategy in the event of downscaling or shutting down operations
- Disposal of obsolete and damaged goods

18.4.4.2   Procedures

The procedures will normally provide the step-by-step guidance on how to manage each aspect of warehousing and may cover:

- Receiving and issuing of supplies
- Quality control or verification
- Storage of goods
- How to control stock movement (stock control)
- Documentation flow
- How to detect and deal with stock losses
- How rejected material will be managed
- How to deal with unwanted material and obsolete and scrap disposal

18.4.5   Transport

In the context of humanitarian organizations, transport is defined as "the activities involved in moving supplies from the point of origin to internal customers or beneficiaries." The aim of transport is to physically move supplies in a reliable and safe manner, on time, cost-effectively, and efficiently to its destination.

18.4.5.1   Operations: Transport Strategy

A transport strategy depends not only on the needs within the organization, but varies from organization to organization and from situation to situation. Some factors to consider when developing a transport strategy are:

- How to identify transport service providers
- How to manage the function, i.e., whether to lease, outsource, or manage own fleet
- Capacity of transport modes available
- Quantities requiring movement over a period of time
- Nature of goods/products/supplies to be transported
- Distances to be covered

- Environmental issues such as climate, government legislature, infrastructure, taxes, etc.
- Number of destinations, hubs, and pre-positioning locations
- Origins and routes
- Available transport modes and their relative costs
- Human resources
- Terrain
- Funding
- Security
- Circumstances – such as nature of disaster

The above factors would be valid for both emergency and nonemergency situations.

18.4.6 Fleet Management

Fleet management is the function that oversees, coordinates, and facilitates various transport and transport-related activities. For the purpose of this document, it will cover vehicles involved in the movement of goods and the management of light vehicle fleets used in the transportation of people and light cargo, possibly motorbikes and other equipment such as generators and warehouse handling equipment. Fleet management underpins and supports transport-related activities through the management of the assets that are used.

Effective fleet management aims at reducing and minimizing overall costs through maximum, cost-effective utilization of resources such as vehicles, fuel, spare parts, etc.

The administration and financial management of fleet is very organizational specific. It largely depends on donor requirements and organizational policies. At a glance, some vehicles are restricted to specific projects, others are utilized in pools to serve all projects, some are strictly organizational driver driven, and others are self-staff driven and coordinated in pools based on administration policies related to pooling. The custodian of the fleet management function is also very much dependent on organizational policies and structures.

18.4.6.1 Fleet Management Systems

In recent times, to address problems in fleet management and the ever-expanding need to monitor usage of vehicles, commercial organizations have designed automated control systems and other approaches to vehicle management. Simple management systems can be designed in-house for internal use to provide a good analysis of the vehicles and driver performance.

Vehicle management systems are structured in a way that enables the capturing of information on various aspects of fleet usage, maintenance, and operations. For example:

- Distances traveled
- Destinations reached
- Distance traveled by vehicle showing official and private mileage
- Fuel consumption
- Repair and maintenance per vehicle
- Rate of consumption of spare parts
- Servicing planned and completed

18.4.7 Cold Chain

Cold chain is a network of refrigerators, cold stores, freezers, and cold boxes organized and maintained so that vaccines are kept at the right temperature to remain potent during vaccine transportation, storage, and distribution from factory to the point of use.

Cold chain management includes all of the means used to ensure a constant temperature (between +2 and +8 °C) for a product that is not heat stable (such as vaccines, serums, tests, etc.), from the time it is manufactured until the time it is used. It involves the equipment and people needed to keep vaccines at the correct temperature (between +2 and +8 °C) during transport and storage from the time they are manufactured up until they are administered.

The cold chain must never be broken. Vaccines are sensitive to heat and extreme cold and must be kept at the correct temperature at all times. Health workers at all levels are often responsible for maintaining the cold chain, while vaccines are stored in the vaccine stores at the province and county levels, or while they are being transported to township and villages, and while they are being used during immunization sessions or rounds. More and more often it is becoming the logistician's responsibility to manage the cold chain as a part of the supply chain.

The logistics staff must be trained to both use and manage these materials. They must acquire knowledge about the cold chain; must develop thorough work techniques, specifically with respect to maintenance; and must be stable in order to ensure better follow-up. This includes having appropriate efficient logistics mechanisms to manage shipping, fuel, spare parts, etc. Without training, the program will be seriously compromised and put at risk.

18.4.7.1 Active Cold Chain (Materials for Producing Cold)

These include active thermal systems that do not use any phase change materials (PCM) such as water/ice or dry ice. These systems use mechanical or electric systems powered by an energy source, combined by thermostatic control to maintain proper product temperatures. The equipment used in active cold chain is split into two categories as follows:

- Compression refrigerators/freezers
- Absorption refrigerators/freezers

Compression Equipment

These are the models most commonly used. They run solely on electricity (220 V/ 110 V or on a battery). These models use little energy, require little maintenance, produce significant amounts of cold quickly, and are easy to repair. They are equipped with a thermostat for setting the desired temperature. Some models require only 8 hours of energy per day ("ice-lined refrigerators").

Solar models are of the compression type (source of energy: solar panels, battery). They are expensive, and maintaining them requires specialized knowledge.

Note These models may only be equipped with an HFC 134a coolant which is not harmful for the environment (the ozone layer). This is valid only for compression models since absorption models function with a water/ammonia/helium (or hydrogen[1]) mixture.

Absorption Models

The energy sources are kerosene, gas, and electricity (heating resistor). They use more energy and require more maintenance. They produce less cold and are slower. However, they are suitable for situations where electricity is not available or reliable.

Since the cooling circuit is closed, it is not possible to fill it with gas or repair it if there is a leak. However, these models are very reliable.

Models used to store vaccines are particularly well insulated and equipped with a temperature-stabilizing device, except for the kerosene model which does not have a thermostat (the best known manufacturers are Sibir and Electrolux). They are used extensively for the Extended Vaccinations Programs (EVP).

Domestic absorption models are generally insulated less well, and it is occasionally difficult to maintain a low temperature for storing vaccines, particularly when the external temperature is high (higher than 32 °C).

The efficiency of the models that run on oil depends on the quality of the fuel. Decanting and filtering are often required. A kit is available to modify certain burners, in order to improve operating efficiency, despite oil of inferior quality.

---

[1] Cannot be purchased locally given the risk that the hydrogen will explode.

18.4.7.2   Passive Cold Chain (Shipping/Storage Materials)

These include passive thermal systems that commonly use phase change materials (PCM) such as water/ice or dry ice. These shipping systems are the most basic and cost-effective. Some of the basic systems in use are as follows:

- Freezers for province, county, and sometimes at the township level
- Refrigerators and, in some areas, the new water jacket refrigerators for province, county, and township levels

Some villages do not have access to a refrigerator for vaccine storage and therefore use:

- Cold and cool boxes at all levels for transporting vaccines.
- Vaccine carrier to store vaccines during the immunization session or round.
- Control materials like paper to wrap the vaccines up when using a vaccine carrier.
- Ice packs or ice, as a last resort, to keep the vaccines at a temperature between +2 and 8 °C.
- A thermometer to measure the temperature inside the vaccine refrigerator and cold boxes.
- A chart to record the day and time of the temperature of the vaccine refrigerator. The chart should be used to record the temperature two times a day (morning and night).

18.4.8   Customs

In the humanitarian sector, particularly during emergencies, knowledge of import and export procedures is a key part of the supply chain process. The Customs Department in most countries administers the customs and exercises laws of a country through an approved legislation. The core business of the Customs Services involves enforcement of prohibitions and restrictions, collection and accounting of revenue, security and trade facilitation, and compilation of trade statistics for economic planning.

How well this aspect is managed will influence the effectiveness and timely response to needs, especially in a rapid-onset emergency. Understanding this aspect and knowing how to manage it is essential in ensuring that goods can move efficiently and in a timely manner. Effectiveness of the emergency response often depends on customs. Understanding of the various customs management issues is essential. To enable this process, it is important that staff carrying out importing and exporting activities understand the particular procedures, rules, and regulations that need to be followed to facilitate the movement of goods in and out of specific countries.

18.4.8.1 Customs and Humanitarian Aid

Any goods coming in and going out of a country have to go through certain government control procedure and formalities. Humanitarian organizations are sometimes at an advantage during emergency responses since the United Nations often assumes the lead role in making appropriate arrangements with governments regarding quick access to emergency supplies. The logistics of emergency relief is contingent upon the abovementioned arrangements and the Logistics Cluster plays a role in each of these. The Logistics Clusters on behalf of the UN Resident Coordinator (UNRC)/UN Humanitarian Coordinator (UNHC) may try to leverage these advantages for all humanitarian organizations in an emergency. Some of the problems encountered by humanitarian organizations during emergencies are:

- Complicated customs procedures cause delays resulting in congestion at port of entry (airport, road borders, seaport) that affects turnaround time for feeder vessels and railway wagons, so affecting the flow of goods
- Complex and nontransparent administrative requirements, often pertaining to documentation
- High costs for processing trade information

18.4.8.2 Role of Customs

Customs covers issues related to import and export. Import is the purchase and shipment of goods into a country, whereas export is the movement and shipment of goods out of the country.

In its efforts to achieve and respond effectively and efficiently to the aforementioned challenges and reduce the gap between reality and limited resources, the customs department has to strategically pursue the following:

- Enhance staff professionalism, integrity, and productivity
- Compilation of trade statistics

The department collects and collates trade data on all imports and exports that the government uses for planning purposes.

- Protects society and the environment using proactive enforcement approaches.
- Prohibitions and restrictions are enforced through import and export controls.

The customs department is the only government agency mandated to take full control of trade imports and exports and in so doing it:

- Protects public safety, health, and morality by barring international trade in illegal substances and materials, e.g., narcotic substances, arms and ammunitions, endangered animal species, hazardous wastes, pornographic materials, and expired, counterfeit, or substandard goods

- Liaises with other law enforcement agencies nationally and internationally to prevent transborder crimes, e.g., movement of drugs, stolen motor vehicles, and smuggled goods
- Enhances voluntary trader compliance through quality client service
- Facilitates legitimate trade through improved and integrated processes applying modern technology

Customs administrations all over the world apply almost the same procedures and processes, and speed of clearance depends largely on what controls are required by legislation and the degree to which information and communication technology is applied.

The customs department is charged with the responsibility of facilitating international trade by providing expedited clearance of goods through simplified and harmonized customs procedures as envisaged under the Revised Kyoto Convention:

- Support professionalism of customs agents and other trade chain participants
- Revenue collection and accounting

The customs department collects the following types of duties:

- Import duties – on imported goods which are dutiable as per the import duty schedule published and revised periodically
- Export duties – on certain exports that may be spelled out in the export schedule

The department also collects certain fees and levies upon importation, based on agency basis, such as:

- Import declaration fees – on imported products
- Petroleum development levy – on petroleum products
- Foreign motor vehicle permit fee – on foreign motor vehicles
- Sugar levy – on sugar imports
- Horticultural crop development levy – on horticultural produce
- Revenue stamps – for certain transaction documents which, by law, require affixing of stamps

The specific activities by customs related to humanitarian organizations are:

- Applying for duties and tax exemption
- Requesting for customs clearance and customs clearance process

18.4.9   Distribution

The distribution chain or channel represents the movement of a product or service from the point of purchase to the time it is handed over to the final user/consumer. This may entail a chain of intermediaries passing the product down the chain within the organization before it finally reaches the consumer or end user. Or it could be direct from the point of purchase to the end user. Each of the elements in these chains will have its own specific needs, which the producer must take into account, along with those of the all-important end user. Reliability of the distribution chain is critical. In the humanitarian context, distribution is viewed from three perspectives:

- Movement of goods from the point of purchase or transfer of ownership (vendor to humanitarian organization) to the point of final use. This is common in sudden-onset emergencies where goods are often taken straight to the end user. The internal distribution occurs at the point the commodity or goods are being handed over to the beneficiary.
- Movement of goods from one location within the organization to another location within the same organization. For example, from hub to hub or hub to end user point, this is common when resources are being mobilized to strategic locations for onward movement to point of use as in the case of preparedness for an anticipated emergency.
- The point at which the goods are handed over by the organization to beneficiaries or partner organization. For example, WFP food distribution direct to beneficiaries or partner agency conducting the distribution exercise.

Some of the distribution activities embrace material handling, storage and warehousing, packaging, transportation, etc. Distribution is sometimes referred to as the "final mile" and is a critical part of the supply chain. This is where the risk of loss and insecurity tends to be high, where communication is the most sporadic, where monitoring is most difficult, where costs require close monitoring, and where the organization sometimes has less direct control but can integrate with the program the most closely. This topic is intended to help develop an understanding of distribution and provides information that embraces all three perspectives above.

18.4.9.1 Distribution Plan

The distribution plan is normally part of general supply planning, but in this case the assumption is that the organization that you represent will be responsible for major portions of the distribution network. With this in mind, care needs to be exercised in formulating the distribution plan. In these guidelines an extended-delivery point (EDP) refers to the point at which your organization actually physically hands over supplies to a counterpart (an NGO, an individual, or even the beneficiaries themselves).

The final overall distribution plan should be easy to read and focused around a distribution table or spreadsheet representing the needs. A successful delivery function can only exist with collaborative planning across functions and entities. There are three levels of a distribution plan.

- The country plan will show the total for the country. The country may be divided into product destinations (whether provincial, regional, or your organization's office responsible areas).

- The secondary level may take into consideration one province and split it into various EDPs that the organization will hand over to.
- At the tertiary level the plan is drawn up by the counterpart, the entity on the ground facilitating distribution. This lists the names of the beneficiaries, or schools, or health posts that the items are destined for. This list reconciles the planned quantities with real beneficiaries, so that for each province, there is a plan one level down.

18.4.10 Monitoring and Evaluation

For logisticians, monitoring and evaluation may be defined as follows:

Monitoring To review on a continuous basis the degree to which the logistics activity is completed and if targets are being met. This allows corrective actions to be taken.

Evaluation To analyze progress towards meeting established objectives and goals. It is done on an ad hoc, monthly, quarterly, or yearly basis. Evaluation provides feedback on whether plans have been met and the reasons for success or failure. It should also provide direction for future plans.

Together monitoring and evaluation provide the basis for performance management. Also key to performance management is aligning performance metrics to the goals and objectives of the program. Without alignment, monitoring and evaluation are ineffective as the direction in which the program is heading is unknown, and therefore M&E is unfocused and potentially disruptive to the program. Without alignment you do not know what to monitor or how to evaluate it.

The logistics function in humanitarian organizations is made up of people, processes, and systems working together to support efficient and effective delivery of services. Controls are normally put in place to monitor weaknesses, poor designs in projects, and improper implementation of programs. Based on continuous monitoring, these weaknesses or shortfalls against targets or objectives set can be corrected or revised in order to continually improve performance, thus reducing the risk of exposure and strengthening the response to needs.

Monitoring and evaluation are integral parts of management and provide a link between planning and implementation. While monitoring focuses on the activities and outputs, evaluation focuses on the outcome and goals.

Monitoring is initiated at the beginning of a program, project, or emergency response and built into the design, assessment, and planning phases of the logistics aspect. It focuses on inputs and outputs and basically tracks and assesses implementation of the logistics aspect of the program, project, or emergency response. It is the continuous process of gathering logistics and program information to measure against preset key performance indicators (KPIs), benchmarks, or previously baselined indicators that are aligned to the goals and objectives of the program.

Evaluation, like monitoring, is a continuous process. The evaluation of the quality of the output should be undertaken in such a way that shortcomings can be identified and corrected. Evaluation should also feed into the planning process continuously so that the planned method of the intervention can be modified to take into account the realities and conditions on the ground. Evaluation provides a tool for management to ensure that focus is maintained.

Monitoring and evaluation have several purposes:

- Provide information to users on the service level they can expect.
- Make an objective evaluation of services and activities.
- Identify problems in the supply chain.
- Determine what measures are needed for improving services.
- Understand the need to increase or decrease resources.
- Objective measurement for calculating reorder levels.
- Define parameters for the periodic review system calculations.
- Evaluate performance of individual staff members.
- Motivate logisticians.

Quantitative and qualitative measures can be monitored for the entire supply chain, from the manufacturer to the beneficiary, as well as for the individual parts of the supply chain. Every link in the supply chain should be seen as a service receiver (from suppliers) as well as a service provider (to users). The management of stocks and the quality of services received will affect the quality of services provided. It is important to make this distinction when there is a requirement to improve service provided to the final user or consumer.

18.5   Conclusion

Managing a humanitarian supply chain crossing international borders and/or cultures is a complex management activity that is yet to embrace the necessity of business supply chain management principles, with very few humanitarian organizations measuring their logistical performance. As with business supply chains, developing a seamless and integrated chain is emphasized which often takes a cost-focused approach aiming to decrease costs, increase efficiencies, and optimize the supply of goods and services with research concentrating on systems, technology, and processes. Humanitarian supply chain management is often linked to sourcing and moving goods to the disaster area but is part of a service-based industry. Interactions and relationships with people are vital, increasing the management complexities. Yet the disaster supply chain consists of managing the movement of both equipment and human resources. Managing humanitarian supply chains is a people business that still appears to be anchored in an efficiency paradigm focusing on cost reduction.

References

Howden M (2009) How humanitarian logistics information systems can improve humanitarian supply chains: a view from the field. In: Proceedings of the 6th international ISCRAM conference, Gothenburg

Thomas AS, Kopczak LR (2005) From logistics to supply chain management: the path forward in the humanitarian sector. Fritz Ins 15:1–15

Pateman H, Hughes K, Cahoon S (2013) Humanizing humanitarian supply chains: a synthesis of key challenges. Asian J Shipp Log 29(1):81–102

Chandraprakaikul W (2010) Humanitarian supply chain management: literature review and future research. The 2nd international conference on logistics and transport, Queenstown

Chapter 19
Peculiarities of Disaster Management in a High-Altitude Area

Ajay Bohtan, Prem Vrat, and A.K. Vij

19.1   Introduction

A disaster is a sudden, calamitous event that seriously disrupts the functioning of a community or society and causes human, material, and economic or environmental losses that exceed the community's or society's ability to cope using its own resource (1).

India has been traditionally vulnerable to natural disasters on account of its unique geo-climatic conditions. Floods, droughts, cyclones, earthquakes, and landslides have been a recurrent phenomenon. These have resulted in astronomical loss of human lives. Loss of property in terms of private, community, and public assets has always assumed staggering proportions in every disaster.

To reduce the far-reaching long-term consequences of a disaster, it is incumbent that adequate steps be taken to reduce the draconian effects of the catastrophe. The abovementioned steps depend a lot on various factors, viz., terrain, weather, local populace, communication links, etc. Studies of previous disasters have brought out that one of the most important factors is the prevailing environment of the disaster area which effects any step taken toward reducing the effects of the disaster.

A high-altitude area (HAA) offers peculiar environment conditions due to which the template of disaster management of other areas cannot be resorted to. A need therefore exists to study the peculiar nature of such an area and examine the effects it would have on the management of disasters.

A. Bohtan
ITM University, Gurgaon, Haryana, India
e-mail: ajaybohtan@gmail.com

P. Vrat (✉)
Pro-Chancellor, ITM University, Gurgaon, Haryana, India
e-mail: premvrat@itmindia.edu

A.K. Vij
Prof Emeritus, ITM University, Gurgaon, Haryana, India
e-mail: akvij@itmindia.edu

© Springer India 2016   273
B.S. Sahay et al. (eds.), *Managing Humanitarian Logistics*, Springer Proceedings
in Business and Economics, DOI 10.1007/978-81-322-2416-7_19

This paper aims at bringing out the peculiarities of a "high-altitude area" and the effects it would have on the disaster management in such areas. The scope of the study is limited to natural disasters occurring in HAA in the Indian subcontinent. However, with a few modifications the results can be extrapolated to other such areas around the globe.

19.2 Disaster

A disaster is an emergency situation gone beyond control. In turn, an emergency is a deviation from planned or expected behavior or a course of events that endangers or adversely affects people, property, or the environment. An emergency becomes a disaster when it exceeds the capability of the local resources to manage it. Disasters often result in great damage, loss, or destruction.

The latest classification distinguishes two generic disaster groups: natural and technological disasters (2). The natural disaster category is being divided into six disaster groups: biological, geophysical, meteorological, hydrological, climatological, and extraterrestrial. Each group covers different disaster main types, each having different disaster subtypes. Some examples of natural disasters include epidemic (biological), earthquakes (geophysical), storms (meteorological), floods (hydrological), droughts (climatological), and hit by meteorite/asteroids (extraterrestrial).

The technological disasters would include unplanned events or accidents that result from human activity or human developments. Examples include chemical spills, nuclear radiation escapes, utility failures, epidemics, crashes, explosions, and urban fires. Some disasters can also be a result of internal disturbances (riots, demonstrations, large-scale prison breaks, and violent strikes), energy and material shortages (strikes, price wars, and resource scarcity), and attack (large-scale terrorism or war using nuclear, conventional, or biological agents).

19.3 Anatomy of Disaster Management

Planning is of utmost importance to analyze and document the possibility of an emergency or disaster and the potential consequences or impacts on life, property, and the environment. This includes assessing the hazards, risks, mitigation, preparedness, response, and recovery needs. The process cycle of disaster management can be divided into six segments (3) as shown in Fig. 19.1.

19.3.1 Prevention

Action within this segment is designed to prevent or impede the occurrence of a disaster. Construction of water channels, dams, fire lanes, etc., is an example of

Fig. 19.1 Disaster
management cycle

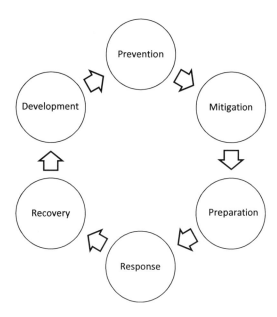

preventing disaster to take place. These are activities that actually eliminate or
reduce the probability of a disaster.

19.3.2 Mitigation

It includes long-term activities designed to reduce the effects of unavoidable
disaster (e.g., legislating appropriate building norms in a potential
earthquake zone).

19.3.3 Preparation

This comprises measures which enable governments, organizations, communities,
and individuals to respond rapidly and effectively to disaster situations and involves
activities necessary to the extent that mitigation measures have not, or cannot,
prevent disasters. In this segment, governments, organizations, and individuals
develop plans to save, maximize lifesaving, and minimize disaster damage (e.g.,
compiling state resource inventories, mounting training exercises, installing early
warning systems, and preparing predetermined emergency response forces). Preparedness measures also seek to enhance the disaster response operations (e.g., by
stockpiling vital food and medical supplies, through training exercises, and by
mobilizing emergency response personnel on standby).

19.3.4 Response

These are activities that are taken immediately following disaster impact. Such activities are designed to provide emergency assistance for victims (e.g., search and rescue, emergency shelter, medical care, and mass feeding). They also seek to stabilize the situation and reduce the probability of secondary damage (e.g., evacuating cracked buildings, securing bridges on a flooded river, etc.) and to speed recovery operations (e.g., damage assessment). Responses are primarily directed toward saving life and protecting property and deal with the immediate disruption, damage, and other effects caused by the disaster.

19.3.5 Recovery

Recovery is the process by which communities and the nation are assisted in returning to their proper level of functioning following a disaster. This includes all activities necessary to return all systems to normal or better. The three main activities under this segment are restoration, rehabilitation, and reconstruction. These activities return vital life support systems to minimum operating standards (e.g., cleanup, temporary housing, and access to food and water). Some of these activities continue for a number of years after a disaster. Their purpose is to return life to normal or improved levels (e.g., redevelopment loans, legal assistance, and community planning).

19.3.6 Development

It is a long-drawn and ongoing process wherein activities to firstly restore and later improve the living conditions would have to be undertaken. The development issues could include sustainable land use, housing repair and reconstruction, business resumption and economic redevelopment, infrastructure restoration and mitigation, long-term health and social services support, environmental restoration, financial considerations, and short-term recovery actions that affect long-term redevelopment as well as other long-term recovery issues identified by the community (4).

19.4 Factors Affecting the Segments of Disaster Management

19.4.1 Pre-disaster Phase

The pre-disaster phase consists of prevention, mitigation, and preparation sub-phases. All factors mentioned herein are taken into effect before the actual disaster strikes.

19.4.1.1 Prevention

  (i) Terrain
 (ii) Weather and climate
(iii) Area mapping
(iv) Population data
 (v) Analysis of hazards and risks

19.4.1.2 Mitigation

  (i) Terrain
 (ii) Weather and climate
(iii) Emergency management program

19.4.1.3 Preparedness

  (i) Terrain
 (ii) Weather and climate
(iii) Storage space availability
(iv) Imparting training
 (v) Attitude of civil administration

19.4.2 Post-disaster Phase

The post-disaster phase consists of response, recovery, and development subphases. All factors mentioned herein are taken into effect after the actual disaster strikes.

19.4.2.1 Response

(i)   Terrain
(ii) Weather and climate
(iii) Ground conditions prevalent
(iv) Surviving communication links
(v)   Urbanization

19.4.2.2 Recovery

(i)   Terrain
(ii) Weather and climate
(iii) Miscellaneous

19.4.2.3 Development

(i)   Terrain
(ii) Weather and climate
(iii) Debris
(iv) Economics
(v)   Agriculture
(vi) Industrialization

As seen from above, all the six segments of disaster management rely a large extent on the terrain, weather, and climate of the place of operation. Accordingly the disaster management process is also peculiar for every different region depending on the geography of that area. The Indian subcontinent can be divided into five physiographic regions: the coastal plains, Thar deserts, Indo-Gangetic plains, Peninsular Plateau, and the Northern Mountains. The height of mountains in India offers a large variance, i.e., from a couple of thousand feet till around 25,000 ft. As the characteristics of mountains change drastically after 9,000 ft, the area above this altitude is generally termed as the "high-altitude area."

19.5 Peculiarities of High-Altitude Area

In India the mighty Himalayan Mountains boast of a continuous belt of high altitudes in the Higher Himalayas. Although most of the high mountains are of the loosely called "wet" type, the Ladakh region is a "dry"-type area and is also known as the "cold desert." The major difference between these two is the annual precipitation which has led to variances in vegetation, living style of the local populace, and accessibility during winters to name a few. Thin air, cold weather, and rugged mountains pose a significant challenge to man's ability to survive at such high altitudes. These characteristics combine to create a unique and unforgiving environment, which can prove as deadly as it seems innocuous.

19.5.1 Rarefied Atmosphere

The phenomenon of rarefied air, caused by low pressure, is an environmental condition unique to HAA. It imposes several physical stresses on men/animals and also alters the performance of aircrafts, generators, pumps, vehicles, etc.

The partial pressure of oxygen falls as well, producing arid air that holds significantly less water vapor and reduces the amount of oxygen available to human tissue. The reduction of oxygen supply to tissue causes hypoxia and can lead to severe physiological effects and other illnesses, some of which can prove fatal.

The most common altitude illness is acute mountain sickness (AMS) which induces headaches and nausea. Most men afflicted with AMS suffer muscular weakness, fatigue, and appetite loss as well. Reduced oxygen causes a wide range of other physiological effects and illnesses. High-altitude pulmonary odema (HAPO) and high-altitude cerebral odema (HACO) are more severe syndromes which can progress to coma and also death in less than 12 hours. Less severe illnesses and physiological effects include sleep disturbance, fatigue, and loss of appetite.

The atmosphere affects vision in several ways. Men could lose much of their natural night vision due to bleeding from blood vessels in the eyes. The drastic increase in ultraviolet light can cause snow blindness and severe sunburn. The time it takes for wounds to heal increases because of the lack of oxygen in body tissues.

All the above inflicts casualties and degrades a person's ability to carry out work. His capacity to move at a certain speed reduces and is always catching breath. Sustained exposure to this can also render temporary loss of memory, and at times his remembering power also comes down.

Aircraft engines produce less power, reducing maneuverability and limiting load capacity. In addition to a reduction in engine power, helicopters lose rotor efficiency in low air pressure. Hovering is difficult and risky, and most helicopters are unable to lift normal loads. The drag reduction caused by low air pressure alters the aerodynamics of a high-performance aircraft. Thin air forces a greater turning radius and increases the height lost in a pullout following a dive. Further, fast changing patterns of winds inside the narrow valleys make flying all the more risky.

19.5.2 Extreme Cold Temperature

Frigid weather is common to most of the India's high mountain ranges. A climb in altitude generates freezing temperatures. Snow and freezing temperatures cause an initial physiological shock and cause incapacitating injuries to men and animals. It also degrades performance of certain machinery due to freezing lubricants and metal brittleness.

19.5.3 Harsh Terrain

Mountains impede both foot and vehicular movement. The rugged and imposing terrain of the mountains with high peaks and ridgelines expose men and animals to severe terrain and thus makes movement very arduous. Rocky, narrow roads make travel a dangerous endeavor. Foot movement is considerably limited and calculated in time, not distance. The movement further gets effected by rain, fog, snow, and blizzards and is much slower and treacherous at nights. Mountains increase the requirements necessary to support the population and make logistics even more difficult. The limited availability of trafficable roads and other choke points like bridges, passes, etc., further makes logistics a planner's nightmare.

Mules and human porters too have a degraded performance in HAA as compared to a regular mountainous terrain.

Mountains affect air operations too, imposing limits on both helicopter and fixed wing flights. Low ceilings, fog, changing winds, and narrow valleys make mountain flying a dangerous task. Terrain canalizes avenues of approach, limiting ingress and egress routes and increasing aircraft vulnerability. Terrain suitable for helicopter landing zones is also difficult to find.

19.5.4 Precipitation

Any type of precipitation above the normal limits of that area is a potential disaster. Excessive rain and snowfall are generally responsible for such catastrophe. Just, for example, during the Ladakh disaster in 2010, the rainfall on August 6 over Leh during the most intense part of the storm was reportedly equivalent to around a year's worth of rain falling in 30 min.

19.5.5 Ultraviolet Radiation

At higher altitudes, a thinner atmosphere filters less ultraviolet (UV) radiation. UV radiation is reflected or scattered to varying extents by different surfaces. Fresh snow can reflect much as 94 % of the incoming UV radiation. In contrast, snow-free lands typically reflect only 2–4 % of UV radiation.

Prolonged human exposure to solar UV radiation may result in acute and chronic health effects on the skin, eye, and immune system. Sunburn is the best-known acute effect of excessive UV radiation exposure. Over the longer term, UV radiation induces degenerative changes in the cells of the skin, fibrous tissue, and blood vessels leading to premature skin aging. Another long-term effect is an inflammatory reaction of the eye. In most serious cases, skin cancer and cataracts can also occur (6).

19.5.6   Axis of Maintenance

There are limited axes of maintenance in mountains. These are further restricted by various choke points like bridges, passes, etc. For example, the Ladakh valley is connected to the rest of India by road by two passes only, namely, Zoji La and Rohtang La. Closure of these passes cuts off the Ladakh valley, which can then only be maintained by using air effort.

19.6   Potential Natural Disasters in High-Altitude Areas

Although a disaster in the making does not look for any time and place, we can certainly rule out some disasters like the tsunami, cyclones, etc., in HAA. Some of the common situations which possess a potential to lead to a natural disaster are as follows:

- Earthquake
- Precipitation
- Blizzard
- Landslides
- Mudslides
- Avalanche
- Drought
- Melting of permafrost

19.7   Effects of High Altitude in Disaster Management

19.7.1   Prevention

(i) To prevent flooding and to control the floodwaters, construction of dams has to be planned. It must be remembered that construction activity can take place only during the summer season, i.e., wef May–Oct. This availability of a 6-month window implies that the time of construction nearly doubles in HAA.

(ii) In a wooded HAA controlled burning of vegetation in a fire-prone area prior to the high fire-risk season has to be carried out to form fire lanes or also to actually prevent the start of a fire or prevent it from reaching threatening proportions, if at all a fire originates.

19.7.2 Mitigation

(i) To avoid damages to buildings in an earthquake, legislations might have to be passed to disallow construction using certain available material, e.g., in Ladakh area maximum houses are constructed using available stones, boulders, and mud. Planning for making appropriate construction material available and at economic rates should be factored in.

(ii) The severe nature of the weather and terrain permits holding of certain hazardous substances like kerosene, diesel, etc. Some control on their holding has to be exercised.

(iii) Any early warning system has to very robust in design. It should be designed to withstand extremely low temperature and high ultraviolet radiations. At places they have to be protected from rains, snow, and blizzards.

19.7.3 Preparation

(i) Certain areas like the Ladakh valley in the state of Jammu and Kashmir remain cut off for 6–7 months due to the road passes covered with snow. Hence stocking of food, supplies, and other material can only be done during the road open period. Effective transportation models have to be devised to ensure timely and efficient stocking.

(ii) In case of rivers and rivulets, a very few crossing points are available. If washed away, it would take a very long time for them to be reconstructed. Similar is the case with roads and tracks in such areas. Hence adequate stocking has to be done at different places including places where the access is very difficult.

(iii) The local population figures of every area are almost constant during the complete part of the year. However, some areas witness a large influx of migrants or tourists during certain parts of the year. Adequate stock levels of food and medicines need to be catered accordingly depending on the location and time of year.

(iv) It has been experienced that during a disaster the disrupted communications cause a further impediment in disaster response effort. Establishing a communication network in a short time in a high-altitude area is a very daunting task. Hence such vital systems such as power supplies, communication nodes, and other key installations should be constructed ab initio with adequate redundancy considering the nature of the existing environment.

(v) Road and air communications are of vital importance in HAA. Hence infrastructure like roads, bridges, airports, and helipads should be conscientiously constructed. Alignment of roads, though restricted due to terrain, should be done so as to avoid disaster-prone areas.

(vi) High-altitude areas are very thinly and sparsely populated. Data of the same needs to be collated ensuring that no one is left out.

(vii) Although the local population is not well aware of impending disaster and the associated drills, adequate awareness needs to be generated by any means available.

(viii) Training of the populace is extremely difficult as they are located at large distances and difficult altitudes. In many circumstances individual and/or family preparedness, where government resources and emergency services are limited, could be very vital for survival during disasters.

19.7.4 Response

(i) The first and the foremost response is the collection of preliminary data of the affected populace and the survivors of the catastrophe. This assumes great difficulty in case proper plans are not in place as the various affected areas are not easily accessible and also not in communication.

(ii) The search and rescue teams from outside the area are not acclimatized and hence face a lot of difficulty in searching and rescuing survivors.

(iii) Most areas are not mapped in details due to very steep altitudes. This raises the degree of difficulty in providing help.

(iv) The rarefied atmosphere lowers the efficiency of machines like bulldozers, JCBs, etc. This leads to further delays in debris removal for rescuing trapped people.

(v) During winter, the diesel fuel in the machinery freezes and therefore poses difficulty in performing the assigned tasks.

(vi) The lift capability of aircraft and helicopters also reduces drastically which is a big limitation not only in evacuations but also in ferrying emergency supplies to affected areas.

(vii) Appropriate locations for storage of the vast relief material may not be available in such terrain.

(viii) Most of the areas in high altitude do not have an electricity supply in all places of habitation. Hence rescue efforts during times of poor visibility are further restricted.

19.7.5 Recovery

(i) Any disaster renders the local population homeless which exposes them to the vagaries of extreme weather. Hence, more than the harm due to the disaster causing events, it is the weather which has an adverse effect on their health. The medical machinery of that area therefore becomes overburdened.

(ii) Restoration of repairable homes and other buildings/installations can only be done during summer time. There would also exist an enormous requirement of special items to undertake repairs. Considering the nature of the calamity, priority for provisioning other essentials like food and medicines would be higher.

(iii) Temporary shelters which are required to be erected need experts from outside that area. Even if they arrive soon, they need acclimatization due to which precious time is lost.

(iv) The shelters also have to be designed to withstand the extreme weather of high-altitude areas, e.g., they have to be insulated from the temperature and be able to withstand heavy blizzards and snowfall. They have to be prefabricated as construction takes a long time in such areas.

(v) Restoring essential services like water supply, sewage disposal, etc., would depend on the type and degree of disaster. Restoration of any service in inclement weather, viz., snow or rain, would take time.

(vi) Physical and psychological rehabilitation of persons who have suffered from the effects of disaster would require greater and special effort. Equipment, infrastructure, and trained personnel would have to be called for, who themselves would be exposed to the perils of the high altitude.

19.7.6 Development

(i) The oncoming assistance for the development of the area has to be regulated and controlled due to paucity of time and space for its utilization.

(ii) Specially designed infrastructure suitable for the peculiar terrain and climate should only be provisioned.

(iii) Extra care has to be taken to ensure that the ongoing development work does not become a potential cause for further disaster.

19.8 Designing a Supply Chain for a Flash Flood Calamity

Any supply chain established to cater for disaster management caters to the following minimum conditions:

- Facility locations
- Resource allocation
- Relief distribution
- Casualty evacuation
- Evacuation of displaced populace

19.8.1 Disaster Response Supply Chain

The classical business supply chain model is used for the pre-disaster and post-disaster activities. In such activities, time is not of utmost importance as would be the case during the response operations conducted immediately on occurrence of the disaster. During the response phase of the disaster cycle, the disaster response supply chain is used to cater a short-term goal achievement. Details of such a supply chain are given in Table 19.1.

A classical supply chain is a coordinated system of organizations, information, and resources which are involved in moving products or services from the suppliers to the consumers. Four variables to be controlled are cost, time, quality, and safety (in this order). In a disaster relief supply chain, the consumer is the population in crisis, and the suppliers are agencies holding the essential stocks of medicines, food, shelters, transport, etc., at a place where the time to transport them to the affected area is the minimum. Moving supplies to the affected area is more complicated than a commercial supply chain. Time of delivery of relief supplies assumes paramount importance over cost and is what is required to be planned in advance. The terminal distribution of the supplies also gains importance. The key challenges to emergency logistics planning as compared to the business logistics case are as follows:

- Additional uncertainties (unusable routes, safety issues, changing facility capacities, demand uncertainties)
- Complex communication and coordination (damage to communication lines; involvement of many third parties, government, and civilians; inaccessibility to accurate real-time demand information)
- Harder-to-achieve efficient and timely delivery
- Limited resources often overwhelmed by the scale of the situation (supply, people, transportation capacity, fuel)

The importance of an already existing disaster plan cannot be overemphasized with a view of mitigating the effects of a disaster by improving the "Response" phase of the disaster management cycle. The coordination of moving supplies to the affected area would initially be done by government agencies. A disaster relief supply chain would then have to be set up at a very short notice with limited resources, man power, information, etc., and so needs to be well planned ab initio. It should possess adequate agility, value, velocity, and visibility to be effective.

The recent disasters in the hills of Uttarakhand during the 3rd week of June 2013 and the one at Leh during the 1st week of Aug 2010 are still fresh in our minds. Both were natural disasters due to cloudbursts resulting in flash floods. While Kedarnath in Uttarakhand is at an elevation of approximately 11,657 ft, the Leh town is at an altitude of 11,562 ft above sea level. Both areas fall under the category of high-altitude area though Kedarnath being the "wet" type and Leh being the "dry" type of high-altitude areas.

Table 19.1 Type of supply chains involved in disaster management

Phase	Pre-disaster			Disaster	Post-disaster	
Operations	Prevention	Mitigation	Preparation	Response	Recovery	Development
Major activities	Identification of potential disaster sites	Evacuation	Pre-positioning, facility location	Relief distribution, causality evacuation, evacuation of displaced populace	Provide road communication	Build houses, generate employment
Type of supply chain	Business supply chain			Disaster response supply chain	Business supply chain	

Ladakh lies on the rain shadow side of the Himalayas, where dry monsoon winds reach Leh after being robbed of its moisture in plains, and in the Himalayan Mountain the district combines the condition of both arctic and desert climate. Therefore, Ladakh is often called "cold desert." The main features of this cold desert are:

- Wide diurnal and seasonal fluctuation in temperature with −40 °C in winter and +35 °C in summer.
- Precipitation is very low with annual precipitation of 10 cm mainly in form of snow.
- Air is very dry and with a relative humidity range from 6 to 24 %.
- Irrigation is mainly through channels from the melted glaciers.

Ladakh is called the Hermit kingdom due to its remoteness and inaccessibility. Ladakh is connected to the mainland through two roads, namely, Leh-Srinagar national highway and Leh-Manali road. These two roads remain open only during summer months, and during the winter they remain closed for more than 7 months due to closure of the passes (Zojila, Rohtang Pass, Baralacha, Changla). Leh district is connected to the block headquarter by roads, through a network of roads. The average distance of the block headquarter from Leh is 180 km. Bus services and other means of communication are very poor. As some of the roads to the block headquarter pass through the world's highest motorable roads, it is frequently closed due to the avalanches and snowfall in the passes. Durbuk Block and Nubra Block remain closed in winter months due to closure of Khardung La and the Changla Passes, respectively.

In order to strengthen the arguments for designing a peculiar disaster response supply chain management plan for a particular high-altitude area, the Leh district in the Ladakh region of the state of Jammu and Kashmir has been taken as a proving ground.

A little information about Leh. Leh district with an area of 45,100 sq km makes it the 2nd largest district in the country. Leh is one of the coldest and most elevated inhabited regions of the world with a total population of 1,17,232 souls as per 2001 census. It is at a distance of 434 km from state capital (summer) Srinagar and 474 km from Manali (HP). The district is divided into nine CD blocks, namely, Leh, Khaltsi, Nyoma, Durbuk, Kharu, Nubra, Saspol, Panamic, and Chuchot and is divided into three tehsils, namely, Leh, Sumoor, and Khaltsi. Leh is the district headquarter and the only township in the district.

An attempt is now being made to design one supply chain during a hypothetical calamity caused by cloudburst and flash flood in Diskit (Nubra valley). The nearest National Disaster Relief Force battalion is located at Bathinda (Punjab). As they will take time to arrive at any disaster area in Leh, the immediate response lies in the hands of the local populace, government agencies, and NGOs.

19.8.1.1 Constraints

The following constraints in establishing a relief supply chain are foreseen in any disaster situation arising:

- No proper command and control.
- Disrupted communication.
- Key roads and bridges washed away.
- Uncertainty of requirement exists in the execution on this supply chain due to no set templates of demand and suppliers.
- Uncertainty of resources available, e.g., the transportation means would vary depending upon their availability and suitability.
- Widely dispersed beneficiaries.

19.8.1.2 Requirements

The first response would involve moving earth and moving equipment to clear debris and extricate trapped people. Thereafter would arise the immediate requirement of relief material consisting of the following items in priority:

- Medical supplies
- Water
- Food
- Shelters

At times supply paradoxes would exist: say, for example, between supply of building material for bridging the cutoff area and supply of food, water, or shelters which cannot be transported without laying a bridge.

19.8.2 Holding of Relief Inventory and Transportation Methods

Although disaster relief material is held at various places under the India Disaster Response Network (IDRN), the same is also available locally at various major places. Transportation of the same needs to be carried out to the disaster-affected area in the earliest time frame by a suitable method of transportation.

19.8.2.1 Road

It is the most important mode of transportation, due to the nonexistence of airstrips and helipads at all places which have been identified as prone to disaster.

19.8.2.2 Air (Fixed Wing)

Airstrip exists only at Leh and at Thoise (Nubra valley). However, advanced landing grounds are available at Fukche, Nyoma, Chushul, and the recently tested Daulat Beg Oldie (16,614 ft).

19.8.2.3 Air (Rotary Wing)

Helipads are available at many places in the Ladakh sector. Also due to the flat nature of the terrain, preparation of makeshift helipads poses no problems. The only problem would be the inclement weather which at time persists for as long as 10 days at a stretch.

19.8.3 PERT Chart for Relief Distribution

Relief distribution consists of bringing relief (medical supplies, water, food, shelters, man power, sanitation, and other related resources) to the affected people. A typical PERT chart data for supply of relief material from Nimoo town to a remote place in Ladakh, say Diskit (located in Nubra valley, en route lies the famous highest motorable pass in the world, Khardung La), shall be as in Table 19.2. The PERT chart has been prepared for one-time transportation of relief material based on the assumption that transport as required is available with undisrupted road communication from Nimoo to Diskit in Nubra valley. In actual the following uncertainties would have to be catered for:

* Inclement weather, which would not allow movement of helicopters and also could slow down road communication
* Blockage at the Khardung La Pass en route would set back the travel time to the Diskit staging area
* Any other blockages en route would also have to be mitigated before the relief supplies could be sent by road

19.8.4 PERT Chart Analysis

Analysis of the PERT chart reveals the following:

* Time taken for each activity is longer than it would have been for an area in the plains.
* Transportation of relief supplies by road from Nimoo to Diskit is expected to take approx. 26 h.

Table 19.2 PERT chart data for relief distribution

Activity	Description	Immediate predecessor	Optimistic time estimate (hours) (a)	Most likely time estimate (hours) (m)	Pessimistic time estimate (hours) (b)	Expected completion time (hours) $\{t_e = (a+4m+b)/6\}$	Standard deviation = (b-a)/6
A	Announcement of disaster relief for Diskit	–	–	–	–	–	–
B	Road transport made available at relief facility at Nimoo	A	2	4	6	4	0.67
C	Man power made available at relief facility at Nimoo	A	2	4	6	4	0.67
D	Identification and segregation of relief material at resource facility at Nimoo	A	2	3	5	3	0.50
E	Loading of relief material at resource facility at Nimoo	B, C, D	1	2	4	2	0.50
F	Transportation to staging area at Diskit by road	E	5	6	24	9	3.17
G	Transportation to airfield/helipad at Leh	E	2	3	6	3	0.67
H	Transport helicopter made available at Leh airfield	A	5	6	12	7	1.17
I	Loading on the helicopter	H, G	1	2	3	2	0.33
J	Transportation to staging area at Diskit by helicopter	I	1	2	8	3	1.17

K	Unloading from helicopter at staging area	J	1	2	3	2	0.33
L	Unloading from road transport at staging area	F	1	2	3	2	0.33
M	Merging and breaking up of relief supplies at staging area	K, L	2	3	4	3	0.33
N	Loading on road transport at staging area	M	1	2	3	2	0.33
O	Transportation of relief supplies to final staging area	N	1	2	5	2	0.67
P	Distribution of relief material to beneficiaries	O	1	2	4	2	0.50

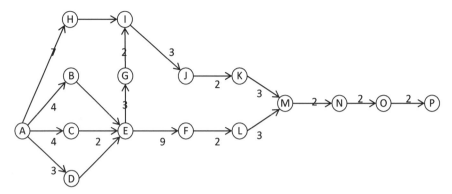

Fig. 19.2 PERT chart for movement of disaster relief material from Nimoo to Diskit

- Transportation of relief supplies by helicopter from Nimoo to Diskit is expected to take approx. 25 h.
- The estimated time taken by road or by air is nearly the same and is far in excess from the ideal time by which the first emergent relief material should reach the disaster-affected area (Fig. 19.2).

In any disaster scenario the initial response for relief to reach the site is of utmost importance.

In the given scenario, the human casualties would be braving inclement weather compounded by the vagaries of the high-altitude terrain. It becomes pertinent that the relief reaches the site in the earliest time frame. Hence the need to minimize the maximum time taken for moving relief infrastructure becomes important. The following is therefore recommended in such situations:

- Time for every action to be crashed, along with consultation from the concerned agencies.
- Forward positioning of various relief facilities to be carried out as dispersed as possible so as to mitigate effects of disruption in road/air communication.
- Alternative routes to be identified to transport relief supplies, bypassing obstacles likely to be created by the nature's fury.
- The time taken due to the effect of high altitude should be factored in the plans.

19.9   Disaster Management in High-Altitude Area: The Way Ahead

In order to realize an effective disaster management plan in HAA, the peculiarity of such areas has to be studied. Wet snow-bound areas like the high reaches in Pir Panjal ranges in Kashmir (India) are quite different than the dry desert like areas of the Ladakh valley in Kashmir itself. Special attention needs to be given while planning and formulating action/activities under each segment of the disaster management cycle.

19.9.1 Planning

(i) Plans primarily address only floods and earthquakes. We need to identify all possible hazards; assess the vulnerability of settlements, communities, and assets to relevant hazards; and finally evaluate the associated risks. Well-thought-out, practically feasible, and flexible contingency plans for an appropriate and quick response at all levels should be drawn out.

(ii) The presence of the Indian Army generally covers the complete high-altitude areas. Army troops are acclimatized, disciplined, and motivated. Any disaster management plans when being formulated should incorporate the utilization of the army. Their immense humanitarian contribution in the recent Uttarkashi disaster is a proof of the same.

(iii) Every available resource in that affected area should be used for assistance. It should therefore be ensured that there is complete synergy and understanding of the capabilities and work culture among the local administration, armed forces, public/private enterprises, NGOs, and the resident community.

(iv) Plans formulated should consider every period of the year separately which has a direct effect on the prevailing environment at the time of the disaster.

(v) Planning for stay and acclimatization of people and animals brought in from plains should be carried out so that they could perform their tasks efficiently.

(vi) As there is a paucity of plain areas in mountainous terrain, locations be earmarked for storage of disaster relief material.

(vii) Any nonessential material coming in would occupy space and also drain the already scarce resources for unloading, transporting, and stacking them. Relief material required should therefore be worked out for every contingency.

(viii) List of donors and vendors to be prepared beforehand. The list would not be reliable as one cannot define the donations, but still a planning figure can be maintained.

19.9.2 Preparation

(i) Pre-positioning should be considered, especially in harsh terrains with minimal communication links. This allows not only faster response but also better procurement planning and an improvement on distribution costs; however, it requires an additional investment.

(ii) "Medical relief bricks" based on the vulnerability of each region to a specific type of disaster could be strategically located in varying combinations to facilitate timely movement and deployment.
(iii) State-of-the-art disaster rescue equipment should be procured which would not get affected by working at high altitudes in extreme climates. They should also enhance the capability to operate at night as well. Detection sensors, based on audio and video display, would considerably enhance the lifesaving capability.

19.9.3 Mitigation

Early warning instruments are also exposed to hazards, and there are chances that they get knocked off first when disaster strikes. To gather information of the disaster, it is important that such instruments are weather hardened to the harsh environment and are placed at places with utmost safety from any hazard.

19.9.4 Response

 (i) The ideal response in such areas can only be carried out when the exact location and extent of damage are identified. Sending a disaster relief force to an area only on premonition is a sheer waste of depleting resources. Aerial surveys using helicopters and unmanned aerial vehicles (UAV) should be carried out to pinpoint areas of distress requiring attention on priority. If possible, satellites can also be used to locate areas of deep distress.
(ii) As the ground communication infrastructure is disrupted first in any disaster, the response teams should be equipped with satellite communication equipment.

19.9.5 Recovery

Rehabilitation material when received should be secured, for utilization in the laid down time frame. Care should be taken that materials like Cement, lime, plaster of paris, which degrade in extreme temperature, are not stocked. If required, stocking should be done in appropriate shelters.

19.9.6 Development

(i) Review of the previously prepared disaster plans should be carried out.
(ii) Care should be taken that any development activity should not create further potential disaster hazards.
(iii) Public education and awareness programs should be incorporated including training to mitigate further such disasters.
(iv) Construction of additional infrastructure from the lessons learned in the current disaster should be carried out, e.g., construction of helipads near population centers.

19.9.7 "Minimax" Modeling

In humanitarian logistics, more than the "minimum" cost optimization, the objective function is to, i.e., "minimax," minimize the maximum time taken to supply a disaster-affected area. This is because the opportunity cost of delay in any disaster is catastrophic, and hence the cost optimization model cannot be implemented in its classical form.

In a "gravity model" the cost of transportation of material is generally taken as proportional to the square of the distance involved. Considering the humanitarian angle involved during disaster (more pronounced in mountainous and high-altitude areas where time is of paramount importance), the cost could be defined in terms of time rather than distance. This aspect gets further emphasized by the fact that travel in mountains is more appropriately designated by the travel time taken rather than the distance involved (due to the nature of terrain). Further, any delay in the relief reaching the disaster-affected area at high altitudes could lead to an increased loss of precious human lives. Hence, considering the opportunity cost involved due to delays, it would not be inappropriate to assume that the cost of transportation is proportional to the "cube" instead of "square" of the time involved.

$$\text{Cost of transportation } \alpha \; kt^3$$

where "k" is the cost per unit time and "t" is the time taken.

Let us assume that from place A to place B (both places being in a mountainous high-altitude area) the cost of road transport is approximately Rs. 400/per hour (by converting the rate per km) and cost of an Mi-17 medium lift helicopter is Rs. 3,50,000/per hour (11). The time taken to reach a particular destination by road is 5 h, whereas it takes only 30 min by air in such a terrain. Calculating the ratio of costs involved for a standard supply load of 3 t, the following is revealed:

$$\text{Cost}_{\text{road}} \; \alpha \; 400 \times (5)^3 \; \text{i.e Rs. } 37,500/-$$
$$\text{Cost}_{\text{air}} \; \alpha \; 350000 \times (0.5)^3 \; \text{i.e Rs. } 43,750/-$$

Hence it can be seen that in such situations it is not very uneconomical to transport by air than by road considering the humanitarian angle. Also, the probability of a road axis not being available is higher during a natural disaster due to landslides, washed bridges, heavy traffic density, etc. Thus, it is quite fair to uphold the "minimax" model in such situations and utilize it for humanitarian logistics in a disaster-affected area at high altitudes.

19.9.8 International Cooperation

Many countries across the globe have, over the years, developed expertise in handling such disaster situations in a high-altitude area. Mutual agreements with these countries could be entered into for providing assistance during all stages of such disasters. The same could also be carried out under UNISDR (United Nations International Strategy for Disaster Reduction).

19.10 Conclusion

Disaster management involves many segments of a cycle right from preparations to the long-term development of an affected area. To have an effective and efficient plan, a holistic view of each and every situation on ground needs to be taken. The case of "one size fits all" cannot be applied in managing a disaster. Handling of a disaster would differ according to various types of disaster occurring at different locations. A high-altitude area presents peculiar conditions of terrain, weather, and environment which pose problems in all stages. Disaster management plans designed for other areas would, if used in high-altitude areas, as per the original design, lead to further delays and hardships in providing relief to the disaster-struck area. These conditions have to be factored in every segment to make the plans practical, economical, and sustainable.

Chapter 20
Relief-Chain Logistics in Natural Disasters

Purvishkumar Patel, Repaul Kanji, and Rajat Agrawal

20.1 Introduction

Disasters have mostly become the price that we pay for the uncontrolled progress that we are making. Both natural and man-made disasters can be explained as direct or indirect consequences of the so-called urbanization and development that we are undergoing at the cost of exploiting the natural cycles. It is often said that the occurrence of disasters cannot be controlled and hence it becomes pretty important that we somehow mitigate its effects and manage the aftermath so as to ensure minimum social and economic loss. It is here where relief-chain logistics comes in handy and plays the pivotal role. This paper would cover the entire spectrum of a successful relief operation using humanitarian aspects as well as technological.

20.2 The Cycle

Before we move into the vitals, we should be aware of the stages that circumscribe a disaster management activity of which relief chain is an integral part. The following figure shows relevance of humanitarian logistics in different phases and stages inside phases of a disaster management cycle (Fig. 20.1).

Of all these stages, we argue that more concentration of efforts is required in the *response* and *recovery* phases, as both these stages have high relevance of humanitarian logistics in disaster management. However, other stages also have

P. Patel (✉) • R. Kanji
Disaster Mitigation and Management, IIT Roorkee, Roorkee, Uttarakhand, India
e-mail: purvishkumar@yahoo.in

R. Agrawal
Department of Management Studies, IIT Roorkee, Roorkee, Uttarakhand, India

© Springer India 2016
B.S. Sahay et al. (eds.), *Managing Humanitarian Logistics*, Springer Proceedings in Business and Economics, DOI 10.1007/978-81-322-2416-7_20

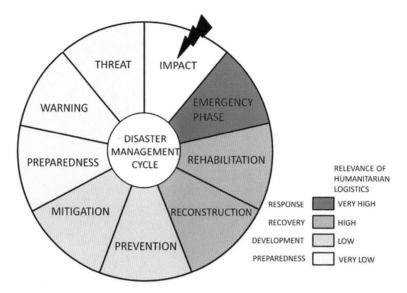

Fig. 20.1 Stages in the disaster management cycle

explicit roles, but they are limited to initial preparations and staging. The response and recovery phases demand agile supply chain and integrated logistics solutions for disaster management. As the further stages of the disaster management cycle are encountered, the supply chain loses agility and becomes more conventional. Humanitarian supply chains should be highly agile as demands are unpredictable and change very fast. Agility is usually defined as the ability to respond to unexpected changes when demand is unpredictable (response and recovery phases).

20.3   Prep Work and Strategic Planning for Disaster Relief

20.3.1   Prep Work

Even before anything goes wrong or a disaster strikes, it is important to stay prepared because, "Prevention is better than cure." There are a lot of things that can be done to increase the preparedness depending on the affluence and ability of the community. First and foremost, a hazard assessment should be done on a local/regional/state/national basis to understand the probable threats and dangers. This is called *hazard mapping* or even *hazard zonation*. Transportation and logistics operations are greatly influenced by spatial structure at the local, regional, and global levels. Given the type and nature of threat(s) along with the spatial parameters, hazard zonation becomes an important input for relief-chain logistics as and when required (Dangermond 1991). In places where threats are prominent (e.g., seismic zones IV and V for earthquakes, villages and towns near mountains with loose soil and rocks for landslides, etc.), the preparations required are a notch higher. The state/district disaster management authority should maintain a proper record of all the resources they have. Resources include everything from contingency fund and relief aid and materials to technological infrastructure. Not only the account but also the sources (where they can be found, in what quantity) need to be recorded. Depending on the geographical spread of the area, the resources should be distributed at different heads instead of storing them at a single source. Storing resources at different heads is not a singular problem but instead involves a very strategic approach, and it is here where technology comes in handy. It is important to have a lineup of responsible people, volunteers who are well versed with the drills, and the actions which are necessary to be taken in an emergency. There could be various such groups of efficient people; however, of them the three majorly required groups are firstly those people who are technologically sound, that is, they are proficient in handling the technological aspects like issuing of emergency signals and warnings, tracking of human as well as relief resources, and coordinating with the external and higher authorities. Secondly, a group efficient in search and rescue operations is primarily required, and it is advisable to have local people recruited for this purpose, as local people would be more aware of the terrain and local dialect of the people easing the rescue operation. And finally, we do need a team of medical practitioners to treat the wounded and affected. Thus, it becomes quite obvious that the service of relief, rescue, and aid to be provided during an emergency/disaster constitutes a humanitarian chain.

20.3.2   Stage-Wise Strategic Planning for Disaster Relief

The strategic plans for a disaster relief activities involve tasks such as determining community needs, estimating disaster conditions, its uncertainties, information quality and complexity, developing coordination plans among various actors of a disaster relief chain, establishing communication channels both internally within the given organization or aid agency and externally within different organizations, logistics companies, army, NGOs, etc., rationalizing the supply base and encouraging trust and commitment among every actors in the disaster relief supply chain. In the preparedness stage, tasks like selection of supply vendors, selection of logistics support vendors, deciding storage amount and locations, temporary storage locations, etc., should be made. Demand distribution, supply chain capacity distribution, lead times, and other relevant parameters should be calculated with the tools of stochastic optimization. In the response and recovery stages, supply purchase plans, availing the supplies at the storage, identifying the demand spots, supplying at the demand spots, and rescue and evacuation plans should be made. In the next section we will see tools and technologies that can be used for drafting these strategies and executing a disaster relief chain (Altay et al. 2009).

20.4 Tools and Technologies for Effective Relief-Chain Logistics

Agility, responsiveness, flexibility, authenticity of demand amount and location, cross-sectional coordination, and satisfying the demand at the right place, at the right time, and in the right quantity are the main aspects of a disaster relief chain. Following are the tools and technologies that can be used for satisfying most of the abovementioned aspects' requirements for running a smooth, efficient, and effective disaster relief chain.

20.4.1 GIS for Contingency Planning in Agile Relief Chains

A GIS (geographic information system) captures, stores, manipulates, analyzes, manages, and presents all types of geographic data. GIS gives a very vivid idea of the area, about its geography, topography, possible means of communications, lifeline services, etc. Although GIS is highly useful in almost all the phases of disaster management cycle, we will see its analytical and decisive power in contingency planning for response and recovery humanitarian logistics actions. To indicate the vulnerability, disaster managers can generate maps both at micro- and macro-level in pre-disaster situation. Locations likely to remain undamaged, unaffected, or relatively safe can be scientifically identified. Such locations can probably be used as temporary warehouses, storage, and/or shelters during the execution of logistic actions in post-disaster situations. Alternate routes to the impact location, relief camps, shelters, and other important locations can be worked out. The involvement of GIS gives an added advantage of zone buffering according to the various levels of risks which in turn would decide the quantity of a particular resource to be stored. Now here is the catch, one might feel that with increased risk, it would be more logical to store a higher amount of relief materials, but often the negative probability gets ignored that with increased risk, the risk of damage of the resources also increases and hence the amount of storage is to be a function of the risk of the area and the demographic factors of the area [amount $= f$ (risk, demographic factors like population density and sex ratio)]. The important demographic factors that need to be considered are population, population density, and sex ratio. In this context, it is advisable to have census blocks; these blocks are geographical regions of which the disaster management authority has complete demographic information (Dunn 1992).

20.4.2   Emergency/Crisis Maps for Improving Responsiveness of a Relief Chain

Generating emergency maps or crisis maps is a run-time phenomenon. Various map providers (e.g., Google Maps) provide various tools (e.g., Google Maps Engine Lite) for creating customized maps for specific application (let us say a rescue/relief operation). These maps are open to edit by authorized persons/officials, or it can even be made editable by anybody who is connected to the Internet. Such emergency maps can be easily integrated with a GIS as a separate layer in it, and hence the combined mathematical, statistical, and analytical power of GIS and emergency maps becomes an important information input for logistics operations. With the help of such emergency digital maps, reliable information can be marked on the map with other important information. For example, if a local person/official wants to share information of a landslide in his area, he can edit the emergency map by marking the impact spot, the probable number of affected people, the nearest hospital, probable temporary relief station, etc. Such information becomes an important asset for decision-making in logistics execution in a relief chain. Decisions like where to stock, what to stock, vehicle routing, fleet size, and fleet type requirements (helicopters, trucks, buses, ambulances, etc.) can be efficiently worked out. Coordination between different bodies like government, military, NGOs, aid agencies, logistics companies, rescue operators, and others can be smoothly made. In general, such emergency maps can play a vital role in making the relief supply chain effective and flexible.

20.4.3   Real-Time Tracking and Monitoring

The success (or failure) of management of a disaster is particularly dependent on how the rescue, relief, and logistical operations are carried out. These operations have to be executed immediately after the disaster strikes, when there is an immense political, social, and psychological pressure and tension. Every decision taken and every second spent on such operations may directly affect many human lives! To ensure the correct execution of such operations, live tracking or real-time tracking technologies can be used. Rescue operators, vehicles (trucks, ambulances, goods carriages, etc.), and relief materials (food, drinking water, medicines, blood bottles, etc.) can be easily tracked for getting information about their current location, their velocity, whether they are moving on correct path, and their probable time of arrival, and other relevant information for managing relief chains can be obtained. A central monitoring station can monitor these tracking activities and can guide the rescue operators to move in a particular direction at a particular spot. Different technologies can be used for live tracking of these assets and actors in relief chains.

20.4.3.1 GPS-Based Live Tracking

A handheld GPS receiver receives coordinates in terms of latitude, longitude, and elevation directly from the constellation of GPS satellites. Along with its spatial coordinates, GPS also gives information about time and hence distance and velocity. GPS receiver works anywhere on the planet except for the places where there is no open sky (e.g., tunnel). Information collected by the GPS receiver can be sent over the Internet through a GSM/GPRS/UMTS network or directly through satellite Internet communication channels. Availability of both spatial and temporal data with the help of GPS makes it extremely easy to integrate it with digital maps and/or GIS (Padmanabhan 2001).

20.4.3.2 Network-Based Techniques

These techniques utilize the service provider's network infrastructure to identify the location of the handset. The advantage of network-based techniques (from a mobile operator's point of view) is that they can be implemented nonintrusively, without affecting the handsets. The accuracy of network-based techniques varies, with cell identification as the least accurate and triangulation as moderately accurate and newer "Forward Link" timing methods as the most accurate. The accuracy of network-based techniques is both dependent on the concentration of base station cells, with urban environments achieving the highest possible accuracy, and the implementation of the most current timing methods (Li et al. 2001).

20.4.3.3 Handset-Based Techniques

These techniques require the installation of client software on the handset to determine its location. This technique determines the location of the handset by computing its location by cell identification and signal strengths of the home and neighboring cells, which is continuously sent to the carrier. In addition, if the handset is also equipped with GPS, then significantly more precise location information is then sent from the handset to the carrier. The key disadvantage of this technique (from mobile operator's point of view) is the necessity of installing software on the handset. Typical smartphones, such as one based on Symbian, Windows Phone, BlackBerry OS, iOS, or Android, would be able to run such software.

20.4.3.4 Hybrid Techniques

Hybrid positioning systems use a combination of network-based and handset-based technologies for location determination (Peuhkuri 2002). One example would be some modes of Assisted GPS, which can both use GPS and network information to compute the location. Both types of data are thus used by the telephone to make the location more accurate (i.e., A-GPS). Alternatively tracking with both systems can also occur by having the phone attain the person's GPS location directly from the satellites and then having the information sent via the network to the person that is trying to locate the telephone. Services allowing such cell phone include Google Latitude. Now these modes might appear to be typically geek-like, but they are not; in fact they are easier to implement once the service provider is involved, and they are asked to customize such emergency services in the name of corporate social responsibility (CSR).

20.5   Estimation and Correction

After the disaster has been averted, it would be equally essential to assess how the entire system faired. Starting from the managerial body of the authority till the last man in the lowest rung, each action requires evaluation. The evaluation must not be so stringent as to rub off the workers, yet should be lenient enough to give them the picture of the importance of their job. By using information systems like GIS, the stored data and the performance metrics of various actors can further be used for evaluation and analysis. The distribution of resources needs to be assessed as well so that it can be understood as to what could have been done more to provide proper and equitable distribution. These results need to be assessed so that in the future proper mitigation can be ensured and better services can be provided. It is almost like taking a feedback, but the only difference lies in the fact that the feedback needs to be incorporated into real-time scenarios and not only be written in some case report.

20.6   Conclusion

The paper might appear to be a logical write-up, good for nothing illustration which cannot be implemented, but here is the fact, only if these certain principles are adopted, the relief operations would become more efficient and fruitful. It might take time to implement the entire scene, but then it needs to start at some point and herein is the efficacy of this paper. This is an attempt to bring to light the need of the best managers in disaster management authorities also and not only in MNCs and the need of technocrats in such authorities apart from being a work geek in some distant land abroad.

References

Altay N, Prasad S, Sounderpandian J (2009) Strategic planning for disaster relief logistics: lessons from supply chain management". Int J Serv Sci 2(2):142–161

Dangermond, J (1991) Applications of GIS to the international decade for natural hazards reduction. In: Proceedings, Fourth International Conference on Seismic Zonation, Oakland, Stanford University, Earthquake Engineering Research Institute 3:445–468

Dunn CE (1992) Optimal routes in GIS and emergency planning applications. Area 24:259–267

Li G, Lam K, Kuo, T (2001) Location update generation in cellular mobile computing systems. In: Proceedings on Workshop parallel & distributed real-time systems, University of Arakansas, San Francisco, p 96

Padmanabhan J (2001) GPS based vehicle tracking system. In: The Asian GPS conference, New Delhi, October 2001

Peuhkuri M (2002) Internet traffic measurements – aims, methodology, and discoveries. Licentiate's thesis, Networking Laboratory, Helsinki University of Technology, Finland

Chapter 21
Humanitarian Logistics of Human Remains of Disasters

Kailash Gupta

21.1 Mass Fatality Management

As Teahen (2012) defines, "A mass fatalities incident is an event that causes loss of life and human suffering, which cannot be met through usual individual and community resources" (p. 1). Mass fatality management (MFM) typically begins once there is no further threat to life (Jensen 2000). However, Neal reported that an Indian official in charge of a response team to the 2004 tsunami said, "Their role was to take care of the dead so that they can then take care of the living. There were bodies all around and the body odor was unbearable, *it was necessary to take care of the dead before taking care of the living*" (Yandek 2011, emphasis added).[1]

Generally, first, there will be the search and rescue for people whose lives are under threat and may be saved. Only after that, MFM may begin. However, seeing human remains and their odor may be repulsive and emotionally disturbing to the responders who want to save lives. Therefore, in cases where rescuers and medical personnel are psychologically unable to take care of the injured people, then first human remains have to be disposed of, before the injured can be attended. Indeed, "sensory or emotional events that are especially difficult for the psyche" (Ritchie & Benedek, 2012, p. 286) are considered psychological toxins.

MFM involves humanitarian logistics aspects of recovery, preservation, communication to the community, identification, and disposition of human remains. I have done a US National Science Foundation-funded MFM research after the 2004 tsunami in Sri Lanka and India (Gupta 2006; Oyola-Yemaiel and Gupta 2005, 2006), 2008 earthquake in Sichuan province of China, 2009 Cyclone Aila in

---

[1] This and next paragraph are drawn from Gupta (2013).

K. Gupta (✉)
Honorary Managing Trustee, The International Emergency Management Society,
Jaipur, Rajasthan, India
e-mail: kailashgupta@my.unt.edu

© Springer India 2016
B.S. Sahay et al. (eds.), *Managing Humanitarian Logistics*, Springer Proceedings
in Business and Economics, DOI 10.1007/978-81-322-2416-7_21

Bangladesh and India (Gupta 2009), and 2010 earthquake in Haiti (Gupta 2010a, b, 2013; Gupta and Sadiq 2010; McEntire et al. 2012). This paper presents the humanitarian logistics-related findings of recovery, preservation, communication to the community, identification, and disposition of human remains.

21.2 Method

A method of field study was used after the disasters in Bangladesh, China, Haiti, India, and Sri Lanka. Field study is the "prototypical method of disaster research" (Stallings 2007, p. 56). One of the field research methods is quick response research in which information is collected "during or immediately after a damaging event" (Michaels 2003, p. 41) because the nature of data is ephemeral or perishable. The method used is case study, which is a "traditional method of studying disaster events" (Comfort et al. 2012, p. 546).

I conducted 186 interviews in Bangladesh, Haiti, India, and Sri Lanka. The interview sample was purposive, and not random, using snowballing (Mutchnick et al. 2009) and networking techniques. The selection of the interviewees was based on their willingness to talk, their knowledge about the research subject, and their potential to contribute to the research. The interviewees were family members of the deceased, physicians, local administrators, military personnel, UN administrators, university administrators, researchers, fire personnel, volunteers, and others. Qualitative open-ended interviews were conducted, sometimes with the help of an interpreter when I did not know the language the interviewee spoke. Some interviews were audio recorded with the permission of the interviewees. Some interviews were transcribed verbatim and entered in the MAXQDA computer-assisted data analysis software. MAXQDA helped in coding the interviews and data analysis.

21.3 Recovery of Human Remains

After disasters, search and rescue of living persons is one of the most important tasks of the responders. Countries send their search and rescue teams to foreign countries to help citizens of their countries who are in that country at the time of disaster involving mass fatalities. This was observed in Thailand after the 2004 Indian Ocean tsunami and after the 2010 Haiti earthquake. In Haiti, more than 60 urban search and rescue teams from 30 nations with more than 1,800 rescuers recovered 132 persons alive. The nationality of the persons recovered is unknown and no data were collected on short-term survival. The number of persons "rescued alive" is not the same as the number of lives saved. The cost incurred and the effectiveness of international search and rescue teams are questionable.

After any disaster most of the lives are saved by the family members, neighbors, and bystanders. The official first responders traditionally considered as fire, police, and medical people take time to reach the disaster sites and are generally less aware of the places people get trapped, compared to the local residents.

Generally, after the search and rescue operation of the living and taking care of them, search for human remains starts. In the June 2013 Uttarakhand catastrophe in India, nearly 5,000 people were missing and their human remains were not found; only about 800 were confirmed dead. After the tsunami human remains were recovered by people who were fishing, largely from smashed boats. A large number of human remains were also recovered from a church in Nagapattinam district of Tamil Nadu. In Haiti after the 2010 earthquake recovery of human remains was largely done by local people. Many human remains were not recovered and were comingled with debris that kept lying. I saw a full-body human remain in a building on the main road of Port-au-Prince, capital of Haiti, after 3 weeks of the earthquake.

21.4 Preservation of Human Remains

Humanitarian logistics requires that human remains need to be preserved for identification and respectful disposition. However, preservation facilities are mostly limited, and after a mass fatality disaster more often than not, human remains are mass buried, particularly in developing countries. An extreme example is that of Haiti in which according to the government of Haiti, 316,000 people died (Brown and Delva 2011). The Haitian government was totally overwhelmed and ordered the National Equipment Corporation (NEC), a government public works department, to dispose human remains. NEC used earthmoving equipment to recover human remains, made no effort to preserve them, and mass buried them in Titanyen. Titanyen is about 24 km northeast from the Port-au-Prince, without nearby human habitation, slightly away from a hill, where trenches were dug and human remains mass buried.

Generally, efforts are made to preserve human remains of foreigners after a mass fatality disaster. This was observed after the tsunami in Sri Lanka and Thailand and after the Haiti earthquake. Sometimes efforts are made to preserve human remains for a limited period for identification. However, if it is not possible to identify the human remains, then they are dispositioned. This was observed after the Kolkata Park Street building fire in 2009.

To preserve human remains, cold storage facilities are required in the morgue. There are limitations how much cold storage morgue facilities the local administration could keep. After the tsunami, a private company from Norway flew a large size cold storage tent for preservation of human remains. Human remains could also be preserved in shallow graves.

21.5   Communication About Human Remains

Local community is informed by the administrator or a representative of the administrator to come for identification of human remains. Local affected community also contacts the administration to find out about the human remains of their family members. This is achieved by various methods. After the tsunami in India and Sri Lanka, photographs were displaced of the deceased persons by the administrators for the local community to identify the human remains of their family members. Human remains were also lined up in morgue and open spaces in hospitals, and people were called to identify the human remains. In Sri Lanka a doctor used *namaz* public address system of the mosque announcing the community that human remains are there in the hospital and asked people to come to the hospital for identification of the human remains.

After the Haiti earthquake, social media was widely used by the Haiti diaspora to help find human remains. In this Facebook, Twitter, and other social media websites were helpful. Google created a people finder website to facilitate people putting information about missing people and search facility to locate missing people. After the Uttarakhand catastrophe in June 2013 in India, initially some photographs of human remains found were put up on the website by the Government of Uttarakhand. However, subsequently those photographs were removed from the website. The list of missing persons was put up by the Government of Uttarakhand and other state governments on their websites.

21.6   Identification of Human Remains

Identification of human remains is important for handing over the human remains to the surviving family members for them to perform the last rites and get compensation from the government, insurance claims, and estate inheritance rights; for the living spouse to remarry; and for other reasons. In case the human remains are not identified, it leaves Zeigarnik effect on the surviving family members. Even after 31 years of ending the Vietnam War, family members were reported to be searching for the human remains of their family members (Phua 2006). In the Western industrialized rich countries, all efforts are made to identify the human remains of disaster victims. The human remains are preserved in cold storages, and different technologies are used for identification of the human remains, including photographs, dental records, X-rays, forensic methods, and DNA profiling.

In Asian poor countries, human remains are preserved for limited periods for identification, and in case they are not identified, they are disposed of. In India and Sri Lanka, simple methods were used to identify the human remains, like clothing, tattoos, photographs, identification by family members or neighbors, jewelry, or other similar methods. After the tsunami, about 45 countries sent their teams to Thailand to identify the human remains of their citizens. Initially, there were conflicts among different country teams and also with local administration. However, subsequently initial problems were sorted out and smooth process was established (Scanlon 2006). Different teams used disaster victim identification protocol of the International Criminal Police Organization (Gupta 2011; INTERPOL 2009).

After the Haiti earthquake, because of the large number of deaths (360,000) and the speed at which the deaths occurred, the government was completely overwhelmed and made no effort to identify the human remains, except of the foreigners and some efforts by the individuals.

21.7   Disposition of Human Remains

Disposition of human remains has to be done with due respect according to the tradition, culture, and religious beliefs and by performing rituals. Generally, defense forces of different countries perform special ceremonies for disposition of human remains of their personnel, known as guard of honor. In the response operations to the Uttarakhand catastrophe, a helicopter crashed killing 12 persons of the National Disaster Response Force, Indian Tibet Border Police, Indian Air Force, and other organizations. A special guard of honor ceremony was organized at Dehradun helipad in the presence of the Home Minister of India, Chief Minister of Uttarakhand, and senior officials of the armed forces that this author watched. After the ceremony the human remains of these people were flown by special helicopters and airplanes for disposition by their families. Do the recovered human remains of the civilians from the Uttarakhand catastrophe not deserve respectful disposition? This is a question that needs to be pondered.

An extreme case of disrespectful disposition of human remains was observed by me after the 2010 earthquake in Haiti. The human remains were dispositioned by earthmoving equipment in long trenches and buried comingled with debris. Pan American Health Organization and World Health Organization has recommended against the mass burial of human remains since it violates the human rights of the family members of the survivors (Pan American Health Organization 2004). However, this recommendation was not practicable in mass fatality situations in developing countries and not implemented after the tsunami in India, Sri Lanka, and Thailand.

21.8   Conclusions and Recommendations

MFM findings reveal that most of the countries are not prepared for the MFM. Even New York City was not prepared for more than 1,000 fatalities at the time of 9/11 (Wachtendorf 2004). Most of the countries do not have a policy of MFM and it is done in a haphazard, by chance, and in a chaotic way, without any strategic planning before a disaster (Pan American Health Organization 2004). Only Indian National Disaster Management Authority has come out with *National Disaster Management Guidelines: Management of the Dead in the Aftermath of Disasters* in 2010 at the national level, although some states in the USA also have policies for MFM.

MFM was severely inadequate in the aftermath of the Haiti 2010 earthquake. According to a senior UN administrator who was interviewed by me in Haiti, "there was no fatality management" (Gupta 2013). Disasters involving mass fatalities are increasing in intensity and number and likely to continue in the foreseeable future, particularly in developing countries. It is imperative that countries learn from the MFM research and evolve policy and practices for MFM.

There is a thriving international illegal trade in human remains and cadavers have been sold for about $10,000 (Carney 2010; Cheney 2006). Human remains of brain dead could be used for transplant. A debate needs to be started for socially accepting legal use of unidentified human remains of brain dead from natural disasters for transplant. This has a potential of removing waiting lists of patients for transplant.

References

Brown T, Delva JG (2011) Haiti revises quake death toll up to over 316,000, p. 1. Retrieved from http://www.reuters.com/article/2011/01/12/haiti-quake-toll-idUSN1223196420110112

Carney S (2010) The red market: on the trail of the world's organ brokers, bone thieves, blood farmers, and child traffickers. HarperCollins, New York

Cheney A (2006) Body brokers: inside America's underground trade in human remains. Broadway Books, New York

Comfort LK, Cigler BA, Waugh WL Jr (2012) Emergency management research and practice in public administration: emergence, evolution, expansion, and future directions. Public Adm Rev 72(4):539–546. doi:10.1111/j.1540-6210.2012.02549.x

Gupta K (2006) Handling the tsunami dead. In: National Institute of Disaster Management (ed) First Indian disaster management congress abstracts. National Institute of Disaster Management, New Delhi, p 132

Gupta K (2009) Cross-cultural analysis of response to mass-fatalities following 2009 Cyclone Aila in Bangladesh and India. Quick response report number 216 http://www.colorado.edu/hazards/research/qr/submitted/gupta_2009.pdf

Gupta K (2010a) A cross-cultural analysis of the disposition of unidentified bodies following sudden catastrophic disasters. In: Nagai T, Conly L, Fontanilla E, Miller D, Ruben M, Stevens K (eds) XVII World Congress of Sociology, Gothenburg, Sweden, 11–17 July 2010, conference abstracts (p 183). International Sociology Association, Gothenburg

Gupta K (2010b). Cross-cultural analysis of the disposition of unidentified bodies in Haiti: preliminary findings. Paper presented at the 17th Annual Conference of The International Emergency Management Society, Beijing

Gupta K (2011) INTERPOL. In: Pennel KB, Staler M (eds) Encyclopedia of disaster relief. Sage, Thousand Oaks, pp 361–362

Gupta, K. (2013). Seeking information after the 2010 Haiti earthquake: a case study in mass-fatality management. Doctoral dissertation. ProQuest dissertation and thesis database.

Retrieved from http://digital.library.unt.edu/ark:/67531/metadc271823/m1/1/?q=kailash%20gupta

Gupta K, Sadiq A-A (2010) Responses to mass-fatalities in the aftermath of 2010 Haiti earthquake. Quick response report number 219. Retrieved from http://www.colorado.edu/hazards/research/qr/submitted/gupta_2010.pdf

INTERPOL (2009) Disaster victim identification guide. Retrieved from http://www.interpol.int/INTERPOL-expertise/Forensics/DVI

Jensen RA (2000) Mass fatality and casualty incidents: a field guide. CRC Press, Boca Raton

McEntire DA, Sadiq A-A, Gupta K (2012) Unidentified bodies and mass-fatality management in Haiti: a case study of the January 2010 earthquake with a cross-cultural comparison. Int J Mass Emerg Disasters 30(3):301–327

Michaels S (2003) Perishable information, enduring insights? Understanding quick response research. In: Natural Hazards Research and Applications Information Center, Public Entity Risk Institute & Institute for Civil Infrastructure Systems (eds) Beyond September 11th: an account of post-disaster research. Special publication no. 39 (pp 15–48). Natural Hazards Research and Applications Information Center, University of Colorado, Boulder. Retrieved from http://www.colorado.edu/hazards/publications/sp/sp39/

Mutchnick RJ, Berg BL, Ireland C (2009) Research methods for criminal justice and the social sciences: practice and applications. Prentice Hall, Upper Saddle River

Oyola-Yemaiel A, Gupta K (2005) Response to mass-fatalities by India and Sri Lanka following the 2004 tsunami. Paper presented at the annual conference of the International Association of Emergency Managers, Phoenix, AZ. In CD format

Oyola-Yemaiel A, Gupta K (2006) India and Sri Lanka's response to mass fatalities following the Tsunami. In: Ammann WJ, Haig J, Huovinen C, Stocker M (eds) Proceedings of the international disaster reduction conference, vol 2. Swiss Federal Research Institute WSL, Davos, pp 413–416

Pan American Health Organization (2004) Management of dead bodies in disaster situations. Pan America Health Organization and World Health Organization, Washington, DC

Phua J (Producer) (2006) Although the Vietnam War ended in 1975, some families are still searching for loved ones missing in action and are turning to psychics for help. Retrieved from http://news.bbc.co.uk/2/hi/programmes/this_world/4989480.stm

Ritchie EC, Benedek DM (2012) Psychological issues and mass fatality. In: Gursky EA, Fierro MF (eds) Death in large numbers: the science, policy, and management of mass fatality events. American Medical Association, Chicago

Scanlon J (2006) Dealing with the tsunami dead: Unprecedented international co-operation. Aust J Emerg Manag 21(2):57–61

Stallings RA (2007) Methodological issues. In: Rodriguez H, Quarantelli EL, Dynes RR (eds) Handbook of disaster research. Springer, New York

Teahen PR (2012) Mass fatalities: managing the community response. CRC Press, Boca Raton

Wachtendorf T (2004) Improvising 9/11: organizational improvisation following the World Trade Center disaster. (Doctoral dissertation). ProQuest Dissertations & Theses database. (UMI Number 3133851)

Yandek C (Producer) (2011) Disaster expert David Neal: 8.9 Japan quake much worse than Katrina. [Audio interview]. Retrieved from http://www.cyinterview.com/2011/03/disaster-expert-david-neal-8-9-japan-quake-much-worse-than-katrina/